Liberation and Authority

Liberation and Authority

Plato's **Gorgias**, *the First Book of the* **Republic**, *and Thucydides*

Nicholas Thorne

LEXINGTON BOOKS
Lanham • Boulder • New York • London

Excerpts from Thorne, Nicholas, "Socratic Wisdom in the Gorgias and the Republic," in *Dionysius* XXXVI (December 2018): 12–24. Reprinted with permission.

Published by Lexington Books
An imprint of The Rowman & Littlefield Publishing Group, Inc.
4501 Forbes Boulevard, Suite 200, Lanham, Maryland 20706
www.rowman.com

6 Tinworth Street, London SE11 5AL, United Kingdom

Copyright © 2021 The Rowman & Littlefield Publishing Group, Inc.

All rights reserved. No part of this book may be reproduced in any form or by any electronic or mechanical means, including information storage and retrieval systems, without written permission from the publisher, except by a reviewer who may quote passages in a review.

British Library Cataloguing in Publication Information Available

Library of Congress Cataloging-in-Publication Data Is Available

Library of Congress Control Number: 2021933842

ISBN 978-1-7936-3904-2 (cloth)
ISBN 978-1-7936-3906-6 (pbk)
ISBN 978-1-7936-3905-9 (electronic)

To Dalhousie's Classics House, as I knew it

Contents

Acknowledgments	ix
Introduction	1
Thucydides: Introduction	5
(1) Periclean Athens	23
(2) Post-Periclean Athens	41
(3) Alcibiadean Athens	55
Thucydides: Conclusion	75
Plato—A Holistic Approach to the *Gorgias* and *Republic* I	93
The *Gorgias*: Introduction	99
Shame and the *Ad Hominem* Arguments	107
(1) Gorgias	117
(2) Polus	127
(3) Callicles	137
How Callicles Is Good: Platonic Doctrine in the *Gorgias*	155
Socrates in the *Gorgias*	171
Republic I	177
(1) Cephalus	181
(2) Polemarchus	189

(3) Thrasymachus	199
Republic I: Conclusion	233
The *Gorgias* and the First Book of the *Republic*: Connections and Comparison	247
Conclusion	259
Works Cited	269
Index	277
About the Author	281

Acknowledgments

Above all, I would like to thank Dennis House, with whom I wrote my MA thesis. This book began in his Plato seminars, and in a conversation I had with him around the turn of the century. In addition to House, at Dalhousie, I would also like to thank the late Robert Crouse, Wayne Hankey, the late Angus Johnston, and Colin Starnes. It was a privilege to be able to study with such great scholars; in subsequent years I have repeatedly found myself returning to the notes I took back then. In the years I spent in Halifax, I gradually came to understand that this gathering of minds was not a chance occurrence, but was rather the legacy of a great philosopher, James Doull. It was with Doull's students that I learned how to read Plato; this book is an attempt to apply that education.

At the University of Pittsburgh I was fortunate to be able to write a doctoral thesis on the *Gorgias* with James Allen. Not only did my time with him sharpen my thoughts on the *Gorgias* in particular, it also improved my writing more generally. In addition to Dr. Allen, I would particularly like to thank Mae Smethurst, Dennis Looney, and James Lennox. I would also like to thank three fellow students: Rhett Jenkins, with whom I read the first book of the *Republic* and much Thucydides in Greek, John Harvey, with whom I read the *Gorgias* in Greek, and Mikio Akagi, who provided helpful feedback on my work on the *Gorgias*.

In addition to the Classics Departments at Dalhousie and at the University of Pittsburgh, I would like to thank the Classics Department at the University of Tennessee in Knoxville, where I worked for a year and was able to begin the final version of the essay on Thucydides contained herein. I would also like to thank Cristalle Watson for proofreading much of the manuscript in its final stages.

Four friends have been giving me feedback on parts of this project from my first attempts to write about these works in 2001 to the final drafts of this book: Jeff Colgan, Eli Diamond, Michael Fournier, and Amod Lele.

I would like to thank Patrick Lee Miller for his comments on parts of the manuscript. For advice and encouragement in the final stages of this project, I would also like to thank Raymond Henning and Matthew Robinson.

Introduction

Plato, when writing the *Gorgias* and the first book of the *Republic*, had in mind a process very much like the one that Thucydides saw taking place over the course of the Peloponnesian War. Both writers give an account of the decline and collapse of the authority of an older ethical order, a development they set out in three stages. This book aims to provide original interpretations of each of these three works—two Platonic dialogues and Thucydides' *History*—taken individually, and the treatment of each work can be read on its own. There is, however, a further intention: to draw attention, through their juxtaposition, to the importance of the similarities between them that arise by virtue of the movement that runs through the whole of each text. This movement is of profound relevance to our own times: Plato and Thucydides give us a distant mirror, as it were, in which we can see an image of our own situation.

Some of the individuals we shall meet in these works would regard the collapse of authority as an entirely positive development. From such a perspective, the release from the constraints of authority seems simply to be a liberation, a source of greater freedom. Whether, or to what degree, liberation thus understood really is an unambiguous good is a question that lurks in the background of all three works. Indeed, we shall see that others regard the release from traditional authority to involve a *loss* of freedom in certain respects, the disappearance of a foundation for a good life. The nature of liberation, then, and its relation to authority, is a central concern here, though one to which we shall explicitly return only in the conclusion.

We shall see that Thucydides, a man of the older generation, and a general in the Peloponnesian War, considered the process an unmitigated catastrophe: the deep counsel of Pericles was abandoned for ever-narrower, more myopic, and more immediate standpoints, and this predictably led to catastrophe, to the collapse of Athens and to immense human suffering along the way. Plato, on the other hand, who grew up during the war, was a member of the next generation, and this no doubt helps to explain his more ambiguous view: clearly, real evil is coming to light as we move through the *Gorgias* and the first book of the *Republic*, but we shall also see that he understands profound good to be coming into view as well, good necessary to his own philosophy. The collapse of the older order represented a challenge which he thought himself able to answer, and one major aim of these two dialogues is to indicate how the Platonic philosophy is a response to this historical situation. Plato and Thucydides, then, give us a more and a less optimistic view of a particular historical development, a more liberal and a more conservative assessment. Their differing approaches might provide some perspective on similar differences of view in our own times.

The three stages through which the overall movement takes place are clearly set out in each of the Platonic works in question in the characters Gorgias, Polus, and Callicles, and Cephalus, Polemarchus, and Thrasymachus. In Thucydides, we find three stages in, first, Periclean Athens, then in the period following Pericles, in which Cleon was particularly active, and finally in Alcibiadean Athens. All three works begin from an acceptance of limits and a standpoint of belief: for Gorgias and Cephalus, belief in normative constraints upon behavior; for Periclean Athens, belief in the city-state and its conventions as the proper center relative to which individuals can pursue their particular ends. All three works culminate in a subjective spirit that abandons limits and proves destructive and inadequate even on its own terms. In Plato this endpoint arises as the result of a skeptical questioning of the older order of belief, one that casts aside constraints that had been passively accepted, with the result that the individual finds himself in unrestrained competition with others. In Thucydides, as citizens find themselves pursuing their own goals in opposition to one another, faith in the city simply falls away.

In Thucydides and in the *Republic*, these three stages are organized into the same structure: the first and last stages are clear beginning and endpoints, essentially opposed to one another, while the second stage is characterized by an incoherent mix of elements from the other two stages.[1] Such an arrangement of three stages is the minimum sufficient to describe a process, an historical development from one state of affairs to another. One might have had five or eight stages, or some other number, but every further stage added beyond the number three would in one sense have been superfluous, as these additional stages would simply have been different versions of the second, intermediate stage. The three stages in the *Gorgias* do not have such clearly opposed beginning and endpoints, but the overall development contains its own peculiar similarity to what we find in Thucydides: it is, in the end, clear that the roots of the final stage can be traced back to the first.

Of course, the main line of comparison between the three works is not without precedent in earlier scholarship. It has frequently been noted that certain similarities exist between them, but usually only in the last of the three stages, which puts forth a 'natural' view of justice. In particular, certain parallels between Thrasymachus, Callicles, and Thucydides' Athenians at Melos are well known.[2] The deeper connections, which run through all three of the works from start to finish, seem to have been scarcely touched upon at all.

In what follows, I show how this view of these works arises out of the detail of each text. In the case of Thucydides, although I believe I have provided a new look at certain individual passages as well as an original account of the ideas that govern the whole, still one most fundamental line I follow—that Thucydides sees a three-stage development at work—is a path well-travelled by previous interpreters.[3] In the case of the two Platonic dialogues, however, my approach is a departure from previous scholarship, for I see the three-stage dramatic structure that runs through each work to be essential to everything Plato is saying: whether we are analyzing the logic of the arguments or interpreting some detail of characterization, if we do so in abstraction from the structure through which Plato has decided to present these aspects, we are missing a great deal.

A NOTE TO THE READER

This book consists, to a very large degree, of commentary on three texts. Those who wish to follow the argument most fully will want to consult a copy of each text. For readers without knowledge of Greek, there are many excellent translations of Plato with the standard Stephanus page numbers (e.g., 517b or 331e) running down the side of the page, but I know of only one English edition of Thucydides—*The Landmark Thucydides*, ed. R. Strassler—that provides the book, paragraph and section numbers (e.g., ii.65.8) needed to follow precise references.[4]

NOTES

1. For a summary of the evidence for these structural claims, see pages 13–15 and 85–86 for Thucydides, and pages 233–234 for the first book of the *Republic*.
2. For example, see Jacqueline de Romilly, *Thucydides and Athenian Imperialism*, trans. Philip Thody (Oxford: Blackwell, 1963), 299–302; Alban Winspear, *The Genesis of Plato's Thought* (Montreal: Harvest House Ltd., 1974), 192; David Grene, *Man in His Pride* (Chicago: University of Chicago Press, 1950),

61–64; W. K. C. Guthrie, *A History of Greek Philosophy Volume IV* (Cambridge: Cambridge University Press, 1975), 85; Richard Lewis Nettleship, *Lectures on the Republic of Plato* (London: Macmillan & Co. Ltd., 1962), 27; Francis Cornford, "Introduction," in *The Republic of Plato*, ed. and trans. F. M. Cornford (New York: Oxford University Press, 1964), xv–xvi. Alexander Sesonske, "Plato's Apology: Republic I," *Phronesis* 6, no. 1 (1961): 35, compares Callicles, Thrasymachus, and Alcibiades. One could give many other such examples; more recently, see Christina Tarnopolsky, *Prudes, Perverts, and Tyrants: Plato's Gorgias and the Politics of Shame* (Princeton, NJ: Princeton University Press, 2010), 8. Kimon Lycos, *Plato on Justice and Power* (Albany: State University of New York Press, 1987), 32, remarks that "it is not implausible to view the succession of characters from Cephalus to Thrasymachus in Book I [of the *Republic*] as a kind of review of the change of attitudes towards justice which Plato thought had gradually come to govern the behavior of Athenian democracy during the [Peloponnesian] war"—though he does not pursue the matter.

3. So, for example, F. Melian Stawell, "Pericles and Cleon in Thucydides," *The Classical Quarterly* 2, no. 1 (January 1908), 46, speaks of the "three figures that dominate the three stages of his history . . . Pericles, Cleon and Alcibiades." Others who have seen three stages include Marc Cogan, *The Human Thing* (Chicago: University of Chicago Press, 1981), Grene, *Man in His Pride*, and Peter R. Pouncey, *The Necessities of War* (New York: Columbia University Press, 1980). Antonios Rengakos, *Form und Wandel des Machtdenkens der Athener bei Thukydides— Hermes Einzelschriften 48* (Stuttgart: Franz Steiner Verlag, 1984), speaks of three stages, but speculates about a possible fourth if the work were completed.

4. I have used the Oxford Classical Text for Thucydides and the *Republic*; for the *Gorgias* I have used Dodds's Greek text.

Thucydides
Introduction

One of the central themes of Thucydides' work is that Athens experienced a decline in the course of the Peloponnesian War, a decline in the conduct of her citizens, in the quality of her statesmen, in the standard of deliberation within the Athenian assembly, and thus a decline in the standard of her government's conduct of affairs. It is through his presentation of Pericles and his successors, above all Cleon and Alcibiades, that Thucydides gives an account of this decline. One after the other, each of these three individuals attained a certain primacy, and Thucydides sees the war as falling into three corresponding stages, in which the decline of Athens is worked out step by step. It is his view that this development provides the most important cause of Athens' ultimate defeat. In what follows, we shall follow this process through certain major episodes in Thucydides' work, focusing primarily on the speeches. The goal will be to present an original account of Thucydides' thought rather than a new history of the Peloponnesian War.

First, however, it is important to outline the conceptual framework that this account will develop and to give an idea of its basis in the text.

THUCYDIDES THE HOLIST

There is a structure crucial to understanding Thucydides' treatment of Pericles and the development that follows him in Athens: the whole is prior to its parts, and greater than their sum. Although my argument for this structure will only be complete at the end of this account, it is in the treatment of Pericles that Thucydides brings the idea most directly to light.

Pericles, in his last speech, claims that he is

> οὐδενὸς ἥσσων ... [A] γνῶναι τε τὰ δέοντα καὶ [B] ἑρμηνεῦσαι ταῦτα,
> [C] φιλόπολίς τε καὶ [D] χρημάτων κρείσσων
> second to no man at [A] recognizing what is needed, or [B] expressing
> these things, and both [C] a patriot, and [D] superior to the influence
> of money. (ii.60.5, bracketed letters mine)

He continues: ὅ τε γὰρ γνοὺς καὶ μὴ σαφῶς διδάξας ἐν ἴσωι καὶ εἰ μὴ
ἐνεθυμήθη; ὅ τε ἔχων ἀμφότερα, τῇ δὲ πόλει δύσνους, οὐκ ἂν ὁμοίως τι
οἰκείως φράζοι; προσόντος δὲ καὶ τοῦδε, χρήμασι δὲ νικωμένου, τὰ
ξύμπαντα τούτου ἑνὸς ἂν πωλοῖτο.

For one who discerns but does not instruct clearly might as well not
even have taken thought; one who has both these virtues, but is ill-minded
towards the city, would in similar fashion fail to advise properly; and if
this is present, but he yields to money, for this one thing he would
sell the whole. (ii.60.6)

There is a logic at work here: without all four of the virtues—A, B, C and D—one will fail in some crucial respect as a statesman. The state of having *all* the virtues mentioned, that is, of having the *unity* of these virtues, is fundamentally different from any lesser state that has only one or some of them, in that the unity alone is able to attain the end of true statesmanship.[1]

Shortly thereafter, Thucydides sets forth the cause (αἴτιον—ii.65.8) of the problems that arose after Pericles' death, and his remarks suggest a similar logic:

> δυνατὸς ὢν [I] τῷ τε ἀξιώματι καὶ [II] τῇ γνώμῃ [III] χρημάτων τε
> διαφανῶς ἀδωρότατος γενόμενος κατεῖχε τὸ πλῆθος ἐλευθέρως, καὶ
> οὐκ ἤγετο μᾶλλον ὑπ' αὐτοῦ ἢ αὐτὸς ἦγε, [IV] διὰ τὸ μὴ κτώμενος ἐξ οὐ
> προσηκόντων τὴν δύναμιν πρὸς ἡδονήν τι λέγειν, ἀλλ' ἔχων ἐπ'
> ἀξιώσει καὶ πρὸς ὀργήν τι ἀντειπεῖν.
> being powerful through [I] his reputation and [II] his judgment, and
> being [III] manifestly most incorruptible by money, he restrained the
> multitude freely, and was not led by them more than he himself led, on account
> of [IV] not speaking to please so as to acquire power from what was not
> proper, but because, having power through his character, he even opposed
> them to the point of angering them. (ii.65.8, bracketed numbers mine.)

Again we have a list of attributes, all of which are necessary to the end in question. In fact, this list has important similarities with the first: virtue A (recognizing what is needed) is equivalent to (II) and virtue D (superiority to money) to (III). Virtue B (expressing things) is a slight variation of (IV): both deal with the way in which things are said. Virtue C (patriotism) is the odd one out here, not having an obvious connection with reputation (I). However, Thucydides' purpose here (i.e., at ii.65.8) is different from Pericles' words above, for the aim here is to explain how it was that Pericles was powerful within Athens. Significantly, Thucydides puts considerable emphasis on the normative aspect: only (II) does not concern action that one would praise in normative terms. The importance of this emphasis should become clearer as we proceed, and will be taken up in the conclusion (see pages 80–2).

As we look at the situation after Pericles, we shall get a clearer view of the problems that arise when particular parts of the whole go missing. But it does seem that Pericles is echoed by Thucydides himself: both suggest a structure in which a unity of all the relevant goods is essential to the end in question; the absence of any of them will fatally undermine the attainment of that end.[2]

Even without Thucydides' own remarks at ii.65.8, we might reasonably inquire concerning the relevance of Pericles' words to the rest of the work.[3] Can we find any further reason to ascribe to Thucydides himself the view that a unity of many essential goods occupies a privileged place, one fundamentally different from any lesser combination of goods? In fact, we shall see that we can find such a reason, and it runs through books ii–vii: one crucial aspect of Thucydides' portrayal of the decline of Athens is the breaking apart of the initial unity of principles, and this portrayal repeatedly calls to mind the specific goods mentioned in the two passages just quoted. A stable safety for Athens is found in the Periclean unity; the most fundamental cause of Athens' subsequent defeat, in Thucydides' view, is the gradual dissolution of this unity, and in the ever more explicit opposition of certain of its parts to one another.

As we follow this development, we shall see something further: there are two types of virtues in Pericles' unity, and these disappear from Athens in two different ways. Specifically, "there are . . . two intellectual [i.e., A and B above] and two moral qualities [C and D]."[4] The "moral" qualities—we will refer to them as *normative* qualities—will simply fade away, while the "intellectual" qualities, which might also be called "instrumental," become opposed to one another. In fact, the latter qualities are not only opposed: by the end of the movement, Thucydides will show how "expressing things" (ἑρμηνεῦσαι ταῦτα—virtue B above) actually becomes destructive in isolation from the other virtues. There is a crucially important difference between, on the one hand, being able to communicate one's views (virtue B above) when this ability is combined with judgment (virtue A), patriotism (C) and incorruptibility (D), and on the other, having a similar fluency of communication without having any of the other virtues. In the former case we have the fully adequate statesmanship of Pericles; the latter case, as we shall see, characterizes the seductive rhetoric of Alcibiades: the fateful decision to sail on Sicily arises out of the isolation of rhetorical genius from the other necessary virtues.

Two generations later, Aristotle will say that an arm is an arm in name only when separated from the body (*Metaphysics* Z.11 1036b30-23)—that is, an arm is only really an arm when it is connected to the whole of which it is properly a part. In what follows, we will see that a similar idea is at work in Thucydides. Like an arm separated from a body, a virtue separated from its proper unity becomes something different—it falls short of the reality it is meant to attain. A virtue that was, in the unity, directed toward its proper end becomes disconnected from that end when separated; what was once simply good becomes much more ambiguous, in certain cases even a means of self-destruction.

BALANCING OPPOSING GOODS

There is another complementary structure at work in Thucydides' account of the decline of Athens, and it involves oppositions. As we proceed through the work, we find ourselves repeatedly confronted with goods that constitute an opposition in that they either appear logically to contradict one another or tend in practice to exclude one another. The requirement, in all cases considered in this account, is to find a way to hold together both sides of each opposition, to attain what has been called "equilibrium in the great antinomies of life."[5] The presence of oppositions, and the need to attend to both sides, has repeatedly been noted in previous scholarship on the Funeral Oration, but the fact that Pericles speaks in a certain way in one speech does not of itself entitle us to the claim that we have found Thucydides' own views. What does entitle us to this claim is the fact that certain oppositions run through the account of Pericles and his successors, and that account implicitly suggests the need to hold those oppositions together. Specifically, we shall see that justice and power; the associated political formations of democracy and empire; passive and active; as well as the good of the individual and that of the state—all of these are held together in some way in Pericles and become separated and opposed in what follows. There is also a related breadth of temporal focus—past, present, and future—in Pericles, which comes apart in what follows.

Just as with the need for the whole, so too with these oppositions: we receive an initial view of the idea through Pericles, and can then watch that idea at work in Thucydides' subsequent treatment of Athens. These oppositions form a particular case of the need for the whole, one that occurs often in Thucydides, in which the "whole" can be understood as both sides of the opposition taken together.

HOLISM, PERICLES, AND HIS SUCCESSORS

This understanding of Thucydides allows a straightforward resolution of what might seem a self-contradictory treatment of Pericles. The praise of Pericles given directly by the author at ii.65 is extraordinary and explicit. In particular, this passage could not be more emphatic in its attempt to place the blame for subsequent Athenian disasters, particularly the one at Sicily, on the shoulders of Pericles' successors, and not on Pericles himself (ii.65.7–11). However, when we look at the way in which Thucydides has actually portrayed the subsequent history of Athens, we find what seems at first to be a very different picture: again and again, implicit connections are made between Pericles and his successors, and they might seem to suggest that the later problems were actually a problem in Pericles himself.

For example, early in book vi, Alcibiades is encouraging the Athenians to undertake an expedition to conquer Sicily, a move that will not only prove catastrophic for Athens, but that also seems, on the basis of the presentation we find in books i–ii, to be an un-Periclean undertaking, for Pericles warned against expanding the empire (i.144.1, ii.65.7). However, as we shall see when we look more closely at the speech that Thucydides has given Alcibiades (vi.16–18), that speech has been written in a way that points back to Pericles in numerous respects. One such respect is that Alcibiades frames the decision to sail on Sicily as a form of activity, and the decision not to do so as a form of passivity. Accordingly, he emphasizes the need for activity as such. He attacks the notion of remaining quiet (vi.18.2), and he disparages the inactive city (πόλιν μὴ ἀπράγμονα—18.7). Furthermore, he makes an appeal to his audience concerning their customary practices (τὰ ἐπιτηδεύματα—18.3), which are understood to incline toward activity rather than inactivity.[6]

In all of this, there are verbal echoes of Pericles. He too made disparaging remarks concerning the man who pursues a quiet life (the ἀπράγμων—ii.40.2, ii.63.2–3, ii.64.4); he too made appeals to Athenian customary practices (ἐπιτηδεύσις—ii.36.4; see also 61.4, 64.2).[7] The speeches of Alcibiades and Pericles thus contain implicit connections to one another (and we shall see that there are further examples). The links between them are not merely verbal, however, for they seem to have the same significance: both Pericles and Alcibiades advocate an active as opposed to a passive course. The catastrophic Sicilian expedition is represented as motivated, at least in part, by a turning away from quietude and toward activity, and Thucydides seems to suggest that this tendency was already present in Pericles.

There thus appears to be a reason to think that Thucydides wants us to understand that Pericles and Alcibiades are simply the same in a crucial regard. The connection might then be taken to suggest that the expedition is to be understood as a *Periclean* undertaking in some sense—perhaps even as a straightforward continuation of Pericles' thought—a strong indication from Thucydides that we should in fact *connect* Pericles with the Sicilian disaster. We would thus have a damning indictment of the elder statesman: Alcibiades, as he convinces Athens to move on Sicily, would bring out a reality concerning Pericles that was not so easy to see when looking directly at the man himself.

We shall see there are other, similar instances of Pericles being echoed by his less distinguished successors. If we were to follow them through the text along the lines just suggested, we would arrive at a schizophrenic Thucydides, one who puts the blame for Athens' later disasters on subsequent statesmen rather than on Pericles (at ii.65), but also suggests that many of their inadequacies were a result of their having been faithful to Pericles in this or that regard. That is, Thucydides might seem first to exempt Pericles from blame—and then to blame him!

This difficulty is resolved from a perspective that understands the whole to occupy a special place above any of its parts. To continue with the example just given, we shall see that it is wrong to understand Thucydides' Pericles as *simply* the advocate of activity, for he is represented as being capable of both activity and passivity, leaning to the one or the other according to the requirements of the situation at hand (see the treatment of ii.21–22 and ii.59–65 in the section on Pericles, *A Balance of Opposites*, pages 24–5, below). His denigration of the inactive sort of person, then, is a moment in a larger picture, whose significance can only be grasped in the context of that larger picture. For Alcibiades, on the other hand, there is no passive moment: his policy and his vision for Athens at the start of book vi is properly described as *simply* active, without room for intelligent restraint upon that activity.

Alcibiades, then, in respect of passivity and activity, has taken only a part of what was found in Pericles but has taken this part for the whole. To do this, however, is to fall short of Pericles in the essential sense. Accordingly, the point of connection does not suggest that the two men are simply the same. Rather, even the similarity proves, upon reflection, to point to a difference, for Pericles' activity was different from the activity of Alcibiades by virtue of being a moment in a larger reflection. The connections really point us to a profound difference between the two men in question. Alcibiades does not give us the reality that was obscurely present in Pericles; rather, Pericles gives us the reality that Alcibiades fails to live up to, the reality of adequate statesmanship, in which activity and passivity both have a place, but a place limited by a wider understanding. Just as an arm separated from its body is an arm in name only, so too can we only say by virtue of an equivocation that Alcibiades is Periclean if he is similar to Pericles only in respect of certain isolated moments that make up the Periclean unity.[8]

Thus we can give full force to the significance of the connections drawn between Pericles and later Athenian politicians, but these connections do not constitute a criticism of Pericles in any sense. They are absolutely consistent with ii.65 in laying the blame exclusively on Pericles' successors, because his successors were able to attain the Periclean standpoint in a merely partial manner. Thucydides' remarks at ii.65 should be seen as indicating to us in advance how we are to understand the subsequent connections between Pericles and his successors.

IMMEDIACY IN THUCYDIDES

As we move through Thucydides' account of Athens we find a progressive narrowing of both the ability and intellectual perspective of Athenian statesmen. Thucydides has represented these later politicians as less able to attain the whole, moving instead toward ever-more limited perspectives. From such a limited perspective, one sees the two sides of an opposition only in their conflict with one another, so that it seems possible to grasp only one side. On Thucydides' account, this intellectual failing lies at the heart of the reason that Athens lost the war.

There are in fact two different kinds of narrowing at work here. One involves the scope within which one understands things (e.g., the ability to conceive of the good of the individual in a wider, and thus more adequate context, involving its proper relation to the state). The other concerns the question of how many different abilities a statesman has, such as the abilities (A) to come up with good advice and (B) to convince others of it. Nevertheless, we shall see in the conclusion that in practice, in the way these oppositions play out in the story Thucydides tells, the intellectual defect—that is, a narrower perspective—is always primary.

This narrowness of perspective is the chief sense in which I will use the word "immediacy": the movement toward more *immediate* forms of thinking causes the destruction of Athens. The "immediate" in this sense is that which has not been mediated through thought. If we take any of the various oppositions that we find in Thucydides, and think through the nature of each side, and the logic of the relation between them, we begin to attain an understanding of the peculiar merits of each side, and of appropriate (and inappropriate) ways of relating them—that is, our grasp of these goods becomes mediated through thought. An *immediate* grasp of the same opposition would be much easier, not involving any such thought, and taking the two sides as they appear on only the most superficial glance. Thus (to take the example used in the preceding section) with Alcibiades in book vi, it becomes a question simply of whether we are to be active or passive, whereas Pericles aims at one or the other having worked out their proper place within a particular situation.

Thucydides is writing at a time when a word for "immediate" as I have just used it is not available. However, he does tell us that "war is a violent teacher, one that drives the character of most people down to the level of their immediate circumstances" (iii.82.2). The words translated as "immediate circumstances" here are τὰ παρόντα, an important term that will reappear at significant moments as we move through the text. Literally, τὰ παρόντα means "the present things," and it points to the second, temporal sense in which I will use the word "immediate": when people react in the moment, we say they react "immediately."[9] More specifically, what is at issue in this case is a *temporal* sort of narrowness, in which one instant is taken on its own, abstracted from any relation to earlier or present times, as when people, reacting in the heat of the moment, consider only the present situation without thinking of the future (or the past). No better are daydreams concerning the future that proceed without reference to present and past realities. Of course, actions taken in such circumstances will tend to be "immediate" in the first sense as well—that is, characterized by a conceptual narrowness of perspective, and thus poorly thought out. The shape of an adequate (i.e., nonimmediate) standpoint has been set forth elsewhere: "in Thucydides' narrative the temporal equivalent of a panoramic view is simultaneity—being able to comprehend a sequence of events all at once to see the present in light of the past, the past in light of the present, the future in light of the past, and the future in light of the present."[10] We shall see this temporal theme develop as we proceed through the work.

Thucydides' remark concerning war and immediate circumstances comes in the context of his most universal reflection on the war (iii.82–83), describing a phenomenon that covers the whole Hellenic world, of which Athens is the most significant part. In fact, much of what Thucydides says at iii.82.4–83.4 can be summarized with the word "immediate" as I have just explained it. As we follow the changing nature of Athens through the Athenian speeches in what follows, we shall see that we get a particularly well-worked-out instance of Thucydides' claim concerning the nature of war: it drives people toward the immediate. Thus understood, the work is, at bottom, a reflection on the decisive importance of thought to adequate behavior.[11]

"Immediacy," then, shall be used to indicate a narrowness of viewpoint, conceptual, or temporal, a failure to grasp a moment in the context of a wider and more adequate reality.[12] In the conclusion (pages 77–8), I shall return to this theme, summarizing its role in the decline of Athens, in particular in relation to significant occurrences of the term παρόντα.

There is one further point to make here concerning the manner in which we are to approach the text: it should be obvious that Thucydides does not want us to judge from an immediate perspective. He does, after all, indicate that his work has been written for (and is therefore to be judged from) the widest possible temporal perspective, as a possession for all time rather than as a competition-piece for the present moment (κτῆμα ἐς αἰεὶ μᾶλλον ἢ ἀγώνισμα ἐς τὸ παραχρῆμα—i.22.4).[13] In particular, this needs to be kept in mind when interpreting those passages in which Thucydides might seem after all to be writing a piece for the present moment, when he is at his most vivid, making us feel almost as though we are spectators at the scenes he describes. Such passages would include the description of the plague (ii.49–53), the end of the Sicilian expedition (vii.84, 87 inter alia), and the end of the Corcyrean stasis (iv.47–48). It would be a cold-hearted reader indeed who could proceed through such passages without being affected emotionally, and the pity that is naturally aroused in us reminds us that the greatness of this war is grounded in the greatness of the suffering that it caused (i.23).[14] However, the perspective of the moment (recall παραχρῆμα—i.22.4) is not the perspective from which adequate understanding arises: we must be careful not to draw conclusions too swiftly and directly from such passages (and the feelings they arouse). This will prove important in relation to Pericles.

THREE STAGES

If we take the speeches reported in direct discourse, and made by Athenians in the Athenian assembly, we find that Thucydides has drawn our attention to three different situations.[15] Those Periclean speeches that put forth a specific policy all represent decisive moments: after each, we hear how the Athenians were persuaded by his advice (i.145.1, ii.14.1, ii.65.2). The next directly reported speeches in the Athenian assembly come in the Mytilenian debate (iii.37–48), and here we have a new situation: the speeches we are given represent the *second* assembly which meets to deliberate on the question at hand. It is responsible for a *change* to a policy that had previously been agreed upon, though it is by the slimmest of margins that the assembly makes its decision (iii.49.1), and it is only barely possible for a ship to reach Mytilene in time to make this decision effective (49.4). Thus, the Mytilenian debate does—barely—give the moment at which the actual policy was decided upon, and the assembly only barely makes its decision effective. The third situation comes in the Sicilian debate (vi.9–23). This is also a rethinking of a previous decree, but this time the debate we are given changes nothing but the scale of the earlier decision (see vi.25–26)—and, of course, Athens will ultimately fail to make the will of this assembly effective (i.e., the Sicilian expedition will fail). These three different situations contain an obvious progression, for the assemblies that Thucydides presents are ever more removed from the moment of the actual decision, and the Athenians are ever less successful at carrying out their decisions. The effect is to emphasize the increasing ineffectiveness of the assembly as a deliberative body.

In this presentation we have an indication from Thucydides that there is a three-step development within Athens, and it is possible to build on this initial indication to a very considerable degree. Again and again we shall see that some aspect of the presentation of Periclean Athens is taken up in the Mytilenian debate and the Sicilian debate, but having changed its form in some way on each occasion, so that we are given a progression in three steps. For example, in his last speech Pericles brushes aside any possible concerns concerning his character by an appeal to his own well-known integrity (ii.60.5). The full significance of this claim starts to become clearer in the course of the Mytilenian debate, for there we find impersonal accusations being made (e.g., iii.38.2, 42.2), and although it is unclear whether they are justified, they are conspicuously not denied outright in the Periclean fashion. In the debate on Sicily, the impersonal aspect has disappeared, for Nicias makes accusations that are unambiguously directed at Alcibiades (vi.12.2–13.1), and in response, Alcibiades names Nicias twice (16.1, 18.6). Thucydides' own remarks (vi.15.2–4) not only confirm that Nicias' accusations are justified but also note that Alcibiades' policy is partly motivated by animus against Nicias. The use of evermore severe, more justified and, in the end, more consequential, *ad hominem* attacks thus give us a development in three steps over the course of these assemblies—and note how it coheres with the three situations mentioned above: once again, the suggestion is of a decline in the assembly.

Sometimes we find a three-step development if we are ready to look a bit beyond the speeches for one of the moments. So, for example, Pericles warns the Athenians against expanding their empire while at war with Sparta (i.144.1; cf. ii.65.7), and the Sicilian debate offers a clear antithesis of this posture in the assertion of the necessity of imperial expansion (vi.18.3),[16] a position shared by the Athenians at Melos. The Mytilenian debate does not touch on the question of expansion, but a bit later one of its participants, Cleon, does: in exchange for peace, he demands (inter alia) the return of four cities that had been part of the Athenian empire two decades earlier (iv.21.3). This is an intermediate position between that of Pericles (no-expansion-during-this-war) and Alcibiades in the Sicilian debate (unbounded expansion). Thus we again have a three-stage development. In similar fashion, we shall see that the theme of the increasing narrowness of temporal focus, that is, immediacy, which is sometimes flagged by the Greek words τά παρόντα, draws us into the Melian Dialogue.[17]

Thus my treatment will focus on the Periclean speeches, the Mytilenian debate, and the Sicilian debate, but it will move beyond them to touch on other portions of the text as necessary. I take the four Periclean speeches (i.139–144, ii.13, 35–46, 60–64) to provide a single standpoint—indeed, I take this standpoint to be the main focus of that section of the text in which Pericles is the principal actor (i.139–ii.65). Further, I think it is broadly correct to speak of the Athens of Cleon and the Athens of Alcibiades as distinct moments.[18] To provide a summary of every respect in which we have a three-stage development would be overly verbose; rather, I will note each one in passing, particularly toward the end.

JUSTICE AND POWER

One of the richest themes in Thucydides is commonly referred to as "justice and power" (perhaps "trust and force" would be better). The phrase points to two fundamentally different ways of relating to other people. Consider, for example, two different bases for an alliance suggested by the Mytilenians in their speech in book iii: on the one hand, they claim that "neither friendship between individuals nor partnership between cities is in any way secure, unless they are convinced of one another's good nature and are in other respects similar, for from differences in judgment come also differences in conduct" (iii.10.1). On the other hand, they subsequently say that "equally balanced fear is the only security for an alliance, for one who wishes to transgress is deterred by the fact that he is not superior if he attacks" (iii.11.2). The first claim would found a relationship with others on mutual respect and goodwill; from this perspective, one might hope to attain one's ends with others through trust. The second claim sees no place for trust but relies rather on strength, on the ability forcibly to compel others to obey one's will.[19]

From the first set of speeches (and not only in the speeches), these two principles are a constant and well-known presence in Thucydides' text. He often presents them in a manner that brings out their apparent mutual incompatibility: to the extent that we forcibly compel others to submit to us, we undermine the possibility of trust with them; to the extent that we put faith in friendship or treaties, we leave ourselves open to violence and treachery. But there is another side: to the extent that we can trust others, we have a source of safety, for we do not need to fear, or arm ourselves, against them; to the extent that we can forcibly dominate others, we also have a source of safety, for we can prevent their doing us any harm. We shall see that Periclean Athens enjoys the advantages of both justice and power—specifically priority given to the benefits of justice at home and to the realities of power abroad— while Athens, as we see her later in the work, increasingly enjoys neither.

More than this, we shall also see how these two principles are not always incompatible with one another: power can come from justice.

The reader should note that in what follows, when I refer, for example, to "justice," it is generally to the relevant concept just described, and not always to the Greek δίκαιος. For example, the Athenians at Melos would define "justice" (δίκαιος) in their own, antinomian, manner, but we do not find room in their words for trust and goodwill to govern human relations. In that sense, "justice" is simply absent from their world.

THE SPEECHES AND THUCYDIDES' THOUGHT

One respect in which Thucydides differs from those who write history today is in his inclusion of speeches in direct discourse that cannot be verbatim transcripts of what was actually said.[20] Not having tape-recorders or scribes writing shorthand to make a word-for-word transcript of what was said, he was obliged to be creative to some degree in his record of the speeches, and the creative space inherent in the situation allowed him to turn the speeches into an investigation of the fundamental forces lying behind the immediate facts of the case, profoundly deepening the view his work provides into the reality of the time. It is in this (deeper) sense that it is correct to say that, though he must often have put his own words into his characters' mouths, he did so "in the service of historical truth."[21] (Of course, in the narrow, more immediate, sense of what words exactly were spoken, Thucydides cannot be said to have served the truth.)

Decades ago, it was common to attribute to Thucydides himself opinions expressed by his characters in the speeches,[22] taking the speeches to be "more or less mouthpieces of the author."[23] Today it is understood that this is too simple, for the views expressed in the speeches are often contradicted or qualified by the narrative, in which Thucydides speaks in propria persona. Indeed, the views expressed in speeches are frequently contradicted by other speeches, since pairings of opposed speeches are not uncommon. Accordingly, many scholars would now agree, with good reason, that "Thucydides' speeches are . . . not vehicles for expressing personal opinion,"[24] and further, that "the few authorial comments by Thucydides, and only such comments, are the evidence from which we can hope to reconstruct Thucydides' own opinions."[25]

There is, however, one way in which we can derive Thucydides' views from the speeches alone: through their interrelation. Scholars have long recognized points of connection, verbal and thematic, between certain of the speeches, and authorial intention in this regard is beyond doubt. In particular, in a brilliant series of papers, the great Oxford classicist Colin Macleod brought to light many connections between Pericles and subsequent Athenian speakers, and his work forms the backbone of my own understanding of Thucydides. Not only has Macleod's work long seemed to me to occupy a special place by virtue of its rigor and depth, it also seemed to me richly suggestive, pregnant with possibilities for further investigation. In particular, implicit in Macleod's work is a larger view of Thucydides' thought, one spanning the first seven books, which comes to light through the Athenian speeches. It will be the work of this book further to develop this larger view, and though I do endeavor to show the connection and coherence of my account with Thucydides' explicit statements, I focus primarily on the speeches to develop an understanding of Thucydides' views.

There is another reason to focus on political speeches, and it comes into focus as we consider their context.[26] They appear at moments in history that are significant in (at least) one of three ways. First, they often come at moments that are decisive in changing the situation.[27] For example, the Athenian decision to reject a Spartan ultimatum, which will mean war, is the occasion of the first speech of Pericles (i.140–144), in which he provides his own insightful reflections upon the situation, and justifies the decision; when the Athenians later make the fateful decision to invade Sicily, we have a set of speeches on the decision (vi.9–23). Second, speeches often point to paradigms, as the Plataean debate (iii.53–67) points to the brutalizing effect that the war is having upon the Spartans, or as the Corcyrean speech (i.32–36) points to the difficulty for neutral states of staying out of the orbit of the two major power blocs.[28] Finally (a specific sort of paradigm), speeches often come at the first instance of a new and continuing reality. The Funeral Oration (ii.35–46) comes at the first burial of those who have died in the war, and thus stands in relation to a practice that will continue, unmentioned, throughout the war; Pericles' indirectly reported speech (ii.13) is given in relation to the first Spartan invasion of Attica, another significant event that will occur regularly in the future. A key to understanding the Melian Dialogue, I will argue, is that it too fits into this account of the speeches. Thus the occasions on which the speeches occur suggest that they have a universal aspect.

The Athenian speeches—both in and beyond the assembly—are a special case, taken together. Most of them represent some decisive new paradigm within Athens, and the Athenian reaction to this; every one of them tells us something significant about Athens at an important moment. Together, they can reasonably be taken to indicate the most important shifts in the state of the city over the course of the war. Now, the fundamental question of the Peloponnesian war was, in Thucydides' view, the question of Athenian power (i.23.6).[29] This power was theirs to lose, and lose it they did, through the folly of their own internal conflict (ii.65.10–12). The self-caused destruction of Athens thus lies at the heart of the course of the Peloponnesian War, and it is through the relation of the Athenian speeches to one another that we get a detailed account of this self-destruction. They bring out in detail the process which took Athens from a seemingly unassailable position under Pericles to internal conflict and ultimate defeat.

In what follows, I hope to be able to justify a number of novel theses, such as the notion of immediacy, or the importance of the whole for Thucydides, particularly when comparing Pericles to his successors, or my treatment of what might be called the Periclean political philosophy, which gives priority to the city, aligns with key statements made by Thucydides in the first person and thus gives a new answer to those who find in the account of the plague a damning criticism of Athens' first citizen. At the same time, I hope I can shed some new light on themes that have often been treated before, such as the three-stage decline of Athens or justice and power; the account I give of Pericles will, I hope, answer some recent "anti-Periclean" work. My treatment of post-Periclean speeches are intended to be new primarily in their relation to the whole (recall that a fundamental idea here is that a thing's relation to the whole changes what it is), and this plays a crucial role in making clear how the larger theses are based in the text. Still, I have, at times, leaned in the direction of setting out explicitly some matters that will be familiar to experts on Thucydides, partly in the hope of making important points clear to those readers familiar with Plato rather than Thucydides, and partly out of a recognition that certain points are of particular importance to the comparison of Thucydides with Plato (for example, the subjective spirit that is characteristic not only of Alcibiades, but of Athens as a whole at this time, and which coheres meaningfully with what we see in Callicles and Thrasymachus).

NOTES

1. Wolfgang Plenio, *Die letzte Rede des Perikles (Thukydides II 60–64)* (Kiel: Christian Albrechts Universität, 1954), 28–34 treats the four virtues considered at ii.65.5–6, finishing with a particularly strong statement of the need for the unity of all four. Georg Friedrich Bender, *Der Begriff des Staatsmannes bei Thukydides* (Würzburg: Konrad Triltsch Verlag, 1938), 36, and Rengakos, *Form und Wandel*, 40–2 (see also 47), both note the importance of a 'unity' at this point, along the same lines I take here, though neither pursue the matter as I shall in what follows. Werner Kohl, *Die Redetrais vor der sizilischen Expedition (Thukydides 6,9–23)* (Meisenheim am Glan: Verlag Anton Hain, 1977), 181, looking back at Pericles from the Sicilian debate, notes the importance of a "unity."

2. Pericles' words at ii.60.2–4 follows a similar logic, applied this time to the city and the individual. We shall consider this passage below, under the heading, *The City as Center* (pages 27–30).

3. Bender, *Begriff des Staatsmannes*, sought to understand Nicias, Alcibiades, and Hermocrates through these words of Pericles, though we shall see that subsequent scholarship has refuted certain of his conclusions concerning Nicias and Alcibiades.

4. Rengakos, *Form und Wandel*, 42. He goes on to say that these qualities are "bound up most closely with one another, so that each of them has its usefulness and efficacy only in connection with all the others." The distinction between the two 'intellectual' and two 'ethical' virtues here was made already by Plenio, *Die letzte Rede*, 31, with a similar emphasis on the need for all four.

5. G. P. Landmann, "Das Lob Athens in der Grabrede des Perikles—Thukydides II 34–41," *Museum Helveticum* 31, fasc. 2 (1974): 65–95. Adam Parry, *Logos and Ergon in Thucydides* (New York: Arno Press, [1981] 1957), in a richly thought-provoking work, gives a treatment along similar lines to λόγος and ἔργον, one of the work's most fundamental oppositions: "λόγος is only right insofar as it has a clear and immediate relation to reality [i.e., to ἔργον]. . . . But ἔργον without λόγος is disastrous and meaningless." Still, "it is impossible *a priori* to determine the relative importance of particular manifestations of the λόγος/ἔργον distinction" (1981: 89; see also 87–88). All this seems to me to be more widely applicable to oppositions in Thucydides; certainly it is true of the particular cases we shall treat in what follows.

6. The Corinthians speaking at Sparta (i.68–71) claim that the national character of the Athenians is particularly adventurous and active (i.70.2–9). Thucydides himself clearly agrees with this assessment, which not only comes out in certain explicit statements (e.g., i.102.3, iv.55.2, viii.96.5) but is also implicitly suggested in the *Pentecontaetia* (i.e., i.89–117). See W. Robert Connor, *Thucydides* (Princeton, NJ: Princeton University Press, 1984), 36–47, especially 45: "the impression that emerges from the *Pentecontaetia* is of the restless energy of the Athenians, their refusal to be stymied, their ability to come out of every setback with even greater vigor than ever before."

7. I take this example from Colin Macleod, *Collected Essays* (Oxford: Oxford University Press, 1983), 82–83. The view I advocate here, according to which the whole has a privileged place, seems to me to be implied, in certain respects, in his work; certainly it is anticipated in certain particulars: see, for example, his insightful comments on Nicias, Alcibiades, and Pericles (86).

8. Thus I mostly agree with Tim Rood, *Thucydides: Narrative and Explanation* (New York: Oxford University Press, [2004] 1998), 158, when he says, "Alkibiades is like Perikles without his honesty, prudence and patriotism; Nikias is like Perikles without his coercive powers. Our sense of (the absence of) Perikles changes, in turn, as we ponder what it means that he was not Alkibiades, nor Nikias." However, I would not stop there, for in my view the crucial point about Alcibiades and Nicias in relation to Pericles is that they each represent only a part of the whole he attained.

9. Adam Parry, "Thucydides' Use of Abstract Language," in *The Language of Achilles and Other Papers* (New York: Oxford University Press, 1989), 193, translates τὰ παρόντα as "immediate, going reality."

10. Emily Greenwood, *Thucydides and the Shaping of History* (London: Duckworth, 2006), 42. Her chapter following these remarks, particularly pp. 49–55, gives examples in support of this claim.

11. Many classicists would disagree with this statement, for they would take the view that Thucydides did not believe in the efficacy of human planning, believing instead that events were unpredictable, and human behavior irrational, to such a degree that "the knowledge of history is the awareness of the domination of the irrational" (Connor, *Thucydides*, 143). For this 'irrationalist' school, the reader of Thucydides acquires insight but is aware of the futility of trying to derive any practical benefit from it. Clearly such a view is incompatible with the claims I have just made. In Nicholas Thorne, "Prediction, Probability, and Pessimism in Thucydides," *Mouseion* LVIII—Series III 14, no. 1 (2017): 45–62, I have presented an answer to the irrationalists by focusing on the work of H. P. Stahl and showing how it fails on its own terms. In seeking to show that history for Thucydides is irrational, Stahl appeals to two different kinds of irrationality, and these contradict one another. On the one hand, he often emphasizes what we might call the irrationality of events, according to which they are fortuitous and unpredictable. On the other hand, he also emphasizes the irrationality of individuals, according to which they judge events poorly. But insofar as people can be said to judge well or poorly, events cannot simply be irrational: the notion of judgment requires that there is something in events which is not simply a matter of chance. Insofar as events are irrational, people cannot be said to be more or less rational in relation to them. Accordingly, Stahl asserts both sides of a contradictory opposition without confronting the question of their relation, producing an incoherent account—and a serious problem for irrationalist accounts of Thucydides. The contradiction, I try to show, can be resolved by a probabilistic account of events in Thucydides which involves focusing less on the specific outcome of a plan than on outcomes in a more general sense, and which also leads us back to the central role of human behavior and thus to the decisive importance of adequate thought. The insights of the irrationalist school can be incorporated into this account. The question of what exactly Thucydides believes to be "man's place in history" requires some exposition; the interested reader can consult that paper for a fuller view than I give here.

12. It is interesting to note that these two senses of 'immediate' as I describe them here have a close parallel in "fidelity and comprehensiveness" as described by D. C. Schindler, *Plato's Critique of Impure Reason* (Washington, DC: The Catholic University of America Press, 2008), 13, as he describes an adequate test for "misology," a radical form of skepticism.

13. Just before this, he makes another remark that harmonizes in general terms with the need for a wider view, as he first shows his awareness of the limitations of a single perspective, and the need for and difficulty of transcending this (i.22.2–3).

14. I am inclined to agree with Connor, *Thucydides*, 31, that the work's "claim to report the greatest *kinesis* is . . . to be judged not by comparisons with the massive operations described by Herodotus, but in the concentration and intensity of human suffering in the long and destructive war."

15. These direct speeches are to be contrasted with the occasions on which Thucydides gives an indirect and summary account of an Athenian speech at Athens, as at iv.21–22 or 27–28.

16. The claim that war with Sparta is not on when the Athenians sail on Melos or Sicily is not one that Thucydides would accept (v.26.2) and does not affect a more fundamental point: Pericles did not feel subject to a compulsion to expand the empire.

17. I have avoided the speech of the Athenian ambassadors at Sparta (i.73–78) and that of Euphemus at Camarina (vi.82–87) partly for reasons of space and partly because they are fundamentally different situations from the speeches that take place in the assembly. The Melian dialogue, however, seems to me to be too tightly tied to the Sicilian debate and expedition to leave out.

18. Rose Zahn, *Die erste Periklesrede (Thukydides i.140–44)* (Leipzig: R. Noske, 1934), 70, fn.14 notes that in addition to Archidamus, only Pericles, Cleon, and Alcibiades are given, on their first personal appearance, a short characterization that encompasses their nature and their importance as statesmen in one or two regards.

19. I began thinking about justice and power in this way after reading Colin Macleod, "Reason and Necessity: Thucydides 3.9–14, 37–48," *Journal of Hellenic Studies* 98 (1978): 64–78, who should be consulted on the Mytilenian speech mentioned here. His work seems to me to have opened up particularly fertile lines of inquiry on the subject of justice and power.

20. Indeed, there is some distance between Thucydides and the discipline of history today: he is a writer working in a genre that seems to have been substantially self-created. If I occasionally refer to him as a 'historian,' this is primarily for reasons of style and because the label is useful to distinguish him from Plato.

21. Macleod, "Reason and Necessity," 64. Christian Schneider, *Information und Absicht bei Thukydides—Hypomnemata 41* (Göttingen: Vandenhoeck und Ruprecht, 1974), 145–53 gives reason to reject the idea that Thucydides at i.22.1 is concerned with the wording of the speeches, and understands Thucydides to be concerned with giving us the overall and most fundamental thought and argument of each speaker, and not with reproducing an 'authentic' text of each speech.

22. For example, Bender, *Begriff des Staatsmannes,* 5 declares that *Pericles'* words at ii.60.5–7 give us Thucydides' means of evaluating statesmen. In fact, I think there is common ground between Pericles' words here and Thucydides' views, but we need to go rather farther than Bender does in order to establish this.

23. Hans-Peter Stahl, *Thucydides: Man's Place in History*, trans. David Seward (Swansea: The Classical Press of Wales, [1966] 2003), 173.

24. Rood, *Narrative and Explanation,* 40.

25. Simon Hornblower, *Thucydides* (Baltimore: Johns Hopkins University Press, 1987), 163; see also 72. Stahl, *Man's Place in History,* 173–89, is well worth reading on this matter.

26. I consider the generals' speeches—such as that of Phormio at ii.89 or that of Nicias at vii.77—to be of a different type, and I would have to specify several qualifications before including them in this analysis.

27. As Colin Macleod, "Form and Meaning in the Melian Dialogue," *Historia* 23 (1974): 52, suggests, as he provides an overview of the different aspects one can find in a Thucydidean speech. I began thinking of the speeches in the manner I describe here as I read Cogan, *The Human Thing.*

28. In fact, Thucydides' work is awash in paradigms. As Connor, *Thucydides*, 144, says, "Mantinea is Thucydides' paradigmatic hoplite battle—as Plataea was among sieges, or Corcyra among revolutions. Thucydides often adopts the technique of presenting one instance of a phenomenon in rich detail, while leaving other examples relatively undeveloped." Similarly, as A. Andrewes, "The Mytilene Debate: Thucydides 3.36–49," *Phoenix* 16, no. 2 (Summer 1962): 77, notes, Cleon is the only demagogue who gets significant treatment in Thucydides (Hyperbolus, for example, is all but ignored). See also Hornblower, *Thucydides*, 41–42: the *Pentekontaetia* stands more generally for Athenian aggression toward her "allies."

29. Martin Ostwald, *ANAGKH in Thucydides* (Atlanta: Scholars Press, 1988), 2–3, finds a grammatical balance in i.23.6 between Athenian power and Spartan fear as equal, joint causes of the war. I agree that "the process of Athenian growth had the development of Lacedaemonian fears as a concomitant," but Athenian power nevertheless has a *logical* priority within this relationship.

(1) Periclean Athens

A BALANCE OF OPPOSITES

Thucydides' portrayal of Pericles consistently depicts the Athenian statesman as maintaining a unity out of opposites, holding together what often appear to be contradictory, or at least contrary, oppositions. This is evident in the speeches given to Pericles, in Thucydides' direct narration concerning him, and also, as we shall see later, in the manner in which Thucydides has implicitly related Pericles to his successors later in the work.

It is in the Funeral Oration that this structure has most frequently been noted in the past.[1] Here Pericles often expresses his praise of Athenian life in terms of a balance between attributes which are usually mutually exclusive elsewhere. Thus he speaks, for example, of a balance of freedom and order: in Athens, public life is free, as is private life, which, despite a certain permissiveness, is free from jealousy (ii.37.2), and yet this freedom coexists with obedience to the laws, written and unwritten (37.3). Furthermore, Athens is an open city, and its citizens live at ease compared to the Spartans (39.1), and yet the Athenians are every bit as brave and capable with arms as their enemies (39.1–4). Athens is not disturbed by conflicts of private and public interest, for Athenians are capable of attending to both public and private matters in an adequate fashion (40.2). There is, in addition, a balance of the intellectual with the active in Athens.[2] Where others would be ignorant while bold, or hesitant while deliberating (40.3), "we believe that words are not a harm to deeds, but rather that it is harmful not to be instructed by speech before going to what must be done." (ii.40.2) One could list further examples, but again, the matter has been treated before.[3]

Less well attested in the scholarship is the fact that this pattern runs right through the characterization of Pericles in Thucydides. This starts with the introduction to Pericles' first speech, where we are told that he was the "most capable at both speaking and acting" (λέγειν τε καὶ πράσσειν—i.139.4). This presents Pericles to us in terms of the unity of an opposition, specifically λόγος and ἔργον (i.e., word and deed), one of the most fundamental oppositions in the work.[4]

Thucydides has structured his narrative so as to show that Pericles navigates between the opposed extremes of activity and passivity according to the requirements of the situation at hand. We see this in two episodes (ii.21–22 and ii.59–65) whose connection has long been recognized, on account of both phrases which echo one another and the thematic link of consistent Periclean judgment versus the inconstant and irrational behavior of the masses.[5] The first episode takes place in the first year of the war, when the Spartans invade Attica, and begin to ravage Athenian land. Under the pressure of events, the city gets into an excited state; the people become angry with Pericles (ii.21.3)—they want action, to go out and attack the enemy. Thucydides, however, has already given another perspective from which to consider the situation: the Periclean plan, which requires that the Athenians do not leave the city walls to defend their country estates (i.143.5). The episode is described in a manner that emphasizes the unreason on the part of the population, and contrasts it with the stable behavior of Pericles. He behaves in a manner that will prevent the people from making decisions through passion rather than judgment (ὀργῇ . . . μᾶλλον ἢ γνώμῃ—ii.22.1). The implication is clear: it is through the agency of Pericles alone that the city maintains its course on this occasion.[6]

In the second year of the war, events move the Athenians in a different manner. Two invasions of Attica and a plague now weigh heavy upon them; eager to end the war, they go so far as to send ambassadors to Sparta. Again, the unreason of the population is emphasized: "at a loss in every respect in their resolution [πανταχόθεν τε τῇ γνώμῃ ἄποροι], they turned upon Pericles" (ii.59.2). Again, Pericles recognizes that the populace is caught up in the heat of the moment, just as he had expected (ii.59.3). He therefore calls an assembly to calm them down, drawing explicit attention in his ensuing speech to his own constancy and their inconstancy (ii.61.4). Again he is successful in maintaining the city on its course (65.2).

Between these two parallel episodes, there is a significant difference: in the first, the Athenian populace swings toward an unreasonable extreme of activity; in the second, toward excessive passivity. In both cases, they would abandon the resolution with which the war was begun. Again, Thucydides has given a perspective beyond the heat of the moment from which to consider these two situations: the Periclean plan. From this standpoint, we see that Pericles can resist unreasonable activity and passivity as the need arises—or, to put it another way, he is capable of being passive and active as the situation requires.[7] Thus his behavior mirrors what we have already seen in other aspects of Thucydides' portrayal of him: we have a balance of opposites, this time in the form of activity and passivity.

Pericles' balance of these two principles is consistent with his words on the subject. The longest relevant passage is in his last speech (ii.63.2–3), where he considers the inactive sort of person (ἀπράγμων). Of course, this passage comes at a moment when Pericles is trying to steer the Athenians away from excessive passivity, so he puts considerable emphasis on the folly inherent in one-sided inactivity, noting that it would destroy a state if in command alone, and that it does not benefit a city when that city is ruling others (if he had been obliged to give a speech at ii.21–22, he would obviously have emphasized the other side). But the key phrase is this: "the inactive element cannot be preserved if it is not marshalled with the active one" (63.3). The inactive element is not eliminated and replaced by the active, but rather joins forces with it, and that is where safety is found (outside of slavery).

The episodes at ii.21–22 and ii.59–65 contain a verbal parallel that is particularly worthy of attention, for it points to the factor that most deeply unifies them. In the first episode, Pericles "saw that [the people] were upset over the immediate situation" (ὁρῶν ... αὐτοὺς πρὸς τὸ παρὸν χαλεπαίνοντας—ii.22.1). This phrase is repeated almost verbatim in the second episode (ὁρῶν αὐτοὺς πρὸς τὰ παρόντα χαλεπαίνοντας—ii.59.3). The words παρὸν and παρόντα return us to the language that we noted in the introduction (see the section, *Immediacy in Thucydides*, pages 11–3), for it is also used to characterize the effect of war in general, which "drives the character of most people down to the level of their immediate circumstances [πρὸς τὰ παρόντα]" (iii.82.2). Accordingly, Thucydides has characterized the behavior of the people in terms of immediacy, a natural result of the pressures of war, while Pericles is presented as unaffected by those pressures—that is, as being moved precisely by what is *not* immediate: he is able to stick to a plan thought out in advance. The balance of intellectual prowess with the ability to take effective action (something claimed in the Funeral Oration at ii.40.2–3; see above) is clearly no empty boast with Pericles at the helm. Certainly, his judicious use of passivity and activity avoids one-sided extremes, but underlying this two-sided Periclean competency is the non-immediate source of his action, that is, thought.

One opposition that runs through Pericles' speeches is particularly worthy of attention. On the one hand, he appeals frequently to that constellation of concepts to which mutual recognition and trust are most fundamental; these we may bring together under the heading "justice." So, for example, in his first speech, right after the opening remarks, Pericles' first point concerns the treaty which he asserts Sparta to have broken (i.140.2), and in the final moments of his speech he returns to this (144.2). The claim is that Sparta's ultimatum fails to treat the Athenians as equals.[8] The speech is thus bookended with appeals to justice. The Funeral Oration turns on a different kind of appeal to justice: a central section praises the justice of life in the city (ii.37–41.1), so we hear that Athens contains freedom, order under the law, openness, and the reconciliation of private and public interest. Indeed, Pericles' own behavior provides an example of the importance of justice: we are told that he was powerful within the city "through his reputation and his judgment, and being manifestly most incorruptible by money" (ii.65.8). Thus his character, the aspect of him most essential to trust, is part of what makes him effective—and we shall see that Thucydides' depiction of subsequent Athenian leaders drives this point home all the more strongly.

On the other hand, the importance of power is never far from Pericles' mind. In his first speech, sandwiched between those normative appeals we just noted, we find an insightful appraisal of the strategic situation, one whose accuracy may indeed have become clearer with time (ii.65.6), but which, at the time, would have been far from obvious. The Funeral Oration is not content only to speak of Athenian justice but also draws attention to Athenian bravery (ii.39.4), military ability (39.2–3) and above all, definite achievements (41.2–5). But it is above all in the last speech that we find an emphasis on the fact of Athenian power (ii.62), culminating in a passage awash in superlatives (ii.64.3–6).

Accordingly, we find both justice and power in Pericles; that he values each and is an advocate of attention to each should be beyond dispute. The principles of justice and power find political expression in the forms of democracy and empire, respectively, and both are part of Periclean Athens. The Funeral Oration focuses on Athens as a democracy, the last speech on Athens as an imperial power; we have just seen how Pericles' first speech makes its argument by means of both principles. An attentive reader might note that the two principles seem to be in tension with one another: if Pericles thinks so highly of justice, how can he support an empire which is, "so to speak, a tyranny," and which it was, perhaps, wrong to acquire?[9] (ii.63.2) This point will prove important when we consider Athens on subsequent occasions.

From one perspective, then, there is a tension between justice and power. Pericles, however, points to another perspective, for it is not the case that he only sets the two principles next to one another, attending now to one, now to the other. Rather, he suggests an essential relation between the two: in the Funeral Oration, he briefly considers the achievements of past generations, who have maintained Athenian freedom and acquired an empire, and then poses a question concerning "the principles by which we came into this position and the form of government from which its greatness resulted" (ii.36.4, trans. Lattimore).[10] He then proceeds to describe the *normative* greatness of Athens, that is, the state of affairs within which a constellation of normative characteristics—trust, justice, mutual regard—can play a decisive role (ii.37–41.1). The power of the city comes from the habits he has outlined

(41.2). The implication is that justice at home is the *cause* of Athenian power abroad—and recall how Pericles' own, conspicuously just, behavior is said to be a cause of his power within the city (ii.65.8). This is a reality whose absence will increasingly be felt as we move beyond Pericles, and to which we shall return in the Conclusion (see pages 80–2).

There is one final point to make about justice and power, something that is not said explicitly in the text. Pericles has attained a balance of these two principles by finding a place in which each one can be emphasized: the main focus for justice is at home, for power, abroad. Justice is appropriate to the internal life of the city, and its presence here can be a crucial source of the city's power. The acquisition and use of power abroad makes the internal life of the city possible by protecting it: if Athens were at the mercy of Sparta or the Persians, the life described in the Funeral Oration would be reduced to docile obedience to a foreign authority. Indeed, it should be obvious that Thucydides cannot be a one-sided advocate of justice. No author ever wrote to greater effect about the folly of pursuing justice to the exclusion of power than Thucydides in the Melian Dialogue.[11] Accordingly, it is very greatly to Pericles' credit that he focuses as much as he does upon power, because he thus avoids the foolish and fatal mistake of a one-sided pursuit of justice.[12] It would be a mistake to attempt simply to trust the Spartans or Persians, as it would also be imprudent to engage in plots against one's fellow citizens. Pericles, given the manner in which he pursues each principle, can draw strength from both justice and power, while avoiding the difficulties that might arise from a one-sided or inappropriate pursuit of either.

One final Periclean balance should be mentioned, though it is not a balance of opposites. The past, in the form of the example of previous generations, finds a place in all of Pericles' directly reported speeches (i.144.4, ii.36, ii.62.3), while all were concerned with deliberation about the future on the basis of present realities. That is, we have here the widest possible temporal frame of reference, in which past, present and future are all given a place: it is not an immediate perspective. There is even the odd glance toward eternity (e.g., αἰείμνηστος, "eternal memory"—ii.43.2, 64.5; ἐς ἀΐδιον, "for all time"—64.3), including the realization that even Athens' empire must one day decline (ii.64.3). This recalls Thucydides' own glance at eternity, when he talks of a "possession for all time" (κτῆμα . . . ἐς αἰεί—i.22.4).

THE CITY AS CENTER

As he begins the Funeral Oration, Pericles points to a possible problem: some listeners, who knew the dead well, may find the praise given insufficient, while others, less well-acquainted with the facts, might be envious and find the praise excessive (ii.35.2). To speak moderately (μετρίως εἰπεῖν—35.2) is therefore difficult. This might seem a strange thing to say, particularly in that it seems to suggest an indifference to the facts of the case—is moderate speaking here to consist in a middle path between knowledge and ignorance?[13] The passage makes sense, however, if it is understood to point to a problem that arises if the individual is the focus and standard of judgment: regardless of the facts of the case, individual interests can conflict with one another—even when the dead are being praised!—and this can produce discord. The speech that Pericles delivers contains an implicit solution to this problem: it spends a great deal of time focused on the city (36.4–42.1) and then declares the greatest part of the eulogy to be complete (42.2). This change of perspective from individual to city resolves the difficulty seen at the start, that is, "to attain the wish and opinion of each of you" (35.3): everyone can partake of the greatness of the city. Thus there is a suggestion consonant with the speech's praise of Athens: the city can resolve difficulties that might result in discord if individuals were simply left to themselves.[14]

This orientation—a focus on the city as prior to the individual—is stressed by Pericles in every one of his speeches. In his first speech, he suggests the citizens should lay waste to their own lands as a gesture of defiance to the Peloponnesians (i.143.5); he later pledges to give his own lands to the state if they alone should be spared by the enemy (ii.13). It is in his last two speeches, however, that he is forced to justify his view, because in these, he is faced directly with the experience of hardship. It is thus in these last two speeches that we are given an account of the end for which sacrifices can reasonably be demanded, and this gives us the reason that the city must be prior.

In both speeches, we get a double answer, of which one part is focused on the hereafter, the other on this life. The first part provides consolation to the dead by pointing to the fame and glory that lives on after those who have accomplished great things.[15] Thus in the Funeral Oration we find praise of the virtue of the dead (ii.42.2–4), with repeated emphasis on the glory (δόξα—42.4, 43.2) and the lasting remembrance they will inspire (43.2–4). In similar fashion, the last speech culminates in an appeal to "everlasting future glory" (τὸ ἔπειτα δόξα αἰείμνηστος—64.5) for an Athens that has "the greatest name" (ὄνομα μέγιστον—64.3), that presents the Athenians with a vision of the lasting fame of their city, of which they may aspire to take part.

There is, however, a second reason why the city can demand great risks and sacrifices from its citizens, and this second reason lies in the present rather than the future (and note the temporal balance here, as mentioned in the preceding section). Pericles' last speech may end with effective rhetoric, but it begins with a substantive argument. After an introductory sentence, he drives right to the heart of the matter:

(1) Periclean Athens

I believe that a city set aright as a whole benefits particular individuals more than when each of the citizens flourishes, but the whole fails. For a man may do well on his own, but when his country is destroyed he is no less destroyed with it, and when he fares ill in a city which prospers, he is much more likely to recover. Since a city is able to bear individual misfortunes, but each citizen cannot bear hers, how is it not necessary that all come to her aid? (ii.60.2–4)

It would be difficult indeed to answer this account—it is never answered in Thucydides—and it has the character of a fundamental truth about political life.[16] It is simply not in the nature of things that the individual can reasonably hope to enjoy the stability necessary to the long-term enjoyment of his own ends if he stands on his own, apart from a community. It is only through a state—here, the city—that the individual can reasonably hope to flourish in the longer term. On this ground, it is appropriate to expect citizens to make sacrifices for the city. As we shall see, the subsequent story of Athens in the Peloponnesian War will show just how correct Pericles is to focus on the city as he does. All this coheres naturally with the more rhetorical aspects of the last speech, which seek to make individuals feel that they are part of something greater than themselves, so that they might reach out beyond the toils and afflictions of everyday life and grasp superlative greatness and eternity in some way.

Those inclined to doubt the truth of Pericles' words should consider them in relation to the situation at hand: he speaks at a moment of supreme crisis, when people are crowded into the city and suffering from the plague. The people of the countryside, though they might be reduced to dire straits by the loss of their land, would be in an even worse state without the city, for they would be eternally and absolutely at the mercy of foreign armies. The same thing is true for the citizenry taken generally: the city, because it can preserve their freedom in spite of the plague and the wasting of the land by the Spartan army, gives them the independence necessary to direct their own affairs, and thus in time to recover what they may lose, whereas once national freedom were gone, their ability to do this—or anything else—would be subject to the whim of stronger foreign powers.

In the Funeral Oration, Pericles is faced with a challenge similar to that of the last speech. Thucydides gives us the speech on the occasion of the first funeral in the war (ii.34.1), and he mentions that the custom was followed throughout the war (34.7). Pericles is thus placed in relation to all the Athenian funerals which went on over the course of the whole war, a fact that implicitly links him to the deaths throughout the war. His speech does not only give "glory" as an answer to the question of what might justify these deaths, for he also points at length to the life of the city, to the possibilities it alone can provide for individuals. So, for example, citizens do not live in a mutually suspicious environment of conflict (ii.37.2); lawlessness does not prevail, because fear produces obedience to the laws, written and unwritten (37.3); while Athenian citizens enjoy a great variety of good things in their city (ii.38). The Athenians and their enemies, he says, do not compete for the same prize, since Athens offers unique benefits (42.1). Thus the life of the city answers the question of why individuals must ultimately subordinate themselves to the demands of the city, risking their lives on its behalf.

PERICLES UNDERMINED?

There is one episode above all in which Thucydides might seem to criticize Pericles, the juxtaposition of the Funeral Oration (ii.35–46) with the account of the plague (ii.47.3–54). Particular attention is drawn to the suffering of the Athenian people, and one of Thucydides' aims here must be to draw a connection between Pericles' plan and this suffering. Certainly, the suffering caused by the war is a major interest of Thucydides—notice, for example, how he justifies his claim that the Peloponnesian War was greater than the Persian Wars by an appeal to the greater number of "calamities" or "sufferings" (παθήματα—i.23.1) in the later conflict.[17] Here we must clarify Thucydides' purpose in connecting Pericles with suffering, and specify the (very limited) respect in which there is a criticism of Pericles in this.

We noted above that the Funeral Oration places Pericles in relation to the reality of death throughout the war. This makes it all the more significant that the Funeral Oration is immediately followed by Thucydides' account of the plague,[18] in which a great deal of what Pericles said about the life of Athens is directly contradicted. Pericles celebrated the self-sufficient individual (τὸ σῶμα αὔταρκες—ii.41.1) characteristic of Athens; in the description of the plague, Thucydides tells us that "nobody [σῶμα ... αὔταρκες ... οὐδὲν] was strong enough for it" (ii.51.3), using the same words as Pericles, but to express the opposite meaning. The Funeral Oration was part of the observance of traditional burial rites (ii.34.1), but with the coming of the plague, burial rites are ignored—bodies lie everywhere, even in temples (ii.52). Pericles declared that Athenians observed the laws, including unwritten ones (ii.37.3), but in the account of the plague, Thucydides dwells at length on the accompanying lawlessness (ii.53). Pericles celebrated sacrifice for the city, and sought to inspire citizens to focus their actions around the city; as the plague makes itself felt, they do nothing of the sort, focusing instead on personal pleasures of the moment. The Funeral Oration described the enterprising and well-rounded spirit of the Athenian (ii.40); the plague brings dejection and hopelessness (ii.51.4–5).[19]

All of this might seem to point to substantial criticism of the adequacy of Periclean judgment along the following lines: "that Athens could have won the war is plausible. But at what cost?"[20]

An emphasis on the cost of victory is appropriate here, but to go beyond this and produce a criticism of Periclean leadership is not in line with Thucydides' intention. To see why, we must return to one aspect of Pericles' thought that we treated above: the necessary priority of the city. Everything depends in the end upon preserving the city and its independence. Only on that basis can individuals reasonably expect to be able to pursue their own ends with any lasting success. There are therefore two perspectives from which we might judge the situation, the first from the perspective of the immediate experience of individuals—it is from this perspective that one would place particular emphasis on the suffering caused by the plague—and the second from the perspective of the city. If we confine ourselves to the former perspective, the fact of suffering might easily seem decisive; to the extent that we allow the latter perspective, it would be difficult to argue that a consideration of suffering alone should carry the day.

The distinction is clearly relevant to Pericles' reaction to the plague, not only because it is crucial to his speech at ii.60–64, but also because Thucydides describes the result of the speech in terms of the contrast δημοσίᾳ μὲν . . . ἰδίᾳ δὲ (ii.65.2). That is, *as a community*, Pericles convinced the people, *but on a private basis*, they remained upset and fined him. Even the Athenians themselves subsequently took Pericles to be the best man from the perspective of the whole city (ἡ ξυμπάσα πόλις—ii.65.4), if not from the perspective of immediate individual experience.

If we keep the private/public distinction in mind, we see that it is not really correct to say, for example, that the plague "changes the situation as a whole . . . such that the situation is no longer defined by previously conceived calculations but rather by the unforeseen element."[21] Certainly, this is true from the perspective of the day-to-day experience of individual citizens.[22] From this perspective—and only from this perspective—it also is correct to emphasize that "the Athenians, uprooted from the countryside, tormented by the plague, confronted with destruction of their land and the erosion of their patterns of life, have found the war anything but easy. Success, it is clear, will have a high price."[23]

From the point of view of the city as a whole (ἡ ξυμπάσα πόλις—ii.65.4), the matter is different. Here one question is paramount: in what respect does the plague prove Pericles' plan to be insufficient to maintain the freedom and independence of the city, and what changes must he make in his policy as a consequence? There can be no doubt about the answer: *no change is required*.

The plan is entirely sufficient to maintain the independence of the city. From the perspective of the city, the situation continues to be defined only by previously conceived calculations and not at all by the unforeseen element: without even the slightest adjustment, Pericles' calculations prove to be absolutely adequate in even the most extreme and unpredictable situation, and this despite the fact that they were made before the war began. The plague has rightly been called "the most sudden, most irrational, most incalculable, and most demonic aspect of war in Thucydides' view of history;" it is correct to say that it "offers the most violent challenge to the Periclean attempt to exert some kind of rational control over the historical process."[24] Thucydides has thus run the Pericles' plan up against the ultimate test: no episode in the entire work provides a greater challenge. This drives home all the more dramatically the adequacy of the plan, taken on its own terms. It is to this aspect that Thucydides calls attention in his overview of that plan in relation to the whole war (i.e., in ii.65.5–13), while he does not believe the plague and the suffering it caused to merit so much as a mention.[25]

Nevertheless, the plague does bring out more clearly than anything else in just what sense Pericles' plan is adequate, and can further be taken to qualify in an important way our understanding of the sort of safety that good judgment can be expected to achieve. Judgment can preserve the city but cannot provide safety at every moment to each individual citizen. The city provides the foundation on which it is possible for citizens to live a good life, and to accomplish that is to achieve a great deal. Pericles' view is clear: in hard times, citizens must make sacrifices and take risks—even risking their lives—so as to preserve the city, because that is the only basis from which their own affairs might subsequently be put right.[26]

But is this *Thucydides'* view? We do not have a direct and explicit affirmation of all this on the part of the historian, but the evidence we do have is very strong. We have already noted how the private/public distinction central to Pericles' last speech is carried over into Thucydides' own remarks at the start of ii.65 (in the δημοσίᾳ μὲν . . . ἰδίᾳ δὲ contrast at 65.2), and in fact, the distinction is central to the whole of ii.65. It remains crucial when Thucydides looks ahead to the reasons for Athens' eventual defeat: the Athenians failed to follow Pericles' advice first of all because of *personal* ambition and *personal* profit (τὰς ἰδίας φιλοτιμίας καὶ ἴδια κέρδη—65.7; note the repetition of the word ἴδιος, "personal"); later, *personal* accusations (τὰς ἰδίας διαβολὰς—65.11) prevented proper support for the Sicilian expedition, and brought about disorder in the *city* (τὰ περὶ τὴν πόλιν . . . ἐταράχθησαν—65.11). The excessive focus on personal interests was fatal: Thucydides not only makes use of the private/public distinction, he gives to it the same significance as Pericles.[27] Clearly, it is Thucydides' view that an overemphasis on the personal side is destructive. Given the nature of this identity of views, it is reasonable in this case to fill out our understanding of Thucydides' views by turning to those sections of the Periclean speech that immediately precedes ii.65—that is, those places where Pericles sets out the reason for the priority of the city (see *The City as Center*, pages 27-30, above). As we shall see, Thucydides' account of Athenian political life after Pericles provides further confirmation of this account.

Because a concern with individual suffering falls on the side of private, as opposed to public considerations, Thucydides' remarks at ii.65 ought to constitute a serious difficulty for anyone who would make suffering the measure by which we judge Pericles' policy—indeed, to judge the Periclean plan only through the lens of the suffering caused by the plague is to enact once again the mistake of Pericles' successors, with their excessive focus on the personal. And recall a point mentioned in the introduction: to proceed directly from a recognition of the emphasis on suffering in the text to the claim that it must represent a Thucydidean judgment, without first placing this emphasis in the context of a much broader reflection is to make judgments on the basis of merely immediate thinking.

We should understand the focus on the hardship that comes as a result of Pericles' plan to point us to the reality that even the right path, the best possible path, may involve great suffering: there are no easy answers. This would suggest that we should cure ourselves of the tendency to demand such answers, and wrestle instead with what is actually possible—indeed, is there any indication that Pericles' plan, or any other plan, should be able to avoid hardship? It seems likely that the alternatives to Pericles' plan would involve greater suffering for the Athenians at some point in the future, as they would become subject to the whims of their more powerful neighbors (the Spartans? Persia?) to the extent that they lost their position of power. From this perspective, it seems that certain things—freedom, for example—are worth a great deal of suffering.[28] Thucydides focuses on hardship so as to give us a richer and more realistic picture: the Periclean plan can preserve the city's independence, and that is a very great achievement, but we cannot reasonably demand anything without paying the price for it.

Nevertheless, in the juxtaposition of plague and Funeral Oration, there is a criticism of Pericles, for Thucydides has pointed directly to the fact that Pericles' words fall short of the truth in one specific instance: his estimation of the Athenian character. However accurate his account of that character (ii.37-40) may be—and while a certain embellishment of the positive side is natural in a Funeral Oration, pure invention would be inappropriate and ineffective—as the pressures of the war begin to make themselves felt, the Athenians prove unable to maintain the habits that brought them their power.

The form which this failure takes is important. The Athenians become focused on the present moment, thinking their bodies and goods to be things of a day (ἐφήμερα—ii.53.2). From such an orientation, it is only natural that the ethical ties that hold the city together should disappear: honor, divine and human sanction are all swept away (53.3–4). The situation is well summarized as follows: "the model of the polis, in which citizens are linked together to a community, because their mutual reliability offers security and prosperity, has lost time continuity as a mainstay."[29] The behavior of the Athenians is thus characterized by immediacy in this episode, in both senses that were set out in the introduction.

Accordingly, the language used by Thucydides to summarize Pericles' response to the situation is just what we would expect. We are told it was an attempt "to lead their resolution away from their immediate afflictions" (ii.65.1); the words used here (ἀπὸ τῶν παρόντων δεινῶν) give a verbal link to language noted in the introduction in connection with immediacy (and above in relation to ii.22.1 and 59.3). This points to a further reality, for while the Athenians in general are affected by the pressures of the war just as we should expect—recall that war moves the character of most men *toward* the immediate (πρὸς τὰ παρόντα—iii.82.2)—Pericles seeks to move them *away from* the immediate (ἀπὸ τῶν παρόντων—ii.65.1).[30] He is thus not only represented as immune to the effects that the war has on most people,[31] he is also represented as an effective antidote to those effects, in that he succeeds in convincing the Athenians as a community. Though the plague may answer Pericles' Funeral Oration, still Pericles can answer the plague.

Nevertheless, even this success leaves us in the end with a problem, for though Pericles himself is able to keep the city on course even in the face of the ultimate challenge, the fact that he needs to be capable of this does not bode well for the future. The vision of the Funeral Oration, of a democratic Athens whose power arises out of the character of her people, is fatally undermined if everything depends in the end on the presence of a particular individual. We are told that Athens was tending toward rule by the first man (ii.65.9), but this gives us reason to fear that the forces that Pericles was able to check, above all, the excessive focus on the merely personal, will become effective once he is gone. In fact, the opposition between personal and public good that first comes into view through the Spartan invasion and plague will become an ever more effective reality as we move through the rest of the work, coming in the end to dominate Athens' fate.

Finally, the juxtaposition of plague and Funeral Oration is not the only place in which Pericles' words are set beside an account of Athenian hardship: the Periclean speech at ii.13 is juxtaposed with the account of the removal of the Athenians from the countryside (ii.14–17).[32] What we have just said in relation to the plague episode must also apply to this case, for here too the distinction between public and private must be relevant, and here too we cannot arrive at Thucydides' view if we focus too much on the private side alone.

THE SUCCESS OF THE PERICLEAN PLAN

Thucydides suggests that Athens' defeat is a consequence of failing to follow Pericles' plan (ii.65.6–13); one might conclude from this that he believes Athens would have won without this particular failing. There is, however, a further indication that the Periclean plan was adequate to win the war, and it is rather less hypothetical: early in book iv, well after Pericles' death, we find that particular emphasis has been placed on a chance to make peace, and the way in which the Athenians refuse to do so is conspicuous for its departure from Pericles' advice.

The first part of book iv is concerned with the Pylos episode, in which a series of fortuitous events causes a seemingly unimportant coastal raid to become a great Athenian success and a potential turning point in the war. Analyses of the episode often focus on the role of chance in it, and Thucydides certainly does emphasize how unexpected events occur repeatedly, and that they do so in a manner that does not accord with any human attempts at realizing a plan.[33] There is, however, another side, for Thucydides has included a speech in direct discourse—always an indication that we are dealing with a moment of some significance—in which certain Spartan envoys make a plea for peace at Athens (iv.17–20). The plea is unsuccessful, and so emphasis falls on the Athenian decision to reject it: however unpredictable and fortuitous the chain of events at Pylos may have been, they come in the end to a question of Athenian judgment, and it is this judgment that will determine the effect the episode has on the larger course of history.

Thucydides' account of the Athenian refusal of peace contains more than one implicit criticism. Attention is drawn to Athenian inconstancy—twice they refuse peace and grasp at more (21.2, 41.4) and twice they repent not having made peace when they could (iv.27.2, iv.14.2).[34] Note that all four reactions here are characterized by a focus on the situation at hand: when the Athenians feel strong, they reject peace; when events seem to be going against them, they become interested in peace (a reality given further emphasis by the Spartans' words at iv.18). That is, their decision-making is characterized by *immediacy*; what is conspicuous by its absence as we look back to Pericles is consistent action on the basis of principles thought out in advance.

There is another, more direct, link back to Pericles in the Athenian rejection of peace: he warned specifically against adding anything to the empire (ἀρχὴν τε μὴ ἐπικτᾶσθαι—i.144.1; the same words at ii.65.7), and at the start of the war he demanded that Athens retain what she possessed in the treaty setting out the Thirty Years' Peace of 446 BC (i.144.2).[35] By contrast, Cleon, who is represented as a decisive force in refusing peace, demands the return of cities ceded by Athens in that treaty (iv.21.3). The implication is obvious: Pericles would have accepted this offer of peace, and Athens, in grasping at more and changing her war aims, has in this respect changed significantly since Pericles' time.[36]

The success of the Periclean plan is thus not left in the realm of the hypothetical. It did in fact succeed when tested against the contingencies of the real world. Thucydides' Pericles cannot have in mind more than the *status quo ante bellum* as a war aim, and this the Spartans offer in the course of the Pylos episode.[37] He never looked ahead to a conquest of Sparta and her allies. Rather, his plan recognizes that Athens occupies a position of extraordinary security, such that it is virtually impossible for the Peloponnesians to conquer her. From this position, it is necessary simply to hold one's ground when the fortunes of war press against Athens (as for example, at ii.21–22 and ii.59–64), and await the moment when they turn against Sparta. The Spartan embassy at iv.17–20 (and 41.3–4), and the offer of peace it brings is thus a confirmation of Pericles' judgment. The plan was a success.

NOTES

1. Above all, see Konrad Gaiser, *Das Staatsmodell des Thukydides* (Heidelberg: F. H. Kerle Verlag, 1975), 31–34 inter alia, who also points out interesting parallels in Greek medicine and in Herodotus (pp. 61–72). Landmann, "Das Lob Athens," 75–92, repeatedly points to the presence of oppositions in the Funeral Oration; see also Dora Pozzi, "Thucydides ii.35–46: A Text of Power Ideology," *The Classical Journal* 78, no. 3 (February/March 1983): 221–31.

2. On the "interdependence—not the opposition—of reason and daring" in Pericles' language both here and in Pericles' last speech, see Daniel P. Tompkins, "The Language of Pericles" in *Thucydides Between History and Literature*, ed. Antonis Tsakmakis and Melina Tamiolako (Berlin: Walter de Gruyter GmbH, 2013), 450–1.

3. Gaiser, *Das Staatsmodell*, 31, gives an overall characterization of this aspect of the Funeral Oration: "in all individual statements there is an antithesis or polarity. In each case it has to do with two diverging, but positive moments that, while they come apart and are only actualized in a one-sided fashion elsewhere, form a tension-filled unity in Athens. The whole description thus has the structure of as-well-as/also, on-the-one-hand/on-the-other, in-fact/although. The advantages appear in Athens without their negative other side; the aggregation of opposed components leads here not to an impairment, but to an enhancement of value."

4. On λόγος and ἔργον, see Parry, *Logos and Ergon*.

5. My attention was drawn to these episodes by Connor, *Thucydides,* 59; he gives a list of verbal parallels. See also Jacqueline de Romilly, "Les intentions d'Archidamos," *Revue des études anciennes* 64, no. 3–4 (1962): 287–99.

6. Thus Plenio, *Die letzte Rede,* 7, sees Periclean judgment (γνώμη) as having passed its first serious test here.

7. Note that ii.65.9 is expressed in a manner that suggests this middle road between extreme passivity and activity. Of course, the idea is not that activity or passivity is *simply* good or bad. They will be good or bad according to the circumstances (e.g., see Rood, *Narrative and Explanation,* 247, on the varied effects of the "dynamism" of Athens). What one needs is thought, and then to be active or passive as a thoughtful evaluation of the situation requires.

8. Note that Pericles' words ἀπὸ τοῦ ἴσου (140.5) and ἀπὸ τῶν ὁμοίων (141.1) are taken up in Thucydides' summary of Athens' reply to the Spartan envoys (ἐπὶ ἴσῃ καὶ ὁμοίᾳ—i.145). These words, which point to a relation of equality, are used at significant moments elsewhere in Thucydides when an appeal to justice is being made (for example, consider i.77.3, 77.4, iii.10.4, 11.1, 12.3, as Macleod, "Reason and Necessity," 76, suggests).

9. Hellmut Flashar, *Der Epitaphios des Perikles: Seine Funktion im Geschichtswerk des Thukydides* (Heidelberg: Carl Winter, 1969) represents an extreme development of this line of thought, finding in Pericles' ethical advocacy mere "embellishments of pure power politics" (p. 30). I have many disagreements with Flashar, but above all, I do not see that he has made his case for the reduction of the ethical side to power politics: he does not examine many possibilities which lie between the reduction of one side to the other. Gaiser, *Das Staatsmodell,* responds convincingly in general and in many particulars to Flashar; Landmann, "Das Lob Athens," also makes good points against Flashar. I follow Macleod in not always trying to resolve logical difficulties within the speeches—that is, I take it the point is often that we are supposed to see a tension between (or a balance of) two logically incompatible principles, and that to attempt to resolve this tension to produce a coherent view is often to miss Thucydides' point. See especially Macleod's comments on Demosthenes' speech at iv.10 and on the Melian Dialogue in "Form and Meaning," 394. See also his account of the Mytilenian debate in "Reason and Necessity," and his treatment of the Plataean debate in "Thucydides' Plataean Debate," GRBS 18 (1977): 227–46.

10. Thucydides, *The Peloponnesian War,* trans. Steven Lattimore (Indianapolis: Hackett Publishing Company, 1998), 92. Plenio, *Die letzte Rede,* 8, speaks of the "inner constitution, out of which [Athens'] external power grew."

11. That is, an obvious point made by that dialogue is that the Melians doom themselves by failing to attend to the realities of power. A. B. Bosworth, "The Humanitarian Aspect of the Melian Dialogue," *The Journal of Hellenic Studies* 113 (1993): 30–44, strongly emphasizes this aspect. We shall see that there is another side to the Melian dialogue, but it is not obvious.

12. This is a point that seems never to be taken into consideration by those, such as Flashar, *Der Epitaphios,* who take Pericles to task for what they consider an excessive pursuit of power politics.

13. Flashar, *Der Epitaphios*, 13–14, has noticed the possible indifference to the facts here.

14. David Gribble, *Alcibiades and Athens* (Oxford: Oxford University Press, 1998), 172: at ii.37.2–3 we have an emphasis on the individual, which is immediately qualified by "the recognition in the second sentence of the danger of such permissiveness for the political life of the city, and of the need for the checks provided by law and an attitude of respect to curb the behavior of the individual." And this balance is in focus in a negative sense at ii.53.

15. This aspect has been noted by Connor, *Thucydides*, 73, who tells us that "in Pericles' view the compensation for the losses of the war is, as we have seen in [book ii,] chapter 64, fame." See also Michael Palmer, "Love of Glory and the Common Good," *The American Political Science Review* 76, no. 4 (December 1982): 825–36, esp. 831. But this is only part of the story, for it is the life of the city above all that can justify the sacrifice needed to maintain it.

16. Rengakos, *Form und Wandel*, 40, finds in ii.60.3 "the correct relationship between state and individual," and sees in it a very old Greek view.

17. Connor, *Thucydides*, 1984, is in general excellent in his attention to the theme of suffering.

18. On Thucydides' description of the plague, see Adam Parry, "The Language of Thucydides' Description of the Plague," in *The Language of Achilles and Other Papers* (New York: Oxford University Press, 1989), 156–76, who argues that Thucydides' intention is not to give a scientific account of the plague, but rather to emphasize the plague as a παράλογον—that is, as something beyond human calculation, unpredictable and overwhelming. This is insightful, although as we shall see, there is reason to disagree with Parry's statement that "Thucydides ultimately leaves it undecided whether Periclean will and forethought—γνώμη—in fact is able to meet this challenge" (p. 176). Morrison Marshall, "Pericles and the Plague," in *Owls to Athens—Essays on Classical Subjects Presented to Kenneth Dover*, ed. by E. M. Craik (Oxford: Clarendon Press, 1990), 163–70, provides an important correction of Parry, arguing convincingly that Thucydides' "motive for emphasizing strangeness and severity is to give an impression that the plague could not possibly be foreseen, so that Pericles can be forgiven for not taking it into account" (p. 169).

19. Such points of comparison are well-known; I have taken most of these from June W. Allison, "Pericles' Policy and the Plague," *Historia* 32, no. 1 (1st Quarter 1983): 14–23.

20. Connor, *Thucydides*, 73. To be clear: Connor does not explicitly say that Thucydides' criticizes Pericles here, though his words certainly point in that direction.

21. Stahl, *Man's Place in History*, 80. The remark is to be taken in the context of his two preceding pages.

22. Georg Rechenauer, "*Polis nosousa*: Politics and Disease in Thucydides—the Case of the Plague," in *Thucydides—A Violent Teacher?*, eds. G. Rechenauer and V. Pothou (Göttingen: V&R unipress, 2011), 241–60: 255, in an excellent paper on the Funeral Oration, sees the turn of the Athenians toward their merely personal afflictions as "a blatant failure and breakdown of the functionality of the Periclean concept of power." As we shall see, I would say instead that it *threatens* to become

(1) Periclean Athens 39

a failure and breakdown, and further that it anticipates what will happen later (but not yet).

23. Connor, *Thucydides*, 73, is focused here on the end of ii.65. The word he is taking up when he says "easy" is ῥᾳδίως at ii.65.13. In fact, 65.13 is referring to the city (τὴν πόλιν), and this at the end of a passage in which (and in reference to a statesman for whom) the distinction between city and individual is of paramount importance. That is, Pericles saw that the city, Athens, would quite easily overcome the Peloponnesians in the war, but this does not carry the implication that he thought it would be easy on citizens taken individually (on the contrary: see i.143.5, ii.13.1).

24. Parry, "Description of the Plague," 176. Similarly, Plenio, *Die letzte Rede*, 14: the plague is "the first and also the greatest *paralogon* [i.e., thing contrary to expectation] of the war."

25. Hans Herter, "Thukydides und Demokrit über Tyche," *Wiener Studien* 89, no. 10 (1976): 106–28, concludes, for reasons different from my own, that "Pericles' plan was . . . not cast aside by the plague, which is to say, by fortune"; he points to its consequent absence from ii.65.11 ff. Similarly, Hans Herter, "Zur Ersten Periklesrede des Thukydides," in *Studies Presented to D. M. Robinson, Vol. II*, eds. George E. Mylonas and Doris Raymond (St. Louis, MO: Washington University, 1953), 620.

26. Odysseus' trip between Scylla and Charybdis is relevant to Pericles not only because it expresses the need to find a way between two opposed poles, but also because even the correct route, the middle way, requires that a price be paid.

27. Pericles, of course, has just drawn repeated attention to the private/public distinction—e.g., πόλιν. . . ξύμπασαν . . . τοὺς ἰδιώτας (ii.60.2); πόλις . . . τὰς ἰδίας (60.4); τὰ ἴδια τοῦ κοινοῦ (61.4). Much later, Alcibiades will be said to aim at personal (τὰ ἴδια) wealth and reputation (vi.15.2), and Nicias will declare himself ready to run the risk of death in the field as an individual (ἰδίᾳ) rather than face the Athenian assembly (vii.48.4), dooming those he commands in the process.

28. Consider Rechenauer, "Polis nosousa," 251: "the *dunamis tes polis* is not an end in itself . . . but its determination is embedded in a higher objective for the political existence of human beings: the attainment of autarky." To this I would add that the attainment of autarky (i.e., independence) not only is essential to the highest ends but also provides the most stable and secure basis for the basic needs of the individual, including safety—or rather, so much safety as is attainable by particular individuals, since an attempt to keep every citizen safe at every moment is an utterly futile quest (and one likely to *cause* suffering in the longer term on account of its preference for fantasy over reality).

29. Rechenauer, "Polis nosousa," 260.

30. When Pericles at ii.64.5 speaks of being hated and disliked "in the present moment" (ἐν τῷ παρόντι), his implicit denigration of the (merely) present moment is consistent with what we see elsewhere.

31. It is in this context that we should consider Pericles' first words, "I hold always to the same judgement [i.e., γνώμῃ]" (i.140.1), a claim made in advance that is dramatically confirmed by the plague. The point is driven home at ii.61.2, where he expands on his original claim, now emphasizing the difference between himself and his audience: "I am the same and do not change; it is you who change."

32. Edith Foster, *Thucydides, Pericles and Periclean Imperialism* (New York: Cambridge University Press, 2010), 174–82, focuses at some length on this situation.

33. See, for example, Francis M. Cornford, *Thucydides Mythistoricus* (London: Edward Arnold, 1907), 82–109; Stahl, *Man's Place in History*, 138–49; and Rood, *Narrative and Explanation*, 24–46.

34. The verb used to describe the Athenian decision at iv.21.2, 41.4 (and also in the Spartan speech at iv.17.4) is ὀρέγομαι, with the meaning "to grasp at." It comes up in other highly significant contexts. Nicias, in speaking against the Sicilian expedition, will warn against grasping at another empire before securing the present one (vi.10.5), and Thucydides describes the successors of Pericles as "grasping at first position" (ii.65.10).

35. Thucydides' emphasis on Pericles' non-acquisitive aims conflicts with the depiction given by Foster, *Periclean Imperialism*, 198–202, of a Pericles focused above all on acquisition ("in Pericles' speeches the acquisition of more becomes in itself the aim and guarantor of Athenian glory and self-sufficiency"). In particular, if it was Thucydides' intention to connect Pericles with πλεονεξία ("greed"), as Foster, *Periclean Imperialism*, 174 (also 201), would have it, it is strange that we never find the word used in relation to him. Foster notes τὰ πλείω (*Periclean Imperialism*, 192) in the Funeral Oration (ii.36.3), but in context this does not seem to me to provide a ground for a claim of Periclean πλεονεξία. ii.65.8 seems also to tell heavily against equating Pericles with πλεονεξία, as does ii.65.10, where the word is applied specifically to post-Periclean politicians. The Athenians at Sparta, envoys sent in Pericles' time, do speak of getting more (πλέον ἔχειν—i.76.2, πλεονεκτῶ—77.3–4), and yet do so in the context of declaring their superiority to such drives: they might have taken more than they have, but have been moderate in comparison to the dictates of human nature.

36. See Rengakos, *Form und Wandel*, 76–82, on how Periclean ideas conspicuously conflict with the picture we are given of Athens at the time of Pylos more generally.

37. See Simon Hornblower, *A Commentary on Thucydides, Vol. 1* (Oxford: Oxford University Press, 1991), 230 on i.144.1 and the verb περιέσεσθαι, which suggests both winning and surviving: "survival was all that Athens had to achieve in order to 'win' the war." See also George Cawkwell, "Thucydides' Judgment of Periclean Strategy," *Yale Classical Studies* 24 (1975): 53–70, and A. J. Holladay, "Athenian Strategy in the Archidamian War," *Historia* 27, no. 3 (3rd Quarter, 1978): 399–427.

(2) Post-Periclean Athens

In Thucydides' account, Cleon rises to the most prominent position in the years immediately following Pericles' death, and yet he does not dominate affairs as Pericles did. We are given only one speech in direct discourse from Cleon, and it fails to carry the day. Like Pericles, he also leads an army in the field, and yet he first achieves this position by accident (iv.27–28), and Thucydides later makes clear that Cleon is no able (or brave) general (v.7.2–3, 10.3–9). One cannot, therefore, speak of Cleonian Athens as one does of Periclean Athens: the period is defined as much by the absence of Pericles as it is by the particular character of Cleon. The ambiguous position of Cleon is, as we shall see, characteristic of the situation within Athens in general at this time, which is really a transitional stage from Periclean to Alcibiadean Athens. Here we shall focus on the Mytilenian debate insofar as it either brings to light the changes in the character of Athens that have come about in the absence of Pericles or contains the beginning of further developments. Where Pericles was able to balance opposites, we can now see that the unity of principles he had attained is beginning to fall away, as his heirs begin to lose their grasp of the whole.

THE MYTILENIAN DEBATE

It is on the occasion of the revolt of the Mytilenians that we are given the first direct speeches in Athens after the death of Pericles.[1] The fact that we now get a debate is itself significant, for in the case of Pericles' three political speeches, only his words were recorded, despite the fact that on most occasions others must also have spoken. The effect is to emphasize the relative unimportance of other speakers in Pericles' time: it is as though their words were of such little consequence that they are not even worth reporting. Now, however, we have *two* speeches. The contrast reinforces once again the impression of the influence which Pericles personally wielded within the assembly (note ii.65.8–9) and puts a corresponding emphasis on the uncertainty and division in the city once the city is deprived of its first citizen.

Cleon

Scholars have often commented upon the many echoes of Pericles in Cleon's speech. The purpose of revisiting them here is above all to show how they exhibit a common structure: Cleon attains to only a part of what Pericles held together, and this means that the connections between them amount in fact to differences (as explained in the introduction, pages 9–11).

The nature of the shift that has taken place since Pericles comes into view with Cleon's first words: "many times before now I have recognized that a democracy is unable to rule others" (iii.37.1). The statement makes a direct opposition of two notions which we saw united in Pericles: justice, the principle of democracy, and power, the principle of empire.[2] Cleon's talk of "democracy" (iii.37.1) echoes Pericles' use of the same word in the Funeral Oration (ii.37.1). The free and law-abiding life described there (see especially ii.37.2–3), because it requires mutual trust, is going to involve behavior that is to some degree indulgent. Empire, characterized by power, involves the forcible ruling of others (Cleon's ἑτέρων ἄρχειν—that is, "ruling others"—at iii.37.1 takes up Pericles' ἑτέρων . . . ἄρχειν at ii.64.5), which is productive of hate (e.g., iii.37.2 and ii.64.4–5). If Pericles did not make the relation of these two principles explicitly clear, still we were able to see how he made use of each according to its proper nature, and he did avoid bringing them directly into conflict with one another in his rhetoric. Cleon, on the other hand, presents us with an explicit contradiction.[3]

Two further echoes of Pericles, one relevant to empire and the other to democracy, deepen this picture. Cleon's phrase, "you hold the empire as a tyranny" (iii.37.2), is an almost verbatim repeat of Pericles' words at ii.63.2.[4] The echo has often been taken as an indication of a straightforward similarity or continuity between the two,[5] but there is a significant difference between them: in context, Pericles' words urge Athenians not to give in, while Cleon aims at a merely brutal policy of a sort not yet seen.[6] The other echo of Pericles, this one focused on democracy, concerns the Athenians' daily life with one another (καθ' ἡμέραν . . . πρὸς ἀλλήλους—iii.37.2). Cleon says, "in your everyday life you are fearless and without plots towards others"; Pericles said that Athenians do not become angry with their neighbors over "that suspicion towards others regarding everyday habits" (ἐς τὴν πρὸς ἀλλήλους τῶν καθ' ἡμέραν ἐπιτηδευμάτων ὑποψίαν—ii.37.2).[7] In context,

Pericles is celebrating this way of life, while Cleon is suggesting that it has corrupted Athenian judgment, causing them to shrink from the brutal measures necessary to empire. In both of these echoes, Cleon is making the same fundamental point: the indulgent behavior characteristic of democracy must be rejected in order adequately to perform the work necessary to empire. What Pericles held together, Cleon presents as opposed to such a degree that it seems necessary to reject one side or the other.

There is, however, a further point: in each of these echoes Thucydides has brought our attention to a similarity, insofar as he has Cleon repeat important Periclean phrases, but also to a difference, which becomes evident as we work through the significance of each phrase in the context of the speech in which it appears. The best interpretation of these echoes will be able to give full weight both to the similarities and to the differences.

To find our way to such an interpretation, let us consider one further verbal connection that brings out the matter most clearly. When Cleon claims, "I am the same man in my judgment" (ἐγὼ μὲν οὖν ὁ αὐτός εἰμι τῇ γνώμῃ—iii.38.1), we have a conspicuous echo of Pericles' words ("I am the same man and do not change; it is you who change"—ἐγὼ μὲν ὁ αὐτός εἰμι—ii.61.2), and in a similar context: both men are contrasting their own constancy with the fickleness of their audience.[8] The phrase has, however, a different significance in each case, and to grasp the difference is to see an example of the logic of part and whole that was set out in the introduction (see pages 5–8).

When Pericles claims to be "the same man," he is pointing to a substantial reality that the reader has seen in action in the related episodes at ii.21–22 and ii.59–65 (see above, pages 24–5) in which he maintains his original plan in the face, first, of excessive activity, and then of excessive passivity, on the part of the populace.[9] Their inconstancy is driven by anger (ὀργή),[10] a characteristically *immediate* moving force (recall τὸ παρὸν—ii.22.1, τὰ παρόντα—ii.59.3); we saw above how Pericles tries to move judgment of the people away from their immediate misfortunes (ἀπὸ τῶν παρόντων—ii.65.1).

With Cleon, the matter is different. His own claim to be "the same man" is technically correct—he does, after all, support the same motion for a brutal punishment that he endorsed the day before—but in comparison with the Periclean case this claim of constancy is little more than a rhetorical motif. More importantly, what lies behind this supposed constancy is precisely the opposite of what underwrote Periclean constancy. At iii.38.1 Cleon effectively recommends ὀργή (anger) as a basis for a decision, and this was indeed a motive force in the initial, brutal decision (iii.36.2). Further, he reproaches his audience for failing to think sufficiently "concerning the immediate circumstances" (περὶ τῶν παρόντων—iii.38.7)—a statement in accordance with anger that suggests the immediate springs of Cleon's activity, a sharp contrast with Pericles.[11] That this is correct is confirmed at the end of Cleon's speech, when he urges his listeners not to be soft in the present moment (μὴ μαλακισθέντες πρὸς τὸ παρὸν), but to get as near as possible to the judgment of the (earlier) experience (ὅτι ἐγγύτατα τῇ γνώμῃ τοῦ πάσχειν - iii.40.7): he is recommending one particular moment of experience as opposed to another, not a broader, more deeply considered reflection as opposed to a merely immediate one (and see below, on the circle of viciousness). In this context it is appropriate to note that Cleon denigrates intelligence, in that he claims that the simpler sort of people (φαυλότεροι) generally manage the city better than the more intelligent (ξυνετωτέρους—iii.37.3). Anger, a drive toward a narrow, merely immediate perspective, a denigration of intelligence—these are not the bases from which one can expect adequate judgment, from which the Periclean virtue of "recognizing what is needed" (γνῶναι τὰ δέοντα—ii.60.5) is possible.

It is accordingly correct to find that the effect is "to establish a contrast between Cleon's superficial resemblance to Pericles and his advocacy of a policy whose *orge* (passion) (N.B. 3.38.1) contrasts sharply with the *gnome* [judgment] of Pericles."[12] But why would Thucydides have brought to light a resemblance as well as a contrast? What positive role does each side serve?

The similarities and the difference are both crucial because the point is that Cleon attains to only *part* of what made Pericles a great leader. The echo of the claim to be "the same man" points to a positive resemblance between Cleon and Pericles, in that both are, as they speak these words, setting themselves apart from—indeed, against—the multitude.[13] This is a quality that Thucydides has mentioned at a significant moment: he told us that two of the keys to Pericles' leadership were the fact that he was "capable through judgment" (δυνατὸς . . . τῇ γνώμῃ) and was also able to speak against (ἀντιειπεῖν—ii.65.8) the populace when necessary, rather than speak to please them.[14] While Cleon does have the latter quality, we have just seen, as we went through the implications of the "same man" echo, that Cleon cannot claim judgment (and see below on the merits of his policy).[15] Thus he has only a part of what we saw in Pericles, and as a result, the nature of that part becomes fundamentally different: the leadership ability that comes with a readiness to speak against the people when necessary is not good if the content of one's leadership is going to be determined by anger and a focus on the immediate. The same is true of democracy and empire: by leaning so heavily toward the latter at the expense of the former, Cleon abandons the balance which above all characterized Pericles. One result of this is the new, brutal policy that Cleon advocates. There are indeed similarities between Pericles and Cleon, but these only highlight Cleon's deficiencies in comparison with Pericles.

At this point it is appropriate to compare the introductions that Thucydides has given to the two men: Pericles is called the "most capable in speech and

(2) Post-Periclean Athens 45

action" (λέγειν τε καὶ πράσσειν δυνατώτατος—i.139.4), while Cleon is "the most violent of the citizens and by far the most persuasive with the people at the time" (βιαιότατος τῶν πολιτῶν τῷ τε δήμῳ παρὰ πολὺ ἐν τῷ τότε πιθανώ τατος—iii.36.6). We do not hear about Cleon's ability in action—his virtues, it would seem, fall entirely on the side of speech: again we have a merely partial attainment of the Periclean example. Even in speech, however, the word πιθανώτατος ("most persuasive") suggests that Cleon is not Pericles' equal. The assertion that Pericles was "most capable in speech" does not distinguish between the quality of his advice and his ability to move others to accept it (i.e., between "recognizing what is needed" and "expressing these things"—ii.60.5). To say that Cleon, by contrast, was "most persuasive" is more specific, pointing only to the second of these virtues and effectively disparaging Cleon's judgment by comparison: once again, Cleon is only a partial heir of Periclean ability.[16] And, of course, as far as judgment is concerned, Cleon's own speech effectively concedes the inefficacy of his deterrent policy, for he admits that the example of previous revolts was no lesson to the Mytilenians (iii.39.3).[17] Nevertheless, the fact that Thucydides tells us explicitly of Cleon's persuasive ability can reasonably be taken to show that Cleon has the virtue that Pericles referred to as "expressing things" (ἑρμηνεῦσαι ταῦτα)—although not as much as Pericles, for Cleon does (narrowly) lose the debate here. The fact that particular attention is drawn to Cleon's violence reminds us that his brutal policy—the slaughter and enslavement of an entire city—represents a development on its own.[18] This will prove a significant point in the next stage.

Before proceeding to Diodotus, we must take note of two points in Cleon's speech whose significance will only become fully apparent once we are in a position to consider the whole movement from Pericles to Alcibiades. The first is a particular kind of bad logic used by Cleon. His emphasis on the present receives its most striking expression in a climactic assertion which is more an expression of anger than an argument (iii.40.5–6). The Athenians, he says, should punish (i.e., annihilate) the Mytilenians, for the Mytilenians did the Athenians an injustice without cause (by making a pre-emptive attack), and, if successful, would have annihilated the Athenians, fearing the danger of letting them survive; for they know that those who suffer wrong without cause are more bitter (and thus more dangerous) than regular enemies. The fact of an injustice without cause, it would seem, puts the two sides into a circle of vicious reaction: each side, because it expects the other to try to annihilate it, must try to annihilate that other side first.[19] But the phrase can be explained another way: the Athenians are angry at the Mytilenians for the revolt; the charge of unprovoked aggression both justifies and intensifies this anger, as does the charge that the annihilation of the Athenians was the goal. Thus, circular logic is working on behalf of circular anger.

Cleon's argument here will prove important in what follows because of the fact that we have circular reasoning, in what we shall refer to from here on as the circle of viciousness. Circular reasoning, of course, must of its nature go on forever: there is a sort of infinity here. On the terms described by Cleon, there can be no end to all this—unless one side exterminates the other. (The conflict within Corcyra (see iii.82–83), will in fact reach its conclusion only through the virtual extermination of one side (iv.47–48).) This circle of viciousness is of a piece with Cleon's focus on the immediate, noted above: the first requirement for escaping such circular reasoning is to step back from the present moment, to take a broader view and recognize that one is caught in a circle of reaction.[20] Alas, we shall see that the next stage in Athens' development involves no such larger view.

The second point concerning Cleon's speech that will prove important as we move forward concerns Athens' allies (or subjects). The Mytilenian debate is significant in part because of the focus it brings to the question of these allies, and the view Cleon takes of them will prove significant later on. One of his central claims is that his policy—the massacre of all the Mytilenians now that their rebellion against Athens has failed—is a just one, but the conflicting statements within his own speech undermine his argument.[21] He urges the justice of his policy first on the grounds that the Mytilenians, enjoying safety, independence and honor from Athens, were not oppressed within the empire, but should have been thankful for it (iii.39.2); and further, that "they did not do harm involuntarily, but plotted knowingly" (40.1). Thus, he can claim that the Mytilenians plotted and rose up rather than revolted—"revolt is characteristic of those who suffer some violence" (39.2). That is, the basic relationship between Athens and her Mytilenian subjects was one of friendship and mutual benefit, for which the Mytilenians could reasonably have been expected to remain gratefully in the empire; it is on the basis of this view that his policy is just. Yet in the same speech, he tells the Athenians that the Mytilenians are conspirators, ruled unwillingly, "who obey not because you gratify them, harming yourselves, but because you are superior to them in strength and not goodwill" (37.2). He further suggests that the Mytilenians are "established from necessity as eternal foes" (40.3). That is, the Mytilenians did not revolt voluntarily against friends, but they revolted by necessity against enemies. Thus, Cleon's speech contains a double view of the Athenians' subjects, first as friends, who, if they were to attack Athens, would do so freely and as aggressors (and thus unjustly), and secondly as natural enemies of Athens, who are forced to rebel in order to defend themselves against an empire which is, as he says, a "tyranny" (37.2). If one side supports his case for justice, the other undermines it.

We can leave aside the reasons that Cleon becomes so tangled up in his own rhetoric.[22] What is important at this point is to note how the double view of Athens' subjects represents a further development of something that was merely hinted at with Pericles. He had talked of how Athens acquires friends by doing good to others rather than receiving it (ii.40.4–5).[23] Perhaps Athens' service in the Persian wars lies behind this; what is important is that a relationship of friendship with others is envisaged. Pericles had also said that it had been wrong to take the empire, and that to let it go would be dangerous (ii.63.2): there is a hint here that the relationship with Athens' subjects is a hostile one, and that they might seek to harm Athens if they were let go. Both sides are taken up by Cleon, and are no longer present as mere hints—and we shall see how his focus on the hostile relationship of Athens toward her "subjects" points ahead to the Melian Dialogue.

Diodotus

Diodotus stands in fundamentally the same relation to Pericles as Cleon does. Just like Cleon, he attains to parts of what characterized Pericles, though not the same parts as Cleon. Diodotus is quite clearly on the side of intelligence, a significant change from his opponent: while Cleon declared "more intelligent" (ξυνετωτέρους—iii.37.3) people to be worse at managing the city than their simpler fellows, for Diodotus, "unintelligent" (ἀξύνετος—42.2) is an accusation with which to discredit others. He defends the idea that "words are the teachers of deeds" (iii.42.2), taking up an idea we heard from Pericles at ii.40.2.[24] Directly taking up Cleon's crude focus on the present, Diodotus declares that deliberation should be "about the future rather than the present" (περὶ τοῦ μέλλοντος . . . μᾶλλον . . . ἢ τοῦ παρόντος—44.3; see also 42.2). He also cautions in particular against haste and anger (τάχος τε καὶ ὀργήν—42.1, taking up the anger—ὀργή (36.2)—which moved the Athenians to their original brutal decision). Anger, characterized by a focus on the present, was precisely the state which Pericles had to counteract (ὀργή—ii.21.3, 22.1; τὸ ὀργιζόμενον—59.3). Clearly, the point in all of this is that Pericles' deliberative ability has an heir in Diodotus. Insofar as he sees the need to take counsel, to avoid anger and a merely immediate orientation, Diodotus has at least the basis to be "capable through judgment" (δυνατὸς . . . τῇ γνώμῃ), one of the keys to Periclean leadership set out by Thucydides (ii.65.8)—the very element that Cleon lacked. And we shall see below that there is reason to think that Diodotus' policy is the better one.

However, Thucydides has also pointed to Diodotus' failure to live up to the Periclean example. Cleon has suggested that the defenders of the Mytilenians have been bribed (38.2), and Diodotus' response to this is conspicuous in its difference from what we saw with Pericles. Where the older statesman could dismiss outright any suggestion of corruption by an appeal to his patriotism and integrity (ii.60.5), Diodotus does no such thing, but tries to turn the subject away from such matters to a consideration of the more general effect of accusations in the assembly.[25] We have been given a reason to expect that this difference will affect Diodotus' effectiveness in the assembly, for Thucydides explained Pericles' political power in part by means of his reputation for integrity (ii.65.8).

This Thucydidean suggestion can be filled out as follows, and it allows us to explain one aspect of the Mytilenian debate that might otherwise seem strange: it occurs as a result of widespread remorse over the earlier decision to kill all the Mytilenians (36.4) and yet is remarkable for the virtual absence of appeals to such feelings.[26] If the assembly is not entirely convinced of Diodotus' integrity, Cleon's accusation of bribery could have effectively primed the audience to ask if an appeal to compassion is not being made from a consideration of personal interest rather than sincere concern regarding the brutality of the initial decision. In such a situation, it could easily be more effective rhetorically if Diodotus were to avoid this concern entirely, and were simply to show how Cleon's policy is inexpedient for Athens. Such an argument is much more likely to be considered on its own merits regardless of any accusations of bribery, conveniently diverting attention away from *ad hominem* considerations rather than meeting them head on. In addition, such a charge could cohere meaningfully with the fact that Thucydides tells us nothing of Diodotus save for a single remark: he also spoke in favor of the Mytilenians in the earlier assembly (iii.41).

Finally, Diodotus' speech contains an element that will prove relevant to the comparison of Thucydides to Plato. The core of Diodotus' argument comes at iii.45, where he sets out a series of internal impulses that propel people forth to action. Differing circumstances might produce daring or greed, or some other passionate impulse, and all these drive people forth into danger (iii.45.4). Fortune (45.6), hope (45.1, 5), and love (45.5) also push people toward irrational daring. Diodotus concludes that it is impossible to stop human nature, when it sets forth eagerly toward some goal, whether by legal means or some other form of intimidation, and only a very simple-minded person would attempt it (45.7). This passage sets out a sort of psychology: there are internal, non-rational drives in every person, and these forces of human nature appear capable of utterly overwhelming rational calculation. These forces are explicitly opposed to the law (νομός—45.7): we have here our first hint of a distinction that Callicles will call νομός and φύσις—that is, custom and nature.

Cleon and Diodotus

Given the links back to Pericles that we have seen, one final question remains: how might Pericles have dealt with a situation like this one? Clearly, Diodotus was closer to Periclean judgment than Cleon, and yet one must concede that if his goal was to prevent further rebellions, the Diodotean policy fails, since other rebellions do in fact follow. It is perhaps pertinent to mention that Cleon, having failed to persuade the assembly of the value of his policy against the Mytilenians, will succeed in carrying it against rebel Scione (iv.122.6, v.32.1): are the people ready to try a more brutal approach once Diodotus' policy has proven incapable of preventing revolts? (The Athenians still fear revolts at v.14.2.) However, Cleon's policy leads quite certainly to what both he and Diodotus feared: a ruined city from which no more revenue can be drawn. Faced with such realities, it might seem the proper conclusion is that "all advice is futile."[27]

In fact, not all advice is futile, and we can see a solution of sorts, particularly in relation to the crucial matter of the revenue that the allies provide Athens, by looking to the example of Pericles' time. In 440 BC, having put down the rebellion of Samos, the Athenians allowed the Samians moderate terms indeed in comparison to the proposals of Cleon: "they [the Samians] took down their walls, gave hostages, handed over their ships, and arranged to pay back by instalments the money which had been used" (i.117.3). Thus, not only was Samos preserved as a source of revenue for the future, but it was made to cover the cost of its own rebellion, leaving the power of Athens ultimately unharmed by an unsuccessful rebellion. The Diodotean policy might therefore claim to be a continuation of the Periclean, and Diodotus alludes to the same solution regarding the matter of the expense of putting down rebellions (iii.46.2). There is, then, reason to find in Diodotus what Pericles called "recognizing what is needed" (γνῶμαι τὰ δέοντα—ii.60.5). The approach to the question of rebellions within the Athenian empire is a practical one: one cannot expect to prevent them entirely, but once they are put down, the damage to Athenian power can be reduced a great deal. There remains, however, a danger in the nature of the source of power in which Athens finds her safety; we consider this below.

The echoes of Cleon and Diodotus with Pericles should be understood in light of two passages discussed in the introduction (under the heading, *Thucydides the Holist*, pages 5–8). These are Pericles' own remarks on the virtues necessary to adequate statesmanship (ii.60.5–6), and Thucydides' subsequent remarks concerning the cause of the failure of Athenian leadership after Pericles (ii.65.8). Let us begin with the latter. Thucydides tells us that "the cause was that Pericles, being capable through his reputation [ἀξίωμα] and judgment [γνώμη], and being manifestly most incorruptible by money [χρημάτων . . . ἀδωρότατος], restrained the multitude freely, and was not led by them more than he himself led [οὐκ ἤγετο μᾶλλον . . . ἢ αὐτὸς ἦγε], on account of not speaking to please, having not acquired power from improper means, but having power through his character, he even angered them by contradiction [ἀντειπεῖν]" (ii.65.8)—a standard which his successors failed to meet.

If we take these remarks as our standard, we see that Cleon and Diodotus present us with a clear division of what was united in Pericles. Cleon has one of the bases of Pericles' effective leadership, in that he is able to stand on his own (οὐκ ἤγετο μᾶλλον . . . ἢ αὐτὸς ἦγε), directly contradicting the people (ἀντειπεῖν), while Diodotus lacks this virtue.[28] Diodotus is, however, the defender of Periclean judgment (γνώμη), as Cleon clearly is not. In respect of reputation (ἀξίωμα), Cleon and Diodotus each represent a falling-away from the Periclean standard: on both sides we now have a suggestion that the other is corrupt, and on neither side do we have an explicit answer to this suggestion of the sort that we saw with Pericles (ii.60.5). Indeed, the conspicuous difference with Pericles constitutes a suggestion that neither Cleon nor Diodotus is altogether incorruptible by money (χρημάτων . . . ἀδωρότατος), and this points to the next stage, where the absence of this virtue will not merely be suggested.

Cleon and Diodotus also paint a common picture in their concerns about the state of deliberative rhetoric in the assembly: Cleon fears that speeches have become mere contests in which speakers vie for the top spot (iii.37.4, 38.4–6), while Diodotus suggests that accusations will prevent speakers from giving the best possible advice (42.2–6, 43.3–6) and will force them to persuade by means of deception (43.2). In all this there is a single underlying message: the interests of the city are falling from view (37.4, 38.3, 42.4, 43.3), since orators look to their own benefit first. We have come some distance, then, from Pericles' straightforward assertion of his own patriotism (φιλόπολίς–ii.60.5) and from his unwavering focus on what was appropriate to the perspective of the city as a whole—and this change is a development that we shall see continued with Nicias and Alcibiades.

We saw how the older statesman set out a list of four virtues necessary to adequate statesmanship: [A] recognizing what is needed (γνῶναι τε τὰ δέοντα), [B] expressing these things (ἑρμηνεῦσαι ταῦτα), [C] being a patriot (φιλόπολίς) and [D] being superior to the influence of money (χρημάτων κρείσσων). As we have seen, Diodotus has some claim to [A] but rather less to [B], while Cleon has some claim to [B] but not [A]. Again, what was united in Pericles is to some degree divided here. As for [C] and [D], it is clear that both Cleon and Diodotus fall short of the Periclean standard: where he asserted his claim to these virtues directly, they do not seem to feel able to do so, giving us instead general concerns about the inadequate presence of both virtues in the assembly.

There is one final theme that will prove important in what follows: a confusion over how to view the subject cities. We saw above how Cleon presents a double view of these cities, on the one hand as friends of Athens, and on the other as natural enemies of Athenian tyranny. Diodotus, on the other hand, claims that the common people everywhere are Athens' natural friends (iii.47.2). If this claim is more optimistic than the facts warrant as regards the immediate case at hand,[29] still Thucydides will himself confirm that the common people often did try to bring in the Athenians as allies (iii.82.1). The Mytilenian debate, then, does not present a single view of the subject (or allied) cities, a significant difference with what is to follow.

NOTES

1. In much of my account of the Mytilenian debate, I am following Macleod, "Reason and Necessity." Even more than his other work on Thucydides, this paper repays careful and repeated reading. Hans-Georg Saar, *Die Reden des Kleon und Diodotus und ihre Stellung im Gesamtwerk des Thukydides* (PhD diss., University of Hamburg, 1953) also provides an excellent treatment, one that is still useful.

2. To be clear: "justice" as I speak of it here is the Thucydidean principle commonly spoken of in the phrase "justice and power" (see the introduction). What Cleon means by the word "justice" in his speech is straightforward retribution, something very different.

3. James A. Andrews, "Cleon's Hidden Appeals (Thucydides 3.37–40)," *The Classical Quarterly*, New Series, 50, no. 1 (2000): 52–53, points to another such case concerning the matter of tolerant freedom and respect for the laws: for Pericles, these are reconciled in Athens (ii.37.2–3); for Cleon (iii.37.3), they present a contradictory opposition.

4. Cleon: τυραννίδα ἔχετε τὴν ἀρχήν (iii.37.2); Pericles: ὡς τυραννίδα γὰρ ἤδη ἔχετε αὐτήν (i.e., τὴν ἀρχήν—ii.63.2). Of course, Pericles' use of ὡς softens the talk of tyranny somewhat.

5. So, for example, consider H. D. Westlake, *Individuals in Thucydides* (Cambridge: Cambridge University Press, 1968), 65: "Thucydides has chosen to draw attention to the affinity between the policies of Pericles and Cleon." Similarly, Hugh Lloyd-Jones, *The Justice of Zeus* (Berkeley: University of California Press, 1971), 139, suggests that the link indicates "that the policy of Pericles was likely to lead, in different circumstances, to the policy of Cleon." Perhaps James A. Andrews, "Cleon's Ethopoetics," *The Classical Quarterly* 44 (i) (1994): 28, is better: "*as regards imperial arete*, Cleon and Pericles do indeed have much in common."

6. Donald Kagan, "The speeches in Thucydides and the Mytilenian debate," *Yale Classical Studies* 24 (1975): 84, calls Cleon's policy "a full-scale attack on the imperial policy of Pericles and his followers." Kagan (p. 83) also tells us that "the Athenians under the leadership of Pericles never imposed so harsh a punishment. The harshest treatment imposed by Pericles, the one the Athenians inflicted on Hestiaea . . . deprived the victims of their lands, but not their lives" (similarly the Aeginetans, expelled from their homes in the first year of the war (ii.27.1–2)).

7. See Macleod, "Reason and Necessity," 68.

8. That Cleon speaks of his judgment (τῇ γνώμῃ) provides us with a verbal link to what is anyway a thematically connected phrase, namely the words with which Thucydides has Pericles begin his first speech: τῆς μὲν γνώμης . . . αἰεὶ τῆς αὐτῆς ἔχομαι ("I am always of the same judgment"—i.140.1).

9. Marshall, "Pericles and the Plague," 165, notes that Periclean constancy is also "an implicit message at ii.13.2, 13.9, 55.2."

10. τὸν Περικλέα ἐν ὀργῇ εἶχον ("they were angry at Pericles")—ii.21.3, ὀργιζόμενον ("being angry")—ii.59.3; see also ii.64.1. In Pericles' own ideal vision of Athens, ὀργή is, of course, not characteristic of how citizens interact with each other (ii.37.2).

11. Macleod, "Reason and Necessity," 70, notes that "the present is preferred to the future" in Cleon's words at iii.38.2–7. Note how this constitutes a temporal narrowing of the sort described in the introduction, pages 11–3.

12. Connor, *Thucydides*, 79, fn. 1.

13. Macleod, "Reason and Necessity," 74, points out that Cleon "dares openly to criticize and contradict the people" (see, for example, iii.37.1–2, 38.4–7), just as Pericles could "bluntly recall to the people that they are responsible for their decisions (i.140.1, ii.60.4, 64.1)."

14. Some examples of Pericles reproaching his audience: ii.60.1, 61.2, 61.4, 64.1.

15. The word for "judgment" here (γνώμη) can also mean "resolution," but we saw above how little Cleon's "resolution" stands comparison with Pericles' in the relevant case.

16. *Pace* Hornblower, *Commentary on Thucydides Vol. I*, 420, who says in relation to this passage that "'persuasive' is not an unflattering word."

17. There is a question regarding Cleon's relation to Thucydides' characterization of the post-Pericleans. Andrews, "Hidden Appeals," 46, notes that although Thucydides at ii.65.10 characterizes the successors of Pericles as committing affairs to the pleasure of the people, the first such successor we see strongly reproaches his audience, particularly in relation to rhetors delighting in speech (iii.40.3) and pleasure (38.7, 40.2). Similarly, A. W. Gomme, *A Historical Commentary on Thucydides, Vol. II* (London: Oxford University Press, 1956), 299: "there is no flattery of the demos by this persuasive demagogue, no letting himself be led by the people." Cleon's behavior in this debate is more consistent with Thucydides' words at ii.65.10 than has often been supposed. We have seen how Cleon makes a *show* of setting himself against the people, a move that is strictly rhetorical, as it was not with Pericles. This move toward rhetoric over substance involves of its nature a greater emphasis on what will move people and a corresponding lack of emphasis on substantial concerns, a change which is at least a necessary first step toward a flattering of the demos.

18. A. G. Woodhead, "Thucydides' Portrait of Cleon," *Mnemosyne*, Fourth Series, 13, Fasc. 4 (1960): 299–300, points out that by 421 the Athenians had implemented Cleon's policy in relation to other revolts (see, for example, the case of Scione at iv.122.6); whether this was as a result of the bloody-mindedness we see in the Mytilenian debate, or simple considerations of expediency (for by then it could be claimed that Diodotus' policy had failed to stop revolts), we do not know.

19. In an oft-quoted phrase, R. P. Winnington-Ingram, "*Ta Deonta Eipein*: Cleon and Diodotus," *Bulletin of the Institute of Classical Studies* 12 (1965): 77, sums this

up as "be beastly to the Mytilenians. Why? Because they would have been beastly to you. Why? Because you would have been beastly to them." This brings out the circular logic nicely.

20. Nor is this the end of Cleon's deficiencies as a thinker. Macleod, "Reason and Necessity," 70, suggests how Cleon's remarks at iii.38.2–7, in attempting to discredit a rethinking of the original Mytilenian decree, overreach, and effectively deny the possibility of deliberation as such.

21. He also claims that his policy is expedient, and here, too, he undermines himself: see Macleod, "Reason and Necessity," 68–72. The double view of the allies/subjects that I discuss here is from Macleod.

22. Again, see Macleod, "Reason and Necessity," 64, 68–72.

23. I understand the remarks at ii.40.4–5 to focus on the behavior of Athenians toward those beyond their city, for the "we" who acquire friends by doing (δρῶντες) become the "doer" (ὁ δράσας) of a favor, who is described in opposition to one who is indebted (ὁ ἀντοφείλων). If the behavior of Athenians within their own city were at issue, there would be a contradiction, for many Athenians would acquire friends by receiving rather than doing good, something that is explicitly denied.

24. Both phrases advocate that λόγοι should inform ἔργα through some form of διδάσκω. Diodotus: τούς τε λόγους ὅστις διαμάχεται μὴ διδασκάλους τῶν πραγμάτων γίγνεσθαι . . . Pericles: οὐ τοὺς λόγους τοῖς ἔργοις βλάβην ἡγούμενοι, ἀλλὰ μὴ προδιδαχθῆναι μᾶλλον λόγῳ πρότερον ἢ ἐπὶ ἃ δεῖ ἔργῳ ἐλθεῖν.

25. It is fair to point out that Diodotus too suggests that his opponents have some private interest at stake (iii.42.2; Saar, *Kleon und Diodotus*, 63, suggests that the interest in question is simply for Cleon to increase his own influence), and that Cleon, no less than Diodotus, fails to dismiss such allegations in the Periclean manner—indeed, iv.28.5 will later make clear that "sensible" citizens would be glad to be rid of Cleon. There is thus a certain balance between the accusations made (iii.38.2, 42.2) and the lack of a Periclean response; still, the order of the speeches, and the fact of Mytilenian influence at this time (36.5), cause the expectation of a response to fall more heavily on Diodotus. The situation is thus characterized more by the appearance of such accusations rather than any certainty of their truth; that will come in a later debate.

26. A.W. Gomme, "International Politics and Civil War," in *More Essays in Greek History and Literature*, ed. David A. Campbell (Oxford: Basil Blackwell, 1962), 324, worries about this. Winnington-Ingram, *"Ta Deonta Eipein,"* 78, and Saar, *Kleon und Diodotus,* 34, argue that Cleon's speech makes straightforward appeals to justice difficult; nevertheless, surely Cleon represents a strong pressure rather than an iron necessity: given that considerations of compassion and justice are the reason this debate takes place at all (iii.36.4), the right orator (e.g., Pericles) would surely appeal to them. After all, we know from Plutarch, *Plutarch's Lives, Vol. III: Pericles and Fabius Maximus, Nicias and Crassus*, trans. Bernadotte Perrin (Cambridge, MA: Harvard University Press, [1986] 1916), 33, that Cleon was active late in Pericles' career, in particular during the episode at ii.21–22, and yet Thucydides tells us nothing of this, suggesting that Pericles' authority was such that he was not much constrained by whatever Cleon was saying.

27. Macleod, "Reason and Necessity," 78. I think Macleod is correct here in theory, but not in practice. The difficulties that he shows to have been brought to light by the Mytilenian debate, above all the double view of Athens' subjects and the consequent nature of Athenian power, which risks undermining itself, are not resolvable in theory. But none of this necessarily dooms Athens. In practice, it is possible to muddle through these difficulties.

28. Saar, *Kleon und Diodotus*, 71, notes that Pericles challenges his audience to be responsible (i.140.1, ii.60.4); Diodotus can only complain that orators are subject to an assembly which is not itself responsible (iii.43.5–6).

29. See Macleod, "Reason and Necessity," 76–77.

(3) Alcibiadean Athens

With Alcibiades, we reach the logical conclusion of the movement that began with the death of Pericles. We also reach a figure who is able to dominate affairs as Cleon did not. However, while the course of history does turn on the person of Alcibiades, it was not merely his stature or his intentions that determined the shape of things: "rather, his behavior, his character, and the reaction it aroused in the Athenians led to a crucial ambivalence in Athenian policy at times of key importance, and to disaster on two occasions."[1] Accordingly, Pericles' normative virtues (e.g., his reputation for integrity) will be brought into relief here. However, before we get to the debate in which Alcibiades appears, we must deal with the Melian Dialogue, for the character of Athens as we see it here helps determine what comes next.[2]

THE MELIAN DIALOGUE

The Melian Dialogue is often (and rightly) studied in connection with the theme of justice and power, but here it is of interest to us insofar as it contains connections—above all, *internal* connections—with the account of the Sicilian expedition (i.e., books vi–vii) that follows. That is, the character of Athens in both episodes is the same in important respects, which represent the culmination of specific developments we can trace back through the Mytilenian debate to Pericles. It is likely that the changing nature of Athens is one reason the dialogue has been included in the text, for although the incident—the crushing of a small island people—is in itself of no relevance to the course of the war, we shall see that the view it gives us of the Athenians is of considerable relevance. We shall also see how Thucydides has suggested the connection of the Melian and Sicilian episodes by means of certain literary devices.

(3) Alcibiadean Athens

There are three main points to cover concerning Athenian character in the Melian Dialogue, each of which reinforces the others. First, there is a suggestive verbal link with important earlier passages that provides our first indication that the Athenians at Melos are characterized by a temporal focus limited to the present—that is, by a form of immediacy as it was set out in the introduction (pages 11–3). Second, there is the central role of fear that we see moving Athens here, and an associated conceptual narrowness (another form of immediacy). Finally, there is the circle of reaction within which this fear comes to light, a significant logical form that we saw in Cleon. Taken together, these three points paint a picture of an irrational Athens, one whose conception of her strategic situation is far too narrow, and thus grossly inadequate, a failing that will soon produce catastrophe.

As the Athenians set the terms of the debate, they demand that it focus only on the present reality (τὰ παρόντα—v.87), specifically excluding the future. This is certainly a rhetorically convenient move, for if the view is restricted to the present alone, the Melian situation seems straightforward, and surrender is the only reasonable option.[3] However, by now we have seen references to τὰ παρόντα at many significant moments in the work, including Pericles' dealings with the masses (ii.22.1, ii.59.3, ii.65.1), Cleon (iii.38.7) and above all in Thucydides' major reflection on the war as a whole (i.e., iii.82–83). Clearly τὰ παρόντα can be a highly significant term in Thucydides, and although its occurrence here cannot on its own determine anything, its presence is not so easy to explain as one might at first think.

It might seem that the Athenians' attempt to limit the discussion's focus to the present is to be explained simply by their desire to win the debate, and yet they conspicuously fail to use it toward this end. Almost immediately, the Melians, invoking justice, mention a future downfall of Athens (v.90)—just the sort of thing that was supposed to be off-limits—but the Athenians do not make good their earlier threat to end the debate (v.87), and they only call their adversaries to order with a reminder of the terms of discussion toward the end, when they contrast present resources—τὰ ὑπάρχοντα—with the future (111.2). In fact, the debate will from this point (i.e., v.90) be *dominated* by speculations concerning the future: the initial attempt to limit the discussion to the present determines nothing.[4] It is just at this point that the Melians take the initiative, for the Athenians will now respond to questions and statements coming from the Melians. We thus have reason to believe that this Athenian insistence on a focus on τὰ παρόντα could contain an authorial indication concerning how we are to understand the Athenians here.

Well might the Athenians want to avoid discussing the future, for the discussion soon brings to light profound inadequacies within their thought. The future, with a possible end of the empire that the Melians suggest, contains a possibility that the Athenians fear: what if their subjects turn and attack them?

It soon becomes clear that this fear dominates and distorts Athenian thinking.[5] They believe that their subjects, seeing tiny Melos maintaining its independence against Athens, will believe that Melos is sufficiently strong to frighten Athens off. If such a weak and vulnerable entity can maintain its independence against the Athenian empire, so the subjects might think, why should they not do the same? (v.97)[6] Athens' great imperial strength thus contains a weakness, and so it is fear that drives the Athenians to conquer Melos, fear of rebellion. From the point of view of this fear, the weakness and insignificance of the Melians, which might otherwise seem a reason not to bother with them, become the reason that they *must* be crushed.[7] This is a new thought, one that we neither heard from Pericles, nor Diodotus, nor even Cleon.

Two aspects here are particularly worthy of note. First, the concern is above all with an *appearance*: the subjective impression that an independent Melos will make upon Athens' subjects is taken to be a decisive causal factor. The importance of this point will become clear when we reach Alcibiades. Second, in the thinking they attribute to their subjects, the Athenians seem unable to conceive of any motive force beyond fear, coercion, and the desire to rule. The possibility that Athens might see no need to conquer Melos seems not to be a possibility here: the notion that the subjects might think Athens fails to rule over Melos because of *indifference* is excluded. We saw earlier how there was at least a suggestion in both Cleon and Diodotus that other cities contained some basis for a relationship of friendship with Athens, and how Thucydides himself confirmed that this was not entirely false (iii.82.1). Now, however, we see no awareness of such possibilities, and so nothing remains but fear and forceful compulsion. If Athens does not want to be thought afraid, then, she had better exert some forceful compulsion: on this basis, it is not difficult to see how the "necessity of nature" (v.105.2), according to which people rule wherever they can, might start to seem a straightforward reality to which Athens is subject. We have here a kind of conceptual narrowing, a form of immediacy as set out in the introduction.

In fact, the Athenians are caught in a vicious circle of immediate reaction. The empire provides safety against external threats—particularly against large powers, such as the Peloponnesians or Persians—but the Athenians no longer find such threats so terrifying: "these are not terrible to the conquered." (v.91.1) What they do find particularly fearful is something that the empire has created: the hatred of the subjects, oppressed as they are by Athenian might. This hatred is supposed to be a sign of Athenian power (v.95), and thus to improve Athenian security, insofar as such signs of power would intimidate the other subjects, and so prevent revolts. But the Athenians seek security by adding to the number of their subjects, which increases the number of those who hate them. That is, the empire is the source of their fear, a fear grounded in hatred, and this very fear drives them to enlarge the empire, which must increase the hatred against them, and thus also their fear. This is a circle of fear, which should remind us of Cleon's circle of viciousness (iii.40.5–6). Further, the logic here points to an unbounded expansion of the empire, at least among islands, creating ever more hatred and fear—the same sort of thing we saw in Cleon's circle. That is, there can be no end to the expansion of the empire, at least until all islands are conquered. And once the need to expand for such reasons has been accepted, what happens when Athens begins to expand against adversaries who have a better chance of winning? The question points us right at the Athenian attempt to conquer another island: the Sicilian expedition.

It also looks back to what we have seen so far and points to a three-step development, in which the focus on the fear and hatred in the empire takes on an ever-greater role. Pericles, for all the power and safety he found in the empire, did also note the hatred inherent in it (ii.64.5) and alluded to the danger posed by the subjects (ii.63.2). In the Mytilenian debate, we saw this perspective deepened, for not only was there a double view of Athens' subjects, but Cleon brought an intensified focus to bear on the negative side, on the enmity of the subjects, and the hatred and violence thus implied. But Cleon did not carry the day. At Melos, the consciousness of hatred and the danger it implies have created a fear that now determines policy. Thus the brutal punishment that Cleon did not quite manage to impose on a city that had rebelled against Athens, the slaughter of a city's men and the enslavement of the women and children, is now imposed on a city that had, on Thucydides' telling, been neutral. One wonders if Hycara (vi.62.3) would have been the only city to suffer a similar fate if the Athenians had succeeded at Sicily. By contrast, we never even saw Periclean Athens propose such a brutal course.

The circle of immediate reaction, the Athenian desire to focus on the present, and their fear—all of these are aspects of a single standpoint. A vicious circle can exist only for those who maintain a narrow focus on their thoughts. For those who look not only to the present but take a wider and longer view, thinking through the future and present in relation to one another, the situation will raise larger questions. Above all, one ought to recognize the vicious circle and to re-examine the thinking behind it. Fear, however, can be an effective deterrent to such reflections, tending instead to keep one's focus on the present reality alone. This, then, is the state of the Athenians at Melos: fearful, too narrowly focused on one temporal frame of reference, and thus caught in a circle of immediate reaction. However sound Athenian reasoning about the present situation may be, this is a profoundly irrational orientation.[8] As we shall see, it is essentially connected to the decision to undertake the Sicilian expedition.

Before moving on, it is important to summarize seven external connections between the Melian Dialogue and the Sicilian episode, for these are literary means by which Thucydides indicates to his readers that we are meant to connect the two episodes.[9] First, the Athenians at Melos boast that they have never yet withdrawn from a siege out of fear of others (v.111.1); they leave the siege of Syracuse fearing they might suffer the enslavement they had planned for others (vii.75.7). Second, the Melians talk hopefully of a factor that might motivate the Spartans to send help: Sparta and Melos share a common heritage (ξυγγενεία—v.104; also 106, 108).[10] When the Sicilian expedition is being considered, the same tie between the Spartans and Syracusans (ξυγγενής—vi.6.2) is put forth with the suggestion that it will motivate the Syracusans to help Sparta against Athens.[11] Third, the Melian suggestion of ways in which the Spartans might help them despite Athenian naval superiority (v.110) turns out to be prophetic in relation to Sicily: Gylippus is able to reach Syracuse despite Athenian naval power, and the Spartans, in fortifying Decelea, do indeed fall upon the Athenians' own land as the Melians suggest, and with considerable effect (vii.27–28). Fourth, the Athenians at Melos push aside hope, chance, and divine aid as sources of safety (v.103, 105); at Sicily, they wind up appealing to all of these (vii.77.2–4). Fifth, the Melians suggest that by attacking them, the Athenians could add to the number of their enemies, as "those currently allied to neither side" (ὅσοι γὰρ νῦν μηδετέροις ξυμμαχοῦσι—v.98) see the fate of other neutrals, and so feel themselves obliged to join the fight against Athens. Although this does not come to pass through Melos, it does as a result of the Sicilian expedition, which eventually causes "the allies of neither side" (οἱ μὲν μηδετέρων ὄντες ξύμμαχοι—viii.2.1) to act as the Melians suggest. Sixth, Thucydides has represented the Athenians at Melos as peculiarly fixated on the fact that they are "masters of the sea" (ναυκράτορες—v.97, 99) and that the Melians are islanders (v.97, 99; also 109). In the Sicilian debate the Athenians are still sure of themselves as "masters of the sea" (ναυκράτο ρες—vi.18.5), but the fact that Sicily is an island (as we are reminded at the start of that narrative—vi.1.1) will become grimly relevant to the fate of the Athenian expeditionary force:[12] a seemingly straightforward thought in the Melian Dialogue points to a catastrophic reality at Sicily. Finally, there is a thematic link: "it is . . . the final disaster in the West which creates the conditions for what the Athenians do confess to fear at Melos, large-scale revolt by the allies, and makes their own survival the crucial issue in the war."[13] Such a list of ironic parallels can hardly be accidental: clearly, we are meant to think through the two episodes in relation to one another.[14]

THE SICILIAN DEBATE

In this debate we see the continuation of the splintering of the Periclean unity of virtues necessary to statesmanship: just like Cleon and Diodotus, both

Nicias and Alcibiades are heirs of Pericles in their own peculiar, and merely partial, way.[15] The debate also takes up themes from the Melian Dialogue, because the decision to sail on Sicily is moved in part by the same forces that led Athens to sail on Melos, and because the decision leads to a result that follows naturally from the effects of these forces.

Nicias

There can be no doubt that Nicias possesses the virtue that Pericles called "recognizing what is needed" (γνῶναί . . . τὰ δέοντα—ii.60.5). Certainly, the expedition that Nicias opposes does ultimately prove disastrous, but Thucydides has made the point more precisely than this. He has given us numerous implicit indications that Nicias brings to light factors that do, in fact, prove important to the expedition: we can profitably compare points made by Nicias against what actually happens. So, for example, Nicias warns about the need to bring adequate cavalry to Sicily (vi.20.4, 21.1, 22.1), and as we read Thucydides' subsequent account of the expedition, we hear again and again about the effect that the superior Syracusan cavalry has on the course of events, either harming the Athenians directly or forcing them to adjust their plans.[16] The implication is clear: Nicias judged correctly in advance. Because these points of comparison have mostly been treated elsewhere, they can be given summary treatment here.[17] On at least six further points, subsequent events show Nicias to have been prescient: the availability of the funds the Egestaeans promise;[18] the danger to Athens inherent in a double war;[19] the distance to Sicily[20] and the consequent problem of supply;[21] the need for naval superiority;[22] the question of whether the Sicilians can or will unite against Athens;[23] and the role fortune can play.[24] In this one respect, at least, in recognizing what is needed, Nicias can claim to be the heir of Pericles.

Despite Nicias' claim to be Pericles' heir as regards knowledge of the right policy, he has three failings that the older statesman did not, and his inability to live up to Pericles' example in these regards has fatal consequences for Athens. First of all, he is conspicuously without the ability to move people. We saw that both Pericles and Cleon had a key to leadership in being able to stand against an audience and reproach them with their shortcomings, but Nicias actually does the opposite of this: "against your character," he says, "my speech would be weak" (vi.9.3).[25] Not only does he fail to persuade the assembly to accept his advice (as Pericles never did), he also makes an ineffectual attempt to manipulate his audience, an attempt which backfires: his second speech in the Sicilian debate (vi.20–23) tries to dissuade the Athenians from undertaking the expedition by means of an emphasis on the need to send forces on a very large scale (24.1)—and yet the result is to make people desire the voyage all the more (24.2). Nicias also offers to resign

(3) Alcibiadean Athens 61

the command (23.1), a gambit he has tried before (iv.28); such transparent attempts to manipulate the assembly are presumably the best he can do in the absence of rhetorical ability. His ineffectiveness is driven home by his exhortation to the old not to worry about how they appear (δόξει—vi.13.1) when they vote: when the time comes, this becomes a description of what actually does happen, for those who have concerns keep quiet precisely because of their fear concerning how they will appear (δόξειεν—24.4). Thus Nicias has neither the ability to express things (ἑρμηνεῦσαι ταῦτα—ii.60.5) that made up part of the Periclean unity discussed in the Introduction, nor does he have the ability to speak against the populace (ἀντειπεῖν—ii.65.8) when necessary.

Even his single success at persuasion—he does get the forces which he desires for the expedition (26.1)—stands in an unfortunate relation to what follows because it is a merely partial success. As he argues for a large armament, Nicias unknowingly makes a darkly prophetic remark: "it is disgraceful to depart having been forced, or to send for reinforcements later, having first planned inadvisedly" (21.2). In the event, Nicias will have to send for reinforcements, and will be forced to depart, and all this despite having got all the supplies he wanted.

Finally, Nicias also proves an unworthy heir of Pericles in his encouragement that citizens take thought for their own property (9.2; also 12.1, which is excusable on rhetorical grounds). Pericles, realizing that such attention to personal property could imperil the whole city, pointed in the opposite direction (i.143.5, ii.13.1). Thus Nicias cannot claim to be superior to the influence of money (χρημάτων κρείσσων—ii.60.5) as Pericles could. This is not a hopeful basis from which to build a claim that other Periclean virtue, patriotism (φιλόπολις), and when we look to Nicias' conduct in the course of the Sicilian expedition, we see his failure as regards this last virtue: as events begin to turn against Athens, he declares that rather than face a hostile assembly at Athens, he would prefer to risk being destroyed by the enemy in the field, as an individual (vii.48.4). The word for "individual" at this point is ἴδιος, the word used repeatedly by Thucydides at ii.65 to point to the destructive role of the attention to private, rather than public, ends. Of course, at this point Nicias is making a decision not only for himself but for the whole expeditionary force. By focusing on himself as an individual, he dooms his city's whole army (just the sort of thing ii.65 leads us to expect). Clearly, Nicias cannot claim patriotism (φιλόπολις—ii.60.5), at least not to the extent that Pericles could.

Alcibiades

It should already be clear that Alcibiades does not have the virtue of "recognizing what is needed" (γνῶναί τὰ δέοντα).[26] We saw seven points made by Nicias that were confirmed in various ways by Thucydides' subsequent account of the Sicilian expedition, and these also reflect poorly on Alcibiades. Nicias rightly warned about cavalry, and about the problems attendant on the great distance to Sicily, in particular, supply; Alcibiades never mentions any of these matters. Nicias expressed his concern about the unreliability of Egestaean funds, a point not addressed by Alcibiades, and when the funds do, in fact, turn out to be negligible, Nicias is not surprised while Alcibiades is (vi.46.2). Nicias presciently warned about the danger of a double war; Alcibiades brushes it off (17.6–8). Nicias is conscious of the importance of naval superiority; Alcibiades complacently takes it as a given (17.8, 18.5). Nicias warned that the Sicilians might unite against Athens; Alcibiades denies that such a thing will happen (17.4).[27] Nicias recognizes the unpredictable role fortune can play; Alcibiades effectively recommends that the Athenians commit themselves to fortune when he says, "do not now be afraid of [my youth], but while I am still in my prime with it, and Nicias seems to be fortunate, use both of us to the full" (17.1).

Alcibiades' failures as a counselor go beyond poor foresight, as his arguments can be very bad indeed, and very much at odds with the facts. For example, his boast concerning the battle of Mantineia (vi.16.6) not only conflicts with Thucydides' account[28] but makes little sense on its own terms, for it contains the claim that the Spartans, though they won the battle against the coalition Alcibiades had put together, have not yet regained their confidence. (How could the Spartans lose confidence through a victory?) In similar fashion, a remark on the Persian Wars suggests that Athens beat the Persians despite having the Spartans for enemies (vi.17.7)—but the Spartans were then allies. Thus quite apart from the basic fact that he recommends an expedition that fails catastrophically, the poverty of Alcibiades' judgment is very much on display in relation to the Sicilian expedition, and we shall see below that his speech has further flaws.

What Alcibiades certainly does have is the virtue of "expressing things" (ἑρμηνεῦσαι ταῦτα—i.60.5): in the Sicilian debate, despite Nicias' accurate foresight, it is Alcibiades who carries the day. That is, his rhetoric is highly effective. There are numerous examples in Alcibiades' speech of claims that clearly do not constitute an accurate recognition of what is needed, but which can nevertheless be expected to be effective rhetorically. For example, Alcibiades echoes the Periclean demand for a unity of desirable qualities. Nicias had appealed to the old to stand fast against the folly of youth (vi.13.1), and in response, Alcibiades can make a claim of uniting young and old (18.6), and thus to make a unity of what are presumably attributes appropriate to each, along with a middle ground: τό τε φαῦλον καὶ τὸ μέσον καὶ τὸ πάνυ ἀκριβὲς. (perhaps, "the trifling, the moderate and the exceedingly precise?")[29] Why each of these elements is desirable, or how some sort of reconciliation of or mean between them might be an end worth attaining, is not immediately clear, but the point does not lie there. Rather, Alcibiades is making a rhetorical appeal to the idea of a balance between various virtues. With Pericles the unity of virtues was a substantial reality, and he could explain the importance of each part (ii.60.5–6)—indeed, by now it should be clear how this unity is a central point of reference in Thucydides' account of Athens (and see the conclusion, pages 75–7). Alcibiades' unity is effective insofar as it allows him to strike a pose as a reconciler of factors that his rival opposed to one another. Where once there was critically important content, now we have a rhetorical motif (recall that we saw a similar replacement of substantial content with mere rhetoric in Cleon's claim to be "the same man" at iii.38.1). The replacement of content with rhetoric points both to Alcibiades' attainment of the virtue of "expressing things" and to his failing as regards "recognizing what is needed" (γνῶναι τὰ δέοντα).

Connected to Alcibiades' rhetorical ability is the fact that his arguments repeatedly depend upon subjective impressions rather than objective facts, a deepening of something we noted at Melos. That is, the distinction between appearance and reality is coming into focus here, with Alcibiades tending toward the former. When he suggests that he has brought "profit" (ὠφελία—vi.16.1) to Athens, he backs the claim up with talk of his personal expenditure at the Olympics: from such displays, he says, "power is inferred" (δύναμις ὑπονεῖται—16.2). That is, the only benefit he can claim is that other Greeks *think* Athens' power to be greater than it actually is: he boasts of creating an appearance. Later, Alcibiades urges the Athenians to avail themselves of Nicias' services while that man "*seems* to be fortunate" (δοκεῖ—17.1, emphasis mine), a turn of phrase that points again to appearance. In similar fashion, the fact that he says "we will be seen" (δόξομεν—18.4) to sail against Sicily shows this tendency at work once more, for he speaks as though the appearance will, of itself, produce results. His account of the battle of Mantineia (16.6), noted above, does not point to an actual victory but tries to make something of the impression the battle supposedly made on the Spartans: again, appearance as distinct from reality. The same is true of the Alcibiadean unity noted above: it is a mere rhetorical motif, useful as an appearance only. Alcibiades is thus represented as peculiarly focused on appearance.[30]

Another defining characteristic of Alcibiades is the role that the individual now takes in relation to the state. Once again, a connection with Pericles brings out the point, for Pericles, in his last speech, struck a note of caution with the reality that Athens was hated by her subjects. He ended with the reflection that "hatred does not long endure, but the brilliance of the moment is left behind to what follows as a glory ever to be remembered" (ii.64.5). Alcibiades, defending himself, says that although brilliant men may be vexatious in their own lifetime, later "they leave behind a claim for other men of kinship with them, even if false, and, to the country in which they lived, they leave behind a boast, not as foreigners or as having failed, but as its own and as having excelled" (vi.16.5). That is, Alcibiades applies to the individual (himself) what Pericles had said about the city. Along the way, he implies that benefit flows to the city from the individual (a view also implicit at 16.1–3), an inversion of Pericles' understanding.[31] Note also how Alcibiades' words here focus on claims and boasts, even false ones: his interest is not in the objective state of affairs, but in rhetorical impact, which is to say that here, too, he leans toward appearances.

Alcibiades' new arrangement threatens the very existence of the democratic order which Pericles had praised, particularly the idea of equality for all (πᾶσι τὸ ἴσον—ii.37.1) under the laws: Alcibiades' claim that "it is not unjust that one thinking highly of himself not be equal" (ἴσος—vi.16.4) will fatally undermine any stable community if applied universally, for if everyone demands a special place simply because he *thinks* himself entitled to it, there will be continual conflict rather than civil society. Note also that we have here a statement dependent upon personal opinion rather than facts: just as with appearances, the determining point of reference is that of the subject rather than objective reality. With Pericles, there was a balance between individual excellence and civic responsibility, for if he did claim a special place for himself, still this was because of his service to the city, and the fact of that service was not merely his own conception of himself (ii.65.4).

The new place that Alcibiades gives to the individual is highlighted in another way, in that his personal habits are the focus of Thucydides' account to a substantial degree. In the remarks which precede Alcibiades' speech we hear that while he managed the affairs of the war very well, individually, citizens were vexed by his behavior, and the city was doomed as a result of their turning the city over to others (vi.15.4). This is not a straightforward endorsement of Alcibiades that lays censure instead upon the citizenry of Athens,[32] for in theme of personal behavior, we have a clear parallel with Pericles. We saw in the Introduction that one of the keys to Pericles' leadership ability was his being "manifestly most incorruptible" (διαφανῶς ἀδωρότατος—ii.65.8). Beyond this, Pericles' private behavior was of no historical relevance, so Thucydides does not record it. With Alcibiades, however, "since his personality generates such suspicions, it is a historical factor of considerable weight."[33] The suspicions show that Alcibiades is *not* manifestly most incorruptible—and note that he must begin both his speeches in this work with a defense of his own character (vi.16, 89). He is thus unable to lead the state as Pericles did, however skillful he might be in other regards.

If the portrait of Alcibiades in the Sicilian debate hints in these ways at the new priority being given to the individual, his speech at Sparta later on puts the matter more bluntly: "I am a patriot [φιλόπολις] not insofar as I am wronged, but insofar as I live safely as a citizen." (vi.92.4) That is, Alcibiades' loyalty to the city is explicitly subordinate to the question of whether his own personal good is being served at a given moment. Once again, the unity of the individual and common good which we found with Pericles has not only fallen apart, but its logic has become inverted. The use of the word φιλόπολις serves to remind us that Alcibiades does not have another of the Periclean virtues we noted in the Introduction (ii.60.5).

Thus we find indications of the new priority of the individual in Alcibiades' speeches, and when we turn to his subsequent career, we find that it provides a straightforward application of this principle to political life. His extravagant personal habits cause him to be suspected of aspiring to tyranny, and this is an essential factor in creating the situation which causes him to flee Athens, for the suspicions of the masses, and their fear of tyranny, form the basis of the investigation which leads to his recall from the Sicilian expedition (vi.53.2–3). We soon find him at the court of Sparta, having fled Athens for fear of standing trial there. His betrayal of his city is total: he recounts the motivation of the Athenians for the Sicilian expedition in a manner most likely to move the Spartans to action (90.2–4); he reveals Athens' greatest military weakness in Attica and urges the Spartans to take vigorous action against it (91.5–92.1); he even dismisses Athens' form of government—democracy—as "admitted foolishness" (vi.89.6);[34] above all, he successfully moves the Spartans to intervene at Sicily, which will prove decisive (in fact, he seems to have betrayed his city even before leaving Sicily, by informing the Messanians of an Athenian plot against them—vi.74.1). Three years later, he has managed to create such animosity against himself at Sparta that he is forced to flee (viii.45.1). He soon becomes an advisor to the Persians, doing all he can to harm his former friends in Sparta (47.1), and subsequently succeeds in being elected general by the Athenian army at Samos (82.1). We thus have a figure who leaps from city to city (or perhaps empire to empire). This is the most absolute inversion possible of the Periclean view that the city is the center relative to which political activity is conducted, for now the individual is the center, and the city is little more than an ornament that can be put on or taken off as need be.

We saw in the Introduction (see *Holism, Pericles, and His Successors*, pages 9–11) that Alcibiades differs from Pericles in his one-sided preference for activity instead of passivity. This orientation is to be connected to the policy that Alcibiades thinks appropriate to his city: "it is not possible for us to control the extent to which we are willing to rule, but insofar as we have gotten to this point, it is necessary to make plots against some, and not to let others go free" (vi.18.3). That is, he sees there is a necessity for infinite imperial expansion, at least until everyone is conquered. This gives us a point of connection with the Melian Dialogue, where the need for a boundless expansion, at least among islands, was implicit. Alcibiades simply makes this explicit, while leaving out any qualifications involving the empire's maritime nature. It also gives another inversion of Pericles, who warned against imperial expansion (i.144.1).

The aspects of Alcibiades that we have noted here—his individualism, his effective rhetoric, the focus on appearance over reality, his one-sided advocacy of activity, and the poor quality of his advice—might seem a casual assortment of random elements, but these elements fit together so seamlessly that it is reasonable to view them in connection with one another. Above all, it is remarkable that we find here a focus on appearances together with the principle of individualism. The notion of appearance requires an awareness of the role of a perceiving subject—that is, an awareness of a principle of individuality—in our experience of the world. What seems blue and black to me might seem white and gold to you: an appearance only exists for a particular subject and can differ depending on the subject. In Plato we shall see the same connection between a new focus on appearances and the move to the individual.

From such a principle of individuality, the other aspects of Alcibiades follow naturally. The problem with a policy of unbounded activity can come to light only to the extent that we are prepared to confront inconvenient realities, above all the fundamental fact that there is a reality that does not depend on us, and to which we must often—passively—adjust our action. Alcibiades' imaginative reconstruction of the past (whether Mantinea or the Persian wars) and the poor quality of his advice are part of the same parcel: however much they may be at odds with reality, they can seem quite convincing appearances, particularly when supported by effective rhetoric. And, of course, the virtue of "expressing things" is not concerned as such with the objective content of what is being said, but rather with the form of expression needed to convince particular individuals of a given view. That is, in the move to rhetoric without judgment, there is also a new focus on the perceiving subject. Thus in Alcibiades we not only have a focus on the individual in political terms; we also find a novel focus on the human subject which we did not see previously, another point of contact with what we shall see in Plato.

ATHENS AS SHE SETS SAIL FOR SICILY

Alcibiades' use of arguments from appearance point to a reality in the situation as a whole. We can see this reality in debate itself, since much that Nicias says points to the reality to follow, but Alcibiades carries the day leaning heavily toward merely subjective impressions—and note Nicias' contrast at vi.13.1 between desire (ἐπιθυμία) which is by nature subjective, and foresight (πρόνοια) which must of its nature deal with objective reality: it is desire, not foresight, that will carry the day. We noted above how Nicias' exhortation not to be concerned when voting with how one appears (δόξει—13.1) is followed by a vote in which opponents of the expedition allow their fear concerning their appearance (δόξειεν—24.4) to determine their behavior: this emphasizes once again how appearance is determining the situation. In addition, although Thucydides twice tells us that the actual aim of the expedition is to conquer the whole of Sicily (vi.1.1, 6.1), and further says that Nicias (8.4) and Alcibiades (15.2) understood this to be the case, the debate on Sicily never mentions this actual motive, focusing instead on the idea that they will help their allies "in seemly fashion" (vi.6.1; this pretense is picked up at 10.5, 18.1). This offers a parallel with the decision to start the whole war, which also involved a distinction between truest cause and pretext (i.23.5–6), but with a crucial difference, for at the beginning of the war, regardless of whether one accepts the truest cause or the pretext, the Spartans were in either case committed to the overthrow of the Athenian empire.[35] In the case of Sicily, the difference between pretext and truest cause turns out to be the difference between the plan of Nicias (vi.47), which has the considerable merit of being very likely to bring the main force home safely, and the plans of Alcibiades and Lamachus (vi.48–9), one of which does, in fact, lead to disaster. In a crucial sense, then, the whole debate on Sicily focuses on the merely apparent reason for the expedition, rather than on the reality, and this is a means by which the actual danger can be concealed.

When we look to Thucydides' account of the departure from Athens (vi.30–2), we see that he has once again made subjective impressions a central theme. The Athenians, taking leave of one another, find themselves thinking about the possible terrors of the expedition more than when they voted for it, but take courage both in the great number of each of the things *which they saw* (τὸ πλῆθος ἑκάστων ὧν ἑώρων—31.1) and *in the sight* (τῇ ὄψει) before them;[36] further, the force was the most costly and *best-looking* of any yet (31.1, emphasis mine). Thucydides is careful to note the figureheads and equipment, the beauty of the ships (31.3), and he records the widespread Hellenic view that the object is to make a display of power rather than a military expedition (31.4). "The expedition," he concludes, "became not less famous for its astonishing boldness and the brilliance of its appearance than for the superiority of the army against those whom it attacked" (vi.31.6).[37]

Of course, the account comes right after the affair of the Hermae (vi.28–29), which will eventually result in Alcibiades' recall, and thus the destruction, of the expeditionary force. Accordingly, we have the juxtaposition of a potent reality with an account focusing on the apparent. The same contrast is also hinted at within the description of the departure from Athens itself, for there are two references to internal conflict: strife (ἔρις) arose from the desire of each crew or company to look best (31.3-4), and when the ships have set out, they race to Aegina (32.2). These are, for the present, harmless trifles, but it is significant that Thucydides records them, as he has just set out the beginning of the fatal episode of internal dissent, which will doom the whole expedition. The contrast between appearance and reality is thus central to the whole of Thucydides' presentation of the motivation to go to Sicily. Accordingly, the focus on the subject that we noted in relation to Alcibiades is not confined to him but is characteristic of the situation as a whole.

MELOS AND THE SICILIAN EXPEDITION

Nowhere in the Sicilian debate do we hear a claim similar to the one made at Melos, that the strong do what they can and the weak suffer what they must (v.89). On the contrary, there remains at least a pretense of an interest in justice in the form of the seemly claim to be going to the aid of the ally Egestaea (vi.6.1, 18.1). We have seen, however, that this is mere rhetoric, and that the real reason for the expedition was conquest. If we look at relations within Athens as she sets out for Sicily, it is clear that the trust necessary to justice is disappearing. We have seen how personal attacks in the Sicilian debate went farther than before, requiring Alcibiades to talk about himself at length. This corrosion of relations within Athens soon bears poisonous fruit in the affair of the Hermae, resulting in the undercutting of Athenian policy (see the conclusion, page 76).

The normative world as the Athenians describe it at Melos is a place in which people relate to one another through forceful coercion alone, whether direct or by means of fear. They are understood to dominate others wherever they can—recall that in the thinking attributed to Athens' subjects, the only reason that Athens might not rule Melos is insufficient strength to do so. No other possibilities are imagined. What we have here is not simply an appreciation of the reality that people often *do* relate to one another through force, but the one-sided and myopic belief that they never do anything else. It is not surprising that an Athens that sees the world like this also produces Alcibiades' claim that the empire must be expanded to parry the blows expected from neutral states (vi.18.3). It is similarly unsurprising that trust between citizens in this same Athens might disintegrate: "as the empire in its purposeful extension first, and in its repressive measures later, becomes violent and tyrannical, so the individual citizen who has personally voted on the imperialistic and repressive plans must have applied its lessons to his own life."[38] If the Melian Dialogue shows the danger of an excess focus on justice in foreign affairs, it also points to a danger that can arise if one ignores justice altogether.

We noted earlier the numerous literary means by which Thucydides has connected the Melian episode with the Sicilian expedition, but by far the most important connection is this: the characteristics that define Athens at Melos go on to destroy her at Sicily. We saw that Athens at Melos was in the grip of an irrational drive (fear), caught in an unthinking circle of reaction, and characterized by a focus on the present at the expense of the future and the past. As the Athenians head for Sicily, the essential facts remain the same, though the accidents do differ. Here, too, they are carried away by the irrational. The difference is simply that fear has been replaced by another emotion: Nicias warns against being "sick with love" (δύσερως) for faraway things (vi.13.1), but at the vote for the Sicilian expedition, however, a love (ἔρως) of sailing away falls upon all alike (vi.24.3).[39] The fact that the reality-based warnings of Nicias are ignored in favor of Alcibiades' empty rhetoric also points to the irrational motivation for the expedition. Further, the circle of fear that we saw at Melos, which tends toward endlessness, is taken up by Alcibiades' explicit demand for an abandoning of limits on imperial expansion. Even Alcibiades' focus on appearance finds a parallel in the Athenians at Melos, who claim to be conquering the city because of the impression its freedom is believed to make on Athenian subjects.

The focus on the present that we saw at Melos, however, is not so obviously duplicated in the Sicilian debate. Nicias advocates that the Athenians preserve their "present resources" (τὰ ὑπαρχόντα) and not run risks concerning things unseen and "yet-to-be" (τὰ μέλλοντα—vi.9.3); the opposition is echoed by Thucydides himself at vi.31.6 (ἐπὶ μεγίστῃ ἐλπίδι τῶν μελλόντων πρὸς τὰ ὑπάρχοντα). Here the idea seems to be that the Athenians are insufficiently focused on the present, and are instead too focused on the future; Nicias' remark concerning a love for faraway things (vi.13.1) plays on the same theme: what is close at hand is ignored in favor of what is far off. Is this not the very opposite of the stance taken at Melos, where the Athenians demanded a focus on the present and derided the yet-to-be (i.e., τὰ μέλλοντα—v.97)? It is not, because the problem in both cases is a matter of temporal narrowness, that is, of becoming excessively focused on one temporal frame of reference to the exclusion of others. Plans for the future must be made with reference to a consideration of present resources (τὰ ὑπαρχόντα), that is, by thinking through both the present and the future together. As Pericles put it, one should trust "in judgment based on present resources [ἀπὸ τῶν ὑπαρχόντων], from which foresight is more stable" (ii.62.5). To focus only on the future without the present is to become lost in a dream; to focus only on the present is to refuse judgment or foresight as such.[40] We noted in our treatment of Pericles that he consistently appealed to all temporal frames of reference, taking such a broad view that he even touched on eternity (mirroring Thucydides himself in this). At Melos, just as in their decision to move on Sicily, the Athenians exhibit a debased form of deliberation, one profoundly different from the Periclean standard, in that their temporal frame of reference has become too narrow, making adequate judgment impossible.

NOTES

1. Gribble, *Alcibiades and Athens,* 184.
2. On the connections between the Melian Dialogue and Alcibiades, see Mary P. Nichols, *Thucydides and the Pursuit of Freedom* (New York: Cornell University Press, 2015), 107–37, who offers an account parallel to my own in certain key respects.
3. See Macleod, "Form and Meaning," 390, on this point. Parry, *Logos and Ergon,* 193–200, is particularly worth reading on παρόντα and ὑπάρχοντα in the Melian Dialogue.
4. Here I focus upon the present in relation to the future, but the exclusion of the past (v.89) is no doubt significant as well. As Connor, *Thucydides,* 155–56, says, not only did the Persian conflict shape Athens into what she now is, "they confronted in that struggle precisely the preponderance of power and the apparent hopelessness that Melos now faces." The question naturally arises: "what if the Athenians had acted against the Persians as they now urge the Melians to act?" The historical parallel reminds us that victory against extreme odds is indeed possible, strengthening the Melian reflection at v.102.
5. The fear is at this point implied. The Athenians start, at 91.1, with the straightforward claim that they do not fear the end of their empire. This statement, however, ends with a semicolon, and is followed by οὐ γὰρ, which brings out the connection of this initial assertion with what follows: rebelling subjects are terrible to the conquered; those who rule others are not. The implication is that the Athenians *are,* in fact, afraid of the end of their empire—if rebelling subjects bring it about.
6. On Athenian fear at v.97–9 see Macleod, "Form and Meaning," 391–92.
7. Bosworth, "Humanitarian Aspect," 38, repeats in one sentence this Athenian argument as though it were simply a reality, and yet the claim finds no confirmation anywhere else in Thucydides. We are never told that Athenian subjects, seeing the example of free, weak Melos, were given any extra impetus to revolt. In fact, the impetus for freedom in Thucydides seems to be universal, arising of itself, not as a response to the example of other, similar states.
8. Both Connor, *Thucydides,* 154, and Georg Deininger, *Der Melier-Dialog* (M. Krahl: Erlangen-Bruck, 1939), 42, see the Athenians at Melos as exhibiting rationality.
9. See Macleod, "Form and Meaning," 392–93, 395, on connections between these episodes.
10. See Deininger, *Melier-Dialog,* 38.
11. Specifically, in the Sicilian debate the notion of Spartan-Syracusan kinship helps build a picture of the Syracusans as naturally hostile to Athens. It thus goes together with Alcibiades' talk of "our enemies" in Sicily who might come and

attack Athens (vi.18.1), and against Nicias' suggestion that the Athenians will bring back new enemies if they go to Sicily, quite apart from the many they already have (vi.10.1).

12. The Athenian army is in the end compared to that small Spartan force which became trapped on the island of Sphacteria (vii.71.7; see iv.14–38 for the Spartans on Sphacteria).

13. Macleod, "Form and Meaning," 393.

14. The end of the Melian Dialogue suggests that what has started there will be finished only in the Sicilian episode. Connor, *Thucydides*, 149–50, has shown that the siege at Melos has numerous close narrative parallels—and also certain significant differences—with the two other major sieges described by Thucydides, that of Plataea in books ii–iii and of Mytilene in book iii; see also his Appendix 5 (255–56), which consists of a chart of verbal parallels between these three episodes, as each progresses through the various stages of a Thucydidean siege. In the case of Melos, there is a significant omission. Connor, *Thucydides*, 92, fn. 30, notes that Thucydides has a "frequent practice of marking the end of a major section or of a digression with τὰ μὲν, a prepositional phrase, οὕτως, and a verb in the past tense (cf. i.139.6)." (Some other examples: i.110.4, ii.54.5, ii.101.6, iii.114.4.) The accounts of the other two sieges conclude with a Thucydidean "rounding-off" sentence, which indicates the end of the episode in question. So, for example, the Mytilenian affair is concluded with the phrase, τὰ μὲν κατὰ Λέσβον οὕτως ἐγένετο ("affairs at Lesbos happened in this manner"—iii.50.3). The Melian episode is concluded by no such final phrase. Where we would expect to find one, we find instead the following words: "in the same winter, the Athenians wished once more to sail to Sicily" (vi.1.1)

15. Gribble, *Alcibiades and Athens*, 188–89, says that the presentation of Nicias and Alcibiades are each complex—"multivocal," as he puts it—with positive and negative strands that might seem to indicate two different views (perhaps from different eras of composition). The presentation of Pericles, by contrast, is more "univocal": we told much the same sort of thing about him whether he is being depicted or we have a direct comment from the narrator. Gribble explains this partly by pointing to the fact that Thucydides was writing about people whose reputations were still disputed, or who were perhaps still alive, and thus he was "in a decisive position for mediating the reputation of individuals whose role in the war was particularly controversial. That is why the depiction of such figures is characterized by a variety of carefully worded, balanced narratorial inventions mixing more positive with more negative analysis." This is my only substantial disagreement with Gribble: my own explanation is that in Nicias and Alcibiades we are dealing with people who attain the whole insufficiently, which means that they are good in some respects and bad in others. This requires the "multivocal" presentation Thucydides gives us; Pericles, by contrast, must be given a "univocal" presentation because he attains the whole.

16. Thucydides first emphasizes the Athenian lack of cavalry at vi.43, where he enumerates at some length the fleet and the army it carries, ending the list with the words "and one horse transport carrying thirty horsemen." Some particularly pertinent cavalry passages: vi.64.1, 66.1, 70.3, 98.3, 101.5, vii.4.6, 6.3, 44.8, 78.6, 81.2, 85.1. Note also how vi.94.4, which recounts the arrival of Athenian horsemen as

reinforcements without their horses, suggests a connection between the importance of cavalry and another of Nicias' points, the difficulty of long-distance supply.

17. See Stahl, *Man's Place in History*, 177–88, and de Romilly, *Athenian Imperialism*, 205–6. Stahl's work here is sufficient to refute Bender, *Begriff des Staatsmannes*, 51, who declares that "Nicias does not possess the ability of γνῶμαι τὰ δέοντα [recognizing what is needed]" and finds in favor of Alcibiades' judgment on Sicily on the basis of a questionable reading of ii.65.11. Bender says that the decision to go to Sicily "is . . . no error against γνῶναι τὰ δέοντα" (p. 66).

18. See vi.22.1 with 8.2, 46.1–2.

19. See vi.10.2–4, 11.6–7 with vii.27.3–28.4. See especially vii.18.2 and vii.28.3, which deal with Spartan and Athenian morale in relation to the double war. Thucydides himself implies the danger of a double war at vi.1.1.

20. See vi.13.1 with vi.68.3 (Nicias finds himself concerned with this distance at Sicily) and vi.88.1 (the distance of Athens works in the Syracusans' favor when the two cities vie for the favor of the Camarinaeans).

21. See vi.20.4, 21.2, 22 with vii.13, 14.2, 25.2.

22. See vi.22, 20.4. Of course, Athens fails to maintain naval superiority. The Sicilians develop a fleet (vii.7.4), and in a series of naval battles (vii.21–3, 36–8.1, 39–41, 51–2, 70–1) go from underdog to victor.

23. See vi.21.1 with vii.15; also iv.65.1. For another view on this point, see W. Liebeschuetz, "Thucydides and the Sicilian Expedition," *Historia* 17, no. 3 (July 1968): 295–6, who sees in the pro-Athenian faction evident in several Sicilian cities a reason to doubt their cohesion. But such factions are characteristic of "the whole Hellenic world" (iii.82.1) at this point, and so show nothing about Sicily in particular.

24. See vi.23.3; Stahl, *Man's Place in History*, 189–222, does at least show that fortune plays a considerable role in what follows.

25. See also vii.14.2 and 48.4, where Nicias again finds his activity confined by Athenian character.

26. In much of my treatment of Alcibiades, I am following Colin Macleod, "Rhetoric and History (Thucydides 6.16–18)," *Quaderni di Storia* 2 (1975): 39–65. The other treatment of Thucydides' Alcibiades that I have found particularly helpful has been Gribble, *Alcibiades and Athens*.

27. Alcibiades is at least correct in his claim that Sicel tribes will come over to Athens (vi.17.6; confirmed at 88.4, 103.2). Liebeschuetz, "Sicilian Expedition," 295–6 suggests that Alcibiades correctly points to the limited military competence of the Sicilians (17.3). In the event, there are indeed indications that Athens' force is of a higher standard than their new enemies (68.2, 70.1, 72.4).

28. K. J. Dover, *A Historical Commentary on Thucydides, Vol. V* (Oxford: Oxford University Press, 1981), 248, summarizes the consequences of Mantineia: "Spartan prestige was enhanced (v.75.3), the Argive alliance fell to pieces (v.81.1, cf. vii.31.1), and oligarchy was temporarily established in Argos (v.81.2), and Sparta intervened to her own advantage in Sikyon."

29. See Macleod, *Collected Essays*, 84–85, on these terms: "the trifling" points to "the easy-going ways of the young," while precision "is a quality of old age;" these

(3) Alcibiadean Athens 73

take up Nicias' "desire" and "forethought" (vi.13.1). "His [i.e., Alcibiades'] argument," notes Macleod, "is seductive, as recommendations of a middle way commonly are."

30. Macleod, *Collected Essays*, 73, drives this point home through a series of antitheses in the Greek.

31. Consider also Gribble, *Alcibiades and Athens*, 206–7: in vi.89, "Alcibiades presents Mantinea as a punishment inflicted by him (*hup' emou*—"at my hands") on the Spartans for personal wrongs. Contrast Pericles' conspicuous exclusion of his guest-friendship with Archidamus from the public sphere [at ii.13.1]."

32. As Connor, *Thucydides*, 164, takes it.

33. Macleod, *Collected Essays*, 71. Macleod's remark contains the kernel of an answer to the thesis of Westlake, *Individuals in Thucydides*, that Thucydides' focus on personalities later in the work is the result of a change of interest as composition proceeded. Gribble, *Alcibiades and Athens*, 159–64, provides a convincing refutation of Westlake.

34. Alcibiades' talk of democracy (δημοκρατία) is to be linked with the use of the same word by Pericles and Cleon: for Pericles, democracy had pride of place in the Funeral Oration (ii.37.1); for Cleon, democracy has started to seem an ambiguous good, for the emphasis was on its conflict with the needs of empire (iii.37.1); Alcibiades completes the movement with his dismissal of democracy as absurd. We have already shown above how this is a consequence of Alcibiades' variety of individualism—e.g., to the extent that "it is not unjust that one thinking highly of himself not be equal" (μὴ ἴσον εἶναι—vi.16.4), the equality for all (πᾶσι τὸ ἴσον—ii.37.1) necessary to democracy cannot survive.

35. On the parallels between books i and vi see the excellent work of Hunter R. Rawlings, *The Structure of Thucydides' History* (Princeton, NJ: Princeton University Press, 1981).

36. A pertinent point of comparison is found in Thucydides' remark that we should not consider the *sight* of cities more than their power (οὐδε τὰς ὄψεις τῶν πόλεων μᾶλλον σκοπεῖν ἢ τὰς δυνάμεις—i.10.3). Sight on its own often gives us only a misleading appearance. This is not the place for a full treatment of the theme of sight in Thucydides, but clearly sight, in its immediacy, can have an effect on people not conducive to judgment. Greenwood, *Shaping of History*, 24, speaks of "the *History*'s sustained illustration of the precariousness of sight, when not disciplined by insight and reflection" (see her chapter 2 for examples). See also Connor, *Thucydides*, 55, who, treating Archidamus' invasion of Attica, notes that "his chief weapon is the eyesight of the Athenians." That is, Archidamus' plan turns on the effect of sight (ii.11.6–7), and sight does prove have the desired effect (ii.21.2).

37. The repeated use of words of perception and belief continues in the account of the affair of the Hermae at vi.60.4–1.3: the Athenian people *supposed* [ᾤετο—60.4] ... it was not *clear* [ἄδηλον ἦν—60.5] ... they *believed* [ᾤοντο—61.1] ... it *seemed* [ἐδόκει—61.1, 61.2] ... the friends of Alcibiades at Argos *were suspected* [ὑπωπτεύθησαν—61.3]. Thus the primacy given to appearance continues to exert a determining role in Athens after the expedition departs.

38. Grene, *Man in His Pride*, 31.

39. Steven Forde, *The Ambition to Rule* (Ithaca, NY: Cornell University Press, 1989), 31, fn. 24, notes that there are only eight instances in Thucydides of words based around ἔρως; aside from Pericles (ii.43.1) and Diodotus (ii.45.5), all the remaining instances come in the story of Aristogeiton and Harmodius (i.e., at vi.54.1, 2, 57.3, 59.1), in which the emphasis falls heavily on the role of the irrational.

40. Macleod, "Form and Meaning," 391, provides some insightful remarks on present and future in Thucydides; see also Macleod, "Reason and Necessity," 70: "the future . . . is for Cleon the domain of hope (*cf.* iii.39.3), and so also delusion . . . at the same time, Cleon himself admits by the word προνοῆσαι (39.6) that if the basis of deliberation is τὰ παρόντα, its subject is the future." The difference, I suggest, between the future as a realm of delusion or mere hope (as at vi.31.6), and the future as the proper subject of deliberation, is a matter of the breadth of temporal reference: an excessively narrow temporal focus produces delusion and mere hope; a sufficiently broad focus is a basis for adequate deliberation.

Thucydides
Conclusion

CAUSE AND EFFECT: THE SHATTERING OF THE PERICLEAN UNITY AND THE SICILIAN EXPEDITION

The Sicilian debate is followed by the account of the Sicilian expedition, in which a total annihilation is visited upon the Athenian force. Certainly, one can speak in a general fashion about how the decline in the standard of deliberation in the Athenian assembly led to poor decisions, and note that the decision to sail on Sicily was just the sort of poor decision one would expect after all this. Thucydides, however, has not left the matter at this. The dissolution of the Periclean unity is directly tied to the decision to undertake the Sicilian expedition, and also to the particular chain of events that bring about the expedition's disastrous end.

We noted in the Introduction how the two "intellectual" virtues in the Periclean unity, (A) "recognizing what is needed" (γνῶναι ... τὰ δέοντα) and (B) "expressing these things" (ἑρμηνεῦσαι ταῦτα), would become opposed to one another, and that this opposition would bring about the decision to attack Sicily. We can now spell this out a bit more fully. We saw how Nicias has virtue (A), for he gives the right advice on the basis of real foresight. What he does not have is the ability to express these realities in a manner that can move the assembly (B). Alcibiades, of course, has virtue (B) without virtue (A). It is precisely this situation—the opposition of recognizing what is needed and being able effectively to express it—that brings about the decision to undertake the Sicilian expedition. If, for example, Nicias had possessed great rhetorical gifts, he might have prevented the expedition from happening.[1]

We can also see how the situation in the Sicilian debate represents a fuller development of something that had already begun in the Mytilenian debate.

Diodotus perhaps retained the Periclean virtue of recognizing what is needed (A), while Cleon clearly did not. Both men have a basis for a claim to be able to express things (B) in a convincing manner: Cleon is the most persuasive man of the time (iii.36.6), but it is Diodotus who actually carries the day in the debate. Still, neither Cleon nor Diodotus can claim this virtue to the degree that Pericles could, as we do not see anything like Pericles' consistent and unqualified ability to get his advice accepted (emphasized at i.145.1, ii.14.1, ii.65.2).

Of course, the simple decision to sail on Sicily was not in itself sufficient to produce a catastrophic result for Athens. That only came about after a long series of contingent events recounted in books vi–vii, and if the accidents in these events had turned out a bit differently, the Athenians would have avoided their force's total annihilation.[2] It is in this chain of events that the other two virtues in the Periclean unity, patriotism (φιλόπολις) and superiority to money (χρημάτων κρείσσων), prove decisively important.

One decisive event that led to Athenian doom was the arrival of the Spartan general Gylippus in Syracuse (vii.2) just when the Syracusans seemed ready to surrender. The reason that the Spartans sent Gylippus is that Alcibiades suggested it (vi.93) after having gone over to Sparta, and it was strife within Athens that caused Alcibiades to switch sides, above all the witch-hunt that followed the mutilation of the Hermae (see vi.27–29, 53, 60–61). Alcibiades' failure as regards the fourth Periclean virtue, superiority to money (χρημάτων κρείσσων), is decisively important here, for Thucydides makes clear that Alcibiades was concerned to gain personal wealth (χρήματα) and reputation (vi.15.2), and further, that his extravagant expenditure caused people to suspect him and to become his enemies (15.4). This is the beginning of the internal Athenian strife that will drive Alcibiades out of Athens. The fact that Alcibiades is prepared to switch sides at all is, of course, the antithesis of Periclean patriotism.

The disappearance of patriotism and of a superiority to money is the culmination of another development we saw beginning in the Mytilenian debate, where, on the one hand, there were indirect and unsubstantiated accusations of wrongdoing, and on the other, Cleon could claim that plots were unknown to the Athenians in their everyday lives (iii.37.2). Cleon's remark does suggest that Athenian life must have been reasonably free from plots to this point: no competent orator will make a claim that his audience will see as obviously false. Something similar must be true of Pericles' celebration of Athens, in which suspicion and anger did not interfere with government (ii.37.2). Certainly, in the view we get of the assembly of his time, personal attacks play no role whatsoever. In similar fashion, in the Mytilenian debate we find with concern in both orators that the interests of the city were falling from view, a concern to which Pericles himself proved an effective remedy.

Thus the dissolution of the Periclean unity is causally related to the eventual catastrophe suffered by Athens. Not only is this dissolution necessary to the decision to undertake the expedition at all, it is also crucial to the contingent series of events that actually brought about the destruction of the Athenian expeditionary force. On Thucydides' account, the Athenian catastrophe at Sicily is self-caused destruction, utterly internal, the product of Athens' internal state at the time of the Sicilian debate, and thus of the changes we have seen since Periclean Athens.

ATHENS MOVES TOWARD THE IMMEDIATE

We have just seen how Thucydides' account of political life in Athens involves an increasing conceptual narrowness—one of the two sense of "immediacy" mentioned in the Introduction—as the war proceeds, for those who come after Pericles are ever less capable of attaining the unity of virtues he set out, instead finding themselves on ever more limited and inadequate bases for activity. We can now turn to the other, temporal, sense of "immediacy."

In the Introduction we noted Thucydides' claim that "war . . . drives the character of most people down to the level of their immediate circumstances" (iii.82.2). Athens herself provides the supreme example of this dictum. We have seen how the words for "immediate circumstances," τὰ παρόντα, appear at significant moments in the mouths of Athenian speakers. Pericles' last speech was summarized as an attempt to move the judgment of the people *away from* their immediate misfortunes (ἀπὸ τῶν παρόντων—ii.65.1), precisely the opposite of what war tends to do (πρὸς τὰ παρόντα at iii.82.2); the continual presence of past and future in the Periclean speeches is part and parcel of this non-immediate orientation, as are Pericles' occasional turns toward eternity. Cleon, on the other hand, thinks the Athenians have not considered adequately "concerning the immediate circumstances" (περὶ τῶν παρόντων—iii.38.7): he wants a greater focus on the immediate, and he repeatedly displays a preference for the present over the future. Of course, Cleon does not quite win the Mytilenian debate, suggesting that the orientation toward the immediate that he represents has not yet quite moved into the driver's seat of Athenian policy (widespread Athenian behavior during the plague is comparable, in that it does not determine policy). Athens as we see her at Melos has gone a step further, for here the Athenians demand that the dialogue focus only on the immediate (τὰ παρόντα—v.87). However convenient this may have been for them rhetorically, we saw that their focus on the immediate connected meaningfully with other aspects of their view of the world, in particular with the circle of fear (v.97) and their implicit belief in the need for an infinite maritime expansion. The circle of fear in the Melian Dialogue was reminiscent of Cleon's circle of viciousness (iii.40.5–6), and we saw the likely connection between this kind of reasoning and a narrow temporal focus. No such vicious circle was seen in Pericles.

With the Sicilian debate, the matter became a bit more complicated. Here we do not have another verbal echo of τὰ παρόντα, for the idea is now that the Athenians are excessively focused on things unseen and "yet-to-be" (τὰ μέλλοντα), and insufficiently focused on their "present resources" (τὰ ὑπάρχοντα—vi.9.3). Nevertheless, we saw that the problem in the Sicilian debate was fundamentally the same as that which had been developing in what preceded: the Athenians have become excessively narrow in their temporal focus. Here, too, we found a vicious circle and a goal of unbounded expansion. Both as regards temporal narrowness, then, and as regards circular or otherwise unbounded lines of reasoning, we have a three-step movement.

The theme culminates in the disaster in Sicily in book vii. If war drives the character of most people down to the level of their immediate circumstances, the myopic and debased judgment that must result from such an orientation can be expected eventually to produce a catastrophic situation in which there is nothing but immediate circumstances left. In such a situation there can no longer be any possibilities for judgment.

It is just this that Thucydides has emphasized in Nicias' speech to the doomed Athenian army at Sicily, which begins, "out of the immediate circumstances . . . it is necessary to have hope" (ἐκ τῶν παρόντων . . . ἐλπίδα χρὴ ἔχειν—vii.77.1). There is no more room for the strategic calculations of Pericles, which might bring an understanding of such principles as money, ships, and walls to bear on the situation, and there is no longer any point to a consideration of the sort Pericles once gave (ii.60.5–6) concerning the need to hold together certain virtues to achieve adequate action, for there is nothing left to reflect on. Such reflections can only be of value, and are only possible, in a wider temporal context. All that is left to the Athenians here are the crushingly immediate demands of the present moment, and out of that nothing can be derived but naked hope.[3] The words Thucydides selected for Nicias suggest just how desperate—indeed, just how hopeless—the situation has become.

FROM CITY TO INDIVIDUAL: TOWARD THE IMMEDIATE

We have seen how the focus of political activity moves from the city, with Pericles, to the individual, with Alcibiades. The Mytilenian debate, in which Cleon and Diodotus both worry that the good of the city is falling from view, occupies an intermediate position, giving us, once again, three steps. This movement from city to individual is itself a move toward the immediate, and the destruction it entails confirms the wisdom of Pericles' focus on the city. This focus is not an immediately obvious truth. One needs to reflect for a time before one can attain a perspective from which one sees that the stable enjoyment of one's own good is possible only within the context of a community which must itself flourish to some degree. The simple fact that one is interested in one's own good, however, is an immediately obvious truth, available without any reflection. An abstract focus on the good of the individual—that is, a view of this good in isolation from any additional considerations, such as its potential connection with the good of other people—is therefore characteristic of an *immediate* standpoint, while the Periclean focus on the city is precisely *not* immediate. Accordingly, as we move through Athens' development, as we leave Pericles behind, and the good of the city falls from view to be replaced by an abstract focus on the good of the individual, we are moving *toward the immediate* (just as the words πρὸς τὰ παρόντα at iii.82.2 would have us expect).

The city, it was said, provides the basis from which individuals can pursue their own ends in a stable manner. Note the broad temporal perspective that comes with the qualification "in a stable manner," a breadth of perspective similar to that required by Pericles' explanation of the importance of the city (ii.60.2–4), in which we step back and look well beyond the present moment. The importance of this qualification becomes clear with Alcibiades, for one might argue that, whatever harm he may have caused to everyone else along the way, he did at least do better for himself than he would have otherwise: surely taking the leap to Sparta was better (for him) than going home to Athens. But Alcibiades' continued pursuit of his own good, as he hops from city to city, could hardly be more precarious: to a considerable degree, he is reduced to reacting to events—that is, to an immediate perspective—as he becomes obnoxious to each of his hosts in turn. In addition, not only is his own great rhetorical ability necessary to keep himself going but a considerable amount of luck besides—and of course, Alcibiades' ways will catch up with him in the end. The problem was present well before the leap to Sparta, in the excessive focus upon the personal (τὰ ἴδια—vi.15.2) that first caused the populace to view Alcibiades with suspicion.[4]

Pericles' approach, by contrast, meant that he never found himself in a position in which he felt forced to abandon his own city. It also had such immense reserves against the dangers presented by fortune that its basis remained in place even in the face of the plague. Further, the focus on the city preserved the possibility of a pursuit of individual ends possible not just for one individual, but for *all* citizens. From a narrower temporal standpoint, it might seem that the suffering attendant on Pericles' plan negates any good it might do, but such a narrow standpoint must of its nature be unstable, hostage as it is to the whims of the moment. The suffering of a given moment must be judged in a much wider temporal perspective: many miserable moments may in the end prove worthwhile or necessary to a good policy (or life). Pericles' plan provides the best possible chance at a good life for Athens' citizens, rather than merely a good afternoon or summer.

One might object to the development set out here on the ground that Alcibiades is just one individual, and an exceptional one at that. It is not the case that all Athenians leap from city to city as Alcibiades did. Even if the matter were so simple, the fact remains that Alcibiades' exceptional behavior does determine the situation as a whole. But we saw something more at work as Athens set out for Sicily, for it is not merely the case that the individual as a political actor becomes an emergent focus here. We also saw how the individual *as a perceiving subject* becomes a focal point that determines the course of events, and this is true not only of Alcibiades' words but of the situation at Athens more generally. This remarkable reality will provide yet another point of connection with what we find in Plato.

We have already seen how Alcibiades' individualism is causally related to the eventual catastrophe at Sicily. We also saw Thucydides' very strong emphasis on the role of the merely personal (ἴδιος) in his own comments on the causes of Athens' decline (ii.65—see page 32). These facts both confirm that Pericles was right to focus on the city as he did. Finally, note that the change of focus from city to individual can itself be considered a taking of the part for the whole, for a city is made up of individuals. As the focus moves from whole to part, the parts can easily come into conflict with one another, something that we saw Pericles to have suggested already at ii.35.2–3.

THE POWER OF JUSTICE

We now have enough material before us that it is possible to make a claim concerning a well-known Thucydidean theme. Let us return to a passage first mentioned in the Introduction, which deals with the power of Pericles within Athens:

δυνατὸς ὢν τῷ τε ἀξιώματι καὶ τῇ γνώμῃ χρημάτων τε διαφανῶς
ἀδωρότατος γενόμενος κατεῖχε τὸ πλῆθυς ἐλευθέρως, καὶ οὐκ
ἤγετο μᾶλλον ὑπ' αὐτοῦ ἢ αὐτὸς ἦγε, διὰ τὸ μὴ κτώμενος ἐξ οὐ
προσηκόντων τὴν δύναμιν πρὸς ἡδονήν τι λέγειν, ἀλλ' ἔχων ἐπ'
ἀξιώσει καὶ πρὸς ὀργήν τι ἀντειπεῖν.
being capable through his reputation and his judgment, and
being manifestly most incorruptible by money, he restrained the

multitude freely, and was not led by them but himself led, on
account of not speaking to please to acquire power from what
was not proper, but because, having power through his character,
he even spoke against them angrily. (ii.65.8)

Consider just how heavily the normative element—the side of "justice"—is stressed here: in a single sentence we hear *four times* about how normative excellence supported Pericles' power. (1) Rank or reputation (ἀξίωμα) is clearly important, as is (2) being clearly beyond the influence of money, and we are then told twice more (negatively, then positively) of his peculiar worthiness: (3) he was not aiming at power through what was not proper or seemly (ἐξ οὐ προσηκόντων) and (4) he had power through his reputation or character (ἀξίωσις, cf. ἀξίωμα, just mentioned). Thucydides is not being subtle here: being powerful (δυνατὸς ὤν) is to be connected to justice.

The full significance of Thucydides' remarks here becomes clear in light of what happens after Pericles: the rise of accusations within the assembly in the Mytilenian debate, and in time the plots against Alcibiades, which play such a crucial role in the disaster at Sicily. There is a double conclusion to be drawn from this: first, that Pericles' successors were unable to occupy a position of leadership as Pericles did because they lacked his conspicuous normative excellence—let us call this his "justice." Second, that the departure of this justice from Athens had disastrous consequences for Athens herself—that is, it greatly harmed the power of Athens. Not just for an individual trying to make himself effective within a city, then, but also for a city itself, justice can be a crucial ingredient of power. If justice and power are often presented in Thucydides in a manner that suggests their incompatibility and conflict, still there are circumstances in which they are not in tension with one another at all.

All of this confirms Pericles' claim that a major cause of Athenian power was the justice of her internal life (ii.36.4–41.1).[5] It also provides another instance of a pattern noted in the Introduction, namely, that the demand, when confronted with certain oppositions, is often to find a way to hold both sides together. The opposition in this case is justice and power, the one attaining its ends through trust and goodwill, the other through force. Having begun, in Periclean Athens, with both sides, Athens ended up with a one-sided focus on the importance of forceful compulsion alone, and the result of that narrower perspective was to undermine Athenian power: the departure of justice from Athens delivers a devastating blow to Athens at Sicily (not to mention Decelea). Obviously, a one-sided focus on justice is no better, as the fate of the Melians after the Melian Dialogue shows us. The Periclean position, which did not always resolve the logical tension between the two principles but was able to attain a balance in which each was emphasized in an appropriate sphere, provides an example of a way to hold both sides together.

There is, then, a sort of power of justice in Thucydides' understanding: trust and goodwill can be effective—and sometimes the most appropriate—means to an end. We have here an utterly unsentimental basis for an interest in justice: it can be a source of power, one that must be confronted by anyone who would make a sober assessment of the realities of this world.[6]

What we do not have is a basis for a claim that one should always strive for justice in foreign relations. We have seen a correlation between increasing brutality practiced against cities beyond Athens with a decrease in the justice of relations between citizens within Athens, and it might seem that this correlation proves that injustice practiced against foreign powers must destroy justice within the city, thus harming the city's power as well. The result would then be a need always to be entirely just in foreign relations. Certainly, it is reasonable to understand the correlation here to have some causal force. The development, however, has been set out by Thucydides in a manner that suggests that the problem did not have its root in Periclean Athens. Pericles does not claim absolute justice for Athenian foreign policy—the empire is like a tyranny and it may have been wrong to acquire it (ii.63.2)—but it is only after Pericles that we begin to see *ad hominem* accusations in the assembly, and these appear together with the brutal new measures proposed against Mytilene; the accusations become a serious problem that decisively affects policy only after the new brutality is actually practiced on Melos. If Athens' later savage behavior toward other cities played a causal role in the decline of trust and goodwill within her own assembly, still it seems that the behavior of Periclean Athens could exist together with a state of affairs in the assembly in which accusations and plots did not rise to a level that affected policy. That is, Periclean Athens practiced at worst a moderate injustice abroad, which did not disrupt the justice within the city. Justice is a concern in foreign relations—one should be careful about straying too far from it, and friendly relations can reduce the need for arms somewhat—but Pericles' relative focus on the necessities of power when looking beyond the city is appropriate.

CUSTOM, NATURE, AND LIBERATION

There is a further theme, related to justice and power, and we must note it here because it provides an important link to Plato. Callicles will show (482c4–483c7) how the arguments used against Gorgias and Polus can be understood in terms of convention and nature (νόμος and φύσις), and this opposition is already at work in Thucydides. Briefly put, the Athenians feel themselves able to master their own nature to some degree in Periclean

Athens, and have available a constraint upon this nature in the form of convention; by the end, these constraints have failed, liberating human (and Athenian) nature from its bonds, so that Athens feels subject to a form of compulsion.

Everything we have seen of Pericles falls on the side of convention as opposed to nature. Of course, he does use the word for convention, for example when he speaks of how fear of the laws (νόμοι—ii.37.3), written and unwritten, keeps Athenians from acting in a criminal manner (παρανομέω). More importantly, the balance of opposites, the unity of virtues, the ability to lean both toward passivity and activity as required, the reliance on justice as well as power—none of this is a direct expression of basic human drives as they will subsequently come to light, but rather it all involves thought at every moment, and requires also that these basic drives be constrained in numerous regards. That is, it all falls on the side of convention rather than nature. In similar fashion, the Athenians at Sparta in book i claim to have acted more moderately than they might have done: that is, they see themselves as *not* having merely followed the dictates of human nature (see *Athens' Development*, pages 86–7 below).

In the speech of Diodotus, we noted how he sets out a series of drives within human nature (iii.45) that seem almost irresistible; certainly, he believes that these drives can overwhelm convention (i.e., νόμος—45.7). In Alcibiadean Athens, the notion of natural drives has been internalized, for when the Athenians at Melos sweep aside Melian hopes of divine aid they point instead to a necessity of nature (φύσεως ἀναγκαία—v.105.2), according to which both gods and men rule wherever they can. The Athenians not only understand themselves to be acting strictly on the basis of nature but are driven by it, feeling compelled by two natural drives—the hatred and fear inherent in the empire—to sail on Melos. The Sicilian debate provides a complementary picture, for Nicias feels unable to restrain the Athenian character (vi.9.3), while Alcibiades not only suggests that the Athenians must simply act in accordance with their active character (18.7), which in this case means undertaking the Sicilian expedition, but also suggests that the choice now is between imperial expansion or an acceptance of subjugation (18.3).[7]

In both Diodotus and the Athenians at Melos, the appeal to nature has the same force as it will have for Callicles in the *Gorgias*: it is something real, and thus something that brings with it a credibility, and an argumentative force, that nothing else seems to equal. Thucydides himself sees considerable explanatory power in human nature (φύσις ἀνθρώπων—iii.82.2), for he sees it at the heart of the horrors of civil war as this swept across the Hellenic world—indeed, he puts particular emphasis on one drive of human nature that Diodotus had mentioned, greed (πλεονεξία—iii.82.8; cf. iii.45.4). However, it is not Thucydides' view that human nature always overwhelms everything, for in his treatment of Pericles he paints another picture entirely: we saw how the great statesman was not driven toward the immediate (the effect of war on most people—iii.82.2), but sought to affect his fellow citizens in the opposite manner (ii.65.1), even in the face of the most unpredictable and overwhelming crisis.[8] The subsequent increase in the influence that basic natural drives have on the course of events does not come about as a matter of necessity but occurs once there is no longer a statesman of Pericles' caliber available: the drives of human nature become liberated from the bonds of conventional understanding, and appear to be ever more irresistible.

In all this we can make out a Thucydidean view concerning the peculiar sort of liberation at work here. It is by actively accepting limits that one escapes the tyranny of the basic drives, limits of the sort inherently present in the balance of opposites we saw with Pericles and in the holism essential to adequate statesmanship, limits exemplified by his advice to avoid expanding the empire. One example of this freedom through the acceptance of limits comes in what might otherwise seem a strange remark, for Thucydides says that Pericles "being capable through his reputation . . . and being manifestly most incorruptible by money restrained the multitude freely" (κατεῖχε τὸ πλῆθος ἐλευθέρως—ii.65.8). In context, the point here is that Pericles enjoys a freedom of action in a way that none of those who came after him did, because he had made himself subject to certain normative (i.e., conventional) limits, as his successors did not. They were therefore constrained as he was not in their relationship with the mass of the people.

In similar fashion, it is correct to say that "the Athenians [at Melos] do what they can because there is no limiting constraint."[9] Of course, to say this is to indicate a failing on their part: they should have an *internal* limiting constraint, like Pericles. It is their lack of such a constraint that gives room to the unbounded compulsions that drive toward Sicily. It is of decisive importance that the Athenians at Melos make "no attempt to do what Thucydides saw as Pericles' great achievement, to control the natural impulses of the Athenian people and empire."[10]

It might appear that the convention-bound understanding typified by Pericles is confining, and that a release from it might be a form of genuine liberation. After all, Alcibiades has possibilities open to him that Pericles did not—jumping from Athens to Sparta to Persia, for example—precisely because Alcibiades is not limited by the earlier conventional understanding. But Thucydides' presentation brings home to the reader not only how deceptive this appearance is, but also how devastating the consequences can be once one has begun to liberate basic natural drives.

THREE STAGES: BEGINNING, END, AND MIDPOINT

The beginning and end of the development within Athens are marked by Thucydides' two first-person commentaries on the two most important Athenian political figures in relation to the fate of the city (i.e., ii.65 and vi.15).[11] The first signifies that we are at the start of the move from a balance with latent tensions to a situation with definite and explicit conflicts; the second, the intellectual completion of the development. From this second standpoint, the question is not what the next stage of the development might be, but rather in what particular form the consequences of the new state of affairs will be worked out. Periclean and Alcibiadean Athens are clear beginning and endpoints, characterized by their opposition to one another; the Mytilenian debate consistently occupies a transitional position. So, for example, for Periclean Athens, political activity centers on the city, while in Alcibiadean Athens, political activity centers on the individual in his opposition to the city.[12] In the Mytilenian debate, we find both speakers united in their concern that the good of the city is falling from view, an intermediate position between the other two. Or to take another example, Pericles warns against trying to expand the empire while at war with Sparta; Cleon demands, as a price for peace, the return of certain states that were once part of the empire; while in relation to Melos and Sicily, Athens actually feels subject to a compulsion to expand the empire with fresh conquests.

Thucydides' choice of the Mytilenian debate, which was so narrowly decided, makes it particularly effective as an intermediate point between two extremes, because he has been able to use Cleon to represent the appearance of a series of related themes at a time when they do not yet determine affairs. These first appear in the Mytilenian debate but do not yet (quite) determine policy as they will in the final stage. We have now seen that this is true of the explicitly negative view of the other cities in the empire, with the increasing consciousness of hatred and danger, of the fear and the brutal policy that follow from this, of the increasing role of emotions, whether anger, fear or a sick love of what is far away, of a limited temporal focus, usually characterized in terms of the immediate (τὰ παρόντα), of vicious circles, and of the role of personal attacks within the assembly. Every one of these elements is either absent or held in check by other considerations with Pericles, and every one of them is present in the end in a manner that decisively determines events. In similar fashion, with Cleon we see the arrival of *mere* rhetoric, of the sort that works by creating an appearance without any substantial content, for example, when Cleon claims to be "the same man," a merely rhetorical echo of Pericles' earlier substantial claim. We saw a much more intensified focus on rhetoric and appearance in Alcibiades—recall in particular his rhetorical echo of the Periclean unity—but again, Cleon does not quite carry the day, while Alcibiades does. The Mytilenian debate is the logical midpoint.

Accordingly, we have a highly schematized presentation of the development within Athens, a beginning point, an endpoint, and a midpoint that is essentially transitional. We shall see exactly the same thing in the first book of the *Republic*.

ATHENS' DEVELOPMENT: AN OLD OBJECTION

We are now in a position to answer an objection made some decades ago to the idea that there is a development in Athens over the course of the war. Specifically, it was noted that "the proclamation of the natural right of the stronger is present already in the first Athenian speech of the work (i.76.2), and it is ambassadors of Pericles who deliver it."[13] That is, the Athenians at Melos are notorious for the dictum that justice is in question only between equals, while the strong impose what they can and the weak submit to it (v.89; see also 105.2); the same idea is already found in the speech of the Athenian ambassadors at Sparta in book one. Athens would seem, on this basis, not to change at all. Indeed, the account given in this essay might seem to strengthen this reflection, since Periclean Athens pursues justice at home, and demands it of the relationship with the Spartans—that is, among equals—while leaning toward the principle of power against the subject cities, who are weaker.

Of course, by now we have already seen a great deal of evidence for a decline within Athens that has nothing to do with the right of the stronger. Nevertheless, quite apart from this it would be too simple to conclude that Athens undergoes no development because of an identical statement of principle in two speeches. "The proclamation of the natural right of the stronger" is but one aspect of Athens at each moment, just as the ability to express things (ἑρμηνεῦσαι ταῦτα—ii.60.5) is also only one aspect of a unity of virtues, an aspect whose nature is to some extent determined by its relation to the whole. We have seen that just as a hand separated from the body is a hand in name only, so too can the ability to express things in a convincing manner become something different—a great evil, rather than a virtue—if it is separated from the other virtues necessary to statesmanship. In similar fashion, though there is a point of similarity between the speech of the Athenians at Sparta (i.73–8) and the words of the Athenian at Melos (v.85–111), this is not of itself sufficient to establish that the two speeches represent positions that are simply the same—might the statement have a different significance in each speech because of its relation to other things said in that speech?

There are differences between the two speeches, for example, the absence of an unbounded argument leading into a vicious circle in the speech of the Athenians in book i. We saw how the circle of fear in the Melian Dialogue took up the circle of viciousness from Cleon, but there is no parallel to be found in the speech of the Athenians at Sparta, nor is there in Pericles. More importantly, there is a difference between the Athenians in the Melian Dialogue and those at Sparta where the "natural right of the stronger" is concerned. At Sparta, they make appeals to a form of justice that does not only exist between equals in strength: they speak of dealing with the allies by means of "customs that have equal force" (ἐν τοῖς ὁμοίοις νόμοις—i.77.1); they say that their allies are accustomed to deal with the Athenians "on an equal footing" (ἀπὸ τοῦ ἴσου— 77.3); they claim that treatment from the Persians was worse (77.5). All of these statements claim that the Athenians have been dealing with the allies on a more equal footing than they had to.[14] To the extent that they believe that "the weaker is held down by the stronger" (76.2), there is no reason for such claims. Accordingly, when the Athenians claim to have recognized a sort of equality with their allies, they are speaking on the basis of some other principle.[15]

In the context of the Melian Dialogue, this other principle, this claim of a relationship of equality with allies, could have been very useful indeed to the Athenians when talking to prospective subjects, and yet they do not appeal to it. At Melos, the Athenians have become utterly consistent in their focus on the right of the stronger.[16] The necessity according to which the weak are ruled by the strong is certainly *part* of the picture of what moves the Athenians at Sparta, but not more than a part. At Melos, this necessity forms the essence of a new position, in which what was previously only a part is now taken for the whole. The purpose of the similarity of expression between the two speeches is the same as that of the verbal parallels we have already seen between Pericles and his successors: they express a superficial similarity which points to a substantive difference.[17]

An explicit consciousness of the way in which the stronger do so often dominate the weaker can constitute a sober recognition of the realities of power, a recognition that can lead to a more adequate thinking about the world, on the condition that such a view is limited and balanced by a grasp of other realities. One other relevant reality is this: if trust and goodwill were excluded from human relations, neither Athens among other states nor Pericles within Athens could be as powerful as they are when the war begins. Athens does not suffer a decline in respect of justice because the "right of the stronger" appears as something entirely new in the Melian Dialogue. Rather, she suffers a decline in the adequacy of her thinking, so that the consciousness of the "right of the stronger" plays an ever greater role, coming in time to affect even the relations of citizens to one another: again, what was once merely a part begins to be taken for the whole.

STATESMANSHIP IN THUCYDIDES AND THE NATURE OF THE PERICLEAN ACHIEVEMENT

It is correct to speak of "the greatness, but also the precariousness"[18] of Pericles' achievement, and further, to note that "the seeds of the Athenian defeat were already latent in the political system and the characteristics praised in the Funeral Speech: a competitive ethic which sought civic strength through the private efforts of individuals, an active posture in the search for wealth and empire, and an almost alarming spirit of daring and indefatigability."[19]

To go a step further, however, and find that Pericles was a poor leader because he failed to set up a structure that was not precarious, would be quite wrong.[20] In Thucydides, it is the *world* that is precarious. Logically, justice and power are very often irreconcilable—and the sort of one-sided thinking that attends only to one or the other tends to result in disaster. Thucydides does not simply leave us with Pericles' claim that a unity of four virtues is necessary to good statesmanship. Rather, he shows us how the breakup of this unity causes disaster—and yet any such unity of virtues will be of its nature precarious, for it will be a rare figure indeed who has them all.

Consider the account of how Athens acquired her walls (i.89–93), which is introduced as an account of how Athenian power grew. Themistocles frames Athens' desire for walls in terms of equality—an equal armament is necessary to fair and equal deliberation (ὅμοιος and ἴσος—i.91.7). However, once Athens has walls, she is on the path toward empire, and all its inherent dangers, including the hatred of the subjects and their tendency to rebel. Very soon, we read of Athens "enslaving" an allied city (δουλόω—i.98.4). Might another kind of safety have been possible for Athens without the empire?[21] If so, it would not simply be better; at best, it would just have a different series of inherent dangers and problems. Great power creates fear and therefore enemies (see i.23.6); lack of power is itself a danger. There is no easy ground here which is simply safe or simply right; the best one can do is to create a moment of stability in a world that is inherently unstable.

The art of statesmanship in Thucydides, then, comes in the end to this: an attempt to create a pragmatic balance of principles that do not sit easily or naturally with one another. Perhaps a unity or balance different from the one we find in Pericles is possible, but its basic, precarious structure would have to be the same.

The problem with Periclean Athens is that it was externally related to the source of its stability. That is, the qualities which kept Athens at her apex did not simply arise out of the life or character of the mass of the citizens but also required the person of Pericles himself to keep things balanced, as we saw. The problem was not with *what* was present but rather with the *way* in which it was present in the city. If the citizenry generally had attained Pericles' unity of virtues, the city could not have been fatally undermined by his death.

NOTES

1. Accordingly, I would like to add something to the insightful remarks of Connor, *Thucydides*, 246: "the anatomy of power in the first book . . . is not rejected but transformed. Naval power and financial strength continue to be important throughout the work but they result not in progress and security but in expansion and vulnerability. Walls come to symbolize not security but siege and defeat. Boldness and innovation are crucial constituents of Athens' growth but also of her overextension and defeat." In every case here, the difference between the positive and negative side to which Connor points is explained by the decline in judgment within Athens. There is every reason to reject the idea that if subsequent politicians had possessed the deep counsel of Pericles, naval power and financial strength, for example, would still have resulted in expansion and vulnerability.

2. Stahl, *Man's Place in History*, 189–219, gives an account of books vi–vii in which chance is the dominant factor. I have answered this in Thorne, "Prediction, Probability" (see page 12, note 11 above). Readers who want a fuller account of my understanding of the way in which both human judgment and chance have a place, and how they relate to one another in Thucydides, should look there.

3. The remarks of Parry, *Logos and Ergon*, 87–89, on λόγος and ἔργον (i.e., word and deed) are particularly valuable in relation to this passage: one needs in a sense to hold λόγος and ἔργον together, so that λόγος is informed by ἔργον, and ἔργα can thus be informed by λόγος. At vii.77 the situation is the radical separation of these two principles: confronted by pure ἔργον, the λόγοι of Nicias amount to little more than fairy tales, an echo of the Melians at the end of book v.

4. Note how δημοσίᾳ . . . ἰδίᾳ ("in public . . . in private") at vi.15.4 takes up δημοσίᾳ μὲν . . . ἰδίᾳ δὲ at ii.65.2, except in the latter case, Pericles stood entirely on the side of the public focus (δημοσίᾳ); with Alcibiades, public competence is conceded, but his own focus was far too much on the side of the private (ἰδίᾳ).

5. Thucydides' remarks on civil conflict (iii.82–83) point in a similar direction.

6. There is a parallel consideration in the opposite direction: natural necessities can affect our understanding of what people ought to do. For example, this is clearly the force of Diodotus' focus on internal human drives at iii.45: to the extent that the Mytilenians have acted on the basis of such compulsions, they cannot be blamed. Nichols, *Pursuit of Freedom*, 16, notes that to the extent we can blame Pericles for the war, the war cannot have been necessary.

7. Nichols, *Pursuit of Freedom*, 109, sees in Alcibiades "a rejection of all limits, which Thucydides captures in the *paranomia* he ascribes to him" (6.15.4).

8. Note that when Thucydides says (iv.108.4) that people are accustomed (εἰωθότες) to entrust to thoughtless hope what they desire, and to push away with sovereign calculation what they do not approve, his manner of expression leaves room for exceptions, such as Pericles.

9. Bosworth, "The Humanitarian Aspect," 40.

10. Macleod, "Form and Meaning," 395. See also Deininger, *Der Melier-Dialog*, 78. Plenio, *Die letzte Rede*, 60, expresses the problem in a manner that connects it to the first of the Periclean virtues: "the Athenians at Melos no longer aim at what is needed [τὰ δέοντα], but at what is possible [τὰ δυνάτα], a policy that then led straightaway to catastrophe."

11. Gribble, *Alcibiades and Athens*, 184, suggests that vi.15 and ii.65 share themes and a scheme of causation: "the decay of political life and the privileging of private interests over the public good, on the part of both leaders and the Athenians."

12. Rengakos, *Form und Wandel*, 121, suggests the possibility of a fourth stage. I am not inclined to think we would find one if the work had been completed, because of the logic internal to the thing itself. Alcibiadean Athens is in most respects the logical conclusion of the movement that began with Pericles' death—there is nowhere left to go. Instead, what we should expect to see is the working out of the consequences of Athens' new condition. This, to my mind, is what we start to see in book viii (and already in book vii). I do not treat book viii here; others have already suggested how it can be seen as a continuation of the movement of the preceding books (e.g., Pouncey, *The Necessities of War*; I have found the treatment in Greenwood, *Thucydides and the Shaping of History*, 83–98, particularly helpful). At some point, no doubt, there would be a new beginning of some kind, though I don't see this in the text as we have it.

13. Hermann Strasburger, "Thucydides and the Political Self-Portrait of the Athenians," in *Oxford Readings in Classical Studies—Thucydides*, ed. and trans. Jeffrey Rusten (Oxford: Oxford University Press, 2009), 217; the paper was originally published in 1958. Flashar, *Epitaphios*, 44–46, similarly argues against the distinction "between an ideal situation under Pericles and a later degeneration," on the basis of the claim that the ideology of power (*Machtideologie*) remains the same. Stahl, *Man's Place in History*, 48–49, makes a similar argument.

14. There are also normative appeals to the Spartans. For example: "we were not angered that you did not come to help us beforehand. Thus we say that we ourselves benefitted you no less that we profited from this" (74.2-3). Why should the Athenians speak of their own *lack of anger* at receiving no help? The possibility of Athenian anger implies that the Spartans *should* have come to their aid but did not—that is, this is an appeal to justice. When they continue to talk of how both sides profited, this points to an unequal balance sheet: another appeal to justice.

15. This confirms the line taken by Macleod, "Form and Meaning," 393–94: "all along they are warning the Spartans . . . but equally it is clear that the whole line of argument is also a self-defense . . . εἰκότως [i.73.1] is . . . designed to imply, but mask, a justification or appeal to morality." See Hans-Peter Stahl, "War in Thucydides: Veneer Remover—Veneer Fabricator," in *Thucydides—A Violent Teacher?*, eds. G. Rechenauer and V. Pothou (Goettingen: V&R unipress, 2011), 35–36, for a different view on the word εἰκότως. Stahl sees the Athenian appeals to justice at Sparta in book i as a veneer, but even so, we have a difference from the Athenians at Melos, for whom the same veneer would have been most expedient.

16. In similar fashion, the Athenians at Sparta speak of three compulsions that led them on to empire: δέος, τιμή and ὠφελία (i.e., fear, honor, and profit). We have seen

how great a role fear plays for Athens at Melos, and we hear of ὠφελία at v.91.2. What has happened to honor? It is the only one of the triplet that involves the recognition of other people, making its absence from the worldview of the Athenians at Melos particularly significant.

17. See also the remarks of Connor, *Thucydides*, 246–47, on the different effect that the doctrine of the right of the stronger has in different contexts.

18. Macleod, *Collected Essays*, 87.

19. Gribble, *Alcibiades and Athens*, 175.

20. Is Thucydides critical of Pericles because the statesman failed to adjust the constitution of Athens or to improve the citizens so as to ensure the long-term stability and prosperity of the city? This is the sort of criticism we find in the *Gorgias* (515d–516d), but it does not have a basis in the text of Thucydides. On the contrary, when he does consider Pericles in light of what happened later (ii.65), he is careful to lay the blame on the post-Periclean politicians only.

21. One thinks at this point of the Delian League, whose various members were able to augment their strength and freedom through some degree of mutual trust. When Athens became first among equals, she removed the danger inherent in this trust but simultaneously took on new dangers by losing the same trust.

Plato
A Holistic Approach to the Gorgias *and* Republic *I*

We have already seen that the idea of a structure that can be understood only as a whole is crucial to an understanding of Thucydides, and this idea is no less important to my approach to the dialogues of Plato. One must first attain an understanding of the whole by working through each of its component parts, and then rethink each of the parts in terms of the whole, perhaps repeating this process many times until difficulties have been worked out.

If the approach to the text that I set out here cannot really be called new—in fact, it seems to be in line with interpretive ideas that are gaining in popularity—still I think it important to explain the reasoning behind it. This reasoning is what ultimately justifies my interpretations of the *Gorgias* and the first book of the *Republic*, which are a departure from most previous scholarship.[1] I find that the philosophical content of these dialogues is inseparable from their literary structure. In both cases, there is a three-step development as we move through a succession of three characters, in a conversation that begins with relatively superficial matters, and with a willingness to make assumptions, but gradually investigates what was previously just assumed, treating in the end profound questions of fundamental importance—and the conversation also loses its initial pleasant nature as it proceeds. A careful study of the detail of these dialogues—the logic of the arguments as much as the literary aspects—is necessary to a full appreciation of this structure, and in turn, this structure is necessary to an understanding of particular details.

The most important new ideas are as follows. In the three-step structure we have an intellectual history, an idealized account of the development of an idea, and Plato is using this to put his own philosophy into context, to make clear exactly what problem he is trying to solve. It can sometimes be the case that finding answers is less difficult than finding the right questions to ask. The *Gorgias* to 499c and the first book of the *Republic* focus on getting the questions clear, and in doing so, bring us to a standpoint from which we can already begin to see something of the form that the answers to these questions must take. The way in which they do this is not what one might at first expect: Callicles and Thrasymachus, though they receive the least sympathetic portrayals of all characters in the Platonic corpus, are nevertheless to be understood as being *good* in crucial respects. Both characters, to the extent they have freed themselves from the shackles of conventional thought, have thought more deeply than their predecessors, and are therefore able to produce a series of novel challenges. As Socrates answers these challenges, we see Plato's own thought coming to light, leading us into the *Republic*. In both dialogues, Socrates himself undergoes a change, from the fellow familiar in the early dialogues, who wishes to "learn" (πυνθάνομαι in both works—447c1 and 328e5) and confines himself to asking questions, to someone very nearly like the figure we see beginning in book ii of the *Republic*, who actively puts forth doctrines of his own. As we shall see, these Socratic changes point toward the relationship between Plato's thought and the problems that come to light in these two dialogues.

The three-step movement is also essential to an understanding of the individual arguments by which Socrates refutes his opponents, as these arguments are themselves essential to the overall movement. In the *Gorgias* to 499c, and in key moments of the first book of the *Republic*, Socrates' key refutations are *ad hominem*—that is, they refute particular characters who are Plato's own creation. We shall see how this kind of argument forms the logical backbone of each dialogue, and we shall also come to understand how, and in what sense, both dialogues ultimately constitute an attempt on Plato's part to form a conviction in the mind of the reader. If Socrates' arguments here do not provide proofs of the sort that might compel any skeptical reader to adopt his conclusions for the reasons he has given, what we do have, in the end, are a number of highly plausible ideas of fundamental importance to the question of how we ought to live. We have also been given a motivation to accept an account of just the sort that Plato is beginning to develop, for it provides an answer to the problem that comes to light over the course of the three-step development in each dialogue, a problem involving a new subjective spirit and its peculiar conception of liberation. The reading of Thucydides given in the preceding pages should suffice to show that this was a matter of critical importance to the time in which Plato was writing.

These, then, are some of the key ideas. It remains to say a few words on the method by which I have arrived at these views. Plato did not write abstract arguments for the consideration of philosophers in one work, and then write another, entirely different work, in which he brought characters to life for the edification of students of literature. On the contrary, in the *Gorgias* and the *Republic*, we find the dramatic and argumentative aspects interwoven with one another, in the context of a dialogue that has quite clearly been conceived as a whole, given the structure running from the beginning to the end. It is an obvious step, then, to seek to understand these aspects relative to one another, grasping as a whole what Plato has presented as a whole.

I see my approach as moved by an attempt to eliminate unnecessary assumptions as far as possible, something particularly important in the case of Plato, who stands near the dawn of prose writing, at a time when conventions for expressing philosophical thought, conventions that now seem self-evident, did not yet exist. The two main prose writers before Plato whose work survives in more than fragments are Herodotus and Thucydides, both of whom are remarkable for expressing their own thought in a manner radically different from anything in use today. The chapters on Thucydides in this book provides an example, as it relies constantly on words and phrases that echo one another in different parts of the text: that these echoes carry implicit meaning has long been accepted by scholars. This manner of expression can be found in other literature of ancient Greece going back to Homer.[2] We shall see the same technique at work in Plato, for example, with the word "good" (ἀγαθός) in the first book of the *Republic*, or with the theme of ruling (ἄρχειν) in both works. Thucydides is also remarkable for his practice of making a point by means of the exceptionally sophisticated use of bad arguments in the mouths of his characters[3]—just the sort of thing we shall find in Plato.

It may be that Plato's work fails to conform to our expectations concerning the manner in which a philosophical work can be expected to express itself. As we can know Plato's intention in each work only through what he wrote, it would be best if we could base every claim we make in the text, and this includes the matter of how exactly Plato speaks to the reader.

It is necessary to assume at the start that Plato wrote what he wrote for a reason. Without this assumption, interpretation cannot begin; if we are to make any further assumption, we had better do so only under the yoke of necessity. If we assume at the start that any character gives us Plato's reasons for Plato's doctrines, we impose an assumption, perhaps anachronistically, about the way in which such an ancient work can be expected to express itself. Certainly, the text will say something on this basis, but by proceeding in this manner, we import the risk that we have imposed a barrier between ourselves and Plato, and because it has been imposed at the start, we might never recognize the way it distorts our view. The presence of a literary aspect contains the possibility of some literary mode of expression, involving symbols, metaphors, and other implicit means of communication. Every claim must be based in the text, and every piece or aspect of the text has the potential to contain a claim.[4]

This is why I have written in the manner that I have: my goal with Plato is to *explain the text*. If we can find a perspective from which it would make perfect sense to write exactly what he has written—including the plain fact that these two dialogues are each well-ordered wholes—then we have the best basis possible from which to claim that we have understood his thought. Certainly, we must analyze the arguments, but we should also aim to say something, for example, about Cephalus' citations of Sophocles, Themistocles, and Pindar, or the various complaints of crudeness (ἀγροικία) in the *Gorgias*, or the exchange in which Socrates replies with mathematical examples (337b) to Thrasymachus' refusal to allow that justice might be the beneficial, the profitable, the gainful, or the advantageous (336d). The inquiry should not stop, however, with a mere claim that these moments say something. We should try to push the matter farther, seeking an understanding from which it becomes evident how these moments are parts of a whole, and contribute to the overall intention of the *Republic* or the *Gorgias*. We should recall that passage in the *Gorgias* in which Socrates gives his account of what it is to be "good," an account, as we shall see, that is also Plato's.[5] Here Socrates contrasts something that is structured and ordered (503e7–504a2) with the notion of acting at random (εἰκῇ–503e1, 3): if one finds oneself claiming that any aspect of the dialogue falls into the latter category, one has a reason to look again at one's interpretation, for one is effectively saying that the dialogue is not "good" according to Plato's own understanding of the word.

The *Gorgias* is Plato's third-longest dialogue; an attempt to set out an interpretation of the whole thing would be a large book on its own, so I have written instead from four different perspectives focused largely on the section of the dialogue (i.e., to 499c) that is most relevant to this book's thesis. The first book of the *Republic*, at just over 25 Stephanus pages, is another matter. Here I have produced what is, in effect, a commentary on the text. At the end of my treatment of Plato I show how both dialogues lead us to the second book of the *Republic*, so as to confirm the line of interpretation I have given, and to provide an idea of the end toward which all this is moving.

NOTES

1. I speak of the first book of the *Republic* as a "dialogue" simply as a matter of convenience. I do not believe it to be a separate work, for reasons I summarize on pages 238–240.

2. Antonios Rengakos, "Fernbeziehungen Zwischen den Thukydideischen Reden," *Hermes* 124, no. 4 (1996): 396–417, gives examples of this Homer-Thucydides comparison.

3. See, for example, Macleod, "Reason and Necessity."

4. I should also like to make clear that this is not a Straussian account of Plato. I agree with the Straussians that we should try to make sense of every word in the text; from that moment, I find myself compelled to disagree with them.

5. See Raphael Woolf, "Callicles and Socrates: Psychic (Dis)Harmony in the *Gorgias*," in *Oxford Studies in Ancient Philosophy*, Vol. XVIII, ed. David Sedley (Oxford: Oxford University Press, 2000): 12, for an explanation of how we have at 503d–504a "a quite general theory of what it is for something to be good."

The *Gorgias*
Introduction

Scholars have long recognized that there is a single structure running through the whole of the *Gorgias*, a movement "from the superficial to the fundamental."[1] The three main characters with whom Socrates speaks "do not represent three distinct forces . . . but three successive developments of the same force: Polus is the spiritual heir of Gorgias, Callicles is the spiritual heir of Polus. Accordingly, each takes up the discussion where his predecessor broke down, carries it to a deeper level, and shows that it involves wider issues."[2] The most satisfactory interpretation of the dialogue would be able to show the essential relation of this structure to Plato's overall purpose—indeed, surely an adequate account ought to attempt this—and yet previous scholarship seems scarcely to have made the attempt.[3] Certainly, we often find that the underlying structure has been noticed, and is mentioned in passing, but on the question of why Plato would go to the trouble of expressing his thought in the context of such a structure, there remains ample room for further insight.

Let us begin with an overview of the basic idea at work in this structure, which we can find in the metaphor of doctor and the pastry-chef. Early in the dialogue, in the course of the argument with Gorgias, the elder rhetor makes a remarkable claim: "if a rhetor and a doctor went to any city you wish, and had to compete in speeches in the assembly, or in any other gathering, concerning who should be chosen as doctor, the doctor would be nowhere, but the fellow able to speak would be chosen, if he wanted" (456b6–c2). Later, in the argument with Polus, Socrates describes a slightly different contest: "if a doctor and a pastry-chef had to compete among children, or among men as foolish as children, concerning which one, doctor or pastry-chef, understood good and bad foods, the doctor would die of hunger" (464d5–e2). Finally, at the end of the dialogue, as Socrates defends his own way of life, the image comes up again:

I will be judged as a doctor would be among children, with a pastry-chef for his prosecutor. For consider how such a man would defend himself if taken among such people, if someone should accuse him, saying "children, this man works many evils on you: he ruins the youngest of you by cutting and burning; he makes you go wanting, slimming and choking you; he gives you the most bitter drinks, and forces you to hunger and thirst—not like me: I feasted you on many and various pleasant things." What do you suppose the doctor could say if caught in this terrible situation? If he should speak the truth—"I did all these things, children, in a healthy manner"—how great an outcry do you suppose such judges would make? Would it not be great? (521e3–522a7)

In these three quotations we have more than a mere three instances of a doctor unjustly losing a rhetorical contest. Rather, over the course of the dialogue the image undergoes a development, both as regards its own detail and as regards its significance. The picture is intensified so as to present us with an increasingly troubling reality. As we move from the first to the second instance, the judges become less competent, the doctor's competitor more obviously unqualified, and the penalty for losing harsher. The third instance treats the matter at greater length, making explicit what the first two instances had left unsaid: we now hear the case against the doctor, and see why he cannot effectively respond. Beyond the development of the image itself, its significance also becomes a more serious matter, for it begins as a hypothetical contest for a position but ends as a trial by jury, and one that alludes to a real trial and death: if we do not actually hear, in the final instance, that the doctor will be put to death, the fact that the result of the trial of Socrates hangs heavy over this part of the dialogue means that death does as well.

The development exhibited by this metaphor is characteristic of the structure at the heart of the dialogue: we begin with a hint, with something seemingly insignificant or merely implicit, and as the dialogue progresses, this initial moment exhibits growth, becoming more fully worked out, often also leading into a richer and weightier matter. In what follows, we shall see one example after another in which such a development comes to light.

Now, if all of this is true, there is an important question that most of the literature seems to have passed by: why would Plato organize a dialogue in this manner? What has he gained by doing so? Certainly, it would have been easier to write a work without such a complicated structure; the fact that Plato took the time to do so demands explanation. The intention in what follows is to show not only how this structure is relevant to the dialogue's content but also how the structure is itself part of that content.

THE STRUCTURE OF THE GORGIAS

Within the overall development mentioned above, the *Gorgias* falls into two major sections. Aristotle (*Nichomachean Ethics* i.4, 1095a32–33) tells us that Plato used to inquire whether a path led to or from the principles. This consideration points to the dialogue's main division. As we proceed from Gorgias, through Polus, to Callicles, we are on a path *to* the principles. From 499c, where it has been agreed that pleasure and the good are not the same, we are proceeding *from* the principles. The "three successive developments of the same force" (mentioned above) are above all characteristic of the first major piece of the dialogue, although the movement "from the superficial to the fundamental" continues into the second portion (and of course, in the second section Socrates is still arguing against Callicles, so that we are still concerned with the culmination of that "same force"). The chapters that follow will focus on the first section of the dialogue, venturing into the second as necessary to complete certain lines of thought.

As we move from Gorgias to Callicles, we find ourselves involved in questions of an ever more fundamental nature. We begin with relatively mundane matters—who is Gorgias, and what is the power of his art? (447c1–3, d1)— but as the dialogue proceeds to Polus, we soon find ourselves involved in the question of "who is happy and who is not" (472c9–d1). As Socrates brings our attention to this new question, he also declares that it is no small matter, but "almost" (σχεδόν—472c7) the noblest about which we might know and most shameful about which we might be ignorant (472c6–8). The qualifier "almost" is dropped in the next stage, against Callicles, when the subject has become what sort of person one ought to be and what one should do (487e9–488a1): here Socrates simply declares the investigation to be "noblest of all" (487e7–8). We move, then, from a relatively superficial matter to a deeply philosophical inquiry. As we begin the movement from the principle, there is a final step: we become explicitly conscious of the fact that we are talking about "how one should live" (500c3–4), as Socrates puts it (and note that just before this, at 500c2–3, he once again stresses the importance of this final question: a person having even a small amount of sense would take it seriously). Of course, the later questions are implicit in the former, something the dialogue suggests by showing a discussion of rhetoric leading naturally into the later, and deeper, matters.[4]

As we move from one character to the next, we also find ourselves in the presence of increasingly rigorous reflections on ethical matters. Gorgias asserts a series of ethical obligations—at 456c6–457c3 the word δεῖ occurs six times, in the sense "one ought"—but he does so in an unreflective fashion, as though such obligations can simply be taken for granted: in conspicuous contrast with what is to follow, there is no explicit discussion of any considerations that might move people to ignore an assertion that "one ought" to act in a given way. As Polus intervenes, a problem with this standpoint begins to come to light: what if these ethical obligations conflict with our interests? With Callicles, we encounter a position from which this problem has been resolved: "justice," as Callicles would understand it, is indubitably in our interest (assuming that we are "the stronger"). In addition, Callicles takes the matter further, for when he introduces his "natural" justice, he calls into question the credibility of *any* ethical obligation of the sort mentioned by Gorgias—that is, quite apart from the question of our interests, why should we believe at all an assertion that "one ought" to act in a given way?

This development is not confined to the question at issue or the rigor with which it is examined. We also see certain themes develop in a similar manner. For example, consider the theme of (tyrannical) ruling. When Gorgias talks about ruling others (452d7–8) and making them one's slaves (452e4–8), this hints at the admiration of the tyrant Archelaus that is to come with Polus (470d–471d), and that notion receives a richer development through Callicles (491e–492c). Of course, just as the later questions are implicit in the earlier ones, so too should we understand the appearance of Archelaus with Polus to give fuller and more conscious expression to something that was already implicitly present in Gorgias. The language of potentiality and actuality is appropriate to this move. Gorgias does not intend actually to advocate the life of the tyrant, but the notion of tyranny is present in potency with him; what we see later in the dialogue is the actualization of this aspect of Gorgias. Thus, it is correct to summarize the relation of the earlier moments to the latter as follows: "men like Gorgias put a deadly instrument into unscrupulous hands for the corruption of simple people. That is why the dialogue is called *Gorgias*, not *Callicles*: Gorgias' teaching is the seed of which the Calliclean way of life is the poisonous fruit."[5] And of course, the theme of ruling is not merely literary, for we shall see how Socrates, in his final schema of skills (517b–519a), takes up the notion of ruling and shows how it is crucial to a good life—a theme which is also of obvious importance to the *Republic*.

All these matters are connected as part of a single movement, a single reflection in which the question "why?" is brought continuously to bear, driving us to an ever-deeper consideration of the matter at hand. Accordingly, the first section of the dialogue brings out how the seemingly mundane matters of everyday life depend on assumed answers to profoundly philosophical questions. It is because of this relationship of dependence of the earlier matters on the later ones that we may be said to be on our way to the principles in this part of the dialogue.[6]

In the second section of the dialogue, from 499c, Socrates presents his own account, as an answer to the challenge set by Callicles. Here the order of inquiry is reversed: the most fundamental matter is treated first, and subsequent questions are treated in a logical order, each depending on what has preceded. More specifically, after some preliminary matters that follow from an agreement that pleasure and the good are distinct, Socrates gives his own account of the nature of the good (503d–505b). This gives him a basis from which he can give an account of the completely good person (506c–507c), which allows him to answer the question concerning the best way to live (505c–509a). When this has been accomplished, he can begin to move toward practical matters: the next question concerns a power capable of saving us either from doing or suffering injustice (509b–511b). After preparing the ground with a consideration of the value of self-preservation, the most fundamental basis of temporal power (511b–513c), Socrates can finally give his own account of politics (513d–517c), and this points to an answer concerning the nature of rhetoric. The remainder of the dialogue completes Socrates' argument, and deals with related challenges concerning his own way of life that have come up over the course of the argument of the first section.

Again in this second section, it is the relationship of dependence that tells us we are now moving *from* the principle. That is, it is only when we have achieved some clarity about what is meant by "good" that we can address the question concerning the good life; practical questions about how we might best attain a good life are in turn dependent on these earlier matters.

The dialogue's structure is tied to one of the major interpretive points to be developed in what follows: the development we observe as we move from Gorgias to Callicles is in certain respects a good thing. Above all, it brings the discussion to the level of principles—that is, to what is by nature prior to all else—and this is a requirement for genuinely philosophical thinking. In addition, we shall see that the culmination of the movement in Callicles produces a number of specific challenges, and that the account that Socrates begins to provide in the second piece of the dialogue (i.e., from 499c) is constructed in a manner that answers these—indeed, key pieces of the content of Socrates' own account are taken from Callicles. We shall also see how Socrates changes in response to each opponent, a development that suggests that without the challenges provided by the succession of three opponents we would not get the Socratic account.

FOUR PERSPECTIVES

The chapters that follow provide four perspectives on the unity of the *Gorgias*' structure and content. The first, responding to work by Charles Kahn, provides a summary treatment of the logic of the arguments that defeat each of the three main characters, and the related theme of shame. These arguments are not attempts on Plato's part to convince the reader to adopt the doctrine set forth by Socrates but are to be understood as the logical backbone of the three-step structure that runs through the first major piece of the dialogue (i.e., to 499c). Shame, which plays a crucial role in these arguments, is not an innate moral sense or a philosophical tool but a profoundly unphilosophical factor that stands in the way of our attempts to understand.

The second perspective is given in the course of three chapters that treat the detail of much of the dialogue to 499c in order to provide a portrayal of each of Socrates' three opponents as they come to light through the arguments. This lends support to the account of the arguments mentioned above and to the holistic view set out in the introduction to Plato (pages 93–6), but will also prove helpful for the comparison of this dialogue to Thucydides and the first book of the *Republic*.

The third perspective addresses a problem that arose in the course of the first: how (if at all) does Plato present his own thought to the reader in this dialogue? The answer, which builds on work by Raphael Woolf, is that Callicles poses certain implicit challenges for Socrates, challenges that cannot be answered by merely *ad hominem* arguments, and there are good reasons to see Plato himself in the answers that Socrates does in the end provide. This chapter also develops an important connection between the *Gorgias* and the *Republic*, for it shows us how Callicles, like Thrasymachus, is in certain respects *good*.

The final chapter on the *Gorgias* provides the fourth perspective, focusing on the changes we find in the portrayal of Socrates as this dialogue proceeds. We shall see that this helps not only to confirm the claim that Callicles is good in certain respects but also to lead us to an answer to the question of why Plato has gone to the trouble of producing a dialogue that includes such a three-step structure. Here, too, we have a point of connection with the first book of the *Republic*, for Socrates undergoes a very similar transformation in both dialogues, and its significance is the same in both cases.

Before going any further, we should address one most fundamental question: to what degree is Plato attempting to demonstrate the truth of certain doctrines in this dialogue? On one extreme, a great many interpreters have felt entitled simply to assume that Plato must be concerned with proving the truth of whatever thesis Socrates is arguing for at every moment. On the other, some have thought that Plato merely wishes to set forth some interesting ideas, with the intention only of provoking the reader to thought. In the case of the *Gorgias* (and the first book of the *Republic*), I think the truth is somewhere between these extremes. Plato does show himself conscious of different levels of discourse, which attain their object with different levels of certainty: in the *Republic*, in the image of the line (509d–511e), we see how one level of discourse proceeds by means of assumptions, and cannot free itself from these (510b–511a), while another is able to get to what is free from assumptions, and can subsequently base everything on this (511b). (The point here is not that the *Gorgias* fits neatly into a specific place on the line, but simply that we can find in Plato a recognition of the existence of different levels of understanding and argument.)

On the account I give in what follows, the *Gorgias* falls short of proving the truth of any doctrine, but this does not mean that it fails to provide us with reasons of any kind for the account developed by Socrates in the second major section (i.e., from 499c). His arguments in this dialogue are all ultimately dependent on unargued assumptions, both in the first section, where we have merely *ad hominem* refutations of three characters, and in the second, which not only proceeds on the basis of those earlier refutations but also contains crucial claims that cannot be said to have been proven (e.g., the nature of the good, as treated at 503d–505b). What we do get are two different kinds of reason that support Socrates' account. The first kind comes to light through the three-step movement culminating in Callicles: Socrates' position provides a way out of the specific inadequacies that we find in Callicles, and these specific inadequacies are not simply a creation of Plato's, but reflect the particular historical situation to which he was responding. The second kind of reason comes in the arguments that Socrates provides in the second section that make his doctrines seem inherently plausible—that is, not true of necessity, but consonant with a great deal of what we know about the world, and based in that reality.

NOTES

1. E. R. Dodds, *Plato: Gorgias—A Revised Text with Introduction and Commentary* (New York: Oxford University Press, [1959] 1990), 4.
2. Dodds, *Gorgias*, 5.
3. Devin Stauffer, *The Unity of Plato's Gorgias* (New York: Cambridge University Press, 2006) does aim to account for the unity of the dialogue, but provides an account very different from mine.
4. Jessica Moss, "The Doctor and the Pastry Chef: Pleasure and Persuasion in Plato's *Gorgias*," *Ancient Philosophy* 27 (2007): 229, fn. 2, takes the questions at 472c9–d1, 487e9–488a1 and 500c3–4 to be "equivalent formulations." This captures something important—we are meant to see how these questions are essentially connected to one another, and not simply distinct—but it fails to capture the development that occurs as we move from Polus to Callicles, a development to which Plato has drawn attention through Socrates' use, against Polus, of a qualifier (σχεδόν, "almost"—472c7) that is not found in the corresponding passage in the argument with Callicles.

5. Dodds, *Gorgias*, 15.

6. It is in this context that we should understand the Socratic comment, "you're fortunate, Callicles, because you have been initiated into the great mysteries before the small ones" (497c3–4). The whole first part of the dialogue deals with small mysteries on the basis of assumed answers to great ones.

Shame and the *Ad Hominem* Arguments

As we have just seen, the first half of the *Gorgias* consists of three stages, as Socrates confounds three increasingly intractable opponents. The arguments by which he does so, however, can easily seem unsatisfactory. Here we shall consider the logic of these arguments, including the related theme of shame, acquiring in the process an overview of the logical backbone of the first half of the dialogue.[1]

In a paper which has rightly exerted a lasting influence, Charles Kahn has shown that a number of the key arguments of the *Gorgias* turn on the shame that Socrates manages to induce in the three characters—Gorgias, Polus, and Callicles—who confront him.[2] These arguments are accordingly *ad hominem*—that is, they expose inconsistencies within the particular character in question. However, if we accept this interpretation, we must face the question of what Plato hopes to achieve by employing such arguments, for inconsistencies within characters who are, after all, Plato's own literary creations, might seem at first to be of little interest to the reader. Here there is room for fresh insight.

The arguments in question are those by which each of Socrates' three opponents is reduced to a passive state, whether this takes the form of removal from the argument or, in the case of Callicles, of a noticeably reluctant continued participation under compulsion (from 499c). Kahn has shown that in the case of the final argument with Gorgias (460a–461a), in a key argument used against Polus (474c–475e) and at a crucial turn in the argument with Callicles (491d–499b), Plato has pointed readers to the role played by shame in the argument. So, for example, we can see a way out of the argument for Gorgias, but he finds himself refuted by Socrates because he makes the fatal—and perhaps unreasonable—admission that someone who has learned just things will be just. There are subsequent suggestions

(461d, 482c–d, 487a–b, 494d2–3) that Gorgias was refuted because he was ashamed to press the argument farther than he did. Polus and Callicles similarly find themselves refuted when they might have continued to hold their own because they are subject to shame.[3]

In his own account of the logic of these arguments, Kahn has assumed that Socrates must speak directly for Plato, so that we would expect to find in Socrates' words the reasoning by which Plato would hope to convince us of a particular position, or at least the position for which Plato is advocating.[4] As a consequence, Kahn feels a need to answer the question of why Plato would try to establish "the central moral claims of the *Gorgias*"[5] by means of the *ad hominem* arguments that Socrates deploys against Polus and Callicles. In answer to this question, he produces an account according to which there is a "deposit of truth" in all of us that allows us to recognize "what is truly good,"[6] and it is the shame felt by each character that points toward a recognition of moral truths. On this view, then, shame in the *Gorgias* points to "a Platonic conception corresponding to our own notion of an innate moral sense . . . an obscure intuition of the good on the part of Socrates' interlocutors."[7] This account has proven persuasive, so that we find another scholar claiming that in the *Gorgias* "pleasure pulls us in the wrong direction, towards false value judgments, while shame pulls us in the right direction, towards the truth."[8] If this is so, it might explain "Plato's interest in [shame] as a tool of persuasion."[9] But shame in the *Gorgias* does not simply serve to orient us toward the truth—in fact, it can point us away from the true and the good as much as toward them. Although it might often exert a pull on unreflective people in the direction of better behavior, it is an impediment in any deeply searching inquiry.

There are two considerations that point decisively to this understanding of shame: first, the manner in which shame fits into the progression from Gorgias to Callicles, and second, Socrates' comments at 487a–e. To begin with the larger picture, each character in the *Gorgias* is willing to go farther than the last; the influence of shame diminishes as the argument moves forward. Gorgias feels compelled by shame to say he would teach virtue; Polus does not feel this compulsion but will at least grant that doing injustice is more shameful than suffering it; Callicles will not even admit this. And yet we saw in the introduction that as we proceed from one character to the next, the discussion itself focuses on ever more philosophical matters, and each character has reflected more rigorously on ethical matters than his predecessor. Implicit in the development from Gorgias to Callicles, then, is the idea that a genuinely philosophical discussion is present to the extent that shame is absent as an active force within it.[10]

Proceeding on the basis of this point alone we might conclude that Plato sees an opposition between shame and philosophy, but Plato has not been content to leave the matter implicit. Polus and Callicles both suggest that their predecessor failed to maintain himself in the argument because of shame (461b–c, 482c–e), and Socrates confirms their analysis (487b2–5, 494d2–3). It is Socrates' remarks at 487a–e that give us an unambiguous indication of how we are to understand the role of shame in the arguments. He believes that Callicles will be a touchstone (βάσανος—486d7, 487e3), by which he may test (βασανίζειν—487a4, e1) his own beliefs. Further, he spells out the reason for his belief. There are three qualities in question: knowledge, goodwill, and frankness (487a2–3), and these indicate, respectively, cleverness (487a4–5, 7), friendliness (487b1, e5) and a lack of shame (αἰσχύνη—487b3, e4). Now, Gorgias and Polus are not criticized in regard to the first two requirements, for we are told that they are clever and friendly (487a7–b1). However, "they are more deficient in frankness and are more shameful than they should be" (487b1–2). The effect is to put particular emphasis on the matter of shame and frankness: it is specifically because Callicles is "the sort of person who speaks freely and is not ashamed" (487d5) that he might be an adequate touchstone. Accordingly, if Callicles fails to be frank, if he gives in to shame, the reader has been prepared by Plato to understand this as a failure, one that carries the consequence that Callicles can no longer be considered a touchstone.

In fact, Callicles does fail in precisely this regard. At 494c, Socrates urges him not to give in to shame (494c4–5), reminds him of the failings of Gorgias and Polus in that regard (d2–3), and appeals to Callicles' bravery (d4)—but shortly thereafter, Callicles brings shame into the discussion (e7–8). The connection of this passage with 487a–e, where Plato set up a specific expectation, is obvious, and it makes interpretation a straightforward matter: Callicles fails to provide Socrates with a touchstone.[11] Plato's intention is to show the reader that Socrates' belief that an agreement with Callicles would have "the end consisting in truth" (487e7) was misplaced, and that the attainment of this end will somehow be compromised. How exactly this end is compromised I shall suggest below.

Now, let us return to the idea that shame in the *Gorgias* should be understood as a means of getting to the truth. The idea is presumably that the increasing willingness of each character to push past shame makes their eventual collective failure to maintain their stance all the more significant. That is, if Gorgias gives way in argument because of shame, and Polus, who pushes things further, does the same, then if Callicles, who goes furthest of all, can also be made to give way to shame, one might believe oneself entitled to claim that shame points to a kind of universal reality that can be brought to bear on all people without qualification. We may leave aside the possibility that a more vigorous and consistent hedonist would push things farther than Callicles does—note how Socrates mentions "someone more vigorous than you" (σοῦ τις νεανικώτερος—509a3)—for there is a more serious difficulty:

if shame is an innate moral sense, how can its absence be a requirement or a touchstone needed for an argument on moral matters, as Socrates clearly suggests at 487a–e? If Plato's intention is that the reader should view Callicles' succumbing to shame as a sort of philosophical success, one that brings out the truth, surely he ought to have made Socrates say, "if you too, Callicles, fail to be frank and become ashamed, as Gorgias and Polus did, then our conversation will have the end consisting in truth."[12]

Plato, then, has made the role of shame in the *Gorgias* quite clear: it is an *anti*-philosophical force, one that *prevents* an argument from getting to the heart of things. There are truths that are difficult or impossible to see insofar as we are under the influence of shame. Later we will see just how important the realities are that Callicles brings to light when he is at his most shameless: the desire to base his views on an objective order, the focus on ruling and on the appetites—these all contain something *good*, if not in the way they are present in Callicles (see pages 155–168).

Still, if shame has no place in a fully philosophical argument, it does seem reasonable to connect it with an adherence to conventional beliefs. We can see this if we look at the role shame plays as the movement from Gorgias to Callicles progresses. That is, Gorgias uncritically accepts everyday conceptions of justice, and he is most susceptible to shame. This is less true of Polus, whereas Callicles, who is least subject to shame, is able explicitly to contrast convention and nature (νόμος and φύσις—see 482e–483a), and presents an unconventional account of justice. That is, shame is an indicator, in this dialogue, of the degree to which each character is willing simply to accept conventional views as given; that a freedom from such uncritical acceptance is necessary to philosophy should be a straightforward matter. To test the soul (βασανίζω—486d4), one cannot be held back by common opinion; rather, one must be frank, saying what one really thinks, however much it conflicts with common opinion. That is why Socrates begs (δέομαι—492d3) Callicles not to slacken in any way once he is speaking frankly (492d1–5).

This view of shame as a force inappropriate for fully philosophical argument, one that serves as a measure of a character's unthinking acceptance of conventional views, finds some support in a parallel consideration concerning manners.[13] Polus, as he enters the argument, is offended by Socrates' very questioning, which has put Gorgias in a difficult position in front of so many people. For this, Polus accuses Socrates of crudeness, or ill-breeding (ἀγροικία—461c4),[14] and Socrates quickly admits that speaking the truth may be "rather crude" (ἀγροικότερον—462e). The point behind this is that regard for manners, or attending to the feelings of others—that is, regard for conventional behavioral guidelines—can be a hindrance to a philosophical argument.[15] We can see the same idea at work when Callicles, speaking frankly to Socrates about the dangers inherent in a life devoted to philosophy, admits that he is speaking "rather crudely" (ἀγροικότερον—486c2), or when Socrates himself, insisting on what he sees as the iron-clad, irresistible nature of the argument, confesses that it is "rather crude" (ἀγροικότερον—509a1) to speak in such a manner. A truly searching philosophical investigation can be uncomfortable, in that it can require that we focus strictly on the demands on the argument; this can conflict with the polite regard for others that characterizes well-mannered conversation.[16]

We shall see a similar point in the first book of the *Republic*, for there too we find a movement through three characters, in which the subject matter deepens as it proceeds from everyday matters to the question of the best life. There too, the characters who confront Socrates are increasingly more adequate to philosophy as we progress from one to the next and leave behind an unthinking reliance on convention. In fact, we shall see that Plato has made the point there in an even more striking manner, for he has been very careful in his use of the word ἀγαθός ("good")—a significant word in that dialogue—to show how each character has a more direct relation to what is good as we move forward from Cephalus to Thrasymachus.

In both dialogues, then, we find the same point: conventional belief— whether shame or the simple piety of Cephalus—has no place in philosophical argument. This is not to say, however, that it has no place in *philosophy*, for the sort of character who will be appropriately motivated for philosophy—and therefore suitable for engaging in a fully adequate philosophical argument—must have a certain sort of regard for the content of conventional belief if not for the lines of reasoning by which that content is usually defended. Turning again to the *Republic*, once Glaucon and Adeimantus have made their challenge to Socrates in book ii, they emphasize that they do not want to give up their belief in justice, even though they are very much aware that they are not in possession of adequate reasons for their faith (366d5–367e5). In response to this, Socrates actually suggests that they have a touch of the *divine* (θεῖος—368a4, 5) in them, an extraordinary compliment. Obviously, the point is not that mindless adherence to a belief is, as such, a virtue. Rather, it is what prevents Glaucon and Adeimantus from abandoning the inquiry into justice the moment the search runs cold, and pursuing instead a narrow conception of their own interests. That is, this "divine" characteristic is what keeps them from becoming Thrasymachus (or Callicles); instead, as a pre-philosophical non-rational force, it motivates their demand for a proper account of justice.[17] It is in this sense that one might call faith in convention an "intuition of the good"[18]—but note that it is not present in all people.

In similar fashion, surely shame is in one sense a positive characteristic within Gorgias himself, for while he may be inadequate for philosophical argument, at least *something* is keeping him back from the "natural" justice of Callicles. Again, the *content* of conventional belief will not be simply rejected by philosophy, and we can find support for this notion by means of another comparison to the *Republic*: it is nothing new to observe that a number of the doctrines of that work are already present in some form with Cephalus[19]; it is the *manner* in which they are present for convention that is fundamentally anti-philosophical.

Now, if we take this line concerning shame, we must confront anew the problem of the positive function played by the *ad hominem* arguments—that is, by arguments that are in an important way flawed—in the *Gorgias*. In the dialogue's structure, as described in the introduction, there is a basis for a new answer to this problem. *Ad hominem* arguments can be said in one sense to succeed, and in another to fail. Socrates' argument with Gorgias does decisively refute the elder rhetor, for it shows him to be attached to two mutually incompatible commitments. It is therefore necessary that he give way. However, because the argument used against him is merely *ad hominem*, Gorgias has been refuted in a manner that leaves room for a further defense of his position. Polus can therefore pick up the argument where it left off, so that we really do have "the same force"[20] running through this part of the dialogue. That is, the *ad hominem* arguments are crucial to the dialogue both insofar as they succeed and insofar as they fail. To say this, of course, is to say that Plato does not expect the reader to be moved by Socrates' arguments to Socrates' conclusions, at least not in the case of the arguments that remove Gorgias, Polus, and Callicles from fully active participation in the dialogue.

This brings us back to a question suggested above: if Plato means us to understand that Callicles fails as a touchstone, and that consequently Socrates' belief that the argument can attain "the end consisting in truth" (487e7) is somehow misplaced, how exactly should we understand that end to be compromised? The answer is that *ad hominem* arguments fail in an important sense: though they may tell us something about inconsistencies within a particular individual's beliefs, they can tell us nothing more.[21] To the extent that the truth is not dependent on the beliefs of three individuals, Socrates' refutations of those individuals do not attain the end consisting in truth, and Plato means his readers to see this.

Of course, if we take this line, we are left with a problem: how *does* Plato communicate his own thought in the *Gorgias*? That is a matter we shall take up when we consider how Callicles is good.

NOTES

1. My account of shame here amounts to a defense of R. B. Rutherford, *The Art of Plato: Ten Essays in Platonic Interpretation* (Cambridge, MA: Harvard University Press, 1995), 149, who sees shame as a "failure in frankness, a reluctance to reveal

one's true beliefs." R. B. Cain, "Shame and Ambiguity in Plato's *Gorgias*," *Philosophy and Rhetoric* 41, no. 3 (2008): 212–37, D. B. Futter, "Shame as a Tool for Persuasion in Plato's *Gorgias*," *Journal of the History of Philosophy* 47, no. 3 (July 2009): 451–61, and Tarnopolsky, *Prudes*, all give more recent treatments of shame in the *Gorgias*.

2. See Charles Kahn, "Drama and Dialectic in Plato's *Gorgias*," *Oxford Studies in Ancient Philosophy* 1 (1983): 75–121.

3. John M. Cooper, "Socrates and Plato in Plato's *Gorgias*," in *Reason and Emotion—Essays on Ancient Moral Psychology and Ethical Theory* (Princeton, NJ: Princeton University Press, 1999), 31–51, takes issue with Kahn's reading of these arguments. This is not the place to take up his objections in detail. Of course, I do think Cooper points us in the right direction when he poses the question, "What is Plato's relation to Socrates in the *Gorgias*?"

4. Kahn, "Drama and Dialectic," 119, finds Plato's case in the first, rather than the second, major section of the dialogue: "the reasons offered in support of this conception of the good [i.e., at 503e ff] are more in the nature of eloquent exhortation than rigorous argument. So far as this dialogue is concerned, the most cogent argument for the Socratic moral position is the total collapse of the Calliclean alternative." In the chapter on how Callicles is good (pages 155–168), I set out the view that Plato's case appears in the second major section of the dialogue (i.e., after 499c). The collapse, or at least clarification, of Callicles' position will help us to see that there is rather more than "eloquent exhortation" at work in Socrates' conception of the good—and that the Calliclean alternative actually contains elements of the truth.

5. Kahn, "Drama and Dialectic," 110.

6. Kahn, "Drama and Dialectic," 113.

7. Charles Kahn, *Plato and the Socratic Dialogue* (Cambridge: Cambridge University Press, 1996), 138.

8. Jessica Moss, "Shame, Pleasure and the Divided Soul," *Oxford Studies in Ancient Philosophy* 29 (2005): 146. Moss continues (pp. 146–47), "prejudices and confusions may hide our deepest value beliefs from our own view, but in our feelings of shame they shine through. Deep down Polus truthfully believed all along that injustice was worse than justice." In addition to the objections given below, we should keep in mind that Plato has emphasized Socrates' failure to convince in this dialogue (as Moss, "The Doctor and the Pastry Chef," 229, notes). If Plato had wanted to direct us to the idea that shame brings out the truth, he could have made the point clearer by eliminating any doubt at all the reader might have about the conversion of Polus and Callicles to the Socratic perspective. In my view, if those two are not entirely convinced, this points to the fact that their beliefs, even deep down, do not fall entirely on the side of their shame. On the notion that pleasure moves us in the wrong direction, see my treatment of Socrates' final schema of skills (517b–519a) on pages 158–165.

9. Moss, "Shame, Pleasure," 140. Tarnopolsky, *Prudes*, argues more broadly that shame can be both a positive and negative influence.

10. One might accordingly expect Socrates to be entirely without shame, but at the end of the dialogue, he tells of one thing that would cause him to be ashamed (522d5): being shown to be wrong about having the form of self-defense that he has by this point set out. Shame here plays a different role than it did earlier, for it is not the basis

on which anyone agrees to any proposition; it does not drive the inquiry but follows after it. In that sense it is absent from the discussion.

11. Plato has also drawn attention to Callicles' failure as regards friendliness. Callicles professed his friendly intentions toward Socrates (485e2), and Socrates accepted this claim on the basis of a conversation he had overheard between Callicles and three other associates (487c1–d4). Now, a consequence of this friendliness was said to be that Callicles would not deceive (ἀπατάω—487e5). But by 499, Socrates finds his hopes dashed: he had not believed that Callicles would deceive him (ἐξαπατάω—499c2, 3), since he was a friend (c4). Clearly, in this he was wrong. Thus both at the beginning and end of this section of the dialogue, we find a connection between friendliness and sincerity, or between deception with the absence of friendliness. By tying the conclusion of the argument back to the beginning with Socrates' expression of disappointment on this matter, Plato emphasizes that friendliness is a second failing of Callicles, again pointing the reader to the conclusion that Callicles fails as a touchstone. In the errors in Callicles' use of historical and literary material—see Rutherford, *Art of Plato*, 163, 166–68—one might also find a reason to qualify Socrates' assertion that Callicles is "clever."

12. There are two passages in which Socrates might seem to contradict this view: 475e3–6 and 508b–c. Both are decisively different from 487a–e, and the difference shows why they cannot give us Plato's view of shame in the dialogue. At 487a–e, the writer is setting up an expectation in the reader in advance of an argument, one to which the argument subsequently refers, as we saw. In this the author's hand is plain to see: he is giving us guidance on how to understand the argument. We have in this a reason to take Socrates' words at 487a–e as a more general, programmatic statement concerning shame. In the case of his words at 508b–c or 475e, we not only have no similar reason to take them as applicable beyond their immediate context, we have a positive reason not to do so: they are dependent on specific arguments (as the comments at 487a–e are not). At 508b–c Socrates returns to the claims he made against Polus and Gorgias, declaring these to be true rather than mere shame-based concessions. But this declaration depends upon the statement that "the earlier matters, Callicles, all follow" (508b3–4)—that is, they follow from the argument after 499c. Socrates has since then introduced reasoning of his own, proceeding from the principle (see pages 102–3), and this, he thinks, allows him to claim as true what earlier had only been conceded out of shame. We see something similar in Socrates' claim at 475e3–6 that it is true (and thus, one assumes, not a matter of a mere shame-based concession) that no man would choose to do rather than to suffer injustice: this is the conclusion of a particular argument, dependent on that argument. It is accordingly to be rejected if the argument is inadequate, as Plato has Callicles suggest it is.

13. On ἀγροικία see also Ann N. Michelini, "Polle Agroikia: Rudeness and Irony in Plato's *Gorgias*," *Classical Philology* 93, no. 1 (January 1998): 50–59, who notes (p. 51) that one aspect of good social behavior in Greek traditional discourse is presented by "charm and socially pleasing manners, covered by χάρις or the verb χαρίζεσθαι. Polus regards 'pleasing' as an honorable aim of rhetoric, while Socrates treats the production of χάρις as a species of flattery, κολακεία."

14. In addition to the argument he specifically refers to, Polus might also have in mind 457c-458e, where Socrates uses Gorgias' genteel nature to make him feel uncomfortable—in fact, ashamed (αἰσχρόν—458d7)—and thus pressures him to continue the argument. But as regards Gorgias' shame at this point, does it not show the argument actually being advanced by shame, since it keeps Gorgias from leaving the argument? I take it that the point here is to emphasize the extent to which Gorgias is subject to the influence of what others think of him. This is to be compared with Callicles, whose (partial) desire for independence from this compulsion will be an important theme later on.

15. I am inclined to view Callicles' use of αἰσχύνη at 489b8 in similar fashion. The fact that Plato uses the word here is surely significant, and I take the idea to be that Callicles is trying to pressure Socrates by bringing against him the prejudices of the audience against over-detailed inquiry, placing him among pedants and quibblers. The idea behind αἰσχύνη here is that if Socrates were influenced by it, he would give up on the details, and thus on the argument.

16. Rutherford, *Art of Plato*, 150: "in Socratic discourse, the interlocutor needs to come out and show himself, to bare his soul . . . Socrates . . . is on the side of Polus and Callicles to this extent, that he wants and insists on frankness, and does not want others to cover up their real opinions with a safe, orthodox morality. He criticizes his interlocutors more than once for this kind of false shame (489a2, 494cd), and he praises Callicles not least for his candor (487 passim, esp. d; cf. 492d)."

17. This motivating force is not a tool, and does not play a role in the arguments that follow in the way that shame does in the *Gorgias*: there are no complaints that the argument fails to investigate a possibility because someone turned away from a possibility on non-rational grounds. In the arguments of the *Republic* from book ii on, neither shame nor an unreflective adherence to conventional beliefs play a role in arguments that are meant to give the reasons for adopting a particular view. This is just the role that shame plays in the relevant arguments against Gorgias, Polus, and Callicles. For Glaucon and Adeimantus, a non-rational adherence to conventional or traditional beliefs motivates the search for such reasons, but does not play a role in the reasons themselves.

18. The treatment of the poet Simonides—also divine (θεῖος—331e6)—in the argument with Polemarchus offers another example of this faith in the content of convention: Socrates does not suggest that Simonides is wrong, just that he has not been properly understood.

19. See Nettleship, *Lectures*, 15–16, and my treatment of the *Republic*, below.

20. Dodds, *Gorgias*, 5.

21. There is no reason to restrict the relevance of Callicles' failure as a touchstone only to the arguments before 499c. Because the argument to that point establishes the claim that pleasure and the good are not the same thing, a claim on which the rest of the argument will depend, and because Callicles remains Socrates' opponent, his inadequacy must affect the results of the entire dialogue: those truths which come to light cannot be said simply to have been proven, but are being established in a provisional fashion.

(1) Gorgias

Socrates' arguments in the first major section of the *Gorgias* (to 499c) are not only important for the insight they may give into the immediate focus of the discussion, such as rhetoric or the good life, but also for the light they shed on the three characters whom Socrates confronts. Here we shall focus on the latter concern, that is, with Plato's characterization of Gorgias, Polus, and Callicles. This will help to fill in the overview, given in the preceding chapter, of the logic of this part of the dialogue. More importantly, it will provide a basis from which it is possible to reflect upon the single force running through these three characters, something necessary to understand the *Gorgias* on its own and also in relation to Thucydides and the first book of the *Republic*.

The crucial point concerning Gorgias' character can be summed up in one word: "*complacent.*"[1] Throughout Socrates' discussion with the elder rhetor, Plato consistently brings before the reader the fact that the old man has not thought things through. Though Gorgias is a genial and respectable fellow, there are suggestions, implicit in his own words, that real evil lurks in his profession. That these suggestions are only implicit is of fundamental importance: Gorgias believes he provides a valuable service, a genuine force for good, even as he takes pride in the power of his art. It becomes clear that there is an ethical order that exerts a very real hold upon him. His superficial thinking has prevented him from recognizing the potential for evil that his art brings with it, a reality that will quickly rise to the surface when we move on to Polus.

As Socrates begins his conversation with Gorgias, the question concerns the nature of rhetoric. The first section of the argument (449a–453a) produces a provisional answer: rhetoric is able to produce persuasion in the soul of an audience (453a), particularly in politics (452e). The argument to this point follows a peculiar pattern: Socrates presses for answers concerning the nature of Gorgias' art, and Gorgias fails to give an adequately specific answer. The question of rhetoric's subject matter proves troublesome: first Gorgias says it concerns speech (449e1), but this will hardly do, since plenty of other arts are also concerned with speech, as medicine is concerned with speech about sick people. Gorgias then says that rhetoric is *wholly* concerned with speech (450b). This too will not suffice, for Socrates points out that other arts also proceed entirely through speech (450c–e). Under pressure, Gorgias changes tack, and gives a peculiar answer to the question of rhetoric's subject matter: he declares it to be "the greatest and best of human affairs" (451d7–8). To do this, however, is to repeat a mistake or a kind that the argument has already seen (against Polus at 448c): answering a "what is it?" question as though it were asking "what *sort* of thing is it?"[2]

Gorgias' difficulties here already tell us a great deal about him. After all, the subject matter is rhetoric itself, and he is supposed to be a master rhetor, one who boasts that "nobody has asked me anything new for many years" (448a2–3)—and yet it takes some pages before Socrates can draw out of Gorgias a basic conception of what rhetoric is. The problem is not that Gorgias has no idea what rhetoric is but that he is not in the habit of giving definitions. It would seem that his usual activity has not required this of him. Instead, it assumes that it will be enough to have a general idea which everyone recognizes. Gorgias is accustomed to skim along the surface of things, focusing on attributes rather than essences, on ποῖον ("what sort?") rather than τί ("what?"). In fact, this sort of thing is often sufficient in practice—so long as nobody thinks too deeply. On this basis, one can make impressive and persuasive speeches, in which one seems to know what one is talking about, without actually being able to give a precise account. Socrates, by contrast, has assumed that an investigation or account will be necessary before one can claim to know what something is.

The argument will subsequently reveal a second (and complementary) explanation for Gorgias' difficulties in giving an account of rhetoric: he believes it to be a sort of universal art, one capable of persuasion virtually anywhere. Socrates has said that medicine is responsible for speech about making sick people well (449e), but Gorgias will soon relate that he has persuaded patients to undergo surgery when doctors could not (456b). That is, rhetoric is also in some sense responsible for speech about making sick people well—and he proceeds to add that the rhetor, speaking before an assembly, will be able to get himself chosen as doctor in preference to a real doctor, something to which he has already alluded (452e). But this points toward a less reputable aspect of rhetoric, its ability to persuade on the basis of something other than knowledge, and thus to wield power unjustly, something that in turn leads toward the argument that will remove Gorgias from active participation in the dialogue (see below). Somewhere in all of this—one might quarrel about where exactly—Gorgias has not thought things through. The crucial point is that he proves able to hold his own only to the extent that the argument fails to be clear about what exactly rhetoric is and how it works: the impression we get in the first few pages will be confirmed in the end.

The argument to 453a, then, suggests that Gorgias has never thought in a significant manner about what he does, however convincing he may be in front of a crowd. By the standard of the average person in the street, he may be an intellectual force to be reckoned with, but once he has entered Socrates' world, it is a different matter. Gorgias is certainly confident in his abilities—we are told that "just now he bid anyone inside to ask whatever he wished, and he said he would answer them all" (447c6–8)[3]—but behind this confidence there is no indication of substantial intellectual ability.

Gorgias' statement that rhetoric is "the greatest and best of human affairs" (451d7–8), proves to be a pregnant statement indeed, for it leads Socrates to make a short speech about "the greatest good" (452a–c). As Socrates speaks, it becomes clear that Gorgias has assumed answers to important questions, for Plato has Socrates speak in a manner that points toward deeper issues that will be taken up later in the dialogue. He brings before us three different kinds of person: the doctor, the physical trainer, and the businessman. Each of these believes his own art to focus on the greatest good, but gives no argument in support of this belief. Instead, each is presented as taking the matter to be *obvious*—note in particular that the doctor and businessman both reply πῶς γὰρ οὔκ ("[of course,] for how not?"—452a8, c5) when asked if their art's work is the greatest good. An active mind would see a problem here: three people each take it as obvious that their own peculiar focus is the greatest good. Surely the situation must produce a contradiction, for they cannot all be right—or could their statements be reconciled? What exactly *is* the greatest good? An answer would require some substantial thinking about the ends of life—indeed, an answer would likely imply an answer to the question concerning the kind of life one should live. That deeper matter, of course, will come explicitly into focus when we get to Callicles (487e), a strong suggestion that Plato is hinting at it here. For a thoughtful person, deep matters lurk in Socrates' short speech.

Gorgias, it would seem, is not such a thoughtful person. Ignoring the implicit deeper issue, he focuses only on the immediate matter at hand, the specific subject matter of rhetoric. Thus he asserts that yet another thing (persuasion) is the greatest good (452d5–8), and although he does at least give *some* account of why his art should have the top spot, he does so in a way that brushes aside the deeper issues. That is, being able to persuade people in various political assemblies is the greatest good (452e) because such persuasion puts its practitioner above all other arts: it can acquire whatever the other arts produce. Gorgias thus ignores the implicit question of ends, and reduces it to a practical matter. That is, there's no *need* to inquire concerning the ends of life, for whatever these might be, rhetoric can get them for you.[4]

In the course of giving his own answer concerning the greatest good, Gorgias makes another remark significant for what is left unclear rather than stated directly. He says that rhetoric "is the greatest good, at once the cause of freedom for humankind in general [αὐτοῖς τοῖς ἀνθρώποις] and, for the individual, of ruling [ἄρχειν] others in his own city" (452d5–8). This statement is ambiguous, for it seems to point toward both collective and individual freedom.[5] If rhetoric is simply a source of collective freedom, it will be unambiguously good. But what is the character of the "rule" (ἄρχειν) over others? Does it seek the good of the whole community, or is it rather a tyrannical sort of rule, which seeks the good of the ruler at the expense of the community? The fact that Gorgias straightaway begins to talk of making other people slaves (452e5) directs us toward the latter case. Plato could easily have eliminated any ambiguity if he had wanted; that it is present will prove significant.[6] Rather than declaring in favor of one or the other side of this statement, we should understand that its ambiguity indicates that Gorgias has (once again) not thought things through. Here he points simultaneously toward both collective *and* individual freedom, because both sides make him look good: collective freedom allows him to be seen to provide something good for everyone, while individual freedom means he can then appeal to each listener, saying, in effect, look what this will do for *you* (see below). Again, it is to the potential for evil that our attention is directed, for Gorgias immediately begins to talk in terms of making people *slaves* (452e).

This talk of making others into slaves gives an example of the sort of complacency that characterizes Gorgias and his activity. He speaks as follows: "through this power, you will hold the doctor as a slave, and the physical trainer as a slave . . . the businessman will come to light as making money for another and not for himself, but for you who are able to speak and persuade the multitude" (452e). Given the use of the second-person singular (e5, 7), this sounds like an advertisement for Gorgias' teaching. On the surface, this power sounds wonderful, as we think of it in *our* hands (and see also 459c3–5, which has a similar effect).[7] It is only those listeners thoughtful enough to step back from the pleasing thought of *themselves* holding this power who will notice a troubling reality: the rhetor is coming to light as a sort of tyrant, one who enslaves everyone else. Gorgias' account might seem on the surface to be good in an unproblematic way, but this appearance will only be effective on an unreflective audience.[8] However troubling the implications might be at this point, there is no sign that Gorgias himself has thought them through.

Although the suggestion of slavery is the first hint of the darker turn the dialogue will later take, we can see that Gorgias himself is sincerely concerned with acting rightly. When he emphasizes the immense power of rhetoric (456a), he gives an altogether praiseworthy first example of how this power might be used: he has persuaded those whom even a doctor could not move to undergo surgery or take medicine (456b1–5). However, we soon find ourselves on more ambiguous ground: a rhetor would be more persuasive than any other artisan, and so could get himself chosen above someone who actually has the relevant skills. Although a reflective reader or listener might already note the capacity for harm implicit in this account–an ignorant quack might get himself chosen surgeon general–nevertheless, Socrates has as yet made no suggestion that Gorgias' art might be an agent of injustice. It is *Gorgias himself* who addresses the issue, on his own initiative, and he thus shows himself to be sincerely concerned with the moral status of his art. The way in which he does so is significant. On the account he gives, there are normative limits that should be recognized, for he stresses imperatives of this sort quite heavily (456c6–457c3: the word δεῖ occurs here six times, in the sense "one ought"). The question of *why* one ought to act in such a manner is (significantly) ignored, although one could reasonably ask at this point why someone who could benefit from doing wrong would choose not to. It is through Polus and Callicles that the dialogue will delve more deeply into the question of why one should act rightly; Gorgias, by contrast, is content simply to assert certain ethical obligations as obvious givens, and though he never abandons these, he also never confronts the deeper difficulties inherent in his position without pressure from Socrates.[9]

Gorgias, then, is shown to have a genuine concern with acting rightly but also to have consistently failed to think things through. With this characterization in mind, we can see how Socrates' final argument against the older man (458e–460e) has been designed with exquisite precision. Socrates first step is to remind us that Gorgias' rhetoric will often produce persuasion on matters of which the rhetor is ignorant. The inversion of the proper order of things that this entails is emphasized by means of a rather labored formulation: one who does not know will seem to know more than one who does know, among those who do not know.[10] Having established this, Socrates makes his next demand at some length, piling up questions (459c8–e8), and ending up with a restatement of his desire to hear the power of rhetoric (460a1–2), the question with which he began the dialogue (447c1–2). All this constitutes an indication that we are coming to an important moment, and Polus (461b4–c3) will soon point to it as the moment that lost Gorgias the argument.

The crucial question is this: when it comes to matters that concern how we ought to act—the just and the unjust, noble and shameful, good and bad—will the rhetor be ignorant and still able to produce persuasion, or must he have knowledge regarding these things? This question points right at the ambiguities we have noted in Gorgias' earlier statements. Does he see in rhetoric a source of freedom for all humankind, or only for its practitioners, who would then be tyrants over everyone else? How far did Gorgias intend to go when speaking of making others one's slaves? If freedom for a few and slavery for others is the true focus, then knowledge of the just and the unjust (etc.) will be irrelevant. On the other hand, if rhetoric is to be a *simply* good and praiseworthy activity, then it *must* have knowledge of these things, at the very least to be able to avoid trespasses against justice (and the noble and the good) while making use of its own tremendous power.[11]

Socrates' argument, given the focus it has put on knowledge and ignorance, sharpens this difficulty still further, for the suggestion is that the ignorant will be able to lead the ignorant over the objections of those who know. Applied to the peculiar focus of rhetoric, ethical matters (454b), this points to some very dubious ethical ground indeed, for it will mean that Gorgias would take people who are wicked and teach them how to seem good. While skilled boxers might attack defenseless people, their skill at boxing will not allow them to make it appear (in court, for example) that such actions were not wrong. By 460a, however, rhetoric goes a step further: in principle, a scoundrel might learn from Gorgias how to commit any sort of crime with impunity. To admit this would involve critical loss of face for anyone who wishes, as Gorgias clearly does, to maintain that rhetoric is a praiseworthy activity. He had not thought it to be responsible for wrongs of such magnitude—indeed, he had probably never dwelt at length upon the harm his art could do. In this context, it is precisely correct to say that "the pressure on Gorgias to claim to teach justice is precisely the pressure to claim he trains only good men, who will not abuse their power."[12] Accordingly, Gorgias answers Socrates' question by saying that a student who comes to him without knowledge of the just and the unjust (etc.) will get it from him.

Plato has given clear indications that we are to understand that Gorgias makes this crucial admission out of *shame* (461b4–c3, 482c–d, 487b–c, 494d), and we have already seen, in the preceding chapter, the importance of the theme of shame to the overall movement through Socrates' three opponents.[13] It is thus important that we properly locate Gorgias' shame. Certainly, he does thrice mention the possibility of a teacher being hated and thrown out of the city (456e1–2, 457b6–7, c2–3), but it is unlikely that this is to be connected to his reaction to the argument, for there is reason to doubt he lives in fear of such a fate.[14] Rhetoric, we recall, has come to light as possessing an extraordinary, even godlike (δαιμονία—456a5) power, one particularly appropriate to courts and assemblies. As an accomplished rhetor, Gorgias would be absolutely in his element in a court of law. However guilty he might actually be, he more than anyone could make himself seem innocent—indeed, one imagines that if not for his own sense of decency, his accusers, however innocent they might in reality be, could soon find themselves on trial for their lives.[15]

Accordingly, when the argument begins to bring out into the open the unjust, shameful, and bad aspect of his professional activity, Gorgias finds himself with genuine misgivings: he is not afraid, but ashamed. Certainly, the matter of Gorgias' interests is not absent, for the conversation is being held in front of an audience. We are twice reminded that prospective students are present (455c5–d5): to admit that the art he teaches has such a disreputable aspect could be bad for business. Of course, the presence of an audience also makes him all the more subject to shame, for it is this that shames him into continuing the argument at a moment when he would like to leave (458b5–e2).

Socrates will later confirm that Gorgias was moved by shame (487b1–5, 494d2–3). To say this is to say that Gorgias was, in an important sense, *not* compelled by the argument to give way to Socrates. This constitutes an indication on Plato's part that he understands the argument at this point to be flawed—that is, that it will not suffice to move the reader to accept Socrates' conclusion. Accordingly, "the outcome, for the reader, of Socrates' discussion with Gorgias is not at all a recommendation to focus on Socrates' arguments in order to discover their truth."[16] The inadequacy in the argument is essential to Plato's purpose here, for it not only gives us a final confirmation of the characterization of Gorgias as we had already understood it, but it also leaves a deeper analysis of the matter at hand for the rest of the dialogue.

Gorgias is sincerely concerned to pursue what is right but is too complacent to have looked beneath the pleasing surface of his own professional activity. His talk of making others one's slaves might be taken to suggest a willingness to give way a little to ignoble instincts (although the dialogue takes place in a world that regards slavery differently than we do), but as soon as any disreputable tendency is brought into the open, Gorgias backs away from it. He remains sincerely interested in the results of the conversation that follows, as is clear from his subsequent interventions (463a5, 463d–464b, 497b, 505c–506c).[17] Later in the dialogue we will encounter the distinction between convention and nature. Gorgias shows no sign of being aware of this distinction—if he were, he would have a basis for considerably greater resistance to Socrates—and lives very much on the side of what Callicles will later call convention. The problem with Gorgias is not that he has any active inclination in the direction of evil, but rather that he is not a thoughtful person. This lack of thought, however, will turn out to be a serious failing indeed; the argument up to 499c is in effect an investigation of its consequences.

NOTES

1. Graeme Nicholson, *Plato's Phaedrus—The Philosophy of Love* (West Lafayette, IN: Purdue University Press, 1999), 39. Dodds, *Gorgias*, 9, also speaks of Gorgias' "complacency."

2. Dodds, *Gorgias*, 200: "Gorgias, like Polus, confuses τί with ποῖον." Elsewhere, commenting on 448c4–9, Dodds, *Gorgias*, 192, notes that "Chaerephon had grasped Socrates' meaning from a single example [i.e., at 447d], but two have failed to enlighten Polus." In similar fashion, the examples given by Socrates at 451a–c fail to enlighten Gorgias.

3. Further indications of self-confidence: 449a7–8, c1–3, c7–8, d7.

4. Note that Gorgias does *not* take the position that ends are a matter of convention as opposed to nature. That move is significantly not given explicit expression until Callicles. The point with Gorgias is that such thoughts are suggested at 452e1–8 as being *implicit*, but that he is *not* represented as having thought so far on his own.

5. Cooper, "Socrates and Plato," 33, fn. 5, translates αὐτοῖς τοῖς ἀνθρώποις as "humankind itself;" Irwin translates it as "a man himself." Cooper, "Socrates and Plato," 33, fn. 5 (see also 40–41), provides a reading of Gorgias at 452d (and in general) which seeks to make explicit the nature of the unambiguous good that rhetoric aims at. In doing so, he develops too fully what is at best implicit in the text. I think the point is precisely that any genuine political good for rhetoric is left on the level of mere implication here, and is *not* given the explicit development which Cooper provides; the evil, on the other hand, will be the progressively more explicit focus of the dialogue to 499c. In addition, the talk of "freedom for humankind in general" does not relate to the preceding three examples so unambiguously as Cooper suggests. Certainly, medicine and physical training provide a good to those *on whom* the expert practices, but surely the businessman (χρηματιστής; Cooper translates with "financial expert," which suggests the sort of person, well-known in our own time, who advises on a stock portfolio) typically provides money *for himself*—note how the thought that the activity might make money for someone other than its practitioner appears as something exceptional at 452e6–7.

6. The distinction between individual and collective good (and confusion over this distinction) will become central to the argument with Polus at 474b–475e, as we shall see.

7. Polus will make similar second-person rhetorical appeals, e.g., 468e6–9, 469b12, a tendency that culminates in Callicles' direct address to Socrates in the second person (485e7–486d1).

8. Perhaps there is a connection here to the theme of long and short speeches (*makrologia/brachulogia*). Rutherford, *Art of Plato*, 146: "in Plato and others, long rhetorical orations are suspect because they cannot be questioned and tested at every stage. The listener is carried away and forgets the details."

9. This is not to assert that Gorgias displays indifference to his own self-interest here, for he is intent on placing the blame for the misuse of rhetoric on the student, not the teacher. James Stuart Murray, "Plato on Power, Moral Responsibility and the

(1) Gorgias 125

Alleged Neutrality of Gorgias' Art of Rhetoric (*Gorgias* 456c–457b)," *Philosophy and Rhetoric* 34, no. 4 (2001): 355–63, provides a reflection on 456c–457b which correctly brings out the immoral nature of rhetoric that lies implicit in Gorgias' own defense. Murray's account is not simply wrong, but it is important to remember that such conclusions are *only implicit* at this point, a fact which becomes all the more conspicuous as the rest of the dialogue unfolds. Gorgias has not thought his own words out as thoroughly as Murray, and will turn away from their consequences as the argument brings these out. His moral concerns are sincere, though in tension with his work as he himself describes it.

10. ὥστε δοκεῖν εἰδέναι οὐκ εἰδὼς ἐν οὐκ εἰδόσιν μᾶλλον τοῦ εἰδότος (459d6–e1). Note also 459c1–2: ὥστε φαίνεσθαι τοῖς οὐκ εἰδόσι μᾶλλον εἰδέναι τῶν εἰδότων ("so as to seem, to those who do not know, to know more than those who do know").

11. That this question of whether rhetoric is a simply praiseworthy activity or a morally dubious one is indeed at issue is confirmed by Socrates' concluding words (460e5–461a2), which affirm the former position. The argument is also preceded by Socrates claim that Gorgias is now saying "things not altogether consistent or harmonious with what you first said about rhetoric" (457e1–3); at 457c4, Gorgias has just given a speech in which he says right out that rhetoric can be used wrongly (457b5–c1), and speaks of a definite wrong a rhetor might inflict on others (i.e., stealing reputations—457b1–4). This clearly conflicts with the earlier suggestion that rhetoric might simply be good—e.g., provide freedom for all humankind. Earlier, the matter had been ambiguous.

12. Kahn, "Drama and Dialectic," 82. Cooper, "Socrates and Plato," 38–46, is correct to note that the controversial agreement that actually dooms Gorgias in the argument is not the claim to know just and unjust, but rather the claim that "the man who has learnt just things is just" (460b7). Why, then, does Polus point to knowledge of just and unjust as the fatal agreement? (461b4–c1) Surely because this is the point at which he begins to take issue with the argument, and it is from here that he will begin his defense. Certainly, if this point is not granted to Socrates, the rest will not follow. And of course, Gorgias will affirm that "the man who has learnt just things is just" for the same reason he concedes he will teach justice: to refuse is to admit that his work has been less than praiseworthy.

13. See Kahn, "Drama and Dialectic," 79–84, who has shown the importance of shame to this argument. Cooper, "Socrates and Plato," 34, believes that Gorgias has already effectively claimed knowledge of just and unjust for the rhetor back at 454b5–7, for there he claims that just and unjust things are part of rhetoric's expertise. But shortly thereafter we learn that rhetoric produces conviction without knowledge (455e), just as cookery, which has foods for the body as its area of expertise (464d), does not have knowledge of these. Socrates later tells us that rhetoric and cookery are knacks rather than skills, and skills are distinguished from knacks in that the former grasp the nature (φύσιν—465a4) and cause (αἰτία—a5) of their subjects, while the latter do not. So, the fact that rhetoric has the just and the unjust as its subject matter does not necessarily imply that rhetoric has knowledge of these things.

14. Fear is what Kahn, "Drama and Dialectic," 80–81, would take as Gorgias' motivation for his fatal admissions at 460a–b.

15. So why, then, is the fate of an unfortunate teacher stressed? At least part of Plato's reason for including this detail is literary, one of the many ways in which what is only hinted at with Gorgias gradually becomes more fully developed in what follows. Gorgias is quite clear that those who use rhetoric wrongly should be thrown out of the city (ἐκβάλλειν—456e2, 457b7, c2) or even killed (ἀποκτεινύναι—457c3), and is concerned with who does and does not deserve this fate. Polus will use these same words, but to very different effect: rhetoric is desirable because its practitioners may kill (ἀποκτεινύασιν—466b11) and throw out of the city (ἐκβάλλουσιν—466c1) whomever they please. Similarly, Gorgias says a rhetor ought not to take away a doctor's reputation or glory (τὴν δόξαν ἀφαιρεῖσθαι—457b2); Polus' rhetors are enviable because they may take away the *property* (ἀφαιροῦνται χρήματα—466c1) of whomever they choose. Callicles speaks of the same penalties using different words at 486b–c: he mentions death and loss of property, although instead of speaking about being thrown out of the city, he speaks of living dishonored within it. Of course, Callicles is now *warning Socrates* that *he* may suffer these things—and see 511a5–7, where Callicles takes up killing and confiscation (ἀποκτεινύναι and ἀφαιρεῖσθαι) in renewing his warning. Finally, the ideas receive their most pointed expression when Socrates turns them on himself (508d2–3, 521b4–c2).

16. Cooper, "Socrates and Plato," 50. Of course, it is *Kahn* who has suggested that Gorgias gave way out of shame; Cooper objects to Kahn on the matter of shame. I agree with Kahn that Gorgias gave way out of shame, but also agree with Cooper when he suggests that Plato's purpose is "a recommendation to question deeply [the arguments'] presuppositions."

17. Such interruptions confirm that his claim to be interested in the truth (458b) is not insincere. Perhaps he is genuinely interested not only because he hadn't thought his position would lead so naturally to Callicles, but also because he's hopeful that Socrates can carry the day.

(2) Polus

Polus is a younger man than Gorgias (note 461c, 463e2), and therefore more open to new ideas which fly in the face of convention.[1] As was the case with Gorgias, Polus is unconsciously caught in a conflict between two opposing sides of his own beliefs; the difference is that the opposition lies further in the direction of a liberation from conventional constraint. On the one hand, he has something of the complacency of Gorgias, since he accepts certain things to be obvious, such as the nature of power, or the fact that certain acts are shameful. On the other hand, Polus presents us with a fuller development of Gorgias' pride in the power of the art of rhetoric: we are now in the presence of someone who is quite unashamed to proclaim his admiration for the most extreme uses—indeed, abuses—of power. These two sides will prove to be irreconcilable.

A certain lack of intelligence is evident in Polus—one scholar has suggested that he is "perhaps the stupidest of all interlocutors with whom Socrates converses throughout Plato's works."[2] Gorgias was able, after some confusion, to focus on the nature of rhetoric rather than its attributes. Polus, by contrast, is impatient to discuss attributes only (462c7–8, 463d3), something emphasized by Socrates (463d5), and the result is that Gorgias must briefly take part in the discussion again so that the dialogue may reach a preliminary conclusion concerning the nature of rhetoric before moving on to related matters (463d–464b). Polus also makes some fairly obvious mistakes (e.g., 462e2, 466a4–5).

In addition, Polus makes a variety of rhetorical appeals—various astonished expostulations, vivid appeals to experience, laughter—that can certainly be effective rhetorically but have no place in the sort of inquiry Socrates has been trying to conduct. These rhetorical responses point to the side of Polus that is prepared to take certain things as given rather than as matters about which there might be discussion and disagreement. Certainly, he does not accept something that Gorgias had taken as given, that is, the old man's repeated insistence that "one ought" (δεῖ) to avoid acting in certain ways (456e–457c). Still, Polus does think he knows what power is, and who has it: he thinks it plain as day that rhetors have the greatest power in cities (466b4–5). He will also prove to take a great deal for granted about the nature of punishment. This is not to say that he presents an argument, or any reason at all, for these claims. Rather, he considers them so obvious that he is bewildered as the argument moves forward (e.g. "you're saying shocking and monstrous things!"—467b10). His sarcastic responses (e.g., "a child could refute you"—470c5) and laughter (473e2) drive home just how much he takes the matters at issue to be obvious: "you're saying things no one would say!" (473e5)[3] There is one particularly important matter that Polus takes as simply given: the nature of justice. He takes it for granted that the unrestrained exercise of power of the sort we find in the tyrant is unjust (on this, see below).

Polus has two very different ways of relating to other people. On the one hand, at certain moments his lack of concern for others comes out in his remarkably ill-mannered behavior. This is apparent right from the start: "thrusting himself forward in Gorgias' place (448a) . . . he treats both Chaerephon and Socrates with a prickly resentfulness (e.g., 448b1, 461d8, 467b1)."[4] Similarly, his entry into his own section of the dialogue is conspicuously less well-mannered than Callicles' will be,[5] for Callicles enters by first making an aside to Chaerephon; Polus simply interrupts in a "syntactically confused outburst."[6] His claim, noted above, that a child could refute Socrates (470c4–5) is not remarkable for its tact. On the other hand, he also shows himself to think the opinions of other people to be very important indeed. For example, he speaks of being envied and thought happy by others (473c7–d1) as though this were something worth having (and see also 466a9–10, 471c8–d2). He also shows himself to be able to bring consideration for others to bear when it suits him, for he ends his interruption at the start of this section of the dialogue with an accusation of bad manners (461c). His regard for the opinions of other people also comes to light when he says, "Don't you think you've been refuted, Socrates, when you say such things as no person would say?" (473e4–5). That is, he appeals to common opinion as if it provided a ground for a belief (see also 474b6–7, which continues this idea).

Polus' double relation to other people coheres with his treatment of the tyrant Archelaus (471a–d). On the one hand, we find here a fuller development of Gorgias' pride in the power of the art of rhetoric—recall in particular the old man's brief talk of making people slaves (452e)—for Polus not only compares rhetors to tyrants (466b11), but is also quite clear about his admiration for Archelaus. On the other hand, Polus recognizes that what the tyrant has done is unjust. It is quite clear that these two sides are meant to conflict with one another, for the whole force of the example of Archelaus is to bring out the disjunction of justice and power: the tyrant is unjust and for precisely that reason is doing so well for himself.

This conflict will, in fact, prove crucial to the key argument that Socrates uses to defeat Polus. This is because that argument will, as we shall see, turn on two different senses of the word "good," and we can see these two senses at work in Polus' treatment of Archelaus. In his admission that this man is unjust (471a4), Polus shows himself to recognize a sense of "good" that Archelaus could not claim to have attained: from the point of view of justice, this man is clearly bad and shameful. Polus, however, is focused on quite another sense of "good" when he expresses admiration for Archelaus: the man represents something attractive when we consider the various material benefits he enjoys—these things are "good" in the sense that they are considered useful or beneficial. It is from this second sense of "good" that Polus says that doing injustice is better than suffering it (474c), that the unjust are happy if they go unpunished (472e, 473b), and would distinguish the good from the noble and the bad from the shameful (474c9–d2). Indeed, it is surely correct to identify Polus' advocacy of injustice with pleasure. "Good" in this second sense will resolve into "pleasure," in that the reason we pursue good things is ultimately that they are conducive to our own pleasure. The tyrant, who can do whatever he thinks fit, is in an excellent position to minister to his appetites, and thus to enjoy the attendant pleasures. A conventional understanding of justice, by contrast, will often require that we discipline our appetites, forgoing pleasure, and even accept the pain of punishment.[7] Again, recall that the whole point of the example of Archelaus is that justice and power, and thus these two senses of "good," are incompatible with one another.

The key argument used to defeat Polus (474b–475e) turns on the two senses of "good" that we see within him. Socrates seeks to show that doing wrong is worse than suffering it, and in the following argument he will make a further claim concerning punishment. These claims will become a repeated point of reference in the argument with Callicles (483a, 508e, 509b, 522d–e, 527b). It might appear that Socrates rests this claim only on the argument that he deploys here, and this would make this argument a keystone in the logic of his position as he explains it over the whole dialogue.[8] This appearance is deceptive: Socrates will give an independent—and more substantial—basis for his claims concerning justice beginning at 503d. Accordingly, the fact that scholars overwhelmingly judge the argument here (i.e., at 474b–475e) a failure is not the last word on Socrates' thesis on justice.

Certainly, the argument against Polus is not sufficient on its own to establish the conclusion that Socrates draws from it, so what has Plato gained from presenting it like this? First, on the level of the dramatic structure of the dialogue, he has not only refuted Polus in a manner that leaves room for Callicles to intervene and take the matter further, he has also confirmed the characterization of Polus as we have so far understood it, a crucial element in the overall development to 499c. Second, the careful reader will be obliged to reflect on the two different senses of "good," something that looks ahead to, and deepens the significance of, Socrates' subsequent treatment of this concept.

Callicles will object to this argument (474b–475e) on the ground that Polus wrongly granted that doing injustice is more shameful than suffering it, and further, that he only made this concession because he was ashamed to say what he really thought (482d–e). Obviously, Socrates' argument here will collapse whatever its trickery if this premise—that is, that doing injustice is more shameful than suffering it—is removed, but Callicles does not stop at this point. He proceeds to distinguish custom and nature (νόμος and φύσις), and to accuse Socrates of craftily switching between the two so as to confound his opponent (482e–483a). Polus, he says, was speaking of the shameful according to custom, but Socrates pursued the argument according to nature (483a6–7).

All these remarks are very much to the point.[9] To see how, it is necessary to consider the ambiguity at work in the word "good" over the course of the argument. The first meaning comes to light as Socrates moves toward a definition of the noble (τὸ καλόν), which he defines by reference to pleasure (ἡδονή—474d8, e2) and utility (χρεία—474d6); "benefit" or "profit" (ὠφελία—474e3) is then used in place of "utility."[10] Polus soon substitutes "good" (ἀγαθός—475a3) for "useful" and "beneficial," and the argument proceeds on the basis of this term thereafter.[11] The substitution is reasonable, for the argument at 467e–468c has already established that behind "beneficial" (ὠφέλιμα—468c4) lies "good" (ἀγαθά—468c5)—that is, the beneficial is pursued for the sake of the good; the same would be true with regard to the "useful." Polus is thus simply making explicit what lies behind Socrates' examples: things which are understood to be good in the sense of "beneficial," "useful," or "profitable" are pursued by people for the sake of the good. It is also on the basis of this sense of "good" that Polus would deny that the "good" and the "noble" are the same (474c9–d2). This is what Callicles would call "good-by-nature." It seems likely that "good" in this sense will be the same as pleasure—recall the suggestion made above that Polus' praise of the tyrant is grounded ultimately in pleasure. "Good" has another meaning, however, and from this second perspective—which would be "good-by-convention" for Callicles—what is normally considered "noble" will also be called "good." This does not, of course, necessarily mean "good for the agent/sufferer" in the sense of achieving some material (and, ultimately, pleasant) benefit, but will mean "good and admirable in the eyes of the community."[12]

If we were to hold throughout to this second meaning, Socrates would produce an uncontroversial and obvious conclusion, that doing injustice is more evil, in the sense of *conventionally* worse, than suffering it, for what is beneficial or useful for the community is what is conventionally considered noble (475c7–8). On the other hand, if we were to hold strictly to the first sense of "good," then "benefit" and "use" would mean "beneficial/useful for the individual." If it is correct to see "good" in this sense to be the same as pleasure, then "beneficial/useful for the individual" would mean "leading ultimately to the individual's pleasure." The distinction between pleasure and the useful/beneficial/good will then become trivial, since these latter things will merely be for the sake of pleasure. That is, the argument depends on switching between two different meanings of "good": to the extent that it does not do this, it merely states something obvious.

That there has been a switch becomes clear in the argument's last steps: Socrates leads us to the conclusion that doing wrong is more shameful than suffering it, not because of pain, but because of "evil." This must be evil in the sense of what is "good-by-convention." But Socrates then adds that many people agree that it is more shameful to do wrong than to suffer it—again "good-by-convention"—as though this were some additional point ["Άλλο τι]. The appearance is thus created that it has been shown that doing wrong is more evil ("good-by-nature") and more shameful ("good-by-convention") than suffering it.

Polus is not clever enough to see the trick that has been played. As Callicles suggests, Polus speaks of the shameful according to convention at the start (474c–d)—that is, the shameful would be worse-by-convention, but *not* worse-by-nature; the noble would be good-by-convention, *not* good-by-nature. The difficulty arises as Socrates leads Polus to the definition of the noble (474d3–475a4), for the examples used suggest that the meaning of "good" in play is the good-by-nature; this is where Socrates "pursues the argument according to nature," as Callicles puts it (483a6–7). But if Polus accepts this, he must contradict the position he began with. Why, then, does he not object? Because it would make perfect sense to define the noble in terms of good-by-*convention*, and Polus, as we shall see, has not thought through the distinction between convention and nature as Callicles has.

These two meanings of "good" both have a sound basis in the characterization of Polus as Plato has presented him. Thus, he is characterized above all by his failure to relate these two sides, for if he were to pursue either one to its logical extreme, he would negate the other. It is precisely correct to say that there is a "*latent* contradiction"[13] (emphasis mine) within him. The purpose of Socrates' argument is to run the two sides of Polus into each other. Once again, then, it would seem that Socrates has understood his opponent well— indeed, the argument is directed with exquisite precision, in the very nature of its error, at the confusion that defines Polus: it is confused precisely where he is, making it most likely to succeed in confounding him.

The final argument against Polus (476a–479e) suffers from the same sort of defect as its predecessor: it presupposes answers to questions concerning the nature of punishment and justice without having actually established anything concerning them. Near the beginning of this final argument, Socrates secures Polus' agreement that "the sort of action that the doer performs is the sort that the thing affected receives" (476e)—that is, if one cuts deeply, the recipient suffers a deep cut; if one strikes hard, the recipient suffers a hard blow, and so on. But Socrates has chosen convenient examples, and his result does not hold in every case. Rather, "this argument from correlatives . . . works only when the property of the action belongs to it intrinsically and non-relationally." For example, "if I inflict pain with difficulty, it does not follow that you suffer pain with difficulty, though it follows that you suffer something done with difficulty by me."[14] The matter at hand is that of "paying justice" and punishment: the question on which the argument depends is thus whether justice and punishment are such that the relation Socrates speaks of holds. That is, what is the nature of justice? What is the nature of punishment? Socrates no doubt knows that Polus, who is inclined to chase after attributes rather than natures, is not likely to ask such questions. His argument is thus once more well-aimed at his particular opponent, while Plato's presentation should arouse in the careful reader questions about the nature of justice and punishment, as the previous argument aroused questions concerning "good."

At this point it is necessary to give a more general overview of the encounter with Polus. With Gorgias, Socrates repeatedly emphasized that the argument was not a personal attack but a sincere attempt to get at the truth (453a8–b4, 453c1–4, 454b9–c5, 457c4–458b3). At the start of the encounter with Callicles, Socrates will express his belief that he has found a person whom he can use as a touchstone to get to the truth (487a–e). Against Polus, this emphasis on the truth swiftly disappears.[15] In fact, Socrates contradicts the younger man as explicitly and fully as possible.[16] One consequence of this is that although Socrates repeatedly takes Polus to task for chasing after the attributes of rhetoric without first grasping its nature (462c10–d2, 463b7–c7, d4–5), he is himself soon guilty of a similar failing. That is, Plato has first primed the reader to be aware of a particular kind of inadequacy, and has then included that very inadequacy in the arguments that follow. Thus, once Polus suggests that rhetors have the greatest power in the cities, Socrates replies that they have the least power of all (466b). There is an obvious question here that does not get addressed: what is power? It is clear enough that Polus thinks "power" is some form of external ability. Socrates' argument does not show that this cannot be good. Instead, he deals with the power of rhetoric by turning straightaway to one of its (alleged) attributes: its goodness (466b6–7).

We saw above that the central argument against Polus (474b–475e) turns on an ambiguity in the word "good," although the argument with Polus does not investigate what "good" is; at 503d–505b it becomes clear that Socrates has his own peculiar conception of "good." So too with the last argument against Polus: it does not investigate what punishment is, and here too Socrates may have something very different in mind from anything set out in the dialogue so far. All of this is in line with the suggestion made in the introduction (pages 101–2) that we are moving toward the principle in this part of the dialogue.

On this basis, one can attempt a brief sketch of what these last two arguments might look like in light of Socrates' later account of the good (503d-505b).[17] On this account, a person would be "good" by virtue of an internal order. Such a person would be good-by-nature—and yet surely such a well-ordered person is just the sort who will also tend to be called good-by-convention,[18] and it is not difficult to see how such a person might be considered happier than his opposite (508b1–2). In this sense, "to do wrong" might be to act in a manner that disturbs one's internal order, which could be both shameful (evil-by-convention) and evil (-by-nature), resolving the conflict of the central argument with Polus (although the specific acts covered by the term "to do wrong" might conceivably change somewhat). "Suffering wrong" might also disturb one's internal order, but not of one's own volition, so that "doing wrong is worse than being wronged insofar as it is more shameful" (508b8–c1). But what would it mean to "pay the penalty" (διδῶ δίκην)? Polus has no doubt what he understands by this (473c), but it should now be clear that Socrates' own conception of "paying the penalty" might be quite different. The matter has simply been left open. On Socrates' understanding, "paying the penalty" would have the effect of removing the greatest evil, the disorder of the soul, from a person. Even if this might not be pleasant, will it necessarily involve physical discomfort? Might it rather involve some kind of purely psychological treatment?[19]

This is a speculative account, and it is significant that it is not made explicit in the *Gorgias*. Still, the point is this: while Socrates' own account of "good" (503d–505b) might allow us, in hindsight, to resolve certain difficulties central to the final arguments against Polus, it could also require that we adjust, perhaps substantially, our understanding of which actions exactly are considered unjust, what is involved in paying the penalty, and so on. Socrates has begun a profound rethinking of normative life, one that may only align with a conventional understanding to a partial degree.

The place of Polus' character within the context of the dialogue should be clear enough: he represents a midway point between Gorgias and Callicles, above all because he is less restrained by shame than his teacher, but more so than the character who will follow him. Gorgias took certain moral limits simply to be given. We have seen how this tendency to take things simply as given is continued in Polus: in his rhetorical appeals, in his concern for the opinions of others, in his acknowledgment that some acts are shameful or unjust, in his understanding of the nature of justice, punishment or power—in all these respects, he takes something to be obvious rather than a matter for discussion. However, Polus also presents us with a further development of something that was only hinted at with Gorgias, when he makes clear his admiration for the tyrant Archelaus. In the process we get a hint of something more, namely, what motivates the tyrant to live as he does. It is with Callicles that this latter hint will itself receive further development, as pleasure and the appetites become the focus of the argument.

NOTES

1. Dodds, *Gorgias*, 221, along the same lines: "Polus represents a new generation, less afraid of the consequences of its own thinking than its elders had been."
2. Nicholson, *Plato's Phaedrus*, 39. Socrates will later make the charitable remark that Polus is "clever" (σοφός—487a7), but the purpose there is to place the emphasis on his most significant failing, his shame or lack of frankness.
3. Rutherford, *Art of Plato*, 155, notes that Polus, in using laughter, is following a Gorgianic precept. Rutherford connects this with the theme of frankness. This can agree, in a general way, with my own account: a failure of frankness is said by Socrates to go along with an excess of shame, which (on my account of shame) is a measure of the degree to which one has not thought about the matter at hand, but takes it to be obvious. In similar fashion, the laughter of Polus at 473e2 takes something simply to be obvious.
4. Dodds, *Gorgias*, 11.
5. As Dodds, *Gorgias*, 260, points out.
6. Terence Irwin, "Notes," in *Plato—Gorgias*, trans. and ed. Terence Irwin (New York: Oxford University Press, 1979), 128.
7. Moss, "Shame, Pleasure," 143–44, summarizes the implicit hedonistic aspect of Polus nicely, pointing to the implicit presence of pleasure as the reason for which Polus would admire the life of the tyrant. Note how we thus have a hint of what is to come with Callicles, for pleasure will be treated explicitly and at some length there.
8. See Kahn, "Drama and Dialectic," 87, who tells us that "in the later confrontation with Callicles, Socrates does not provide an independent argument to show that doing is worse than suffering injustice: he describes this thesis as established 'in our previous discussion (*logoi*),' where the conclusion was 'fastened and bound by iron and adamantine arguments (*logoi*)' (508e3–509a). The reference here can only be to [474c–479e]." In fact, there does seem another possibility. From 508a8, Socrates talks about the consequences of "this" argument, the one he has been developing since at least 503d, on the basis of the assumption that pleasure and the good are different (499c). What are the consequences of this argument? "All those earlier things, Callicles" (508b2–4), including the things Polus had been said to admit because of

shame. That is, the claim is not that the argument at 474c–479e has established these things, but rather that the argument since 499c has done so (perhaps by filling in a missing premise in that earlier argument). At 508e6–509e2, then, we hear how "the things that back there in the earlier arguments [i.e., 474c–479e] seemed so . . . are held and bound . . . by steel and adamantine arguments [i.e., by the arguments since 499c]." Socrates can make such strong claims for his arguments because he knows Callicles cannot answer, something to which he draws attention by suggesting the possibility of someone more vigorous than Callicles (509a3).

9. Joseph Patrick Archie, "Callicles' Redoubtable Critique of the Polus Argument in Plato's *Gorgias*," *Hermes* 112, no. 2 (2nd Qtr., 1984): 167–76, has provided the best treatment of this argument that I have read.

10. The mention of pleasure at this point is, of course, altogether appropriate to Polus: recall the suggestion made above that his praise of the tyrant is grounded in the end in pleasure.

11. As Kahn, "Drama and Dialectic," 88, Archie, "Callicles' Redoubtable Critique," 170, fn. 4, and Moss, "Shame, Pleasure," 140–41, fn. 10, have noted.

12. Dodds, *Gorgias*, 249, suggests that "use" or "benefit" (χρεία, ὠφελία—474d-e) could imply use or benefit *for the community*, which would mean that this second, conventional meaning of "good" has been ambiguously present even before Polus introduced the word "good" (475a3). One need not agree with Dodds to accept what I think is the crucial point, that "good," a concept crucial to the argument, is left undefined.

13. Kahn, "Drama and Dialectic," 95. Curtis Johnson, "Socrates' Encounter with Polus in Plato's *Gorgias*," *Phoenix* 43, no. 3 (Autumn 1989): 201–7, disagrees with this, presenting a view according to which Polus' true view would be entirely on the side of the tyrant. He does this, however, by focusing on Callicles' talk of shame, which, while correct, is not *simply* correct. The whole point with Polus is that he has not thought things through as thoroughly as Johnson.

14. Irwin, "Notes," 159.

15. Socrates does at least begin with the hope that Polus will set him straight if he has stumbled (461c-d).

16. Kevin McTighe, "Socrates on Desire for the Good and the Involuntariness of Wrongdoing: *Gorgias* 466a-468e," *Phronesis* 29, no. 3 (1984): 221–28, suggests that we find in the argument and example of the purgative dialectic discussed in the *Sophist* (230a–231b). See also Roslyn Weiss, "Killing, Confiscating and Banishing at *Gorgias* 466–8," *Ancient Philosophy* 12 (1992): 302–3: "Socrates' manner of speaking is exaggerated and extreme: he chooses . . . the more shocking rather than the more sober way of refuting Polus' views."

17. We will consider 503d–505b itself in a bit more detail on page 157.

18. See *Republic* 442e–443a, where, after the order of the soul has been investigated at much greater length than in the *Gorgias*, it is decided that this order will produce conventionally just behavior.

19. It is not clear to me that the matter is resolved in the *Gorgias*.

(3) Callicles

The movement that has been taking shape beginning with Gorgias, and continuing with Polus, reaches its climax with Callicles. One might have thought, then, that whereas the two earlier characters were defined by the contradictions that we saw running through them, Callicles might represent a more stable and adequate position. Certainly, there is something new in his ability to grasp the preceding argument in terms of certain principles that governed it, but it is not at all clear that he is more consistent than his predecessors. The argument to 499c is an investigation of his position, one that ends with the conclusion that Callicles is in fact deeply committed to two irreconcilable ideas.

This part of the dialogue has three main sections. First, there is an introduction, in which Callicles makes the initial statement of his position, and Socrates sets out his hopes for the argument to follow (481b–488a). Next, Socrates tries to find the principle underlying Callicles' initial statement, revealing, in the process, its two-sided nature (488b–494e). Finally, the tensions are shown to lead to a contradiction, refuting Callicles (495a–499b).

OPENING REMARKS (481B6–488B1)

After a preliminary exchange between Socrates and Callicles (481b6–482c3), we come to what will henceforth be called Callicles' "initial statement" (i.e., 482c4–486d1). This has four sections: the first (482c4–483c7) reviews the argument so far; the second (483a7–484c3), and third (484c4–485e2) set out Callicles' position proper; while the fourth (485e3–486d1) turns to a practical matter, the possible fate of Socrates.

In the first section, Callicles reviews the argument so far, and this can profitably be taken as a hint from Plato that we should reflect on the context within which Callicles is being presented: he represents the third and final moment of a larger movement that began with Gorgias, the culmination of the single force[1] running through the dialogue. We noted in the introduction how the initial complacency of Gorgias is implicitly called into question by Polus and then by Callicles, producing two subordinate questions concerning the basis of Gorgias' normative claims. First, why should we act in accordance with ethical obligations if doing so conflicts with our interests? Second, what gives any credibility at all to claims about what the just and unjust, the shameful and the noble, are?

We are now in a position to appreciate that an additional aspect has come to light. Polus focuses our attention upon definite and indubitable facts when he speaks of the power of the tyrant (471a–d) or in the torments suffered by his victim (473c). Next to this focus on the actual, Gorgias' mere assertions of "one ought" (456c6–457c3) must seem empty indeed.[2] A position that can make clear its basis in reality occupies a position of immense strength in comparison to a series of pious ought-to-be's that provide no benefit at all. Whatever one might believe Socrates to have established against Polus, his arguments have certainly failed to address this consideration directly. Why would anyone choose to be logically consistent if the price of this is to be burned in pitch (etc.—see 473c)?

Understood in this context, it seems that Callicles is dissatisfied with Polus for having focused with insufficient rigor on the realities of everyday life. Callicles can point—accurately, as we have seen—to the principles that determined the argument against Polus, νόμος (convention), and φύσις (nature—482e–483a). It soon becomes clear that "convention" must refer here to the basis of a set of beliefs. That is, laws, or notions in general of how one ought to act, are, on this view, a creation of a group of individuals (483b4–7), a series of mutual agreements. From such agreements we should distinguish the objective order of the natural world, according to which lions, for example, always hunt down and eat lambs while lambs never hunt and eat lions. In hindsight, we see that the argument with Polus has already drawn out a *practical* problem with conventional beliefs: apart from the will and ability of people to enforce them, they have no power to affect the world. But as Callicles makes the difference between convention and nature explicit, another problem comes into view. If one were to ask, "do lions eat lambs, or the reverse?" the answer would have a basis in an objective order of the world, one in no way dependent upon the wishes or decisions of people anywhere. But if one accepts a conventionalist account, with any question of what one ought to do, one is conscious precisely of the fact that the answer is *not* grounded in an objective order. Instead, there are only agreed-upon opinions, which could be changed at any moment if the appropriate people so chose.[3]

Thus, from the perspective of Callicles' νόμος/φύσις distinction, we can now see the full force of the second problem with Gorgias' assumed moral standards: what makes these imperatives believable in the first place? How are they not mere "papers, trickery and spells?" (γράμματα καὶ μαγγανεύματα καὶ ἐπῳδὰς—484a4–5) Even if they were shown to be not altogether at odds with our interests, what gives them any credibility at all? Surely appealing to them amounts to "enchanting and bewitching" (483e6) one's audience, as opposed to presenting reasoned arguments with a foundation in reality.

Because he is fully conscious of the distinction between νόμος and φύσις, as Polus was not, Callicles thinks he can avoid the confusion of nature and convention that confounded his predecessor, and also avoid the problems concerning interest and credibility. By founding his views only upon nature, he might hope to attain consistently—and therefore unassailably—the argumentative strength that Polus was beginning to achieve, that is, a strict basis in the concerns of everyday life. We thus have a continuation and deepening of a theme that runs through the dialogue so far.

The question is how exactly Callicles' views will be grounded in nature. Somehow, the natural world should suffice to provide a basis from which he can derive everything he wants to say about justice and injustice, the shameful and noble, the better and the worse, and thus the question to which he turns the dialogue, what sort of life one should live. But are these matters to be resolved by appeals to an order of nature in the same straightforward manner as in the case of the question of whether lions hunt lambs? As Callicles makes his initial statement, it is not yet clear how this might be possible.

Callicles' position is set out in the middle two sections of his initial statement, and it is to these that we must now turn. The second section (483a7–484c3) is unproblematic as regards the relation of justice and injustice to the order of the natural world. Here, he gives an account of various normative expressions in purely descriptive terms. For example, he does not say that a (real) man *ought* not to allow himself to be wronged, or that this is not fitting or proper; rather, he says that this *is* not the experience characteristic of a (real) man (483a8–b1). "The just" is not defined with the claim that the strong *ought* to rule the weak, but rather with the fact that they *do* (483d1–6). We also have the explicit claim that "nature herself shows" (φύσις αὐτὴ ἀποφαίνει—483c9) what the just is, suggesting that facts evident in the natural world are sufficient to establish his conception of justice. Note also that the next (third) section begins with the phrase, "well that's how things are" (Τὸ μὲν οὖν ἀληθὲς οὕτως ἔχει—484c4), as though what has preceded is a straightforward description of reality. Callicles can claim, at this point, to be appealing in an unambiguous manner to an objective order of things; anything he might say from this standpoint about the just and the unjust, about how we ought to live, would not merely be laid down as an assertion, but would rather claim a basis in reality. Thus he can speak about "the nature of justice" (φύσιν τὴν τοῦ δικαίου—483e2) since justice appears here as something real, that has a nature, and not something that might change from one moment to the next because people changed their minds. His account so far would seem to be strictly on the side of nature (φύσις) as opposed to mere convention (νόμος). Later, when the argument reaches pleasure and appetite (491e–492c), we find the most fundamental ground of this perspective. That is, if we inquire as to the reason one might rather be a tyrant than burned in pitch, there is an indubitably real basis within the individual for such a wish: pleasure. This reality provides the hope for Callicles of founding all action in facts as opposed to arbitrary imaginings.

However even within Callicles' initial statement of his own position, it is difficult to see how everything he says might be derived from the realities of nature. In the next (third) section of his speech (484c4–485e2) we suddenly find ourselves awash in words that express how things *ought* to be: δέω ("one ought"—484c7), χρή ("one ought"—d1), προσήκει ("it is fitting"—485b3), πρέπον ("fitting"—485b5, c4), ἀξιόω ("to be worthy"—c7). Unlike in the preceding section, here it is not clear how Callicles' use of each of these words is to be derived from an objective order, nor is it clear that such a derivation is possible. So, for example, he says that philosophy is a delightful thing at the right time of life, but if one spends more time at it than one ought, it is a man's destruction (484c7). Callicles does explain how philosophy can contribute to one's destruction (484c8–e7): it can take precious time away from the pursuits Callicles thinks important (although even here, why one should value these things is not made explicit); Socrates' own demise would no doubt provide an example of the sort of harm philosophy can do in the worst case. But how is philosophy a "lovely thing" (χαρίεν—484c6) at an earlier time of life, how is it "noble" (καλόν—485a5), how could it be "fitting" (πρέπειν—485c4), and why would Callicles admire it (ἄγαμαι—c4) or think that anyone, ever, is illiberal (ἀνελεύθερος—c6) because he does not philosophize?

When we look to the example Callicles uses in explaining the positive value of philosophy—children who do or do not mumble (485b–c)—the difficulty deepens. "The implication," we are told, "seems to be that slave-children exhibited an enforced precocity as a result of being set to work very young, whereas for a child to continue mumbling was [worthy of a free person], since it showed that his parents could afford not to force him."[4] That is, the emphasis is precisely not on the innate qualities of the child in question, but rather on his upbringing, on his conventional standing within society. Surely Archelaus the tyrant (471a–d) would be a perfect exemplar of a strong nature that tramples on all opposing charms and incantations, and thus rises to be master (as Callicles describes it at 484a). Archelaus, however, is the son of a slave (471a5–6): he would not have mumbled as

Callicles would like—nor would he have practiced philosophy at the appropriate time of life.

There is thus reason to believe that Callicles remains very much in the grip of convention, for all his trumpeting of the virtues of nature. Accordingly, when he refers to the ideal of a gentleman of good reputation (καλός κἀγαθός καὶ εὐδόκιμος—484d1-2), one with the proper experience of the laws of the city and human custom (d2-7), it is an open question whether we are to interpret this as an expression of the natural virtues Callicles endorsed at the start, or as a straightforward appeal to conventional understanding. Is he really going to be able to explain everything said in his main statement from the brute facts of nature?

Strictly speaking, we do not have an answer to this implicit problem until 494e, but Callicles' initial statement points to what will from now on be called his "realist" and "aristocratic" sides.[5] The former contains all that can be derived from an objective order of nature, such as we find at 483a7-484c3, and is "realist" by virtue of this derivation. The "aristocratic" side would contain all that Callicles believes that can*not* be derived from natural reality. One might try to understand the word "aristocratic" in a natural sense—that is, aristocrats would be those who, if the natural order of things were allowed to play out without the interference of artificial conventional agreements, would naturally rise to top place, perhaps because of their superior strength and ability. However, if there does turn out to be anything that Callicles believes that is not derived from an objective natural order, we can appeal to another sense of the word: aristocrats are, in an important sense, those *most* in the hold of convention, for they have the best manners, and are acutely sensitive, as the lower classes are not, to social cues that demonstrate education and upbringing—precisely the consideration which seems to govern the third section of Callicles' speech (i.e., 484c4-485e2). From this perspective, Archelaus, for all his natural strength, could never be more than a *novus homo*.

This is not the place to take up the final section of Callicles' initial statement (485e3-486d1), for the practical problem that it brings to light concerning Socrates' life does not receive any attention until after 499c, which is the beginning of the Socratic account that will culminate (at 521a-522e) in Socrates' defense of his own life; we are at present concerned only with the argument to 499c.

FINDING THE PRINCIPLE IN CALLICLES (488B-494E)

Before Callicles can be refuted, one must be clear on what exactly he believes. We have seen that it is very much a question of whether his initial statement presents a coherent position, so Socrates' questioning now aims to discover what exactly this position is. In particular, we have already seen that there is a question about whether everything that Callicles wants to say really can be derived from the order of nature. If not, perhaps Callicles will prove to be most fundamentally interested in the seemly world of the gentleman of good repute. As we shall see, to clarify Callicles' views is tantamount to refuting him; the actual refutation that follows simply requires that Socrates apply the contradiction he has found in Callicles' most fundamental beliefs.

The question of the principle behind Callicles is what unifies this section of the text.[6] There are three steps to the argument here. Step (a), running from 488b2–489b6, pursues the idea of grounding moral precepts in reality as opposed to mere agreements; this takes up the corresponding section of Callicles' speech (i.e., 483a7–484c3). Step (b), from 489b7–491a6, focuses on the subsequent section of Callicles' speech (i.e., 484c4–485e2), which made a series of claims concerning how things ought to be, claims that were not obviously derivable from facts. Step (c), at 491a7–494e8, turns again toward the realist side, bringing to light pleasure as the principle underlying much that has been said so far, and testing whether or not Callicles will hold consistently to it.

It is important to be quite clear that on the account given here, the argument of this section concerns only Callicles and his position. Doctrines such as hedonism or the law of nature enter the argument only insofar as they are relevant to this focus, so that Plato only engages with these doctrines in the particular form in which they appear in Callicles. Accordingly, we do not find here, for example, The Platonic Refutation of Hedonism—although that is not to say that we learn nothing relevant to a consideration of this and other matters.

The Good as the Stronger (488b2–489b6)

Socrates begins by focusing on the realist side of Callicles, specifically on the idea of grounding things in readily observable facts. How do we determine who exactly is favored according to the law of nature? This question is what drives Socrates' questioning (488b3–d3) concerning the relation of the words κρείττων ("superior"), βελτίων ("better"), ἀμείνων ("better," or perhaps "nobler" or "abler" in context) and ἰσχυρότερος ("stronger").

Here, the argument investigates the possibility that "stronger" determines "better"—that is, people would be "better" (and thus deserve more) because they are "superior," where "superior" means "stronger" (note the order in which Socrates connects these at 488b8–c7). The idea behind this is the one set forth in Callicles' initial statement (at 483a7–484c3), when he suggested that his idea of justice by nature (τὸ δίκαιον ... κατὰ φύσιν, as Socrates puts it at 488b2–3, cf. 483e2) had a straightforward basis in an objective order: in nature it is clear who is stronger because one can see them actually prevailing. Accordingly, the argument now puts this idea in the spotlight, applying it to people: the stronger sort of people would be those who actually prevail, and it is this that underwrites the normative claim that they are "better," and thus "deserving" of more (insofar as it is possible to speak of a normative claim at all in this context).[7]

To say this is to eliminate any difference between what ought to happen, and what actually does happen. On this view, the fact that the multitude does in fact establish laws over every individual, then, makes the multitude superior to, and therefore better than, any one man, however strong he might be on his own. Accordingly, their laws acquire the same justification as Callicles' "law of nature" (483e3). That is, an appeal to reality might in some cases show us the stronger sort of individual having more than the weaker, but it also shows that the view "that it is just to have the same amount and it is more shameful to do wrong than to be wronged" (488e8–489a1) is itself a substantial reality, actually enforced in real places. Now, if Callicles were most fundamentally concerned with founding his position in the facts of nature, he could simply rest with the results of the argument at this point, and discard all that conflicts with it. That he does not do this shows that his views are not so simple as a straightforward deduction from observable realities.

One could respond that Callicles means to appeal to an order of nature in a rather different way, believing that the stronger sort of people are those who *would* be on top *if* we would just stop obstructing the natural order with our conventions; it is in this sense that the comparison to animals (etc.) should be understood, since animals are never obstructed by convention. To do this, however, would be to abandon Callicles' pretense that he is simply basing his account on what is in fact the case. Instead, he would be setting up his own view of the way things *ought* to be. The argument will now proceed to deal with a consideration of this very sort.

The Good as the More Intelligent (489b7–491d3)

The second step of the argument investigates the possibility that "better" might be prior to "superior." That is, people would be "better" in some way, and on that basis, could be called "superior." We could accordingly recognize them as people who *ought* to have the top place even if they do not yet have it. This develops the aristocratic side of Callicles, as he himself emphasizes with a particularly heavy-handed statement of his view that not all people are equal—"a rabble of slaves and of every sort of person worth nothing except as regards bodily strength" (489c3–4). As in the second part of his initial statement (484c4–485e2), the move to the aristocratic side brings a proliferation of language that emphasizes that Callicles' position must now be understood to express what *ought* to be rather than what simply *is* (δεῖ—490a2, c2, d7, d11, e2, e7, προσήκει—491d1; ἄξιος at 489c5 takes up ἀξιόω at 485c7).[8]

In the first step, the question was simply who the better sort of person might be. In this second step, things have become a bit more complicated. Socrates begins by suggesting (1) that the "prudent" (φρονῶν—490a1) are the better sort, but then continues on to say (2) that the wise ought to rule (ἄρχειν δεῖ—a2), and further (3) that they ought to have more (πλέον ἔχειν—a3). That is, we are now concerned with three questions, who is better, who should rule, and what they should get as a result. All three of Socrates' suggested answers come from Callicles' initial statement.[9]

The move to this composite statement is explained by the move from a claim concerning what simply *is* to a claim about what *ought* to be: questions concerning who should rule and what they should get thereby only come up when we turn to what ought to be. Socrates naturally does not dispute the claim that those with some sort of intellectual virtue, here called "prudence," are the better sort of person and should rule. Instead, he focuses on the matter of having more.

The argument soon takes a strange turn: Socrates makes a series of absurd suggestions, that doctors should get more food and drink, cobblers more shoes, weavers more cloaks, and so on (490b–e). The idea in each case is that "the person who is more intelligent with respect to a particular sort of thing should have more of that sort of thing."[10] It would be difficult to defend all this as an attempt to discover or elucidate the views of Callicles. On the contrary, Socrates seems simply to be foisting absurdities on Callicles, to be ridiculing rather than engaging with his opponent here.[11]

However, there is a method to Socrates' apparent madness here, and in two different ways. First of all, the passage needs to be considered in the context of a broader view, one that encompasses the whole dialogue. Socrates has chosen to interpret "prudence" in terms of skills, and skills are a recurring theme in the *Gorgias*. In the next chapter, we shall consider the passage in which this theme culminates (517b–519a), and we shall see that it contains implicit connections to Socrates' apparent absurdities here, and helps to explain them. In particular, it will become clear how it is reasonable for Socrates to bring skills to bear in the current passage: it gives him a basis—a basis in familiar facts—with which he can answer the latter two questions we noted above, that is, who should rule and what they should get for ruling. The reason that those with the appropriate intellectual distinction[12] should rule is clarified at 517b–519a, and what they get is a properly ordered, and thus good, result. For example, the medical art is a sort of rule of the body, and properly aims at the healthy order of the body. Indeed, it is a fact familiar to everyone that doctors prescribe according to the case at hand (see 505a), so that the prudence of the doctor does not lead to having more, but rather to having an amount appropriate to his own body. Socrates, in suggesting that a doctor will consume more than some people and less than others so as to avoid damaging himself (491c), is pointing to a *reality* (and is thus engaging with Callicles' realist side). From this perspective, the idea that a ruler would take more for himself is absurd. Talk of the doctor gorging himself or the cobbler getting the most shoes is a powerful piece of absurdity precisely because of its difference from what everyone knows to be the case. There is a hint here, then, of the case that Socrates will develop in response to Callicles.

Secondly, in a narrower context, Socrates' examples serve as a fruitful provocation of Callicles' aristocratic side: the talk is of cobblers, doctors, farmers and weavers, people who must gain their living by their labor, and who thus lack the status that Callicles' ideal man must enjoy.[13] Later on, the dialogue will touch explicitly on Callicles' contempt for those who do manual work, and how he would not want to be related by marriage to such people (512c3–7). Here, Socrates' examples, provocative not only in their importation of the lower classes into Callicles' account but also in their inherent absurdity, serve to drive Callicles more deeply into his aristocratic side: he now makes an active attempt to explain just what makes his preferred sort of person better.[14] The result is a new composite statement: the better sort of people are prudent with respect to the affairs of the city *and* brave *and* capable of accomplishing what they intend *and* not inclined to hold back on account of being too soft (491b1–4).[15] The scope of "prudence" has now been limited to a political occupation appropriate to the upper classes, so that we have here a list of *virtues*, qualities in which one might take pride—indeed, about which one might be inclined to boast.[16] That is, Callicles has felt compelled to assert that aspect of his position by which it seems an admirable and worthy thing, a fuller statement of what *ought* to be.

The first section of the argument ended with the result that Callicles' pretense to be basing his position simply in readily observable realities was too simple: clearly his views force us to talk in terms of the way things ought to be. The second section, however, has produced a different sort of conclusion: far from forcing any kind of rejection of Callicles' aristocratic side, it has produced a deepening and intensification of that side. The result is an appreciation of just how much Callicles is concerned with what ought to be rather than what is, and of the degree to which he is intent on the worthiness, the dignity and superior status of his ideal sort of person. On the basis of the argument so far, then, it would seem that the aristocratic side of Callicles is more important to him than the realist side. The question for the next section will be whether he will hold consistently to this tendency or not.

Socrates' brief statement to the effect that Callicles never says the same thing (491b5–c5) is an indication that we are moving to a new step in the argument. Although Socrates focused on part (3) of the position he suggested—that is, the matter of having more—Callicles has disagreed with part (1), the notion that the prudent are the better sort of people. Callicles began by agreeing that the more prudent are the better *simpliciter* (489e8), but ended by saying instead that only those who are prudent with respect to political affairs are the better people—and further, that several other virtues are required (491b1–4). The position considered at the start of this section has thus been abandoned.

Pleasure and the Appetites (491d4–494e8)

In response to Callicles' new attempt to define those for whom it is fitting to rule and have more—those who are prudent-in-respect-to-the-city and brave—Socrates does not try to refute the new position by means of an investigation of bravery. It is assumed from this point that Callicles has adequately indicated who he thinks the better people are: Socrates will not contest this combination of virtues but will return to them once he has finished clarifying Callicles' position, taking them as a basis for two arguments. First he will speak of knowledge and bravery (ἐπιστήμη and ἀνδρεία—495c6–7), and the final argument against pleasure will proceed in relation to the prudent (φρόνιμοι—497e4–5) and the brave.[17]

Having satisfied himself on the matter of who Callicles' superior people are, Socrates now turns to the second of the three matters suggested in the preceding section, the question concerning ruling (the third was the question of one's reward for ruling, which Callicles took to be having more; that will be addressed here as well). Callicles took ruling to be a fairly straightforward matter: it describes a relationship between people, and of course he believes his superior people should rule. However, in the *Gorgias*, the question of how exactly we think about ruling (ἄρχειν) will prove to be an important one. Here the theme takes a crucial turn as Socrates introduces the notion of *self*-rule (491d4–9), a move that drives the argument toward the internal, psychological motivation behind Callicles' position.[18]

Callicles is at first bewildered (491d5, 7, 10), but the talk of self-rule and moderation (as well, no doubt, as the provocations of the preceding section, and his frustration at not holding his own so far) quickly drives him into his final attempt to set out his position at length (491e5–492c8). Plato has taken care to emphasize that this final attempt is remarkable in particular for its *frankness*: Callicles remarks on just how frank he is being (παρρησιαζόμενος—491e7–8), and Socrates not only confirms this remark (παρρησιαζόμενος—492d2), but also continues with a reminder of how this frankness connects to the purpose of the argument (as he did at 487a–488a): because Callicles is saying what others think but won't say, it might become clear how we should live (492d2–5). Callicles is also now saying what he himself thinks, but has not yet been willing to emphasize or say: we are getting to the heart of the matter (or to *a* heart of the matter, as we shall see).

Callicles rejects the idea of self-rule in no uncertain terms: "how could anyone be happy while a slave to anything?" (e5–6) That is, the idea at work here is of an absolute liberation, a sort of pure freedom from constraints, even from *self*-restraint.[19] As he continues, it becomes clear that his account has a new focus: the fulfillment of appetites (ἐπιθυμίαι—491e9, 492a2–3), with particular mention being made of pleasure (ἡδονή—492a8). Of these two factors, pleasure is the more fundamental, for it is for the sake of pleasure that people want to fulfill their various appetites. Pleasure also provides a ground for Callicles' concern with bravery and intelligence: they provide the means by which one has the ability to minister to the appetites (492a1–2). Certainly pleasure and the appetites were mentioned in Callicles' initial statement (484d5), but their significance has changed since then: by bringing Callicles to the point where he is provoked into speaking so frankly, the argument has brought out pleasure as a fundamental foundation of his position, the principle from which many other elements can be derived.[20] This view represents a profound challenge to the philosophical life of Socrates; to the extent that Callicles holds to it, the dialogue will become a rigorous and genuinely philosophical investigation of a matter of principle.[21]

Pleasure is significant in another regard. When Callicles describes how the inability of the multitude leads them to praise justice and moderation, and when he then asks rhetorical questions about tyrants and kings (492a3–c3), he not only reveals pleasure to be the ultimate foundation on which his account of justice is developed—after all, it is the inability (and cowardice—492b1) of the multitude to fulfill their appetites that leads them to enslave those better by nature and to praise (conventional) justice and moderation (492a3–b1)—he also assumes pleasure to be the universal human end. That is, he takes it as obvious to everyone that pleasure is the ultimate reason that we act. When we recall his earlier implicit attempt to derive his account from facts, as opposed to chimerical claims of what merely ought to be, the universality of pleasure takes on further significance: it is unquestionably real. Both the appetites and the pleasure that they promise are facts, indubitably present to each individual, just as much as, or even more than, the facts of history or the animal kingdom that Callicles alluded to before (at 483d–e).

By 492d, then, the argument has shown Callicles to be deeply attached to two different things. On the one hand, the preceding section produced a renewed emphasis on the ideal, that is, on the virtues one ought to strive for to become the better sort of person, and on the worthiness and dignity appropriate to this ideal figure. On the other hand, his frank speaking has brought pleasure to light as the ground of his position. The question on which all shall now turn, and on which Callicles will ultimately founder, is this: how do these two sides relate? Certainly, bravery and intelligence *could* be grounded in pleasure, as Callicles has already suggested. That is, the reason that one would want to be brave and intelligent, and to focus one's activity on the city rather than on shoemaking or weaving, would be in order to better indulge one's appetites, and attain the most pleasure possible.[22] But is Callicles really prepared to follow this view to its logical conclusion?

This question explains the peculiar turn that the discussion now takes. From 488b to 491a Socrates has used arguments to analyze Callicles' position, but from 492e–494e, we have a series of images, the purpose of which is to suggest with increasing intensity the inadequacy and lack of dignity in the appetitive life. If Callicles will hold consistently to pleasure in the face of all the indignities that Socrates suggests here, if there really is no line he won't cross, then pleasure alone will constitute the foundation of Callicles' position. This would mean that his realist side, the side derived from the facts of nature, would turn out to be Callicles' true position. The aristocratic side, of course, consists of everything that can*not* be derived from facts of nature. If Callicles turns out to be inconsistent in his adherence to pleasure in a manner that does not appeal to other facts of nature, it will prove the fundamental incoherence of his position—that is, he will be shown to be wholeheartedly attached to two different types of commitment, convention and nature, and it was his claim from the start that these were generally opposed to one another (482e5–483a8). In this case, all Socrates needs to do to refute Callicles is to repeat the sort of performance Callicles complained about, playing convention against nature.

Socrates begins with an image that focuses on the futility of the appetitive life, comparing it to having to carry water in a sieve to a leaky jar, the sieve being the soul itself (493a–c). No end is ever actually attained; the means are hopelessly inadequate to their task, with the result that there can be no rest from unceasing toil. The next image, focusing on jars (493d–494a), retains this result, but now compares it to another possibility, that of the temperate life, which promises a limit to the work of filling the jars. Callicles is undaunted by the prospect of this extra work, for he locates pleasure in the flowing itself, so that the temperate man lacks it once he has filled his jars. One wants as great a flow as possible.

With such an aim in mind, it is easy to produce images that aim directly at conventional notions of a dignified life. "If much flows in," says Socrates, "much must also flow out, and the opening for the out flow must be great." (494b3–4) If this is so, must the appetitive life not be the same in principle as that of a χαραδριός? ("a bird of messy habits and uncertain identity,"[23] apparently known for excreting as soon as it eats.) What about the life of someone forever scratching an itch? Scratching his head only? What about the life of a catamite?

(3) Callicles 149

At this point Callicles can go no further, and declares Socrates' questioning shameful (494e7–8). In doing so, Callicles proves that the side of him that spoke of a "gentleman of good reputation" (484d1–2) *always* exerts its own pull on him: it can even overrule pleasure, which, we now see, underwrites only a certain portion of what he believes. Pleasure is therefore not *the* principle of his position, but rather *a* principle of his position. There are two sides to him, and they pull ultimately in different directions. Far from having resolved the tension between convention and nature, he is every bit as caught in and defined by this tension as Polus was, even if on somewhat different terms.

The most important consequence of this move was set out earlier (pages 108–110): because Callicles has given in to shame—indeed, he has actively brought it forth of his own account—he cannot be an adequate touchstone for Socrates, and the argument cannot have "the end consisting in truth" (487e7). Instead, Socrates will be able to use merely *ad hominem* arguments, and the conversation will fail to investigate the nature of crucial subject matters, such as justice, power and punishment.

Callicles' expression of shame is also a turning point as regards his own activity: from this moment, he effectively retreats from the argument. He begins to qualify his answers as he did not before, making his reluctance to participate all too evident—for example, his next answer begins with the proviso, "in order that my account is not inconsistent" (495a5). Soon Gorgias must intervene, twice, to keep him in the conversation (497a–c, 505c–506c), and for a time (505c–509c), Callicles leaves Socrates to carry on the dialogue on his own for a bit. His uninterested responses (see, for example, 510a1, 513e1, 516b4) continue right up to his final words (522e7–8), and at the very end, Socrates makes clear that he understands that Callicles is not convinced (527e5–7).[24] We see nothing more of the man who boldly entered the conversation, and tried to determine its result. It is altogether natural that the change should come right after his admission of shame: once it is clear that Callicles is firmly attached to two incompatible considerations, the game is up. At the moment Callicles expresses shame, and thus falls short of the frankness that Socrates demands, he fails to be a touchstone, and also ceases actively to challenge Socrates in an argument.

The three steps of the argument to 494e, then, show us that Callicles is both the smasher of conventions and one scrupulously concerned with them. The end of action for Callicles is pleasure—and yet so is the ideal of a gentleman, who shuns any association with tradesmen, and worries about accents and the appropriate time of life for philosophy. Thus, the argument has shown that Callicles does not fundamentally differ from Gorgias or Polus: he is defined by a commitment to two conflicting ideas. If he is willing to go farther in the direction of liberation from convention than his two predecessors, still he has failed to resolve the tension between his aristocratic and realist sides.

(3) Callicles

The result is that Socrates can now pursue the very strategy that Callicles complained of in the beginning (483a2–4): he can play convention and nature against one another so as to produce a contradiction. In the two arguments that follow (to 499c), this will take the form of the two Calliclean virtues of prudence and bravery on the one hand, and the Calliclean end of pleasure on the other. As our aim here is to develop Plato's characterization of Socrates' opponents, we need not investigate these arguments here, but one point should be made clear: the principle on the basis of which the rest of the dialogue will proceed—that is, that pleasure is not the good—is established in a merely *ad hominem* fashion. This means that the *Gorgias* provides a *provisional* investigation and treatment of its content; little or nothing can in the end be counted as simply proved.

NOTES

1. See Dodds, *Gorgias*, 5.
2. Before Polus, there were anticipations of his focus on what is real, for example when Gorgias was focused on the power of rhetoric, on its ability to have its way even against experts in their own fields. Of course, "real" in this context is "what Gorgias, Polus and Callicles take to be real," that is, reality as it is understood in everyday life.
3. One might argue, and provide a variety of accounts, about what the basis is of conventional beliefs. Within the context of the dialogue so far, however, the answer would seem to be *nothing*: Gorgias provided no reason at all for his beliefs, and Polus similarly failed to be clear about his beliefs' basis in this sense. Socrates has provided arguments that might be taken to touch on this matter, but they have been merely *ad hominem*. The dialogue so far has brought out convention as what is simply given, that is, grasped in an unreflective manner. It is also worth noting that Plato does not seem to be interested here in the notion that the content of conventional behavior varies from one group to another. The text treats convention as if it has a definite content—e.g., Callicles will say simply that by convention (νόμῳ—483a8) it is more shameful to do wrong than to suffer it.
4. Dodds, *Gorgias*, 274.
5. In finding two sides to Callicles, I am following Raphael Woolf, "Callicles and Socrates." He speaks of "Callicles 1" and "Callicles 2;" these are equivalent to my "realist" and "aristocratic" Callicles. Here and in what follows I am trying further to develop his account of Callicles. See his paper for further support for this line of thought. Note in particular his suggestion (pp. 4–5) that through Socrates' words at 481c–482c, which discuss internal contradiction and immediately precede Callicles opening statement, "we have been primed to go through Callicles' speech with the likelihood of his self-contradiction at the forefront of our minds, so that if the text seems to reveal an inconsistent position on his part, we have been given a large authorial hint to accept it as such."

(3) Callicles 151

6. Woolf, "Callicles and Socrates," 7–8, has already suggested in a more general way how it is possible to make sense of this portion of the text in light of the two sides of Callicles.

7. Note how the opposite possibility—that the superior and better might be weaker and more wretched, which would require a non-factual basis for "better"—is explicitly passed by at 488c7–8.

8. Cooper, "Socrates and Plato," 53, fn. 33, is incorrect to assert that Callicles' first use of the word προσήκει comes after "instruction" from Socrates. In fact, he used the word before, at 485b3, and Socrates, in using similar language of what "ought" to happen, is showing his characteristic precision in this dialogue in directing his inquiry at exactly what the other characters have said. Cooper does point to a use of δεῖ by Socrates (488c2) in the preceding section of the argument (488b2–489b6), in which (on my view) the focus is the realist Callicles, but notice how Socrates qualifies this with οἷόν μοι δοκεῖς . . . ἐνδείκνυσθαι ("the sort of thing you seem to me to indicate"—488c3–4)—that is, the δεῖ is explicitly a Socratic development of Callicles' realist side.

9. That is, Callicles' talk of being prudent (φρονεῖν—486c6) is taken up by Socrates at 489e8 and 490a1; Callicles was also concerned with ruling (ἄρχειν—483d5; Socrates: 490a2) and having more (πλέον ἔχειν—483c2–5, c8, d1, d6; Socrates: 490a3). Callicles' interest in an intellectual, as opposed to physical, form of superiority was also suggested when he spoke of "experience" (see ἔμπειρος—484d1; also ἄπειρος—484c9, d3, d6) in a manner that suggested it was a mark of the better sort of person.

10. Jyl Gentzler, "The Sophistic Cross-Examination of Callicles in the *Gorgias*," *Ancient Philosophy* 15 (1999): 34.

11. See Gentzler, "Sophistic Cross-Examination," 34, who also notes how Socrates at 490d demands yes/no answers at moments when this seems unreasonable.

12. For Callicles, these are the prudent (φρονῶν); in the end, Socrates will speak of knowing (εἰδέναι–517e7).

13. Dodds, *Gorgias*, 290, notes how Callicles "does not like to have the ἀμείνους [better] compared to anything so low." See also Dodds, *Gorgias*, 349, on the contempt felt by upper-class Greeks for the laboring occupations; "the stigma attended in practice even to what we now call liberal professions"—that is, it would apply also to doctors.

14. Note that near the beginning of this section, Callicles explained who the βελτίους ("better") are simply by saying that they are ἀμείνους ("better"—489e5), presumably having previously taken it to be obvious. This brought things to a bit of an impasse, so that the formulation that the prudent should rule and have more came from Socrates rather than Callicles.

15. Note that all of these elements were present in his initial statement. Callicles' talk of ruling cities (491d1) recalls Gorgias' talk of ruling others (452d7), as well as his references to various particular affairs of the city (452d–e, 455d–456c): once again, what we find in Callicles existed *in posse* earlier in the movement.

16. We are presumably to read "capable" and "not-too-soft" as glosses on "brave," for at 491c6–d3 Callicles restates his new position simply in terms of prudence and

bravery. The argument here, by focusing on a particular kind of ruling, takes a turn similar to what we find in the *Republic*, where Thrasymachus responds to Socrates' use of the skill-analogy with a focus on ruling as a unique or unusual kind of skill (343b–c): in both cases, a turn is made toward a special version of the phenomenon in question.

17. It should also be clear that Callicles' new definition does *not* free him from the first step in the argument, that is, the one in which it was shown that, because the multitude is stronger than any individual, Callicles' position must involve talk of how the world *ought* to be, and cannot claim a basis in nature in the manner that he had at first suggested (this is driven home by Callicles' use of the word προσήκει at 491d1). After all, on Callicles' initial account, the multitude often succeeds in scaring the better sort of man (484b4–c6), so that in these cases the multitude will be braver as well as stronger, giving their edicts the same basis in nature as Callicles claims.

18. We shall see in the next chapter how ruling (ἄρχειν) proves to be the crucial concept in Socrates final schema of skills (517b–519a), a further development of an idea Callicles had taken to be simple and self-evident.

19. Nicholas P. White, "Rational Prudence in Plato's *Gorgias*," in *Platonic Investigations*, ed. Dominic O'Meara (Washington, DC: The Catholic University of America Press, 1985), 140, is quite right to note that Callicles "rejects any and all forms of temperance." Similarly, George Klosko, "The Refutation of Callicles in Plato's *Gorgias*," *Greece & Rome* 31, Second Series, no. 2 (Oct. 1984): 128.

20. At 494a Callicles will reject Socrates' orderly and temperate life on the ground that it does not involve pleasure, which again suggests the centrality of pleasure to his view of things. Irwin. "Notes," 196, notes that "this view requires pleasure to be at least the predominant component of happiness, that is, no other combination of components must ever outweigh the value of pleasure."

21. Klosko, "Refutation of Callicles," 131, points out that Callicles' position here is more extreme than it needs to be, presenting an "unsophisticated" hedonism. By modifying this position so as to allow for *some* restraint on the appetites, Klosko produces a position that Socrates fails to answer, that would be much harder for him to refute, and would (perhaps) also more closely represent "what others think, but refuse to say" (492d2–3)—although I am inclined to think that the multitude, like Callicles, has not thought things through so well as Klosko. It is important to be clear on the question of Plato's purpose here. On my view, the point is to develop toward its logical extreme the idea of freedom as a liberation from restraint. The idea of the individual will opposing itself to everything external, the pursuit of arbitrary individual whim, represents the full flowering of the idea of power as it lay implicit in Gorgias. The important question for the dialogue is whether or not Callicles will actually hold to this idea in its most extreme form—and note that this view does not require any modification to the text to get rid of any "unsophisticated" ideas.

22. The alternate reason one would aim at prudence, bravery, and center one's activity around the city is the one suggested in the previous step of the argument: because of the conventional status these things bring.

23. Dodds, *Gorgias*, 306.
24. Dominic Scott, "Platonic Pessimism and Moral Education," *Oxford Studies in Ancient Philosophy* 17 (1999): 22, and Cooper, "Socrates and Plato," 52, fn. 32, both note that the present tense is at work in this final passage: it is not that Callicles was not convinced, but that he *is* not.

How Callicles Is Good
Platonic Doctrine in the Gorgias

On the basis of the interpretation of the *Gorgias* given so far, in which Socrates' arguments fall short of full adequacy because they are merely *ad hominem*, and in which dramatic detail plays such a central role, it might seem as though Plato has become a sort of skeptic, putting forward interesting ideas but without any of his own. In fact, Plato is intent on setting forth doctrines here, but they come to light in a most unexpected place: in those aspects of Callicles that are most at odds with conventional beliefs, and thus most shameful.

Most interpreters seem to have taken it to be self-evident that we are to put a white hat on Socrates and a black hat on Callicles, so that Plato's views are to be found in Socrates' negation and rejection of everything Callicles stands for. Here we shall see that an approach along these lines is supported only to a limited degree by the text, because there is ample evidence that we are to understand Callicles to be good in certain respects that might seem to represent his worst: in his demand for natural justice, in his interest in ruling, and in his focus on pleasure and the appetites.

Of course, the point is not that Plato accepts that the strong should rule the weak, or that he shares Callicles' enthusiasm for tyranny, or that he advocates an unleashing of the appetites. Rather, in all three cases, Callicles has a grasp of an important reality, though in an imperfect way. The challenge for Socrates is to take up the truth in what Callicles says while eliminating all that is harmful—and note that *ad hominem* arguments, of the sort that Socrates employed in his refutations of each of his three opponents, will not suffice here.

In what follows, I am extending an approach to the *Gorgias* that has been set out elsewhere. We have seen that there are two sides to Callicles, the realist and the aristocratic, and that these contradict one another. Raphael Woolf has shown how these two sides provide, of themselves, an implicit challenge for Socrates, and that Socrates has implicitly answered that challenge. That is, on Woolf's account, one side of Callicles would smash laws and conventions so as to maintain its own integrity (this corresponds to the "realist" side developed in the preceding chapter), while the other finds itself in need of laws and conventions because it seeks good relations with other people (the "aristocratic" Callicles on my account).[1] These two demands—for integrity and friendship—are present in Callicles in a manner that requires them to conflict with one another. Socrates, as he gives his own account, does not question the importance of the two demands, but, taking them up into his own account, finds a way to satisfy each demand in a manner that eliminates its conflict with the other.

There is no need to rehearse in detail the substance of Woolf's account here. What is important is that it is reasonable to see Plato's own thought coming to light through all this, particularly given that no character questions the importance of the demands for integrity and friendship. This pattern, as I will try to show in what follows, is repeated in other themes, so that rather than simply ascribing directly to Plato every word of Socratic argumentation, we find Plato speaking to us indirectly in the *Gorgias*, through certain implicit challenges and the implicit answers to those challenges given by Socrates.

SOCRATES' NATURAL JUSTICE

We saw in the preceding chapter how Callicles sought to ground his own account of justice in an objective natural order. Having made the difference between νόμος (convention) and φύσις (nature—482e483a) explicit, he showed how there were two quite different accounts of justice available, one based in convention, and the other in nature. Natural justice, on this account, is founded in well-known facts, and derives its credibility from its basis in such facts. Conventional justice is the product of an agreement between people, and has no such credibility: to call an account of justice "conventional," on this view, is precisely to recognize that it has no basis in facts, but could change the instant that the relevant people changed their minds. Thus Callicles speaks derisively of "papers, trickery and spells" (484a4–5): conventional justice appears here to be a sort of enchantment, with no basis in reality.

If Callicles could make good on his pretense that his own account of justice is founded in nature, it would put him in a position of great strength. Of course, he fails to do this: the very first step of Socrates' argument shows just how empty is Callicles' implicit claim to ground his own account of justice in reality (488b2–489b6). However, the challenge has been made, and if Plato were to fail to rise to it, his own account of justice would lack credibility. Accordingly, Socrates' own account contains an implicit answer. From 503d–505b we get an account of what it means for something to be good, and one remarkable feature of this account is that it is not founded upon an intuition, upon a merely subjective belief, but rather finds confirmation in a readily observable order of the world. The craftsman, we are told, aims to produce in his work some form, setting it in some arrangement, and forcing each part to fit with and be suitable to every other, so as to produce something structured and ordered (503e7–504a2). This idea is specifically contrasted with that of acting at random (εἰκῇ—503e1, 3; see also 506d6). Skilled activity does seem to be characterized by the production of order, and this is not only true of human inventions, such as ships or houses, but also of attempts to improve the body, whether through training or medicine. A poorly built house will leak, allow drafts, or collapse; a well-made ship will better survive a storm; a trainer might aim to correct a muscle imbalance. Even the move from order and structure as productive of health and strength in the body to the same things as productive in the soul of mental health and strength (504b–c) is a highly plausible one, and does seem to conform to many facts of life: people who act simply at random, who are utterly unpredictable, seem mad; those who have regulated their passions, and are capable of self-control, can respond reliably to even the most stressful situations. There does seem to be a notion of "good" according to which a great many things—perhaps all—are better off when they attain the order appropriate to their nature; skilled activity aims to produce this. This "good" does not arise as a matter of agreement between individuals but is simply a feature of the world.

Accordingly, we find another case like that of friendship and integrity: Callicles has presented a demand that he himself fails to satisfy, and Socrates is able to address this demand in a substantial manner. In this case, Socrates has taken for himself the strength that Callicles had sought to claim, namely the grounding of assertions concerning how one ought to act in an objective order of the world.

Plato, then, is interested in the logical basis of our ethical views here. There is no appeal in the *Gorgias* to subjective intuitions or an innate moral sense—on the contrary, Plato would join Callicles in deriding such things as "papers, trickery and spells" (484a4–5). Instead, the interest here is in finding an objective basis from which we can think about living a good life, and he has used Callicles to bring to light the need for such approach. We shall see below that this interest in an objective basis can also be found in Socrates' final account of skills; later, when we compare the *Gorgias* to the first book of the *Republic*, we shall see that the idea reappears in that longer work.

PLEASURE, THE GOOD AND RULING IN THE *GORGIAS*

There are two further instances of this challenge-and-response pattern: Callicles represents something good even in his focus on the appetites, and in the *Gorgias* a consideration of the appetites must be considered in relation to a theme that runs through the whole dialogue, that of *ruling*.

The theme of ruling, like so many others, exhibits a development as we progress through the work. As we noted in the introduction, Gorgias claims that his art of rhetoric will provide its practitioner with rule over others (ἄλλων ἄρχειν—452d7), and when he goes on to describe how others will become the slaves of the rhetor (452e), he hints at the life of the tyrant. When we get to Polus, the tyrant is no longer present merely as a hint but becomes the explicit focus of discussion in the account of Archelaus (470d–471d), who rules (ἄρχειν—470d7) Macedon. In the argument with Callicles, Socrates brings in a novel conception—*self*-rule (491d4–e1)—as part of the work of clarifying and thus refuting Callicles; in response, Callicles provides the richest development of the conception of rule (ἀρχή–492b3) so far, relating it to its alleged end, the unlimited satisfaction of the appetites (491e–492c).[2]

The theme does not end there, however, for Socrates takes up the notion of ruling, together with the appetites, in his final schema of skills—that is, his account of the relationship between genuine skills and lesser forms of activity. In fact there are *three* schemas of skills in the *Gorgias*, and before we can make full sense of the last one, we need first to deal with its relation to its predecessors. It is not immediately clear that they can be reconciled with one another, but we shall see that we have here yet another instance of a theme that develops over the course of the dialogue.

A Problem: Socrates' Schemas of Skills

It is above all necessary to reconcile the first and last of these three schemas if Socrates' account of skills and non-skills in this dialogue is not to be incoherent. Against Polus, Socrates gives a lengthy speech (464b–466a) in which he provides a schema relating genuine skills to an inferior sort of activity that he refers to as "knacks" (ἐμπειρία—465a2) and forms of "flattery" (κολακεία— e.g., 465b1). Skills, such as medicine and gymnastics, understand the object of their attention, and aim at its good, while mere knacks, such as cookery and cosmetics, have no such understanding (464c4–5, 465a2–5). Furthermore, because they aim at pleasure, with no thought for the good, these knacks are forms of "flattery" (464d1–2, 464e2–465a2). Socrates does not hold back in his condemnation of the lesser sort of activity: he calls cookery "shameful" (αἰσχρός—465e2), and cosmetics "harmful, deceptive, ignoble and illiberal"

(465b3–4); he has already called rhetoric "bad and shameful" (κακός, αἰσχρός—463d3). This account, then, sets up a clear opposition between skills and the lesser activities known as knacks. There is no suggestion that gymnastics, for example, might somehow include, or make use of, cosmetics, for the two have different aims, proceed on the basis of unequal understandings, and one is a praiseworthy pursuit, while the other is most emphatically not. We thus seem to have two fundamentally different types of activity that exclude one another.[3] Furthermore, because pleasure and the good seem to fall entirely on opposite sides of this division between two types of activity, pleasure here appears only in its opposition to the good, and only as a means of seducing the soul away from its proper concerns. So, for example, Socrates tells us that "flattery . . . has no thought for what is best, but chases after foolishness and deceives by means of immediate pleasure, so as to seem to be most worthy" (464c5–d3). If certain pleasures can be good, there is no suggestion of it here.

Toward the end of the dialogue, however, Socrates returns to the matter of genuine skills and activities that fall short of these (517b–519a), and the latter sort of activity is now called "serving" (διακονική). It soon becomes clear that this is not simply another word for knack, and that serving activities are included, rather than excluded, by genuine skills. We shall see in what follows that this later schema shows how pleasure is often good, and how the good life must be, to a considerable degree, pleasant.

It is possible, I think, to reconcile Socrates' differing accounts of skills and non-skills, although I believe that the dialogue's literary structure (as well as the nature of the problem) requires us to do so on the terms of the last passage in question. Recall that the movement is "from the superficial to the fundamental":[4] it would be entirely appropriate, in the context of this movement, if Socrates' earlier statements represent a relatively superficial overview of a given matter, while his later statements deliver a fuller and more adequate account.[5] In keeping with this suggestion, I will focus on Socrates' final treatment of skills (517b–519b), and I shall try to show that his initial treatment (464b–466a) should be understood to occupy a limited place within the final treatment. It is because of the way the final schema includes and even depends on those aspects of Callicles' position that might at first seem most opposed to Socrates—the appetites, pleasure, and the focus on ruling—that it gives further examples of my suggestion above concerning the way in which Plato speaks to the reader in this dialogue.

The Final Schema of Skills in Context

It will prove helpful in determining Plato's purpose in giving Socrates multiple, and possibly conflicting, speeches that treat a schema of skills, if we begin by discussing the context in which the final speech occurs. First of all, its position toward the end of Socrates' own positive account is significant. From 503a–517a we have a self-contained portion of the dialogue, recognizable as such from internal cues. In response to Callicles' claim that there really are people who speak while concerned for the good of the citizens (503a2–4), and that the Four Men—Miltiades, Themistocles, Cimon, and Pericles—are examples of these (503c1–3), Socrates produces a lengthy account of his own that culminates in the astonishing conclusion that none of these men were skilled practitioners of rhetoric (517a). In the course of this account, however, Socrates provides an answer to Callicles in a much deeper sense, for he develops a position that provides an alternative to Callicles' view of the world, one that takes up certain fundamental concerns of that view and incorporates them into itself. (The twin demands of friendship and integrity, as well as the notion of basing an ethical theory in an objective order, are examples of such fundamental concerns.) I shall try to show in what follows that the final discussion of skills, in which they are contrasted with "serving" activities, is to be understood as a final moment in this deeper answer to Callicles.

Plato has drawn our attention to the relevance of the dialogue's overall structure to this final treatment of the schema of skills, for Socrates pauses to note that "we do not stop continually coming round to the same thing" (οὐδὲν παυόμεθα εἰς τὸ αὐτὸ ἀεὶ περιφερόμενοι—517c6).[6] With this reminder in mind, we can appreciate the significance of the fact that this is the *third* time that the schema has come up: in addition to the first passage, mentioned above (464b–466a), in which knacks and skills were described in opposition to one another, and in which there was no hint that pleasure and the good might be reconciled with one another, Socrates also brought this schema up right after a crucial turn in the argument, in which Callicles agreed that pleasure was not itself the good (i.e., after 499b–c). In this return to the schema of skills (500a–501c) the basic idea remained the same, and yet there were important differences in comparison with the first schema.

In the first place, whereas against Polus, Socrates had simply to assume a difference between pleasure and the good, after 499c Callicles has just agreed to the distinction, so it now has some basis in the preceding discussion. In addition, Socrates now allows that some pleasures are good (499c7), something not explicitly ruled out in the first exposition of the schema but left significantly unsaid there. Socrates also now explicitly declares that one does pleasant activities for the sake of the good (500a2–3). This too does not contradict anything said against Polus but requires us to see it in a different light: the impression earlier was that pleasure was simply to be avoided, but now the door is opened to the possibility that someone aiming accurately at the good might want to do pleasant things. Thus even as the schema is now more firmly grounded in the argument than it was before, a new difficulty is coming into view: how, given the examples that Socrates is using, might pleasure be reconciled, at least in certain situations, with the good? How, if cookery and medicine are our paradigmatic activities, might one do pleasant activities for the sake of the good? Surely cookery achieves pleasure, and does not achieve any good, while medicine, which is decidedly unpleasant, does achieve a good. It is this difficulty that will be resolved in the final treatment (517b–519a). Accordingly, we can see in Socrates' three treatments of the schema of skills (4664b–466a, 500a–501c and 517b–519a) an ordered progression, in the course of which the initial, apparently straightforward, account becomes more complicated, and finally takes on a significance very different from what we would originally have expected. This is not to say that the first schema of skills is entirely abandoned at the end, for I will try to show how it can be included in the final treatment. With all this in mind, we may now turn to the passage on which my account depends.

Servile and Master Arts (517b–519a)

At the start of Socrates' exposition of serving (διακονική) we find a suggestion that "serving" is not simply another word for knacks and forms of flattery (i.e., for ἐμπειρίαι and κολακείαι). Rhetoric was said in the first schema to be a kind of flattery (e.g., 464e2) that aims at pleasure. Now we hear that the Four Men did not really practice flattering rhetoric (ῥητορική . . . κολακική—517a5–6), but were servants (διακονικοί—b2–3) of the desires of the city. Serving, then, is different from rhetoric as understood earlier but seems to aim at the same thing, assuming that satisfaction of the desires produces pleasure. This might seem to suggest that we have an account of skills that is simply different from what went before, but Plato has included a suggestion of continuity: Socrates, having used the examples of food, drink, cloaks, and shoes, claims, "I'm speaking to you through the same images on purpose, so that you may understand more easily" (517d5–6). Now food, drink, cloaks, and shoes were used earlier in the argument with Callicles (490b–e; also 496c–e for food and drink alone), but they were *not* used to illustrate Socrates' schema of skills and knacks. Their use in such a context is novel, and if we are more easily to understand through them, it is evidently not by looking back to Socrates' original schema at 464b–466a. The talk of walls, harbors, and dockyards, which come up a little later (519a2–3; also 517c2–3), presents a similar case: these things were also mentioned earlier in the dialogue (455b–e), but not in the context of skills and knacks. The full significance of all these images will be taken up below, but already we can see that Socrates' remark points toward continuity, in that he is using "the same images," but also, for the careful reader, toward difference, since these images are being used in a new context. (In the context of the original schema at 464b–466a, "the same images" would suggest medicine, cookery, justice, rhetoric, etc.)

The notion of "serving"[7] is filled out by providing (ἐκπορίζειν—517b4, c4, d2) that for which one has an appetite (ἐπιθυμεῖν—b5; also ἐπιθυμία—b5, d5).[8] Now, the appetites (ἐπιθυμίαι—491e9, 492a2–3) lay at the heart of Callicles' conception of things: after he has begun to feel the force of the argument, he is driven to a particularly frank (παρρησιαζόμενος—491e7–8; also 492d1–2) expression of his own views (491e5–492c8), in which the appetites take center stage. Here we see that the appetites are to be utterly unrestrained, and the Calliclean virtues of bravery and intelligence are to be put at their service. Since we are told in this context that "wantonness, intemperance and freedom ... this is virtue and happiness" (492c4–6), we see that there is a fundamentally appetitive conception of human ends at work in Callicles. Socrates' new talk of "serving" activities accordingly takes up, in the notion of appetite, a foundation stone of Callicles' position. Furthermore, if "serving" is an activity that provides what the appetites demand, then it will be an activity that produces pleasure: the examples of food and drink were used as part of an argument about the nature of pleasure (496c–e), where it was asserted that "need and appetite" (ἔνδεια καὶ ἐπιθυμία–496d4) are unpleasant, but that pleasure arises in the satisfaction of such needs.

Now, insofar as "serving" produces pleasure, it would seem to be the same as the knacks of Socrates' initial account (464b–466a), which aimed at pleasure. However, the differing images used to illustrate each account seem to point in quite different directions. Whereas cookery and cosmetics were used in the first account to suggest pleasures that were independent of—or even opposed to—a good, the examples Socrates now uses, desires for food, drink, clothing and shoes, must often be in accord with the good of the body. A body without food, drink or clothing will starve or freeze to death: we now have necessities vital to survival. If food, drink, cloaks, and so on are objects of bodily appetite (d4–5), then a new view of appetite has emerged, one that shows how the appetites (and also the pleasure that arises in their satisfaction) must sometimes be in accord with the good, not independent of or opposed to it. Plato, by having Socrates speak of "the same images" (517d5–6) actually points the careful reader toward what is new in this account.[9]

As Socrates continues, it becomes apparent that this interpretation of his images is correct, for he now describes true skills—gymnastics and medicine are the chosen examples—as properly ruling over, and using the work of, the other, lesser activities (517e6–7). The idea, then, is that the baker, weaver, and shoemaker provide things that are necessary for a healthy body, and that gymnastics and medicine are not wholly self-sufficient, but stand in need of the products of these lesser activities. If one of the subordinate activities were to acquire control of the activity of the body, they would focus too much on their own products, and the result might be an overindulgence in bread, or an excessive acquisition of cloaks and shoes. In fact, we find in this thought a means of making sense, in hindsight, of an earlier passage that might merely have seemed absurd: that at 490d–e, Socrates suggested that the weaver is to have the biggest cloak and the cobbler the largest and most numerous shoes.

It is in the sense that they are properly subordinate and not of themselves directed toward their ultimate end that these arts only *seem* to care for the body (517e2–3); in reality (τῷ ὄντι—e5), there are other, genuine skills— medicine and gymnastics—that can properly be said to care for the body. These understand the nature of the body and, according to what is just (κατὰ τὸ δίκαιον—518a4), should direct the servile (διακονικάς—518a2) arts so as to achieve bodily health. That is, a doctor will use the work of the baking art to give the proper quantity of bread to a body, and a gymnast will use the weaving and shoemaking arts to make sure that the body is properly clothed. There is, then, a hierarchy of practices, each of which properly aims at least at some partial good, but it is crucial that the genuine skill be in charge of all the others.

The idea determining Socrates' account here is that of *rule* (ἄρχειν— 517e6); we noted above that this represents the final moment of a theme that runs through the entire dialogue.[10] In the previous two accounts (464b–466a, 500a–501c), the distinction between knacks and genuine skills was underwritten by the distinction between pleasure and the good. Now, however, we see that this was not the final word on the matter, and we can see what was not clear in the second account, namely how exactly some pleasures could be good. Baking or shoemaking satisfy appetites (and so will produce pleasure), but can achieve good only if they maintain their appropriate place subordinate to and directed by the appropriate master art (e.g., medicine). If, however, an art that should properly occupy a subordinate place comes to occupy the top spot, in the place of the art that ought to rule, all sorts of evil results. It is not the question of whether or not an activity aims at pleasure that ultimately determines its goodness, but rather the question of whether or not it occupies its proper place in a hierarchy of serving activities and master arts—and note that this notion itself harmonizes with the sketch we get at 503d–505b of what it means to be good.

There is a place within the new schema for the earlier one. The arts that properly rule, because they know what is useful and base for the excellence of their subject (517e7–8), will always, and of their nature, aim at the good. The serving arts, because they satisfy appetites, will always and of their nature aim at pleasure, and will achieve good only when directed and limited by a proper master art. Accordingly, the distinction that governed the earlier schemas (464b–466a, 500a–501c), pleasure and the good, is not only still present in the new one but also continues to provide a means of distinguishing true skills from lesser activities. However, it does this in a different manner than we would have expected. Previously it might have seemed that pleasure was simply evil, a perilously seductive force that could lure us away from the good. Now, however, it appears that pleasure need not be avoided as such, and can in fact lead us toward the good as much as away from it—indeed, surely the reason that we have appetites is that we have needs for food, drink, and so on. Still, pleasure does not necessarily lead toward the good, and will in many situations exert a seductive pull in the wrong direction.

We can find a place for the flattering knacks of Socrates' original schema of skills (464b–466a) at the very bottom of this hierarchy, for there we find practices that aim at creating only an appearance of the good where the good is in fact absent, such as cosmetics, when it aims to make an unhealthy body appear fit, or flattering rhetoric, when it tries to make bad things appear good.[11] In the original schema, the distinction between appearance and reality is fundamental to the whole: knacks proceed by means of impersonation, pretense, and deception (464c7–d4); they have only the empty appearance of being skills. Even here, the good is in a sense present as an end, but now it is only the appearance of the good that is present. In this way, flattery (κολακεία) could find a place in this scheme of things, but could only be said to be a sort of serving (διακονική) by virtue of some equivocation. There is an anticipation here of the necessary/unnecessary appetites of the *Republic* (558d–559c)—flattery points to an unnecessary, serving, to a necessary appetite.

Socrates' earlier remarks on the work of doctors can be connected with this new view. Doctors, he said, typically allow healthy patients to eat and drink as much as they like, according to hunger and thirst, but almost never allow this to sick patients (505a). We also hear later of a doctor who compels patients to go hungry and thirsty (522a). The idea behind this (as Socrates at 505b suggests) is that a healthy body is properly ordered, so that its appetites align with its needs (and therefore with its good), whereas a disordered, sick body will have inappropriate appetites, which tend toward its own destruction: all will depend upon the type of order present within the body. Again we should note here how Socrates is building on the account of the good he gave at 503d–505b, and also how he is able to find confirmation for this account of the hierarchy of skills in realities that should be plain to all.

The really important thing, then, is to have properly ordered appetites. Once this has been achieved, individuals can make use of various serving arts to see to their needs. Here too we find that appetites are not to be avoided as such; here too we find that it is the order of the soul—for a type of rule points to a particular order of the soul—that determines whether appetites lead us toward good or evil.[12]

The fact that Socrates is taking up and reworking ideas from Callicles is driven home in the final schema of skills by certain key words from Callicles' main statement which are thrown back at him. Callicles' ideal man was to show himself to be master (δεσπότης—484a6); Socrates' master arts will similarly be masters (518a4—δεσποίνας). Callicles believed that clear speech on the part of a child was something befitting a slave (δουλοπρεπής—485b7), and also that failing to philosophize when young was illiberal (ἀνελεύθερον—485c6, with b4, c5), while philosophizing too late in life was just as bad; Socrates finds the serving arts to be slave-like and illiberal (δουλοπρεπεῖς, ἀνελευθέρους—518a2). Callicles' interest in a fine and good man (καλός κἀγαθός—484d1-2) is thrown back at him at 518b1 and 518c4-5. In similar fashion, Callicles dismissed philosophy as "nonsense" (φλυαρία—486c7), having made clear that it had a limited place in the scheme of things, though one altogether subordinate to what he believed really to be important. He also later called food and drink "nonsense" (φλυαρία—490c8–d1), and when Socrates spoke of a person intent on wearing the biggest and the most shoes, Callicles replied, "you're talking nonsense" (φλυαρεῖς—490e4). Here too, the point cannot be that food, drink, and shoes are simply undesirable, but rather that they are unimportant relative to what really counts. Socrates will also speak of "nonsense" (φλυαρία—519a3), though he will apply the word to harbors, dockyards, and walls. Let us now consider the passage in which he does so, where will shall see that he no more means to suggest that these things are inherently harmful to a city's health than food, drink, or shoes would be to a body.

Servile and Master Arts and the Four Men

Socrates follows his final schema of skills with his final verdict on the Four Men, and this allows us to work out the consequences of the interpretation just given. Callicles provoked Socrates into giving the final schema of skills when he spoke of the "works" (ἔργα—517a8) of the Four Men; the word is echoed at the end of that schema when Socrates says that the ruling art will make use of the "works" (ἔργα—517e7) of the others. Now, the specific works of the Four Men are said to be ships, walls, and dockyards (517c2). This would carry the implication that these are not simply bad things. As a body needs clothes and shoes, so does a city need ships, walls, and dockyards to survive; as a body has an appetite for its needs, so too does a city. A city that ignores such necessities can expect to be conquered by its neighbors. From this perspective, the problem with the Four Men would seem not to be that they provided ships, walls, and dockyards, nor that the city's appetite for such things was simply evil as such. Rather, the problem was that they focused on these things "without justice and temperance"

(519a1–2), perhaps focusing on them to an excessive degree, like one who, recognizing food and drink as goods, gorges himself until sick. A true statesman, then, would also have provided ships, walls and dockyards, but would have been careful to subordinate these things to the overall order and health of the city.

But does Socrates not contrast the provision of such naval apparatus with "changing the course of the appetites and not yielding to them, persuading and forcing them toward what will make the citizens better" (517b5–7), saying that the latter activities constitute the "only work" (μόνον ἔργον—c1) of a good citizen? That is, the work of a good leader might seem *not* to involve ruling over various subordinate skills and using their works; rather, it is *only* a matter of directing the appetites of the citizens. However, the reference to the "only work" of a good citizen is to be interpreted in the light of Socrates words at 517d6–e6: many arts might seem to be the care of the body, but in reality (τῷ ὄντι—517e5) medicine and gymnastic are the arts that care for the body. This is not to say that the baker or the shoemaker fail to care for the body in any sense—their works will, after all, be needed by the ruling arts—but rather that they fail to do so in the strictest sense. The force of the words "only work," like the words "in reality" is not to point to an actual form of activity that aims at the good as opposed to a practice that ignores (or opposes) the good entirely, but rather to a fully adequate form of activity as opposed to a merely partial (and thus potentially destructive) form.[13]

We can therefore summarize certain of Socrates' views in this dialogue. He does not want simply to turn people away from pleasure as such, but believes it important to understand the proper place of pleasure in the larger scheme of things, so as to be able to recognize those circumstances in which one ought not to be led by it. The difference, for Socrates here, between a person leading a good or a bad life is not that the one will avoid satisfying the appetites while the other will strive to do this, and not that the one will shun pleasure while the other pursues it. On the contrary, the person living well will constantly be satisfying appetites, as he eats an appropriate kind and quantity of food when hungry, drinks a suitable drink when thirsty, clothes himself warmly in the winter, and keeps his feet from harm with proper footwear. Such appetites play a crucial role in helping us to lead a good life, and so the pleasure that results from their satisfaction helps lead us toward the good. A bad life is distinguished from a good one not by the pursuit or avoidance of pleasure, but by a difference of ruling principle: when a practice that is properly subordinate, such as baking, becomes dominant, the result is a focus on inappropriate appetites, and consequently on that particular variety of pleasure that leads us away from the good.

SUMMARY

At 491d, Socrates introduces a novelty into the dialogue's theme of ruling. He speaks of self-rule, and his final schema of skills should be taken as a further development of this idea. This final schema takes up and reforms Callicles' concern with ruling and his focus on the appetites. The problem in both cases was not that Callicles was entirely wrong to be interested in these things. On the contrary, they represent crucially important concepts; the problem was rather the way in which Callicles conceived of them. In the *Republic*, the notion of ruling—including self-rule—will of course be central, and the first we shall hear of it will be with Thrasymachus, who plays a role analogous to that of Callicles here.[14] We saw above how the treatment of the appetites here looks ahead to the necessary and unnecessary appetites of the *Republic*. We have also seen how Callicles' attempt to found his understanding of justice in reality was not simply wrong but rather in need of reformulation.

Thus in all of these respects, Callicles has performed a considerable service: he has brought crucially important ideas into the argument. In doing so, he has done something good. This coheres with something we saw earlier, in the account of shame and certain arguments (pages 108–110): Socrates praises Callicles for his lack of shame (487a–e). Clearly this lack of shame is in a sense a good, for it means that Callicles is willing to say things that other people are not. This means that he can bring the discussion to places it would not go otherwise. Although he is not as shameless as Socrates might like, he is sufficiently frank that he has brought natural justice, ruling and the appetites into the argument. In all of this, then, Callicles is good. Of course, Callicles does not exist in a vacuum, but comes at the end of a development, as we have seen for each theme treated here. If Callicles is in certain respects good, so too must be the process that culminates in him.

Of course, the various doctrines that Socrates produces in the final part of the dialogue cannot be said to have been proved true. It is still possible to refuse to accept them. What we do have is a series of compelling answers to a particular situation. So, for example, once Callicles has implicitly brought out the possibility of grounding a view of justice in facts, any merely conventional account will have a credibility problem. Socrates' account of the good is not necessarily true, but the fact that it finds confirmation in facts means that it is particularly effective as a response to Callicles. This is in general the case: Socrates in the *Gorgias* provides effective answers to Callicles but does not prove the truth of any doctrine. Thus we arrive, in the end, at a series of contingent truths: if we find ourselves unsatisfied with Callicles, whether we find certain elements inherently objectionable or cannot affirm his self-contradictory standpoint, divided as he is between his realist and aristocratic sides, then Socrates has, in the end, provided us with a superior alternative, one that takes up central Calliclean truths.

NOTES

1. See Woolf, "Callicles and Socrates." The two sides of Callicles are anticipated in Gorgias and Polus. Consider, for example, the hint of the tyrant we saw in Gorgias, which developed into the praise of Archelaus with Polus: this leads to the side of Callicles that seeks integrity. On the other hand, the shame of Gorgias and Polus, and the (differing) degree to which they are still held by the authority of conventional morality—these aspects become, in Callicles, the side that holds friendship to be of fundamental importance.

2. Rule is an idea that runs right through the investigation of Callicles' position: he spoke of ruling in his main statement (483d5), and the idea was then taken up by Socrates, and included in his criticism of Callicles (490a2–3, c2) even before he turned the conversation to self-rule.

3. Moss, "The Doctor and the Pastry Chef," 244: "the *Gorgias* draws a polar opposition between flattery, which is both persuasive and pleasant, and correction—including dialectic—which is both unpersuasive and unpleasant." I agree with this, but note how Moss is careful to oppose flattery and correction, rather than pleasure and the good. Her paper is helpful in working out the opposition she identifies: it is so strongly present that we can see how easy it would be to attribute to Socrates a polemical aversion to pleasure in general.

4. Dodds, *Gorgias*, 4.

5. Such an approach is also consistent with the changes we see in Socrates: see the next chapter.

6. Dodds, *Gorgias*, 5, uses this quotation to point to the fact that "the movement of the dialogue is not rectilinear like that of most plays (and most philosophical treatises) but spiral."

7. Irwin, "Notes," 238, tells us that "the term 'serving' [διακονική] is ambiguous between (1) 'serving the whims of the audience,' and so an irrational knack; (2) 'serving the aims of the superordinate science.'" If there is any ambiguity, it serves Socrates' pretense, which I take up below, that he is simply extending the same case he has been developing all along. In fact, as we shall see, it is meaning (2) that determines his account at this point.

8. Socrates' ἐκπορίζειν (517b4, c4, d2) takes up Callicles' use of the same verb, although there is a significant change of voice: Callicles was concerned that one should be able to provide *for oneself* (ἐκπορίζεσθαι—492a8) pleasures and also (ἐκπορίσασθαι—492b3) some form of rule. Note that the two things Callicles mentions that he wants to provide—pleasure (i.e., appetite satisfaction) and rule—are the very two things that are found below to be taken up by Socrates in the final schema of skills.

9. The dialogue is concerned with rhetoric, but the passage in question deals only in analogous activities, and leaves it to the reader to work out the consequences for rhetoric. See Gabriela Roxane Carone, "Socratic Rhetoric in the Gorgias," *The Canadian Journal of Philosophy* 24, no. 2 (June 2005): 221–41, for a treatment of rhetoric that takes account of the final schema of skills, one in many ways complementary to my own account here.

10. The two sets of images from earlier passages mentioned above also have connections to the idea of rule. The first mention of walls, harbors, and dockyards (455b–e) included the first mention of Themistocles and Pericles. In the passage that contained the food, drink, cloaks, and shoes examples, Socrates repeatedly mentioned ruling (ἄρχειν—490a2–3, 8, c2).

11. Cookery might seem to represent a problem, for the cook (ὀψοποιός) is mentioned at 517e1 in the context of serving, but was also an important example of flattery in the first schema of skills (e.g., ὀψοποιός—464d6). I would resolve this as follows: cookery might serve the good by making unpleasant but beneficial things more pleasant, as some honey on the rim of a cup would make the bitter medicine within easier to swallow; cookery might also produce unhealthy but delicious dessert treats that tempt people toward sickness through overeating. In the former case, cookery would be a serving activity, in the latter, a mere form of flattery. In the same way, any serving activity might become flattery when disconnected from its proper master art. If this account requires that we work things out that are not directly stated in the text, that is acceptable: Socrates' schema of skills is an analogy, and as such requires that we work out the consequences of the particular examples he give in order to get to his point.

12. Accordingly, there is reason to disagree with Moss, "Shame, Pleasure," 146, when she says that "pleasure pulls us in the wrong direction, towards false value judgments." An appetite properly subordinated to its master art will pull us in the right direction, for example, toward eating an appropriate quantity and type of food, or toward wearing something warm in the winter. Accordingly, the pleasure that comes from the satisfaction of appetites in such cases will pull us in the right direction, toward correct value judgments. One imagines that the philosopher, intent on the true, the beautiful and the good, might forget to eat and drink if deprived of his appetites, and might thus die of hunger or thirst.

13. In this context it is pertinent to quote Gabriela Roxane Carone, "Socratic Rhetoric," 234–35, who reminds us that "Socrates talks . . . of the right kind of rhetoric as being able to change (*in the sense of re-directing—μεταβιβάζειν—rather than suppressing*) the citizens' desires (517b)" (emphasis mine).

14. See also Rachel Barney, "Callicles and Thrasymachus," *The Stanford Encyclopedia of Philosophy*, ed. Edward N. Zalta (Fall 2017 Edition), URL = https://plato.stanford.edu/entries/callicles-thrasymachus/, who notes that "in the *Republic* we see that Plato in fact agrees with Callicles that the many should be ruled by the superior few—that is, the intelligent and courageous—and that it is only natural and just for the latter to have greater happiness and pleasure than the many. Where they differ is in the content they give to this shared schema."

Socrates in the *Gorgias*

It is not only the subject of discussion and Socrates' three opponents that present us with an ordered progression as we move through the *Gorgias*. We see such a development in Socrates himself, as he changes from the character of the early dialogues, who questions others without putting forward doctrines of his own, to someone who is trying actively to establish theses of his own.[1] Here, too, there is room for fresh insight; here, too, Plato has obviously gone to considerable trouble to weave this structure into the text: the rigorous interpreter will aim to explain why.

Let us review the main changes. As the dialogue begins, Socrates is recognizable as the fellow from the early dialogues. He seeks to learn from Gorgias (πυθέσθαι παρ' αὐτοῦ—447c1), and proceeds only to ask questions. When Polus gets involved, there is a change: Socrates does give his own opinion, although at first (462b–465e) he does so having been asked for it, and the view he gives is to a substantial degree a logical consequence of the admission which separates Polus from Gorgias.[2] There is then another step (466a–481b), in which he actively puts forth radical new claims of his own, which not only do not follow from what Polus has already said but are characterized by their opposition to what he says, as we have seen.[3] Finally, when we get to Callicles, it is pertinent to keep in mind Socrates' earlier admonition to Polus: "would I not suffer something terrible, if I am not allowed to go away and not listen to you?" (461e–462a) By 497a, Callicles would very much like to go away and not listen, but Socrates and Gorgias *will not let Callicles go* (see also 505c–506c). Indeed, Socrates reaches a point (506c–509c) at which he alone *is* the argument, since Callicles wants nothing to do with it.[4] Thus we can see an ordered progression of increasing activity within Socrates.

Plato has drawn the reader's attention to the change in Socrates over the course of the dialogue through a well-known theme, namely that of lengthy speech (μακρολογία—449c5). On the dialogue's first page, Socrates asks for a discussion rather than a display (447b–c), and from this point on there are repeated references to the length of the speeches characters make. Thus Polus is criticized for his failing at discussion (διαλέγεσθαι—448d) while Gorgias, having agreed to a discussion (449–bc), is praised for the shortness of his answers (449d). The same demand to restrain long speeches is made of Polus (461e–462a). However, when Socrates first begins to give his own views, he gives a long speech, but then apologizes for it, saying that he needed to do so in order to make himself understood (465e–466a). By the time we get to Callicles, not only do both characters speak at some length at the start (481c–488b),[5] but by 506c, we have a dialogue no more, for Socrates takes over the argument completely on his own for several pages—and by this point it should be clear that there is a connection between this theme and that of Socrates' increasing activity. Socrates later excuses himself for such long speeches (519e) on the ground that Callicles refused to give answers. Thus Plato has introduced a theme right at the start, one which might seem at first to be irrelevant to the purpose of the dialogue, but its effect is to point us to the change in Socrates over the course of the dialogue.[6] All this helps us to see that Socrates has become active by the end of the dialogue, in that he is setting out his own doctrines, but further, that he is so active, he is declaiming these doctrines at length.

There is another aspect to his characterization that is important here: his failure to convince. He proves unable to move Polus and Callicles.[7] If we take the *Republic*, from book ii onward, as a point of comparison, we note that there, the other characters are convinced by Socrates' arguments, which are not *ad hominem*, and even Thrasymachus remains interested in the argument (i.e., at *Republic* 450a-b; see also 498c–d).[8] There is nothing easier for the writer of a dialogue than to show all of his characters being moved by his arguments to his preferred conclusion,[9] and yet in the *Gorgias* this is precisely what does not happen. Instead, Callicles makes it abundantly clear by the end that he has lost interest in the argument, and is unmoved by it. In fact, Plato has made this particularly conspicuous, for he has Socrates set himself a standard: "if I do not provide you, one person, as a witness agreeing with the things I say, I do not believe anything worthy of account has been achieved by me concerning the things on which we argue" (472b6–c2; see also 474a, 487e6–7).[10] Socrates' actual achievement of this aim is ambiguous, for other characters have a double relation to the argument. The final exchange with Polus can stand as a paradigm for the result of the whole dialogue in this regard (480e):

Polus: [The result of the argument] seems to me bizarre, Socrates,
   although perhaps in your eyes it agrees with what went before.

Socrates: Well either one must resolve those [earlier] matters, or these necessarily follow.
Polus: Yes, that is so.

That is, Plato presents Polus as unable to answer the argument but ultimately unmoved by it: he does *not* say, "I am convinced by what you have said, and will live my life according to your principles from now on." The same is true of Callicles, who goes further, making clear his lack of interest in the argument and trying to escape participating in it.[11] Plato did not need to present the results of the arguments in this manner, so what might he have gained by setting things up like this?[12]

On the basis of all this, we should say that the Socrates of the *Gorgias* develops into a *semi*-Platonic Socrates, one who has doctrines, but whose arguments fail to establish all he claims for them, and whose dialectical victory is significantly qualified. It is in the second book of the *Republic* that these qualifications on his philosophical activity will be removed, and we will have a fully Platonic Socrates, one who speaks for Plato in a more straightforward manner.[13] The *Gorgias*, then, through its portrayal of Socrates, locates itself in between the "early" dialogues and the *Republic*—and note how this view of Socrates coheres with the account of the sort of argument that the *Gorgias* has been found to make. That is, in the previous chapter, we found that the *Gorgias* is not concerned with establishing certain theses as necessarily true, but rather with contingent truths, a response to a particular situation. From a fully Platonic Socrates one might expect more than this.

But why would Plato present a Socrates who actually undergoes a change within the dialogue itself? What is gained by presenting him as *developing into*, rather than simply *being*, a semi-Platonic Socrates? We can find an answer in the context within which this takes place, that is, in the overall movement of the dialogue as explained above. Socrates presents his own views as a *reaction* to Polus and Callicles. This is the idea behind the changing Socrates of the dialogue. It is the need to respond to the destructive new position we find coming into being with Polus and Callicles that provokes Socrates into increasing activity, and thus into giving his own account. This is one of Plato's ways of indicating that the philosophy he will develop, of which we get an image in this dialogue, and which will be set forth at much greater length in the *Republic*, is a response to this particular development. In addition, we see here, once again, how the movement that culminates in Callicles is a good thing: it produces an active response from Socrates, something that a conversation with Gorgias alone could never have done.

NOTES

1. Dodds, *Gorgias*, 16–17, has drawn attention to certain Socratic changes in this dialogue.

2. Kahn, "Drama and Dialectic," 85: "by tacitly admitting that the orator need not *know* "what is just and honorable and good" (461b5–6), even though this is his official subject matter, Polus yields to the charge of cognitive emptiness which Socrates has been pressing against Gorgias throughout Act One. He thus lays himself open to Socrates' new onslaught in Act Two: his claim that such a technique of persuasion is not a *techne* at all, not the rational mastery of a definite subject matter, but merely an empirical knack of flattery and influence."

3. John Beversluis, *Cross-Examining Socrates: A Defense of the Interlocutors in Plato's Early Dialogues* (Cambridge: Cambridge University Press, 2000), 319, points us toward the change when he reminds us in this context that Socrates is "the philosopher whose wisdom consists in the fact that he knows nothing."

4. See also Dodds, *Gorgias*, 16–17, and Charles Kaufmann, "Enactment as Argument in the *Gorgias*," *Philosophy & Rhetoric* 12, no. 2 (Spring 1979): 120–21.

5. Rutherford, *Art of Plato*, 157–58, notes that the phrase, "there's nothing like asking him," occurs both in the initial scene of the dialogue, where Gorgias is the one to be asked, and at the start of the Callicles section, where Socrates is the one to be asked (447c5, 481b9). I take the point of this to be a nod toward Socrates' increasing activity.

6. Beversluis, *Cross-Examining*, 364, again brings our attention to the inconsistency within Socrates by referring to him as "the man who cannot tolerate long speeches."

7. On Socrates' failure to convince, see Kaufmann, "Enactment as Argument," 116–22.

8. I think the overall picture of Plato's corpus given by Kahn, *Plato and the Socratic Dialogue*, is very much in the right direction. Though I take a view of the purpose of the *Gorgias* different from Kahn's, I still think my interpretation fits into his overall framework for what is traditionally regarded as the early/middle Plato.

9. Indeed, Plato often leans so heavily in this direction that readers today complain that he has set up a "Yes man" to affirm everything the principal character says. It seems the complaint has been around since Plato's time, as Xenophon's recognizable parody of the Platonic dialogue shows: Socrates is shown asking a question requiring an affirmation, and everyone replies "certainly;" six more questions follow, each receiving the response "certainly." Then he asks, "would someone who is able to make others pleasing to one person be better, or someone who can make others pleasing to many people?" At this point there is a division, with some answering, "it is clear that he is better who can make others pleasing to many," and some saying, "certainly" (see Xenophon's *Symposium*, iii.56–9).

10. George Klosko, "The Insufficiency of Reason in Plato's *Gorgias*," *The Western Political Quarterly* 36, no. 4 (Dec. 1983): 587, makes a similar point.

11. Note also that unlike Gorgias, Polus does not reappear later as an interested onlooker. As Klosko, "Insufficiency," 593, says, "having explicitly made the point that his opponent must be convinced if he is to be accounted successful, Socrates is unable to convince Callicles of anything." Similarly, Rutherford, *Art of Plato*, 143: "an important feature of the *Gorgias* is Socrates' ultimate failure to convince."

12. Rutherford, *Art of Plato*, 141, suggests that the direct form in which the *Gorgias* is reported is to be contrasted with dialogues narrated by Socrates (specifically the *Protagoras*): "it is less natural for us to align ourselves with Socrates; he is not present as a friendly narrator inviting our sympathy." In fact, the Socrates of the *Gorgias* is a flawed character. For example, already in antiquity people noticed that his attack on the Four Men (513d–517a)—that is, on Cimon, Miltiades, Themistocles and Pericles—fit Socrates himself like a glove: see Olympiodorus, *Commentary on Plato's Gorgias*, trans. and eds. Robin Jackson, Kimon Lycos and Harold Tarrent (Boston: Brill, 1998), 261 (lecture 41.3), and Dodds, *Gorgias*, 355; more recently, see Kaufmann, "Enactment as Argument," 122–24.

13. See Tarnopolsky, *Prudes*, 44–46, for a different account of the changes in Socrates over the course of the dialogue. She sees him changing into a fully Platonic Socrates.

Republic I

Plato has expended an extraordinary amount of care on the first book of the *Republic*. There is not a detail, not a phrase—scarcely even a word—that is not crucial to his purpose. The dramatic and argumentative aspects of the dialogue present a seamless web throughout, revealing an ordered movement through three standpoints, one each for Cephalus, Polemarchus, and Thrasymachus. Many have struggled to make sense of what can seem a muddle of bad arguments and superfluous literary detail. The first book, however, is a *masterpiece*. Important though the particular arguments with Polemarchus and Thrasymachus may be, it is in the overall movement taken as a whole that the argument of the first book lies, and it forms, as we shall see, the perfect introduction to the *Republic*.

The inadequacies in Socrates' arguments fall into a consistent pattern, and are precisely appropriate to the requirements of both the first book and the rest of the work. Just as in the first part of the *Gorgias*, the arguments are generally *ad hominem*, and do successfully refute the particular characters at whom they are directed—indeed, thus understood, they usually cut with the precision of a surgeon's scalpel, right to the heart of the position in question. Of course, at the same time, they can hardly be an attempt on Plato's part to move the reader to Socrates' position. There is, however, another aspect. Previous scholarship has called attention to the "proleptic" character of the first book of the *Republic*, that is, to the way in which aspects of the first book look ahead to doctrines that appear late in the work.[1] We shall see new instances of prolepsis in what follows, and in particular, we shall be concerned with the *logically proleptic* character of the arguments of book i: though they overlook crucial considerations, and thus cannot be expected to convince a careful reader, these crucial considerations subsequently become a focus of the rest of the work at some point in books ii–x.[2] This is one sense—though not the only one—in which the whole *Republic* is a response to the challenge set out in book i.

The view of book i that prevailed for a time considered its purpose to be merely negative, clearing away conceptions of justice which might rival Plato's own, or perhaps providing an implicit critique of the method of earlier Socratic dialogues. This need not be wholly false, but neither is it wholly true, for the overall movement from Cephalus to Thrasymachus presents us with an intellectual history, one whose purpose is to locate the *Republic* relative to the intellectual crisis of Plato's time. This movement brings out the problem which the *Republic* must answer, the critical necessity of finding an answer, and also shows something of the form the answer will take.

One aspect deserves to be introduced right at the start: the movement from Cephalus to Thrasymachus is in a crucial respect a movement toward the good. Plato has been very careful indeed with his use of the word ἀγαθός ("good") in this first book, the same word that will be used for the ultimate principle later on in the *Republic*.³ We shall see that Cephalus answers a question about good (ἀγαθός) in terms of the useful (χρηστός): he has no active connection to the good. Polemarchus uses the word "good" the moment he is forced to think for himself, although he understands it to be something that one does to other people, and he has not entirely worked out the difference between the useful and the good (we shall see how the argument with Polemarchus gradually purges the useful from the good). Thrasymachus uses the word "good" at the very moment he is finally driven to say what he really thinks, and we shall see how everything he says and does is grounded in the good as he understands it. It is Socrates, however, who in the end gives expression to the closest relation of all to the good, for he speaks of "good" as something one can *be*. The movement of the first book is not just a matter of different definitions of justice, but also of different, and ever closer, ways of relating to the good.

NOTES

1. Charles Kahn, "Proleptic Composition in the *Republic*, or Why Book I was Never a Separate Dialogue," *The Classical Quarterly*, New Series 43, no. 1 (1993): 131–42, gives an overview of this aspect of the work.
2. Kenneth Dorter, "Socrates' Refutation of Thrasymachus and Treatment of Virtue," *Philosophy and Rhetoric* 7 (1974): 25–46, seems to have been the first to suggest this, though he was focused only on the last three arguments against Thrasymachus (348a–354c). Christopher Rowe, *Plato and the Art of Philosophical Writing* (Cambridge: Cambridge University Press, 2007), 186–97, shows how the argument at 349b–350c is proleptic, requiring the rest of the work to address the

differences in assumption between Socrates and Thrasymachus (I shall give a different account of what exactly that difference in assumption is). We shall see how earlier arguments also fall into this pattern.

3. The relevant passage begins in book vi at 505a2: ἡ τοῦ ἀγαθοῦ ἰδέα μέγιστον μάθημα ("the greatest learning is the form of The Good").

(1) Cephalus

The first page of the dialogue (to 328b) is a dramatic introduction to the *Republic* as a whole; we shall return to it in the Conclusion. We begin, then, with Cephalus, the voice of a traditional order, who has lived a life that seems to a substantial degree to have been virtuous. However, though he speaks words which do contain a sort of wisdom, he cannot give an adequate account of his virtue; between his life and his thought is a gulf he can neither recognize nor bridge.

The initial description of Cephalus gives us two main impressions: first, he is very old (328b; the point is emphasized from 328c–e) and second, he is pious: we meet him wearing a wreath, having just performed sacrifices. His exit from the dialogue will confirm this opening impression of piety: he will go off to perform more sacrifices.[1] The picture is thus of someone in almost continual communion with the gods, and his concern for the divine order comes up again when he speaks of punishments in the afterlife (330d–331b). This is an important point in relation to what follows: the gods are quite real for Cephalus, whatever doubts he may have concerning the exact truth of traditional stories (330d–e). Achieving a proper relation to the divine is a matter of genuine concern to him, a matter to which he clearly devotes a significant amount of time. His dutiful relation to a traditional order is also emphasized in his frequent reference to great figures of authority: he quotes Sophocles (329b–c), Themistocles (329e–330a) and Pindar (331a).

The conversation with Cephalus is remarkable—particularly in light of what is to come later—both for its pleasant tone and for its repeated expressions of agreement. It begins with the old man welcoming Socrates and expressing his desire for more frequent visits (328c6–d8); in return, Socrates makes clear that he sees in Cephalus a valuable source of insight (328d9–e8). This opening sets the tone for the whole encounter with Cephalus. It is not

(1) Cephalus

only a pleasant encounter in which both sides show continual regard for one another but is also a discussion rather than an argument, punctuated by declarations of agreement from both men (329d8, 329e7, 330c10–d1).[2] Even Socrates' most direct criticism of Cephalus begins with the words "you speak splendidly" (331c). The pleasant nature of the conversation, and the continual expressions of mutual regard give us reason to disagree with those who would paint the encounter with Cephalus in an unsympathetic fashion;[3] the emphasis on agreement that we find throughout will prove still more significant.

As the conversation with Cephalus moves forward, it soon becomes clear that there is more reason for Socrates' respect for Cephalus than mere deference to old age. In addition to his piety, there are other indications that Cephalus is genuinely virtuous: he believes his temperament to have made old age less painful for him than for many of his fellows (329a–d), and if wealth has helped him in this, he sees it as necessary but not sufficient for contentedness[4]—a sort of balance involving both a decent man (ὁ ἐπιεικής) and adequate means is required. Such balance and moderation appears again when he describes his relation to money as a mean between the extremes of his father and grandfather; Socrates himself then confirms that the old man is not overly concerned with money (330b–c). Pious, mindful of great authority figures, moderate and balanced in conspicuous aspects of his life—and above all, old—Cephalus is meant to represent an older world of Hellenic virtue. His relation to this order is, as we shall see, unbroken by critical thought.

It has long been recognized that

> in Cephalus' simple utterances some of the philosophical results of the body of the *Republic* are anticipated. In him the delight of philosophical discourse has taken the place of the pleasures of the flesh (328d, cf. 485d–e); he has thereby got rid of "a raging and cruel master" like the "tyrant love" of book ix (572e sqq.). In the course of a long life he has come to see that, though poverty can mar happiness, no material prosperity can command it, and that character is the arbiter of happiness (330a–b, cf. 591e).[5]

In three cases listed here—an appreciation for the pleasures of discourse, freedom from bodily appetites, and the importance of character—Cephalus has indeed hit upon truths central to the *Republic*, and yet in each case there is also an inadequacy.

First of all, when we look at the sort of discourse which is present throughout the encounter with Cephalus, we see that it is in fact only superficially philosophical. It consists of speeches—on philosophical subjects, one admits—in which conflicts and disagreements are avoided: when Socrates gently suggests a criticism of Cephalus, by setting up an opposition between him and "the many" (329d–e), Cephalus responds not with a refutation of

(1) Cephalus 183

those who contradict him, but shows how both sides are partly right, removing or at least reducing the opposition (329–e330a; he even begins with "you are correct"). However, when Socrates sets up a more direct and explicit opposition (331c), Cephalus simply leaves the dialogue. It is a relatively easy matter to give and admire lengthy speeches; a truly philosophical form of discourse could maintain itself in the face of direct criticism, giving a satisfying account of particular ideas and their mutual relation, in the sort of question-and-answer format into which the dialogue moves after Cephalus, in which each major point—and sometimes minor ones—is approved by participants before moving to the next. If Cephalus were to disagree openly with Socrates, he would have to give some *reason* for his differing opinion. Instead, it takes only a single direct question to remove him from the discussion. His frequent reliance on authority figures, already noted, further confirms the impression of a discussion which is only superficially philosophical.

Second, as for Cephalus' relation to bodily pleasures, it is true that he has achieved a certain independence from them, but there is a double problem in this. First, his current situation has come about through the accident of old age rather than a determined and premeditated effort on his part—in fact, this is true also of his increased desire for discourse (328d)[6] and his concern with Hades (330d–e). Secondly, Cephalus' relation to his bodily appetites is simply a matter of negation—they fade away (ἀπομαραίνονται—328d), and he is free from many mad masters (329c). Although the passions, unchecked, can grow despotic (as we see in books viii–ix), it does not follow that Plato advocates a simple retreat from or repression of them. On the contrary, virtually all the positive doctrines of the *Republic* come after 372d, when the appetites of the healthy, moderate city are allowed to become inflamed: a significant goal of the work will be to establish an appropriate relation to the appetites while still allowing them a place in the scheme of things.[7] Although Cephalus has attained a stability relative to his appetites, this is not as a result of having worked out his own relationship with them, actively relating them in turn to their proper end, but simply through their having been negated. Thus while Cephalus has achieved a sort of inner order, something which is indeed desirable, behind this lies a double flaw in his means of achieving it.

Third, it is significant that Cephalus' first speech, in response to Socrates' request for some thoughts on old age, brings out the central doctrine of the *Republic*: the importance of character (ὁ τρόπος τῶν ἀνθρώπων—329d), a theme to which he repeatedly returns. The conversation focuses on old age and money, two external relations particularly well-suited to bringing out one's ability to stand firm in response to outside pressures.[8] Cephalus is less fortunate in relation to one, and more fortunate in relation to the other, and this should allow him to demonstrate his steadfastness in relation to both good and bad fortune. However, it is difficult to be impressed by Cephalus' account of character: what is its content?

We hear of a man who is ἐπιεικής ("decent"), κόσμιος ("orderly") and εὔκολος ("content/sweet-tempered"),[9] and also of one "having sense" (ἀνδρὶ νοῦν ἔχοντι—331b). These words suggest an agreeable nature, though not an active one. At this point, we can begin to draw together various details which we have already laid out: the pleasant and agreeable nature of the conversation with Cephalus and the superficially philosophical discussion which goes along with it; the accidental manner in which Cephalus' escape from the passions, his desire for discussion and his concern with Hades have all arisen; the fact that his freedom with regard to the passions is a matter of simple negation—all these things suggest, not strong and active character, but its opposite. In his last speech, Cephalus concludes that the greatest use of money is that it helps keep one from unwillingly (ἄκοντα331b) deceiving, lying and owing things to gods and men. This advantage is not only passive; it is negative: there seems to be a series of things one should *not* do, rules set up by the gods to which one must conform. As in his release from the passions, which was itself a merely negative achievement, the aim here seems to be to experience the absence of evil, not actively to seek the good.[10] True character, surely, consists in preserving one's integrity in the face of external pressure, not in conforming as closely as possible to an externally given order, and in actively seeking one's proper end, not in fear of external punishments.

Thus, although Cephalus may bear old age more easily than his fellows, and may have a more moderate relationship with wealth than many others, nothing that we see suggests a will deliberately setting things in order according to an actively acquired understanding. For all his talk of character, Cephalus represents an extreme of passivity. His contentedness arises as a result of an incidental correspondence between his natural state (old age) and what he understands to be appropriate to proper living (release from the passions), not as a result of calculated and conscious action. It seems reasonable to infer that his talk of character comes from the maxims of some great figure of authority, a Themistocles or a Solon, and that the gulf between this talk and what we see of Cephalus' actual life is a matter of his inadequate understanding of the words he has received. With its passive and negative tendencies, the actual content of Cephalus' own character consists substantially in being determined by what is other than him. It is true that there is a certain minimal level of active thought in Cephalus, for he has been able to think his way past those of his fellows who simply bewail old age—and yet even here we do not see him holding his own in debate with them.

In the course of his final speech, Cephalus' external orientation is confirmed in another regard, and in a most significant manner. It is not correct to say that "the greatest good Cephalus has enjoyed from money is the avoidance of injustice and impiety,"[11] for this misses a crucial distinction. Socrates asks what the greatest *good* is (μέγιστον ἀγαθὸν—330d)[12] which Cephalus has enjoyed on account of his great wealth, and Cephalus responds in terms of *utility*: wealth, he concludes, has many other *uses* (χρείας), but it is most *useful* (χρησιμώτατον) in the regards he has mentioned. The only time Cephalus ever uses the word "good" is incidentally, when mentioning the "good nurse of old age" (ἀγαθὴ γηροτρόφος—331a) at a moment when he is citing Pindar. The word ἀγαθός ("good") is, of course, a significant one in the *Republic*, and the fact that Cephalus doesn't show much interest in it will prove to be important. But we should also note the nature of his confusion in answering Socrates. What is good is desired for itself, while what is useful is desired for the sake of something else, and thus looks to what is external to itself. Cephalus talked of character, but is himself actually quite externally oriented, the opposite of what character should be; his conception of ends involves the same confusion.

With all this in mind, we can see that the criticism which Socrates makes (331c) goes right to the heart of what is at work in Cephalus. The definition he ascribes to Cephalus,[13] telling the truth and giving back what one has taken,[14] is itself focused on external relationships: it requires that we know nothing of the nature of the people with whom we deal, only our relation to them. Earlier, Cephalus had said that one "sums up and considers if one has done anyone some wrong" (330e), a phrase that brings out nicely his idea of how morality works: it is essentially an economic conception—not surprising for a businessman—and one entirely consistent with his preference for words of utility rather than goodness.[15] Socrates' counter-example involving someone who has gone mad calls Cephalus' whole view of the world into question: where Cephalus' external orientation has him considering only abstract relationships between individuals, Socrates' criticism requires that we take into consideration the nature of the particular person with whom we are dealing. At this point philosophy requires activity of those who grasp the problem. Cephalus can indeed see that there is a problem here but is not much interested in it: he is content to bequeath the conversation to his son, and is so far from being disturbed by Socrates that he laughs as he departs (331d). However, Socrates' single critical question (331c1–10), even though it is far gentler than what we will see from him later on, is like a pebble thrown on still water, shattering the order that had so far been present.[16]

Finally, it is appropriate to consider Cephalus in terms of a political community. Starting at 368e, the argument of the *Republic* will explicitly involve an analogy between the individual and the city; in book i, the matter of the political aspect of principles of justice also arises (beginning at 338d). Accordingly, although Cephalus is clearly focused on proper living as it relates to him as an individual, it is entirely within the spirit of the *Republic* to ask a question of what we have seen of Cephalus' thinking: what sort of community would it produce? The answer should be obvious. If everyone strives to act honorably, to refrain from deceiving others, to pay back all they owe, then we have a community at peace with itself, free from the divisions caused by political strife. In this context of the times, this will mean that we're dealing with a city.

The problem with what Cephalus represents lies less in the content of his life than in his inability to give an adequate account of it. He has an unconsidered "knowledge" of right and wrong, acquired through the experience of his life and the wisdom of tradition and authority.[17] Uninterested in philosophical debate, he can hardly be troubled by it. As Cephalus departs, no doubt he remains secure in his maxims received from poets and great men, sacrificing to the gods and conforming to the divinely given order.

NOTES

1. Julia Annas, *An Introduction to Plato's Republic* (New York: Oxford University Press, 1981), 20, sees in Cephalus' exit a "polite fiction that he has to attend to the sacrifice (which is in fact over)." If this were what Plato wanted to communicate, we might expect to hear that Cephalus then did something other than what he said he would (e.g., "he went off to bed"). Instead, Socrates—the narrator—tells us that Cephalus then went off "to the sacred rites" (πρὸς τὰ ἱερά—331d), echoing the word Cephalus had just used to describe his intentions: "I must take charge of the sacred rites" (τῶν ἱερῶν—331d). How could Plato more clearly indicate that Cephalus is as good as his word as he leaves?

2. I can't resist noting 330c10–d1: "You speak truly," he said. "I certainly do," I replied. (Ἀληθῆ, ἔφη, λέγεις. Πάνυ μὲν οὖν, ἦν δ' ἐγώ).

3. As does Annas, *Introduction*, 18–23. In particular, she claims that in declaring his enthusiasm for conversations (328d), Cephalus is paying "a back-handed compliment," and "saying, in a tactless and insensitive way, that this sort of thing is fine once you have nothing better to do." As we shall see, Annas is correct to emphasize the unphilosophical aspect of Cephalus, but the spin she puts on it is inappropriate: within the context of the first book of the *Republic*, the conversation with Cephalus is not conspicuous for its lack of tact and sensitivity, but rather for the mutual regard and agreement repeatedly expressed explicitly by both characters. John F. Wilson, *The Politics of Moderation* (Lanham, MD: University Press of America, 1984), 2, describes Cephalus' behavior here as "polite."

4. Beversluis, *Cross-Examining*, 187, gives a different account of Cephalus' relation to wealth, reminding us that Plato and the Platonic Socrates often seem to look down on those who spend their lives in pursuit of wealth. Such misgivings, he says are "unmistakably implied" in relation to Cephalus (see also Mark Gifford, "Dramatic Dialectic in Republic Book I," *Oxford Studies in Ancient Philosophy* 20 (2001): 68–69). In the context of the *Republic*, however, it is not

(1) Cephalus 187

correct to say, with Beversluis, that "such people have no place in the ideal city." The various kinds of artisans (all of whom work for wages, thus spending much of their time pursuing wealth) form the appetitive class, which is not only necessary to the ideal city, but also the largest class within it. This sort of activity becomes problematic only when it proceeds without moderation, but clearly Cephalus has this virtue. Following Dorter, "Refutation of Thrasymachus," 26, I take Cephalus to foreshadow the appetitive class, its peculiar virtue, and the associated part of the soul.

5. Nettleship, *Lectures*, 15–16. The comments of Edward Urwick, *The Message of Plato: A Reinterpretation of the Republic* (London: Methuen & Co., 1920), 43–44, on Cephalus seem to me to get the spirit of the matter as well.

6. Mark Gifford, "Dramatic Dialectic in Republic Book I," *Oxford Studies in Ancient Philosophy* 20 (2001): 63, makes a similar point.

7. A full treatment of this view is beyond the present work, but see pages 161–65, for an account of how Plato takes this approach in the *Gorgias*.

8. It is interesting to note here that Plato remarks in the *Phaedrus* (267e) that Thrasymachus deserved the prize for bewailing the evils of poverty and old age.

9. Three words can be combined in twos in three possible ways; each combination can be found once in the conversation with Cephalus: κόσμιος and εὔκολος at 329d; ἐπιεικής and εὔκολος at 330a; and ἐπιεικής and κόσμιος at 331a. Note that we do not find the word ἀγαθός ("good") here.

10. E. L. Harrison, "Plato's Manipulation of Thrasymachus," *Phoenix* 21, no. 1 (Spring 1967): 28, notes that "for a time negative forms come thick and fast: ἀδικήσαντα (330d), ἠδίκηκεν (330e), ἀδικήματα (330e), ἄδικον (331a)."

11. Alan Bloom, "Interpretive Essay," in *Plato, Republic*, trans. Alan Bloom (1991; Philadelphia: Basic Books, 1968), 313–14.

12. Bernard Bosanquet, *A Companion to Plato's Republic for English Readers* (London: Rivington's, 1906), 40, and Stanley Rosen, *Plato's Republic: A Study* (New Haven, CT: Yale University Press, 2005), 28, both note that the significant word ἀγαθός is used here, the same word which Plato will use for the Good later in the *Republic*, but neither has grasped the full significance of it here. Beversluis, *Cross-Examining*, 191, has noted the difference in Cephalus' vocabulary, but would not allow it the significance I give it here.

13. Of course, Cephalus does not, strictly speaking, *define* justice. To give a definition would be to leave his world of pleasant speeches for the more demanding realm of precise thought and argument. As soon as the discussion moves in this direction, Cephalus leaves. On the fairness of Socrates' attribution of a definition here, see Gifford, "Dramatic Dialectic," 73.

14. Even Socrates' positive restatement points to Cephalus' negative orientation: Cephalus spoke of unwillingly lying and fearing to depart while owing things; Socrates speaks of telling the truth and giving back what one has taken.

15. On the economic aspect of Cephalus, see Gifford, "Dramatic Dialectic," 77, fn.58.

16. Traditional wisdom could no doubt deal with a madman demanding his weapons back, perhaps with a different maxim. There is no suggestion that the content

of tradition is wrong, but it is not present in a way that can enter Socrates' world of definitions.

17. The fact that he does use the word "good" when citing Pindar (331a) drives this point home all the more strongly: the poetic tradition from which he derives his "wisdom" has some of the most important content which will later prove so central to the *Republic*, but Cephalus has not adequately understood it.

(2) Polemarchus

Well over a century ago, the essential point concerning Polemarchus was understood, the one through which the whole encounter with him can be grasped: "when we come to Polemarchus we pass from the old generation . . . to a new generation which has inherited the experience of the old, but in a partial way."[1] This is the dramatic expression of Polemarchus' position: he is divided in his relation to the older order. We shall see that this division expresses itself in many respects.

The opening moments of the argument with Polemarchus point to this division: he is caught between a loyalty to what Cephalus represented and a liberation from the confines of that loyalty.[2] On the one hand, his entry into the conversation distinguishes him from Cephalus: he interrupts (331d), showing an interest in, and an active relation toward, the argument. A young man, Polemarchus is not set in his ways as his father is, so that philosophical questions can have a genuine and vital interest for him.[3] The change from father to son is also reflected in the disappearance of the constant expressions of respect and agreement which we noted with Cephalus: the argument with Polemarchus is not ill-mannered or impolite, but it is indeed an argument. On the other hand, we hear twice that he is the heir (κληρονόμος—331d–e) of Cephalus, suggesting that he will take up what his father has left behind. In addition, Polemarchus begins with an appeal to the poet Simonides (331d), continuing the use of authority figures which characterized his father's speeches. Finally, the first definition advanced by Polemarchus, that "it is just to give back to each the things which are owed" (ὀφειλόμενα—331e3), effectively restates the view which Socrates was criticizing, reusing a significant word which Cephalus had used (ὀφείλοντα—331b2).

However, the conversation soon brings out a difficulty in relying on the words of any authority: even if a critic such as Socrates is willing to agree that

189

the authority speaks the truth,[4] it is necessary to interpret the poet's words. The responsibility then falls to Polemarchus to clarify his meaning. This leaves him completely on his own, the words of the poets an empty help, true though they may be. In the speeches of Cephalus, one did not worry too much about definitions—indeed, one felt secure in the immediate knowledge of a divine order—but Polemarchus, ready as he is to enter into a more rigorous form of discourse, finds himself cut off from the gods and the insight inspired by them. This is the last we shall see in book i of the trusting and credulous use of poets and other traditional figures of authority.

Polemarchus parries Socrates' objection with another traditional notion, that of doing good to friends and harm to enemies.[5] There is one particularly important change here: we saw that Cephalus ignored the word "good" when Socrates used it; Polemarchus brings out the word "good" (ἀγαθός—332a10) of his own accord the moment he's left to himself.

In explaining what is due to enemies, Polemarchus continues to steer the argument onto a new course: "I suppose what is owed [ὀφείλεται] by an enemy to an enemy is just what is fitting [προσήκει]: some harm" (332b7–9). The notion of doing certain people harm is a shift worth noting, for it was never even hinted at in the discussion with Cephalus. Another shift, from "owed" to "fitting," is also significant, for it is emphasized in Socrates' response: "Simonides, as it seems, said poetically, in riddles, what the just is. For he thought, as it seems, that it is just to give what is fitting to each person, and he called this 'what is owed'" (332b10–c3).

Because Plato has drawn our attention to the distinction, we must attend to it. "What is owed" (τὸ ὀφειλόμενον) requires only that we know a relationship between two people. We do not need to know whether the one who is owed something is good or bad, friend or enemy, sane or mad—none of this affects the fact that something is owed. As Socrates says, "what he deposited, this is surely owed" (332a1). "What is fitting" (τὸ προσῆκον), on the other hand, requires that we know, not simply a relationship, but something of the nature of the person or thing we are dealing with: harm, in Polemarchus' view, is fitting only for a certain *kind* of person. This represents a dramatic step away from what Cephalus was saying, leaving behind the externality that characterized him, and beginning the move inward which will ultimately characterize the whole *Republic*. Thus we have many respects—the active introduction of the words "good" and "fitting," the talk of harm, the move beyond authority figures, and the move inward—in which Polemarchus represents something quite different from Cephalus.

Plato's emphasis on the change from "owed" to "fitting" helps us to make sense of the direction in which the argument now turns: Socrates suddenly proceeds on the basis of an analogy to skills, a move that has seemed unreasonable and unfair to many readers. After all, Polemarchus never mentioned

(2) Polemarchus 191

skills, and a few of his answers seem rather noncommittal as Socrates brings the skills analogy to bear on the argument concerning justice (332d4–6, d9, e5–6). The suggestion is that he is going along reluctantly: this wasn't what he thought he was saying. Accordingly, it is not surprising to find interpreters criticizing the introduction of the skills-analogy with such comments as "Socrates in fact fathered on him assumptions which he neither made nor was committed to."[6]

In fact, the matter is not so simple. On the basis of Polemarchus' move to "what is fitting," Socrates' introduction of the skills-analogy to the argument is far from implausible. Consider: when we are talking about merely external relationships—the "what is owed" of Cephalus—we don't need to know anything about the nature of the person to whom something is owed. With "what is fitting," however, the matter is different. Different things are fitting for different natures, and to know what is fitting for a particular nature is to be competent in the art or skill (τέχνη) relevant to that particular thing. To use Plato's examples, one who has the art of medicine knows what is fitting for the body (332c–d); the art of cooking knows what is fitting for meats and other foods.

The skills-analogy also picks up on something suggested by Polemarchus' definition: the conception of the good at this point threatens to instrumentalize it—that is, good is something one does to friends, it is *for the sake of* friends. The good is still confused with the useful to a considerable degree. It is not yet seen simply as something desired for itself. We shall see below how this understanding is confirmed by the argument with Polemarchus, which gradually changes its focus from the merely instrumental (i.e., useful) to what is simply good. Still, if the skills-analogy is plausible here, it has not explicitly been agreed upon.

It is not hard to find another interpretation of Polemarchus' words: when he says that doing some good is owed to friends (332a9–10), and some evil is owed to enemies (b7–9), one imagines he thought he was describing an imperative rather than a form of skilled activity. His definition, then, would indicate what one ought to aim at, rather than what one must actually achieve: if we tried to do good to a friend but failed, our activity could still count as just. The skills-analogy is only required if we assume (1) that we need to answer the question of what exactly is fitting for a particular nature, and (2) that beyond this, it is not the fact of having tried, but of having actually given what is fitting that is important. In the case of this second requirement, Polemarchus has not been explicit, but he also does not make any objection to Socrates' interpretation at this point.

How are we to make sense of this move by Socrates? Perhaps there is an answer in the *proleptic* nature of book i: it anticipates, in various ways, matters that will be treated more fully later in the work. We have already seen how Cephalus anticipates certain doctrines that come later in the work. In the current case, the question of whether we understand "giving what is fitting to each person" as a moral imperative or as a sort of skill turns on the unstated questions of whether we know what is fitting (or good) and whether we are able to achieve it. These are not just any questions but point to a matter that will lie at the heart of the whole *Republic*: what is good, and how is it to be achieved? We shall see that justice will not consist of a series of pious ought-to-be's, but rather will have the characteristics of a skill that come into play here: the work will aim to show that it is possible to know what is good, and to achieve it. We shall also see how Socrates develops his own views in response to Thrasymachus, but without explicitly addressing the assumptions that provide the basis of his disagreement with Thrasymachus; here, he makes a similar move against Polemarchus, implicitly introducing an assumption that may not be appropriate to the younger man, but that will lie at the heart of the account that we see later in the work. In both cases, the move is to be understood relative to the nature of book i, a consideration that will become clearer in the conclusion.

Polemarchus does not understand any significant shift to have taken place with the move from "owed" to "fitting." The fact of an unrecognized ambiguity here is typical of him; we have seen how he partly looks back to Cephalus, and partly looks ahead to something quite different. There are indications that his thought is basically confused, conflating principles that are in fact opposed. Where "the owed" and "the fitting" (ὀφειλόμενον, προσῆκον) are concerned, we have seen that Socrates draws attention to the distinction (332b10–c3), but he then allows Polemarchus the pretense that the position has not changed, twice bringing the two terms together (ὀφειλόμενον καὶ προσῆκον—332c6–7, c11) as if they were two aspects of the same thing, when the reality is that the latter term is the one determining the argument.

Soon Socrates will play along in similar fashion with the combination of ἀγαθὸς καὶ χρήσιμος ("good and useful"—333b1; also the comparative forms, χρησιμώτερός τε καὶ ἀμείνων—"more useful and better"—at 333b4–5; see also 333b7, c7). In the subsequent argument, which focuses on whether or not friends are actually good (334c–335a), he switches between the terms χρηστός ("useful") and ἀγαθός ("good") as though they were simply interchangeable with one another; the same is true there of πονηρός ("base" or "useless") and κακός ("evil"). A more deeply thoughtful character than Polemarchus would object that there is a difference between the owed and the fitting, between the good and the useful, but by means of such ambiguities Plato is creating an utterly consistent characterization of an essentially divided figure, a son who has inherited his father's world, but in a partial way. We shall see that the distinction between the useful and the good is relevant to the arguments here.

(2) Polemarchus

The bulk of the argument with Polemarchus can be divided into three parts according to the sort of argument used. First, there is the argument from the analogy to skills (τέχναι, 332c–334b), then an argument from the difference between appearance and reality, emphasizing the difficulty of human knowing (334c–335a), and finally an argument from the nature of virtue and justice (335b–d). These same forms of argument will be repeated, significantly in a different order, with Thrasymachus.

The argument from the analogy to skills focuses first (332d–333e) on the question of how justice might be useful (χρήσιμος).[7] This focus is driven home with all the subtlety of a sledgehammer: the conclusion finds justice to be "*use*less in *use* and *use*ful in dis*use*" (emphasis mine—ἐν μὲν χρήσει ἄχρηστος, ἐν δὲ ἀχρηστίᾳ χρήσιμος—333d12). There appears to be a difficulty where utility is concerned, for there already exist skills whose purpose is to be useful in respect of every particular activity, and anything that justice might do on this account would already seem to be provided for by another skill. There might seem to be a place for justice either in war, or for storing things safely in peace, but this doesn't seem to capture the notion of justice terribly well. The argument here points to a problem that will receive an answer later in the work, when we find that justice is not a particular skill like all the others, but is concerned with ordering the whole (433a–434c, 443c–444d).

The first part of the skills-argument suggested a problem concerning the utility of justice; the second part (333e–334b) suggests that justice, as Polemarchus understands it, might actually be a *bad* thing. That is, we now turn away from the question of utility, and begin to think in terms of the good. The problem here follows directly from the analogy to skills, at least within the context of Polemarchus' view of things: wherever anyone has a skill, there he is most able to do both good *and* evil. If justice is merely an instrument, it will not simply be good. Thus Socrates concludes that "it would seem justice . . . is a certain stealing, for the benefit, to be sure, of friends and for the harm of enemies" (334b). This rather disreputable conclusion comes out of the particular conception of justice—guarding things in peacetime—that the argument has developed. However, the indeterminacy that Socrates brings out here could have been taken much farther, for justice as Polemarchus has described it sets no limit at all to what could be done to enemies. We can broaden the conclusion in principle: murder, torture, blackmail, every form of treachery and betrayal—all of this is sanctioned and much more besides, so long as they are directed at enemies. The fact that acts of a more brutal nature are allowed to lurk, implicit, beneath the surface of what is explicitly said is part of the place of Polemarchus within the dialogue: with Thrasymachus, the liberation from normative restraint will no longer be implicit.

Even without such a broadening of the conclusion, Socrates has shown Polemarchus that his view of justice allows for more liberation from normative restraint than he finds comfortable. He does not dig in his heels and defend his words, as he did earlier (332a), but relents: clearly, he is in the grip of sentiments which do not agree with this interpretation of the great poets. Polemarchus does not seem to want to admit himself an advocate of stealing: at least to this extent he remains his father's heir.

The next argument, dealing with the difference between appearance and reality (334c–335a), shows that the position in question allows for greater liberation still from restraint, and yet also introduces the first basis we have seen for limiting such liberation. Who exactly are friends, and who are enemies? Polemarchus says, "it is reasonable to love those whom one believes useful, and to hate those whom one believes base" (334c4).[8] From this it follows that for those who err in their belief concerning who is their friend, "it is just to act wickedly towards those who do no wrong" (334d). No relation to the actual goodness of the person in question is required; it provides no protection for an enemy. Again, if we follow this line of thought in principle, we see that all normative limits on behavior toward anyone who merely *seems* to be an enemy have been removed, so that such people can be subjected to torture, execution, etc. Even without setting all this out explicitly, the argument is enough to get Polemarchus to change his definition.[9] As before, it is unstated convictions that have moved him, for he might very well have maintained his position by declaring that it *is* in fact just to harm those who do no wrong. Instead, Socrates has brought him to acknowledge what is good as the standard.

At this point we can appreciate that there is a progression in the argument from the useful toward the good. The first argument, which considered justice as a skill, was focused on utility. This focus is an inheritance from Cephalus, who spoke of the useful—χρήσιμος (331b9)—in response to a question about the good. Next, the argument begins a move away from mere utility, with the conclusion that justice is a "certain stealing" (334b), the first suggestion of an inadequacy as regards what is good. The next step in the argument (to 334d) begins a move away from this inadequacy by getting Polemarchus to change his position so that it focuses on what is actually, rather than just apparently, good (335a). The final argument (335b–e) completes the movement, producing a conception of justice that is focused only on the good.

This final argument has been criticized, but convincing the reader to adopt Socrates' conclusions is not Plato's purpose here, something suggested by Thrasymachus, when he complains, in effect, that Polemarchus has not been properly refuted (336c). The argument is to be explained through the necessities imposed upon Plato by the nature of the first book. Polemarchus must be removed from conversation, his position must be refuted—and yet, the problems which have come to light must *not* simply be resolved, or there would be no need to say anything more. Plato has accomplished this in a particularly interesting way. As it is presented, the argument is not likely to convince a careful reader, as it invokes, without explanation, premises which are far from self-evident. In particular, two concepts crucial to the argument, excellence or virtue (ἀρετή—335b–c) and function (ἔργον 335d), are used as if no explanation were needed (in the refutation of Thrasymachus, ἀρετή will appear in two arguments, at 348c2 and 353b2; ἔργον in one at 352e3). Considered from the point of view of the whole *Republic*, one can see how these premises make sense (in fact, ἔργον will be explained in more detail at the end of book i). Thus understood, the argument is *logically proleptic*—that is, it looks ahead to the rest of the work to give an account of its premises. On this basis we can show that Plato is not as foolish here as he has sometimes seemed to critics.

In the first place, this argument (335b–e) is directed at Polemarchus, and we have seen in his position an ambiguity, a failure to think through the distinction between the instrumental and what is good in itself, between skill and virtue. To note that "the argument apparently equivocates between justice as a virtue . . . and justice as a practical craft"[10] is therefore to note that the argument proceeds on the basis of Polemarchus' position as we have understood it. Next, there are two premises which may seem controversial: (1) people, when harmed, become worse with respect to human excellence (i.e., ἀρετή); (2) justice is human excellence (335c). Few readers are likely to accept these premises so easily as Polemarchus (or even to be sure what exactly is being said).[11] From the point of view of the later doctrine of the *Republic*, however, justice—the proper ordering of the soul—is what is most essential to a good life; external things, such as health, reputation, or wealth, are not so necessary. On this view, the way really to harm someone would be to make him less just; external forms of "harm" physical, financial, etc.— would represent a different, and less significant, sense of the word.[12] It is fair to object that the case has not yet been made in relation to Polemarchus, but that is the point: *only if* the whole *Republic* presents a convincing case will Polemarchus have been answered. An argument that is dense, difficult to follow, and, if abstracted from the work as a whole, unsatisfactory, seems to fit Plato's requirements here quite well.

The point of Socrates' argument here is to bring out how, on Polemarchus' definition, it is in the nature of justice to bring about injustice. Anyone for whom the hostility of enemies is of such fundamental importance that it is part of the definition of justice will want not only to cause pain to enemies but also to harm them in such a way as to make them less effective as enemies. If they are less effective as enemies, they will be less able to help their friends and harm their enemies, which on Polemarchus' view of justice would mean making them less just, and thus worse.[13] On this view, then, the just man, using justice, will make his enemies less just. This would make justice produce its contradictory opposite. And yet, surely nothing can of its own nature produce its own contradictory opposite: if it were the "function" (ἔργον—335d) of heat to produce cold—that is, if heat of its nature produced cold—it could hardly be heat; if the function of dryness were to make things wet, it could not be dryness. Since justice cannot be justice if its function is to produce injustice, Polemarchus' definition cannot be correct—and yet, along the way we have heard the two claims noted above concerning human excellence, leaving a good deal more to be said.[14]

The notion of a function proper to each nature will prove important in book ii, where one of the most fundamental notions in the ideal city is that each citizen should have a particular function (ἔργον) appropriate to his particular nature (φύσις) (369e–370c). The function of a shoemaker (τὸ τῆς σκυτικῆς ἔργον—374b) can hardly be to destroy shoes, nor can the function of the guardians, which is the greatest of all (μέγιστον τὸ τῶν φυλάκων ἔργον—374d), be to attack the city. In the same way, the function of justice (τοῦ δικαίου . . . ἔργον—335d) cannot be to produce injustice.

Two points in particular from the argument with Polemarchus will prove important to the dialogue as a whole. First, we have seen how his definition of justice led to an almost absolute liberation from the moral limits of the world as Cephalus understood it: we saw how Polemarchus' definition would deem it just to do any kind of harm to anyone who simply *seems* to be an enemy. Second, the sort of response we see from Socrates is important, for it involves bringing objective reality to bear on the problem. It is in fact the case that people make mistakes, and it is taken to be a reality that each thing has an excellence (ἀρετή) and a function (ἔργον). This sets the stage for the whole *Republic*, for in reaction to the liberation from conventional moral restraint that takes place over the course of book i, a liberation that culminates in Thrasymachus, we will not be given a series of pious imperatives, but rather an account that is founded in reality.

It remains only to consider the political aspect of Polemarchus' position, as we did for Cephalus. Clearly, Polemarchus' position cannot describe a community at peace with itself. Instead, on Polemarchus' principle, the only law outside of themselves which people would acknowledge would be immediately apparent self-interest: groups of people—"friends" to one another—would band together to protect more effectively their mutual interests against all other people, who would be "enemies." This is the logic of party strife within a city.[15]

Polemarchus' feet do not rest upon solid ground. He is divided between his own readiness to involve himself in argument and his desire to be faithful to the ideals cherished by his father. The side that actively involves him in the argument, and the position that he tries to articulate, would liberate him almost completely from his father's world, but such a radical liberation is not what he wants. Polemarchus represents a development which can be seen as both good and evil. The good is evident in his interest in genuine argument and in his active introduction of the notion of good (ἀγαθός), however impoverished his conception of that idea may actually be; the evil is evident in the near-total liberation from normative constraints which Socrates shows to be the consequence of his own words. We have also seen how this picture of Polemarchus as an essentially divided figure finds expression as the argument proceeds, in the conflation we find of good and useful, owed and fitting, skill and virtue. Unlike his father, as a consequence of the inadequacies which Socrates has brought to light out of his position, Polemarchus will remain interested in the argument which follows, intervening later on to keep the argument going later in the *Republic* (449b).

NOTES

1. Nettleship, *Lectures*, 16, in lectures given between 1885 and 1888.
2. For a different view, see Annas, *Introduction*, 18–34, who believes that Cephalus and Polemarchus represent the same position, one of moral complacency. In this she follows A. E. Taylor, *Plato: The Man and His Work* (1926; London: Butler & Tanner Ltd., 1963), 265.
3. In the introduction, it is Polemarchus who requires Socrates to stay with him (327c–328b), which also suggests his interest in the philosophical conversation Socrates is likely to offer.
4. As he does (331e); it is eventually decided not that Simonides is wrong, but that Polemarchus does not understand him (335e). For an account of how Simonides' view turns up later in the *Republic*, see Terence Irwin, *Plato's Ethics* (New York: Oxford University Press, 1995), 173–74.
5. This was a traditional view, widely held prior to Plato: see Kenneth J. Dover, *Greek Popular Morality at the Time of Plato and Aristotle* (Berkeley: University of California Press, 1974), 180–84.
6. R. C. Cross and A. D. Woozley, *Plato's Republic: A Philosophical Commentary* (London: Macmillan Press, 1964), 11. The view that there is failure in the argument here seems to prevail in virtually all commentary which touches on this argument. Kenneth Dorter, *The Transformation of Plato's Republic* (Lanham, MD: Lexington Books, 2006), 28–29, notes that both Cephalus and Polemarchus have treated justice like a skill insofar as they take it to be something that could be attained by means of rules like "pay back what is owed," or "help friends and harm enemies." Terry Penner, "Socrates on Virtue and Motivation," in *Exegesis and Argument: Studies in Greek Philosophy Presented to Gregory Vlastos*, eds. E. N. Lee, A. P. D. Mourelatos and R. M. Rorty (Assen: Van Gorcum & Comp. B. V., 1973), 137, fn. 5, suggests that, to some extent, Polemarchus is committed to looking at justice as a skill.

(2) Polemarchus

7. It is interesting to note that when Socrates speaks briefly of the useful in book ii, when discussing verbal falsehood, he does so in terms of friends and enemies (382c5–7).

8. Note the focus on the individual subject as the measure here, which looks ahead to Thrasymachus. It is also comparable to the focus on the subject that we saw in Alcibiadean Athens, though of course Polemarchus turns away from this, just as we saw the Mytilenian debate introduced new forces that were not yet dominant.

9. Although note that he objects that the argument is πονηρός ("base"—334d8), which we could take to mean that the argument is not his friend, but is doing him harm! If this were his meaning, it would give another regard in which something in Polemarchus is amplified considerably in Thrasymachus.

10. Charles M. Young, "A Note on Republic 335c9–10 and 335c12," *The Philosophical Review* 83, no. 1 (January 1974): 106, fn. 17.

11. Cross and Woozley, *Introduction*, 20–22, and Evelyne Méron, *Les Idées Morales des Interlocuteurs de Socrate dans les Dialogues Platoniciens de Jeunesse* (Paris: J. Vrin, 1979), 132, object that the argument depends upon an ambiguity in the Greek verb βλάπτειν; see Andrew Jeffrey, "Polemarchus and Socrates on Justice and Harm," *Phronesis* 24, no. 1 (1979): 54–69, for a detailed answer to this. I make use of Jeffrey's answer below: Polemarchus' just man will not only cause pain to his enemies, but will also make them less effective as enemies, making them less just.

12. Paul Friedländer, *Plato, II*, trans. Hans Meyerhoff (New York: Random House, 1964), 59, sees this argument as invoking "the kind of internal order that, according to the *Republic*, is the nature of justice."

13. Again, see Jeffrey, "Polemarchus," 1979, on this line of thought.

14. Note that Socrates has gone from mirroring Polemarchus—skills were understood earlier to be capable of good and evil (332d–e, 333e–334a)—to correcting him. This new view of things looks ahead to the eye later on (352e–353c), which is entirely focused on the good, as Polemarchus was not; in similar fashion, when Socrates next treats skills (from 341c), they will not be Polemarchan skills, which might cause either good or evil, but will be focused directly on the good. We shall see below (*Socrates in Republic I*, pages 240–3) how Socrates develops over the course of this book, and it is of a piece with this development that not every statement he makes will agree with every other.

15. Leo Strauss, *The City and Man* (Chicago: The University of Chicago Press, 1964), 73, has interpreted Polemarchus' principle politically so that it describes two cities opposed to one another. This application of the principle is not consistent with what we see elsewhere in the *Republic*, which is characterized by a turn inwards: the focus is working out the consequences of a principle in the individual or a single city (see, for example, books viii and ix). In book i, when political divisions become an explicit focus (e.g., at 351a–352b), we are to think of them as divisions within a single entity. Accordingly, we should understand Polemarchus' definition to imply parties within a city.

(3) Thrasymachus

It is not immediately clear how we are to understand Thrasymachus.[1] He says first that justice is the advantage of the stronger (338c1–2), and soon suggests that this is to be understood in terms of obeying the laws (338e1–339a1), but later says that justice is the good of another person (343c3–6). Though he claims to be saying the same thing all along (341a3, 344c7), we shall see that his various explanations of his thesis do not sit easily with one another. There has been some controversy over the question of whether Thrasymachus holds a consistent position in the course of his argument with Socrates, and if so, what that position is.[2] Interpretations of his position have been quite various; for example, he has seemed an ethical nihilist,[3] and an advocate of legalism[4] or of natural justice.[5] It might seem important to find a coherent position in Thrasymachus, for if his position is incoherent, would that fact not fatally undermine the work of the first book?

I do not find that Thrasymachus holds a position consistently, but there is a more fundamental matter,[6] one suggested by the very variety of opinion concerning Thrasymachus' definition of justice: if such a great diversity of interpretations can seem plausible, it might seem that Plato did a very bad job of writing this section—unless those interpretations have mostly been made on the basis of an erroneous assumption about how to approach the text. In fact, one such assumption does seem to have exerted considerable influence: the notion that Plato's purpose with Thrasymachus must be reducible to a particular doctrine concerning justice. Against this view, there are two lines of thought that suggest that the focus on Thrasymachus' position on justice should not take center stage alone.

First of all, if we compare book i with book ii, we are confronted with a two-headed question concerning the manner in which Plato has had Thrasymachus present his views and the fact that he has included him at all. In book ii, Glaucon declares (358b7–c1) that he is going to revive Thrasymachus' argument. There follows a straightforward and systematic exposition of a position, in three steps: what justice is (358e–359b), why people reluctantly practice it (359b–360d), and whether the life of the just or unjust man is better (360e–362c). Thrasymachus, on the other hand, is made to present his views in an altogether *un*straightforward and *un*systematic manner, touching on the same matters as Glaucon, but also making a number of statements that are (at best) difficult to reconcile, as we shall see below. To the extent that Plato is interested only in presenting a position on justice, the manner of expression he achieves through Glaucon would seem on its own to be adequate to his purpose—indeed, it would seem to be *necessary* to use *only* the Glaucon-presentation, for the manner of expression found with Thrasymachus obscures rather than clarifies a doctrine on justice. Assuming that Plato wrote what he did for a reason, what has he gained by having Thrasymachus present his views in a less-straightforward manner, and further, by having the same position (or at least something said to be the same) set forth twice?[7]

A second consideration tells against focusing excessively on the question of Thrasymachus' doctrine: he is not presented simply as a disembodied philosophical position, but as a *character*, one who shouts, blushes, and demands praise. If these aspects were not essential to his purpose in the work, we should not expect to find them. Again: what has Plato gained by including such detail? Of course, the point here is not that the question of Thrasymachus' position on justice is unimportant, but rather that that question must be approached in the context of these additional considerations. From what perspective would it make perfect sense to present the argument with Thrasymachus exactly as Plato has done it?

It is best to set this perspective out at the start: Thrasymachus stands above all for a particular conception of the good.[8] In his view, certain things are good, and one seeks to acquire them in competition with other people (this underlies 343d1–344a3). Money and other material goods, political power, praise: all of these can be understood in terms of a zero-sum game, in which one person acquires what is good at the expense of everyone else. The characterization of Thrasymachus is founded upon this conception of the good, and it is this characterization that is consistent, not the position on justice to which he gives expression. Indeed, his definition of justice can be seen as a sort of guide to getting what is good, and thus as embodying a claim of practical wisdom. Thrasymachus will never give up on this claim. Everything else follows from his conception of the good, not only the position he takes, but also his failure to express it in an entirely consistent manner, as well as a number of turns the argument takes, such as his refusal to take the escape offered by Cleitophon; we shall summarize these at the end of our treatment of Thrasymachus.⁹ Plato has woven all of these aspects into a seamless tapestry that make the encounter with Thrasymachus utterly necessary to the *Republic*.

The main change of position that Thrasymachus makes comes with his outburst at 343b–344c, and one adjustment made at this point should be set out at the start. Before this point, Thrasymachus talks about the benefit his position would confer in practice in terms of *advantage* (συμφερόν—338c1, 339a1, a4, etc.). In the course of the outburst, however, as he gives a more frank account of his views, he suddenly speaks of *good* (ἀγαθός—343b2, 4). That is, what lay behind the notion of "advantage" all along was "good": Thrasymachus is moved by the desire to get what is good. The full significance of this shift in language will become clearer as we proceed.

Two aspects of Plato's characterization of Thrasymachus will prove particularly important. The first is his desire for praise. Socrates tells us that "it was clear that Thrasymachus wished to speak so that he might be held in esteem" (338a6–7), and Thrasymachus soon asks, "why don't you praise me?" (338c2–3)¹⁰ This desire, itself an expression of his conception of the good, allows us to give a preliminary explanation of his failure to express himself in a consistent manner. Consider certain of the features of his two main positions. The first (338c–339a) is said to apply to all forms of government, and thus has a place for a wide variety of different beliefs.¹¹ The position taken at 343b–344c explicitly takes tyranny as its paradigm, praises injustice, and then makes clear just what this means: taking away the property of others, whether sacred or profane, public or private, by stealth and by force. Anyone who wishes to be praised will have a much easier time of it from the first position, partly on account of the room it has for a diversity of political belief, so that many different people can see themselves in it, but also because many people will be repulsed by the second position. Even those who agree with Thrasymachus' admiration of the tyrant and of injustice might hesitate to admit this to others, and accordingly might not want to be seen giving praise to him. It is therefore natural for Thrasymachus to begin from the first position. It is unlikely that he had any intention at the start of revealing his sympathy for tyranny and injustice, but once he finds himself losing the argument, he becomes upset (note how he insults Socrates just before his outburst—343a4, 7–8). No doubt this emotional state creates the conditions for his rather more frank account at 343b–344a, but more important still is his desire to win: he can hardly expect praise if he is bested by Socrates. Thus he switches to ground which, although it may be less likely in itself to garner praise, now seems to offer the best chance of besting his opponent. A bit later, Socrates gives an indication that his opponent was less than candid at the start when he suggests that Thrasymachus is now saying what he really thinks (349a5–8).¹²

(3) Thrasymachus

Second, Thrasymachus is portrayed as inappropriately active, even aggressive. Polemarchus entered the argument by means of an interruption, showing his eagerness to take part in the discussion. Thrasymachus has been trying, not simply to interrupt, but to *lay hold of the argument* (ἀντιλαμβάνομαι τοῦ λογοῦ—336b2), and has to be restrained by those around him who wished to hear the discussion (336b3–4). That is, he has been *so* eager to take part that he has already threatened the ordered progression of the debate. As he makes his entrance, we are told that "he gathered himself together like a wild beast, and threw himself upon us as if to tear us to pieces" (336b5–7). This aggression threatens the possibility of having a debate at all, for we are twice told of how Socrates is frightened by Thrasymachus' display (336b, d): if Socrates becomes too fearful, or goes "speechless" (336d7) as a result of Thrasymachus' demeanor, he will be unable to oppose whatever Thrasymachus is going to say. The gathering could become dominated, not by reason and mutual consent, as it has been so far, but by emotions and a forceful personality. On several occasions, Thrasymachus must be subjected to some external compulsion or plea in order that the argument may proceed (336b, 337d, 338a, 344d). Here is a nature which threatens the peaceful and rational order of the discussion, and which must be kept in check by force if the order is to be preserved.

This second element of Thrasymachus' characterization—his aggressive nature—is to be connected with the form that the debate now takes: it is *eristic*, a struggle to win rather than a search for truth. It is clear that Plato was aware of a distinction between two different approaches to argument: "practitioners of [eristic] treat it as a game; they argue for victory rather than to establish the truth; and, in the process, they are harsh and uncooperative toward their opponents . . . cooperative dialectic is the opposite on all these counts."[13] As appropriate to an eristic disputation, we have a discussion about the rules before the argument proper begins. There is disagreement about who is to give answers (336c2–7, 337a4–8, 337e1–338b4), what sort of answer is to be allowed (336c7–d4, 337a9–c11) and the prize for victory (337c2–d12): "Thrasymachus and Socrates are not merely beginning a discussion of justice; they are vying for roles in an organized activity."[14] Later on, when Thrasymachus, "instead of answering" (343a3), insults his opponent, Socrates responds by saying, "what? Shouldn't you give an answer rather than ask such a thing?" (343a4–6) The point is that "by not replying Thrasymachus is clearly violating the rules of the discussion."[15] Later still (at 350d–e), Thrasymachus will try "to hide behind the conventions of question and answer debate, by declaring that he could answer Socrates' arguments, but that this would entail a lengthy speech, which is forbidden by the rules."[16] One characteristic of an eristic debate is the use of bad arguments: "where victory is the goal fallacious arguments are employed as a matter of course."[17]

Thrasymachus expresses "his suspicion that Socrates will use fallacious arguments against him (338d, 340d, 341a–b, 341c),"[18] and we shall see in what follows that the arguments that Socrates uses are indeed not sufficient to move a careful reader to the desired conclusion, though as a response to Thrasymachus they are entirely effective.

In all this there is a point that will in the end prove significant, for the eristic nature of the debate with Thrasymachus follows from his character. With such an aggressive, praise-oriented person, for whom argument is not a search for truth but a contest to win, an eristic disputation is all that is possible—and note that such a disputation, in which one combatant wins at the expense of the other, corresponds with Thrasymachus' conception of the good. The point to which we shall return in the conclusion is that Socrates pursues an eristic disputation *as a reaction to Thrasymachus*.

THRASYMACHUS PART ONE: CLARIFICATION

It was suggested above that Thrasymachus' expression of his position falls into two main parts, the second coming with the speech at 343b–344c. Following this division of expression, the argument is itself divided into two parts. The first (338c–347e), in which Thrasymachus' failure to hold his own eventually drives him to be more frank about his real beliefs, has a double outcome: it clarifies his position, and also brings into view, in embryonic form, the sort of refutation of Thrasymachus that the entire *Republic* will provide: a contrary account of justice and of the end toward which activity is to be directed. The second part of the argument (348a–354a) is a refutation of Thrasymachus, and though it has significant failings if regarded as an attempt to convince a skeptical reader, it also has a positive aspect: not only do we encounter, for the first time, a clear explanation of a crucial concept (ἔργον), we also begin to get a glimpse, the merest outline, of the Good.

Justice of the Ruling Party (338c–339e)

The argument proper with Thrasymachus begins in the same way as that with Polemarchus did (at 331e): he gives his definition—justice is nothing other than the advantage of the stronger (338c)—and Socrates immediately shows that the definition is subject to interpretation: a few words are not enough; it seems that they must be accompanied by an account.

When Thrasymachus does begin to clarify his position, we see a connection with Polemarchus, for the talk of particular forms of government—"some cities are ruled tyrannically, some democratically, some aristocratically" (338d7–8)—points in most cases to a dominant faction within a city:

democrats are friends to one another, and to remain in power, they must help one another against enemies. The same is true of aristocrats—and also of oligarchs and most other arrangements you could name. That is, the position here would generally produce factions or parties, the same level of political community which we saw Polemarchus' position could maintain. There is, however, an exception: tyranny. The tyrant differs in a fundamental way from a faction, in that he is not a member of a group in which members seek mutual benefit. There is, then, an ambiguity in Thrasymachus' position as it stands here. It will be resolved in what follows.

Just like Polemarchus' "helping friends and harming enemies," the Thrasymachan position at this point would place no limits on action aside from those imposed collectively by the realities of friendship or rule in common. It represents a change from that of Polemarchus less in the freedom it accords the rulers and more in its self-understanding. Polemarchus, in the end, recoiled from the liberation from normative constraints that proved to be inherent in his words; it soon becomes clear that Thrasymachus is aiming at just such a liberation. Thrasymachus is conscious, as Polemarchus was not, of the derivative status of moral constraints: the laws are created by the rulers. Is it right to return what is owed? Ought one to have an orderly character? Ask the rulers. Where Cephalus would understand his various received maxims to be objectively true, here that is false of every maxim: the rulers determine whether particular actions are right or wrong. The center of gravity has shifted, for the actions of the rulers now determine the ethical order rather than the other way around. Thrasymachus appears to have found a position of genuine independence for his rulers, who determine what lies beyond themselves.

The position, as Thrasymachus describes it, has a peculiar strength. It is not simply a collection of exhortations, of ought-to-be's, of appeals to authority or to some imaginary (though lofty) principle or feeling, but is grounded in the world as we actually experience it. Who can deny that rulers make the laws? Thrasymachus describes his principle so as to emphasize that it is an accurate account regardless of whatever particular party is in power, twice stressing that his view is not limited to a particular place, but holds everywhere (ἐν ἁπάσαις πόλεσιν—338e7; πανταχοῦ—339a3). He also twice suggests that the simple fact that the rulers actually make the laws is what makes them just for the ruled. First, he says, "by legislating[19] the ruling parties showed that the advantage of the stronger is just for those being ruled" (338e3–5). Soon we find another telling phrase: "this [the established government] rules, so that . . . justice is the advantage of the stronger"[20] (339a). The claim is that his definition follows from the fact that the government rules.

Thus it seems that Thrasymachus wants to talk about what he takes to be *reality*, about readily observable facts, and would take his position's clear basis in such facts as an important factor in its favor. There will be further confirmation of this later in the argument, when, having failed to hold his own against Socrates, Thrasymachus appeals again to how things actually work in the world of observable facts (343b ff.), even though this is irrelevant to the argument he is trying to answer. The authority for the position here is not that of great men, nor of belief in gods or a traditional order, but rather of facts which are plain for all to see. Here, then, we have a position similar to the natural justice of Callicles: by looking to observable realities in the world rather than pious beliefs, one sees that the stronger rule.

The criticism that Socrates now brings forward (339c) cuts right to the heart of Thrasymachus' position. Socrates' objection—that rulers sometimes make mistakes (all real people do)—is itself a fact as much as the actual forms of government to which Thrasymachus has pointed. And while Thrasymachus was fully conscious of the derivative status of the laws, making all depend on the rulers, Socrates' objection breaks in on that view of things, for the rulers are themselves seen to be inadequate, dependent on an objective reality that they imperfectly understand (for otherwise they would not make mistakes).

The argument here has the same form as that used against Polemarchus at 334c–335a: by drawing attention to the possibility of human error, it forces a move from a view which would admit a limit only by agreement within the group of rulers to one in which an objective limit is recognized. This has an important consequence for Thrasymachus, for when he does begin to respond to this criticism, he does so in terms of "the precise sense" (ὁ ἀκριβής λόγος—340e1–2). The precise doctor, calculator, or grammarian is not someone who exists in the real world, but rather an ideal figure: Socrates has forced Thrasymachus to argue, not from reality, but from ideality.[21]

Cleitophon (340a–b)

The interruption from Cleitophon is present to help give us a clearer view of Thrasymachus: Plato is emphasizing to the reader that there is a means by which he might have escaped the argument. The position which Cleitophon suggests, that "the advantage of the stronger" is what the stronger *believes* to be good for him (340b), could be a difficult position to refute. At the very least, an argument beyond anything found in the text would be required.

So what has Plato accomplished by pointing out to the reader that Thrasymachus refuses this escape route?[22] By taking it, Thrasymachus might have held his own against Socrates—and clearly he wants to win the argument—but this would have come at a price. Note how the episode emphasizes the importance of the difference between the real and the imaginary by means of its focus on *false* belief: Cleitophon takes "the advantage of the stronger" to be what the stronger *believes* to be good for him, and, quite appropriately, he is inaccurate in his account of the preceding argument (340b7–9)—for of course, from the point of view of what he *believes* to be correct, he is no doubt right! So the episode itself reminds us that believing something does not make it so. This is why Thrasymachus does not take Cleitophon's path: it would require him to give up his claim that his understanding provides real, rather than imaginary, advantage.[23] Indeed, when Thrasymachus goes on to introduce skills into the argument, he repudiates Cleitophon completely, for the very idea of a skill presupposes the possibility of getting something wrong—if everyone always got everything right, nobody could claim to be skilled.

The Cleitophon scene, then, shows that Thrasymachus does not *just* want to win the argument. He will not try to do this without maintaining his focus on getting *actual* advantage.[24] The focus on reality is not so straightforward as he had thought. Nobody can deny that the rulers actually rule, but the claim that they also attain their own advantage does not follow as readily as he had supposed. Socrates' argument has driven a wedge between these two assertions, and Cleitophon's interruption shows us just how attached Thrasymachus is to the latter.

The Precise Sense (340c–343b, 345b–347a)

The argument from 341c–347a has frequently been criticized, but the criticisms have missed a good deal. Thrasymachus is in a difficult position at this point. Some other character might say that although rulers make mistakes, still most rulers make few enough that they do, on the whole, attain their own advange. Why does Thrasymachus not say this at this point? Because it conflicts with his claim that justice is the advantage of the stronger, and thus with his desire to win and receive praise. Though both intelligent and stupid rulers make the laws, rulers who are sufficiently stupid will bring about their own extreme disadvantage by their very lawmaking. Only sufficiently intelligent rulers will realiably command their own advantage, so that intelligence, at least as much as justice, is the advantage of the stronger—and, by a similar argument, intelligence is also the advantage of the weaker, perhaps making it a more universal source of advantage than Thrasymachus' justice.[25]

In fact, Thrasymachus will soon produce an account based in part on the idea that the perfection and scale of injustice will be sufficient to make up for miscalculations (344a–c), but it takes the failure of his "precise sense" gambit and the frustration that comes with this to drive him to the point that he will say this.

To maximize his chance of getting praise, he must appear to preserve his initial claim, so he must find a way to maintain his claim about justice while taking into account the matter of intelligence. This he can accomplish by defining justice so that it includes intelligence, and he does this by claiming that a true ruler is an artisan (a δημιουργός—340e3, 4, 5) of the highest skill.[26] By this move, he has solved a problem which confronted Polemarchus in the previous argument, to find a field for justice: justice is evidently a sort of rule over all the other artisans—and note that we have an anticipation here of a later doctrine of the work, according to which justice will turn out to be a sort of rule over the parts of the soul or city (444d). Thus the argument turns to consider the nature of arts.

The key is that, in bringing forth the "precise sense," in which rulers never make mistakes, Thrasymachus has turned from the world of everday experience to an ideal world.[27] In everyday life, rulers do in fact make mistakes; in the world of this argument, they do not. It is on this basis that Socrates can create an account in which rulers never look to their own advantage. We cannot respond to Socrates by appealing to how things work in practice in everyday life, because to do so is to abandon the basis on which Thrasymachus began his argument, leaving him facing once more the problem that rulers make mistakes, and so command their own disadvantage.

For example, to object that "even as a gardener, the gardener knows that he grows vegetables for use and profit"[28] is no help to Thrasymachus. Certainly, it is true of gardeners we regularly meet, who make mistakes, but Socrates can simply respond that the precise gardener knows nothing at all except what is required to bring plants into a certain state.[29] A precise doctor is not a businessman (341c5–7), even though in the everyday world an actual doctor may be more concerned with his fee than with the good of his patients, and a precise captain is not a sailor just because he sails in a ship (341d1–4), even though in the world of everyday experience he might also be referred to as a sailor on account of his place in the ship. So too with the gardener. Thrasymachus will make a similar objection: shepherds "fatten and care for [sheep] looking to [nothing] other than the good of the masters" (343b2–4). This is no doubt often true in the world of everyday experience, but not in the precise sense.

It is instructive to go beyond what Thrasymachus says, and sharpen his objection as follows: "the Shepherd aims at the good of his sheep at best incidentally. He fattens them not because it is good for them to be fat (although it may be good for them), but because fatter sheep fetch higher prices or are better to eat. He would still fatten them even if doing so made them wretched. Hence a Shepherd is not someone who 'provides what is best for the object of [his Craft's] care' (345d1–3). That description does not capture his essence."[30] Important questions are raised here, but Plato has his reasons for not asking them at this point in the *Republic*. First of all, to inquire concerning an essence is to pose the very sort of question that Plato will flag as not having been satisfactorily addressed in book i (specifically, "what justice is"—354b5). In addition, the *specific* question at issue here is itself a highly significant matter: what is good? Is "good" to be understood in terms of what is beneficial for the sheep, or in terms of their price and taste? How, and in reference to what, are we to define "good"? The question of what is good will, of course, be a central concern of the *Republic*: the unaddressed difficulty in the argument, a difficulty of the sort that Thrasymachus (significantly) never raises, looks ahead to the rest of the work.[31]

It is in book ii that Plato will have Socrates address the problem of what exactly it is through which "good" is to be defined in the case of arts: these exist because of our need (369d10)—there too we are dealing with skills (e.g., 370b5) and craftsmen (370d6)—and so their essences are defined relative to our good, not the good of their objects. That is, within the context of skilled activity, what is actually good for the objects is not of interest, but rather what is good in reference to some human need. Thus, Socrates' account of the arts here is not Platonic doctrine; rather, it is to be understood in the context of an eristic argument whose aim is to refute Thrasymachus, and its inadequacy looks ahead to the *Republic* after book i.

One further aspect of Socrates' account deserves consideration. His theory of the arts would seem to have the consequence that nobody would ever want to become an artisan, for only the person or thing ruled by the art is benefitted. Accordingly, he introduces the wage-earning art, which provides benefit to its practitioner.

This step has been criticized as follows: "Wage-earning must benefit its practitioner. Consequently, Wage-earning is itself a counterexample to the claim that no Craft can do this."[32] But Socrates never said that no Craft can do this. He claimed that skills are themselves perfect, and so cannot look to their own good (341d8–342c6), and then began to talk of skills as forms of rule: they *rule* (ἄρχουσί) and *command* (ἐπιτάττει); a recipient of their activity *is ruled* (ἀρχομένου—342c8–d1). From this point, the examples of practitioners of skills were all qualified with rule-words: the doctor *commands* (ἐπιτάττει) and *rules* (ἄρχων—342d4–8), the captain *rules* (ἄρχων) and *commands* (προστάξει), while the sailor *is ruled* (ἀρχομένῳ—342e2–4). Socrates concludes that no one in a *position of command* (ἀρχῇ), insofar as he is *ruling* (ἄρχων), *commands* (ἐπιτάττει) his own advantage, but does so for the person *being ruled* (ἀρχομένῳ—342e6–11). The point about all skills being perfect no doubt applies to all skills. The point about skills not benefitting their practitioners does seem to be restricted to skills that are forms of rule. When Socrates later introduces wage-earning (346b), an art that benefits its practitioner, he is being consistent, for wage-earning is not said to be a kind of rule.[33]

In Socrates' second pass over the account of skills (345c–347a), in which wage-earning arises, the same distinction is at work. Here he starts by reiterating the point about skills being perfect in themselves (345d1–5), and then returns to talking about rule (from 345d7–346a1 the text is awash in various forms of ἀρχή). When Socrates summarizes his argument, he once again speaks insistently about ruling and commanding (346e3–347a5). It is between these two sections that Socrates introduces the skill of wage-earning, as he speaks about how each skill has its own peculiar power, and produces its own peculiar benefit (346a2–e2). It is reasonable to understand a distinction to be at work throughout all of this, between skills that are forms of rule and those that are not.[34]

The argument from the "precise sense" is remarkable in that it both focuses on skills as forms of rule, and also has to make a special case, wage-earning, in order to address the question of how a skill's practitioner can derive benefit from its practice. In all this, one possibility is neither excluded nor investigated: ruling *oneself*. If self-rule can be shown to be a matter of skill, then surely one could, at least *qua* ruled, enjoy the benefits of one's own rule. Of course, self-rule is a central idea of the *Republic*: once again, lurking in the realm of relevant and important points that are not addressed, we find an anticipation of what is to come later.

Socrates' argument is magnificently appropriate as a response to Thrasymachus. One could escape the argument by denying the connection between ruling and certain skills, but this is precisely what Thrasymachus cannot do, since the connection was his way out of his previous difficulty. We should also note Plato's ingenuity as a writer: the notion of ruling is not only crucial to the logic of the argument here but also has roots going right back to Thrasymachus' first attempt to provide an account of justice. In addition, the focus on ruling leads us, by means of the conclusions reached by Socrates, directly into his subsequent discourse on good men who do not want to rule (347b–e), a passage long noted for its anticipation of a central theme of the whole work, the philosopher king.[35] All of these aspects brought together show us a seamless tapestry: the characterization of Thrasymachus (the connection between a focus on ruling and his competitive conception of the good should be obvious), the detail of the argument, its conclusions—all these together point to the heart of the whole *Republic*.

Finally, everyday experience does seem to partake of the distinction that Socrates is getting at with wage-earning. Everyday life shows us that there is no necessary connection between being an artisan of the highest skill and receiving an adequate reward—or any at all. Often those who are less skilled, but better at ingratiating themselves with colleagues and superiors, or at taking credit for the work of others, make it to the top spot.[36]

The Thrasymachan Outburst and the Socratic Response (343b–345b, 347b–e)

Thrasymachus' great tirade at 343b–344c represents a clear break with the immediately preceding argument. Above all, he now appeals constantly to the world of everyday experience: shepherds think of their own good rather than that of their flock; the just man gets less than the unjust in numerous fields of activity; the tyrant is admired by many who cannot match his infamy. This is precisely the sort of consideration that was excluded by Thrasymachus' earlier appeal to the precise sense. Accordingly, Thrasymachus' new outburst does not free him from the preceding argument, something that Socrates will point out (345d1–3). From 345e–347b, Socrates will continue to appeal to the "precise sense," and is entirely justified in doing so, since Thrasymachus never disowns it–he cannot, for such an admission of failure would conflict with his desire for praise.

There are further indications that Thrasymachus' position has changed, for he now begins to express himself in a new way on a number of matters. Earlier, he emphasized that his account covered all forms of government, and we saw that these generally maintained some level of community, with tyranny being the exception. Now, this universality has disappeared, and the exception has become the rule, so that tyranny is the only form of government Thrasymachus is concerned with.[37] The notion of ruling has been a focus from the start, but while it previously implied, for the most part, a principle of cooperation among the rulers (338c–339e), now the only relation between people is domination and subjection, as between masters and sheep. Before, there was no praise of injustice; now there is. Before, he spoke strictly of advantage (τὸ συμφέρον); now, we hear about good (τὸ ἀγαθόν—343b4, c4). In addition, this new speech has brought the conversation to a new level, for when Thrasymachus devotes attention to the comparison of the outcome for the just and unjust men (343d1–344a3), and speaks about the most perfect injustice (τὴν τελεωτάτην ἀδικίαν—344a4), he pushes the argument toward focus on justice and injustice as *principles*, on the effect that they have *in themselves*. This represents a significant step for the argument, as it anticipates a demand that Glaucon (358b3–5; note τέλεον—360e4, τῷ τελέως ἀδικῷ τελεωτάτην ἀδικίαν—361a) and Adeimantus (367e2–3) will make in book ii.[38] Both previous speeches (338e–339a, 340d–341a) were focused on the reasoning that justified their claims; this final speech, by contrast, presents us with a long string of vehement assertions, connected, to be sure, by an underlying idea, and related to experience, but with little emphasis on the reasons for their truth.

All of this suggests that Thrasymachus might now be saying something different about justice than he said earlier, and in fact, his position on justice here conflicts with what went before. When he talks about the outcome for the just and the unjust man (343d1–344a1), he must have a definite idea in mind of what it means to be just. This is incompatible with what we heard at 338e–339a, where anything could be just so long as it was determined by the rulers. For example, it does seem correct to say that justice at 343b–344a is to be understood by means of a conventional notion, ἰσότης ("equality"), which means that everybody gets his due.[39] On this understanding, all that Thrasymachus says during his tirade (i.e., at 343d1–344a1) about the outcome for the just and unjust man will make sense. But if the rulers (perhaps making a mistake, since Thrasymachus has abandoned the precise sense) declare *in*equality, and acquiring the most wealth, to be just, then the just man would have more (perhaps simply by definition).

Anyone who wants to argue that Thrasymachus has a single, consistent position on justice throughout must address all the indications listed above that something has changed. Plato might have given Thrasymachus one single, obviously coherent speech in which to set out a position. What has Plato gained by having Thrasymachus express himself differently, in all of the ways just mentioned, in this final speech?

The beginning of an answer to this question was suggested above: Thrasymachus expressed himself earlier in a manner more likely to acquire praise. His position at the start was vague enough that many could read their own views into it, and it also cohered in one respect with convention, in the idea that obeying the laws is just.[40] However, now that he finds himself losing the debate, he is driven to a position in which he praises injustice, and speaks of tyranny, of temple-robbers, kidnappers, housebreakers, defrauders, thieves, and also of crimes (344b3–5) in a plainly adulatory manner; soon he will talk of purse-snatching (348d). This is a less promising basis from which to attain praise: even those who agree with him in all this might hesitate to be seen to do so.

This understanding coheres meaningfully with two remarks made a bit later on. When Socrates says that Thrasymachus *dares* (τολμάω—349a2) to set injustice with virtue and wisdom, he is pointing to the inhibitions that kept Thrasymachus from setting out his true beliefs from the start. The same idea is at work in the remark that if Thrasymachus had not gone so far, there would have been something to say against him on a conventional basis (κατὰ τὰ νομιζόμενα—348e9): Thrasymachus' position has now attained a liberation from convention about as completely as one can. Furthermore, when Socrates subsequently says that Thrasymachus is now saying what he really thinks (349b6–9), he suggests that Thrasymachus might not have been giving voice to his true thoughts earlier.

By presenting Thrasymachus in this manner, Plato has built an essential moment into the overall movement of book i, for one aspect of that movement is a gradual liberation from conventional ethical constraint. Cephalus knew no such liberation; Polemarchus' position began to bring this to light, but he recoiled once the significance of his position started to become clear. Thrasymachus, by contrast, is so liberated from the constraints to which most people feel subject in everyday life that he must begin by expressing himself in a manner that conceals something of his real views, hence the relatively palatable position he begins with (338e–339a). Still, he is not absolutely liberated, for he still needs other people in a parasitic manner, for the recognition that they can confer on him through praise (just as a tyrant needs people to rule). It is this desire for recognition that makes him subject to the argument, and this that explains why he is now driven to give a more candid account of his views: the emotional response he feels at having been seen to be beaten makes him less inhibited about admitting his real beliefs to those from whom he hopes to receive praise. In this state, he insults Socrates (343a) and launches into a speech that is more a vehement string of assertions than a careful and logical exposition of a position.

On this understanding, then, Thrasymachus' real views have come to light in this final speech. One point in particular that becomes clear is his conception of ends, for just after he starts to talk about "good" (τὸ ἀγαθόν—343b4, c4), he tries to explain how the just man is always worse off than the unjust (343d1–344a1), and the reason is the same throughout. The just man "has less" (ἔλαττον ἔχει—343d3) than the unjust everywhere; in partnerships he will nowhere "have more" (πλέον ἔχοντα—343d6), but less. Throughout we are talking about *getting* and *having* things, whether money or influence with friends; the final claim is that the unjust man is the one able to get more than his due (πλεονεκτεῖν—344a1) in a big way. Clearly, the good is understood here as something one gets in competition with others; the point of action is to *acquire* good *things*.

This not only represents a more intense focus on the good than we have so far seen, it also presents us with a new conception of the good. In so doing, it resurrects a theme that has been present from the beginning: the question of the reward for justice. Recall that the matter of justice came about in response to Socrates' question of the "greatest good" (μέγιστον ἀγαθὸν—330d2) that Cephalus' wealth had brought about. Cephalus' response suggested that the reward for justice was that it allowed people to avoid worrying about the possible truth of stories about the afterlife. This is hardly the most compelling basis for action. Thrasymachus, by contrast, right after he mentions the word "good" (τὸ ἀγαθόν—343b4, c4), gives a far more impressive basis for (unjust) action: the just man everywhere has less than the unjust man (343d1–344a1). Credulous simpletons may worry about unverifiable stories, but the man who defrauds his partner *knows* that he has more money as a result. Once again, Thrasymachus' position has as a strength its foundation in the world of everyday experience, in a readily observable reality. The more conventional accounts of justice given earlier seem deeply deficient in comparison.

The argument to 347b has certainly had the effect of bringing out what Thrasymachus really thinks, but by the time we reach Socrates' rival speech at 347b–e, it is clear that something else has also been going on: Socrates has been putting forth a position of his own, and his speech takes the opposition between him and Thrasymachus to its extreme. Thrasymachus has given a most candid description of the life of extreme injustice as he sees it, a view which might not be praiseworthy by conventional standards, but which does seem to be based on a realistic appraisal of the way in which things work in everyday experience. Socrates now makes a counter-speech about the rule of the truly good, which is certainly not based in everyday experience. One particularly telling difference between the two positions is the way they talk about the good. We have already seen that for Thrasymachus, it is something that one *gets*. Socrates, by contrast, now starts to talk about a city of *good men* (πόλις ἀνδρῶν ἀγαθῶν—347d2–3). That is, the good here is not something external that must be acquired, but is rather an aspect of what these people *are*: Socrates talks about "being good" (εἶναι ἀγαθοί—348d3–4).[41] This is not only the most direct relation to the good in book i, it is also an anticipation of a later idea of the work, according to which considerable emphasis is put on one's internal state (e.g., 443d–444a).[42]

These two different ways of relating to the good were anticipated earlier when Thrasymachus demands that Socrates should not define justice by saying that it is the needful, the beneficial, and so on (336c–d); in response, Socrates compares this to asking what twelve is, and not allowing the answers two times six, three times four, etc. (337a–b). That is, Thrasymachus puts forth examples of possible attributes, which may or may not belong to justice, just as possessions or praise may or may not belong to a person; Socrates gives examples of necessary relations, things that are essentially related to what it is to be twelve. The difference precisely corresponds to the differing views of the good we find between Socrates and Thrasymachus: if it is something one acquires, then Thrasymachus' examples will be appropriate; if it is part of what a person is, then Socrates' examples will be.

Of course, insofar as Socrates has presented an argument at all for his view, it is founded upon Thrasymachus' "precise sense." This, we have seen, is entirely satisfactory as a response to Thrasymachus—that is, as an *ad hominem* argument—but those who cannot accept the premise on which the whole account is built will require rather more. What we have been given is an anticipation, a glimpse, not only of a doctrine that lies at the heart of the work,[43] but also of the *manner in which* the whole *Republic* will be an answer to Thrasymachus: by setting up a contrary account of justice and the good.

THRASYMACHUS PART TWO: REFUTATION

The pause in the argument indicates that we are entering a new phase. There is a brief reconsideration of method (348a6–b4), and a recapitulation of Thrasymachus' views (348b8–349a3). Socrates' remark that Thrasymachus is now saying what he really thinks (349a6–8) indicates that the business of clarification is now over. On the basis of his now-clarified views—that is, that injustice, rather than justice, is a virtue, and that (completely) unjust men are wise and good—the last pages will present the sort of refutation of Thrasymachus that is appropriate to book i.

The opposition between Socrates and Thrasymachus, which attains its greatest extreme with the rival speeches at 343b–344c and 347b–e, remains in what follows, and colors—indeed, *corrupts*—the arguments. The two combatants occupy different worlds, with radically different conceptions of the good, and these result in very different ideas concerning how life should be lived. Between these two solitudes, no communication seems possible, at least not within the context of the current standoff. In the arguments that refute Thrasymachus, we see these two standpoints talk past one another, with the result that Thrasymachus is defeated, but by means of arguments that fail to examine crucial matters, looking ahead to the rest of the *Republic* for a treatment of their premises.

At the same time, each argument does give us some insight into the position Socrates has implied. He has suggested that it is possible for people to *be* good, and no doubt this is to be connected to the question concerning justice, but the question of what exactly is meant by "good" or "justice" looms over the entire first book. Buried within these three arguments are three hints concerning an answer.

The Unjust Man as Wise and Good (348a–350e)

The divergence of viewpoints concerning the good determines the outcome of the first argument, in which we hear how the unjust man will try do outdo everyone, in both what he does and has, while the just man seeks to attain the same objective measure in what he has and does as other just people do. That is, the unjust man embodies precisely the competitive conception of what is good that we have seen in Thrasymachus, while the just man aligns with Socrates' conception. Plato draws attention to this as the argument begins: In the course of a review of the position, he has Thrasymachus give a series of answers at odds with the suggestions of Socrates (348c5–d2), culminating in a question concerning whether the unjust are wise and good (φρόνιμοί . . . εἶναι καὶ ἀγαθοί—348d3–4). Here too, Thrasymachus does not simply go along with Socrates' suggestion, for he does not echo the talk of *being good*, but speaks instead of profit (λυσιτελεῖ—348d8). The contrast is between a concern with what one is and an acquisitive conception. In addition, Thrasymachus takes a moment here to clarify his own view: purse-snatchers attain some profit, but what he's really interested in are those who can subject whole cities and tribes (348d5–10). That is, both the purse-snatcher and city-enslaver are concerned with getting what is good, but the latter gets far more by virtue of his greatly superior action. This is what is the issue for Thrasymachus when the subsequent argument speaks of how the unjust man will try to outdo the just and unjust action (the just man, of course, will not even be snatching purses).[44]

The argument has been wrongly criticized as exploiting an ambiguity in the Greek verb πλεονεκτεῖν, which can mean both "having more" and "get the better of."[45] Certainly, these are two different concepts, but we have just seen how Thrasymachus unites them: it is the supremely effective action that allows the supremely unjust man to get the most good things; having more is thus part and parcel with outdoing, or getting the better of, others.[46] For Socrates, things will be a bit different: the distinction between having and doing is not only irrelevant but misleading, for both are subordinate to what really matters, that is, *being* good. It will become apparent that being good seems to involve meeting some objective standard. Socrates' would believe himself to have outdone only those who fail to meet this standard (i.e., unjust people), whether we're talking about having or doing.[47]

The logic of this argument has been adequately treated elsewhere,[48] but one aspect of it in particular does not seem to have been noted: Socrates is developing a position here that takes for itself Thrasymachus' greatest claim to plausibility, that is, its basis in the world of everyday experience. A musician tuning a lyre (349e12–15) does not seek to outdo another musician; rather, they both aim to achieve precisely the same sound. In similar fashion, a doctor making a prescription (350a1–2) does not aim to outdo another doctor; instead, both aim at producing health in a body. That is, these activities both aim at an objective state, one recognized by all knowledgeable people. Furthermore, this state is characterized by the notion of a limit: a string tightened excessively will be out of tune; a person who takes too much of anything will harm his health.[49] Knowledgeable people, by producing the appropriate state, will equal one another, and will believe themselves to outdo those who fail to produce it (i.e., those without the necessary knowledge). Only an utterly ignorant person would aim to outdo the experts, perhaps tightening a string until it breaks, or consuming an excess of something until sick. Unlike Cephalus' tales of the afterlife, these examples appeal to readily observable facts—how many Athenians would not have experienced for themselves the effects of too much wine?

Thrasymachus' competitive conception of the good, of which the tyrant is the supreme exemplar, and in which one tries to get as much as possible, is characterized precisely by an attempt to transgress, to break through, any and all limits. Socrates' argument, then, points to a reality, in the world of everyday experience, that such behavior can harm its practitioner. We shall see later that this Socratic move, taking for himself Thrasymachus' attempt to ground his views in a reality that all can observe, anticipates the more substantial answer to Thrasymachus we begin to see in book ii.

The fact that there are two different conceptions of the good at work here, and that this difference is never explicitly addressed, allows us to explain Thrasymachus' failure to respond to the argument—and recall that he previously showed himself most capable at such responses. Consider how this argument must seem to him: it begins from premises that seem fair enough, and each step seems fair enough, at least for someone who has not previously thought through these matters (and who does not have the leisure of the reader of a text). Somehow Socrates is able to produce the conclusion that the just man is good and wise (350c10–11), but this must seem to Thrasymachus to be mere playing with words.

If Thrasymachus were conscious of the difference between his conception of the good and Socrates', he would have a basis for a reply regardless of whether he were able to pinpoint the moment at which the argument takes a wrong turn. Socrates' argument deals with knowledge that aims to produce a certain desirable state; though it is not said explicitly, clearly this state is thought to be good, for to put a string in tune, or to produce health in the body, is to produce in each its appropriate good. That is, Socrates' argument aligns with the good as Socrates understands it.

Thrasymachus could concede that a "good" of this kind exists but still refuse to change his mind about anything. When he speaks of injustice as good counsel, and accepts the suggestion that the unjust are wise (348d2–10), he has in mind a sort of practical wisdom, above all a recognition of his view that people are in competition with one another for goods. What counts for Thrasymachus is the fact that no specialized skill—neither music nor medicine, nor even the skill of the general or prize-fighter—can hope to preserve the good things its practitioner possesses against a sufficiently unscrupulous rival, and all individuals who rely on such skills will be utterly at the mercy of the tyrant. If our end is the possession of good things, then being "wise" and "good" as Socratic suggests may well be irrelevant. Of course the question of our proper end is not the sort of thing that is taken up in book i.

Thrasymachus claims he has some things to say in response to Socrates, but that this would require making an oration (350d9–e2). But the objections just mentioned do not require an oration, and anyway, Thrasymachus has shown himself able to make an oration when he wants (i.e., at 343b–344c), regardless of the wishes of those around him. If he does not respond here, it must be because he is not fully able to: he does not grasp the most fundamental difference between Socrates and himself—indeed, given that he never tries to justify his own view of what is good, it is unlikely that he imagines any other view to be possible. Although Thrasymachus is the most thoughtful of Socrates' opponents in book i, there are still limits to what he has thought through. We shall return to this below.

Socrates and Thrasymachus, then, each anchored in his own conception of the good, are talking past one another here. Socrates' argument here points toward a thin outline of an alternative to Thrasymachus, but far more is needed. Within book i, the failure to confront such fundamental matters as the question of what is good will result in a refutation of Thrasymachus that fails to deal with the substance of his position. Accordingly, there will be a need for Glaucon and Adeimantus to take that position up again in book ii.

Justice, Injustice and Strength (351a–352d)

Thrasymachus said that injustice is stronger (ἰσχυρότερον—344d5) than justice. Socrates now takes this up with a straightforward argument: no group of people, whether a city or a group of robbers, can accomplish anything to the extent that they behave unjustly toward one another. To the degree that the members of any group are engaged in cheating, robbing (etc.) one another, the group will be less effective in any action its members attempt in common. If we assume an individual to be composite, then injustice within the individual will have a similar effect, causing him to be at odds with himself and thus rendering him incapable of action.

We have been given no reason to agree with this assumption: "it is a glaring lacuna in his argument."[50] Of course, book iv will give an account of a composite soul, filling in the lacuna that Socrates leaves open here. In particular, in book iv we will read how injustice is a sort of civil war between the elements of the soul (444b), and justice is a matter of the proper arrangement of the elements of the soul (444d7–9)—just the picture we get here.[51]

Like its predecessor, this argument proceeds on the basis of Socrates' own conception of the good, rather than that of Thrasymachus. That is, we are once again concerned with *being* rather than *acquiring*. Again this explains why Thrasymachus offers no resistance: he has done plenty of thinking about the effect justice and injustice have insofar as getting things is concerned, but here Socrates is talking about how the two principles might affect the nature of a person (or group). This is a manner of thinking utterly alien to Thrasymachus.

Indeed, the fact that Socrates' argument proceeds only on the basis of his own conception of the good might be the cause of another weakness: it is concerned only with the effect justice has on the nature of its practitioner, and does not address the effect it might have beyond this. Accordingly, "it is not clear that a polis cannot treat its members justly, thereby producing the desired cohesion, while treating its nonmembers unjustly. If it can the argument collapses. For someone could then treat himself justly (so to speak), while treating others unjustly."[52] This objection assumes that justice is concerned with external actions as much as an internal state, an assumption that the work will later criticize (443c–444a). Still, in book iv we shall encounter an attempt to address this problem with the claim that doing just things produces justice, and doing unjust things produces injustice (444c9–d1; see also e3–4), but Socrates' argument as it stands here does not go so far.

Thrasymachus' claim (344a4) was that the *most perfect* injustice would be most effective. If Socrates' case for justice leaves something to be desired as it currently stands, still it is able to show that this Thrasymachan claim cannot be applied to a city (something he is ready to do—351b5), for a city must have some justice within itself if it is to act effectively—and so must the individual, if the soul is composite.[53] The previous argument showed how Thrasymachus' acquisition-oriented conception of the good was harmful in certain circumstances: Socrates is at least chipping away at Thrasymachus' view of things.

Finally, this argument suggests a comparison with Thucydides. Given the way that Socrates develops the position, starting with a city enslaving other cities (350a), and quickly developing the point that its members will hate one another and form factions,[54] one is reminded of Thucydides' presentation of the Sicilian expedition in books vi–vii and ii.65, according to which Athens' attempt to enslave the cities of Sicily fails for precisely such reasons. We saw how, on Thucydides' account, the decline of justice within Athens was a crucial contributing factor to the catastrophe in Sicily. Not only is this an historical example of the principle in action that would be very much in the minds of all Greeks in Plato's time, but depending on when exactly one dates the dialogue, it might have been unfolding as the discussion in Cephalus' house was proceeding.

Justice, Injustice and Happiness (352d–354c)

The first two arguments in the refutation of Thrasymachus contain significant deficiencies, simply assuming controversial premises that will receive a fuller treatment later in the work. Nevertheless, these two arguments have gotten some good hits in against Thrasymachus' conception of the good and of justice—that is, concerning the two most fundamental principles the discussion touches on. The final argument will contain the same sort of deficiency, but also a positive element of an altogether different kind. Socrates has become more active as the dialogue has moved forward (a phenomenon to which we shall return below), and has even gone beyond the criticism of others by giving his own opinion, for example, about how in a city of good people there would be a quarrel over not ruling just as there is today over ruling (347d). Just like the logic of his arguments, however, these positive statements of Socrates' own views looked ahead to the rest of the work for their justification. Now, in this final argument, Socrates explains a concept, and it can stand on its own.[55] It provides an explanation of something that was not sufficiently clear in earlier arguments, and it also provides a *basis* for claims made after book i. We do not yet have arguments that can stand entirely on their own, but we have at least gotten to the point at which one important concept can do so.

In the final argument against Polemarchus (335b–e), the word "function" (ἔργον—335d3, 12) popped up without any explanation. Against Thrasymachus, in the argument concerning the "precise sense," we heard that each skill has its own function (ἔργον—346d6), and in the preceding argument it was suggested that the function (ἔργον—351d9) of injustice is to produce hatred wherever it is. Readers could be forgiven if they were not entirely sure what was being said at these points, for just as throughout the rest of book i, these arguments looked ahead to a point later in the work for a fuller treatment. The case of function, however, is unique, because the more adequate treatment is found in the first book, in the course of this final argument. Furthermore, the notion of function "is the implicit basis of Socrates' subsequent argument that each person is suited by nature to a specific pursuit (ruling, fighting, or one of the commercial trades), each of which has a specific virtue (wisdom, courage, or temperance, respectively) and that justice consists in living in accordance with this principle (433a1–6)."[56] We also noted above, while discussing the final argument against Polemarchus, how function proves important in book ii.

Each thing, Socrates says, has some work which it alone can do, or it can do best.[57] Thus, eyes see, ears hear, a pruning knife cuts vines, and so on (352d–353a)—one cannot see with the ears, and though a butter knife might be able to cut vines, it would not do it nearly so well as a pruning knife. The virtue of each thing is that by which it does its work well: it is by the virtue of the eyes that they see well; a nearly blind person would indeed see, but not well, as his eyes, deficient as regards their proper virtue, do not do their work very well. The virtue of the soul, we are told, is justice, so without justice, the soul cannot live well. Thus the just man, with his just soul, will have a good life, and the unjust man, a bad one.[58]

Just like in the preceding two arguments, Socrates develops a view in line with his own conception of the good. If the good is understood in terms of external things that we must seek and acquire for ourselves, then "living well" must involve then acquisition of these things. On this basis, Socrates' argument here is saying something rather far-fetched, for there is always a certain degree of contingency involved in acquiring external things.[59] The claim that there is some form of activity that *necessarily guarantees* the acquisition of certain external things must therefore seem inherently implausible—surely even Thrasymachus would regard his unjust man (and tyrant) to have only a (far) better chance of getting what is good, rather than the absolute certainty of getting it.

On the other hand, from the point of view of Socrates' conception of the good, his argument here is altogether plausible. If the good is not something external that one acquires but rather has to do with what one *is*, then "living well" can be understood without any reference to what is beyond the self. In this case, it is natural to speak of an excellence that alone allows one to live well, just as the excellence of the eyes alone allows one to see. Once again, the different conceptions of the good explain Thrasymachus' failure to respond to the argument, as well as the fact that he is not convinced by it. From his perspective, Socrates must seem once again to be engaged in mere word games, and yet to make a proper response one would need to grasp the difference between the two conceptions of the good at work here.

The argument has not shown us what justice is, but it has offered some further refinements of the account that Socrates has hinted at in the course of his refutation of Thrasymachus. The place to look for justice, it would seem, is in the soul, and justice itself is to be understood as a causal power rather than a series of agreements among members of a community about how to behave. However, the argument as it stands at this point cannot be expected to produce many converts to the Socratic position. It has been criticized for the assumption that justice is the excellence of the soul,[60] and for the application of the concept of "function" to human beings. Of course, these ideas will be filled out later in the work.[61]

GLIMPSES OF THE GOOD

The three arguments by which Socrates refutes Thrasymachus have significant failings, as we have seen, but they do give three glimpses into the sort of thing that might lie behind his talk of goodness as something that one is, as opposed to something one might acquire. The first argument (349b–350e) shows that there already is a notion of "good" in common use according to which people often aim to bring about an objective state—health in a body, proper tuning in a string—and this state is characterized by the achievement of an objective limit. The second argument (351–352d) goes farther, showing how a properly ordered soul or city will achieve a sort of strength through the harmonious ordering of its parts. Finally, the third argument (352d–354c) suggests how such an order can function as a causal power, producing of its nature the activity of living well. Thus Socrates in the first book does not leave the notion of being good entirely empty. Implicit in his last three arguments is a more developed view concerning the sort of thing "being good" must involve.

THE POLITICAL ASPECT

Unlike Cephalus and Polemarchus, the political aspect of Thrasymachus' position is continually present in an explicit manner.[62] Before the argument had begun to impinge on what he could say, Thrasymachus described his position in terms mostly of parties within a city (338d–339a), the same level of political community we saw in Polemarchus. His position at this point was what he *wanted* to be seen as defending, but after his failure in argument caused him to become upset, he described his position in terms of the individual (343c–344c), singling out tyranny for particular praise (344a). It is after this that Socrates indicates that he believes Thrasymachus to be giving his true opinion (349a5–9), and shortly thereafter we have an argument which shows that Thrasymachus' position is incapable of maintaining any sort of community at all (351b–352a).

This, then, is what Plato wants us to understand to be the truth of Thrasymachus' position: it cannot maintain any sort of community—indeed, it must tend toward the destruction of every sort of community. In political terms, here the individual stands alone (insofar as he is not himself torn apart by injustice), liberated from any sort of obligation to other people.

HOW THRASYMACHUS IS GOOD

The characterization of Thrasymachus is remarkably unsympathetic—he has even been called "top contender for the title of Socrates' Most Obnoxious Interlocutor."[63] Nevertheless, Thrasymachus is good in crucial respects. Above all, by following Plato's careful deployment of the word ἀγαθός ("good") we have seen that Thrasymachus is more actively interested in the good than the two characters that proceed him—indeed, there is no aspect of his position or his action that cannot be explained by reference to his conception of the good.

We can now summarize the most important respects in which "good" is the center around which Thrasymachus' world turns. It is at 343d1–344a3 that he makes clear what he has in mind by "good," and the picture we get here is of things that one acquires at the expense of other people—for instance, if the unjust man avoids paying his full share of tax, the extra money he gets is denied to the state. There is no talk of goods that can be enjoyed by all, such as civil society or the discovery of the truth. His conception of the argument as a struggle to win goes naturally with such a zero-sum conception of goods, as does his desire to acquire praise, as well as with his attempts to denigrate Socrates. Thrasymachus' attempt to leave (344d) after his final tirade, before he can be refuted, is of a piece with this. His refusal to take Cleitophon's suggested path could be seen as a qualification on his striving to win, but in fact it reinforces his focus on the good: he clearly wants to win *with the claim to get actual good*, and not with any random claim—this claim of getting actual good is one thing with which he will refuse to part, however much he may adjust his position in other respects. We saw how his changing definitions of justice follow from his conception of the argument, and the argument from the "precise sense" has the question of whose advantage is served as its central disagreement: behind "advantage" lies "good." His failure to respond to Socrates' last three arguments is not simply a matter of his dialectical defeat to that point, but also a matter of Socrates' having used a novel conception of the good without explicitly introducing it. The problem with Thrasymachus is not that he fails actively to pursue the good—he could not be more active in this regard—but rather what he takes the good to be.

There are five other respects in which Thrasymachus must be understood to be good. First, it is Thrasymachus who brings the conversation about justice to the point where it touches on principles, when he speaks of the *most perfect* injustice (344a4), and considers the lives of the just and unjust man as the standard by which the question should be judged. In book ii, the matter of perfect injustice will be sharpened a bit by Glaucon into the demand for an account of the effect that justice and injustice each have in themselves. Second, Thrasymachus presents an account of justice that avoids a shortcoming found in the conversation with Polemarchus, which revealed some confusion about the proper field for justice. Thrasymachus found a place for justice in the activity of ruling, and in this he is not wrong: justice will indeed turn out to be concerned with a sort of rule, but a turn inward will be needed, so that the focus becomes *self*-rule.[64] Third, Thrasymachus' account of justice also gives us an answer to the question of why we should act at all: the unjust man gets what is good. This is a great step forward—Cephalus and Polemarchus did not address this matter at all. Fourth, Thrasymachus bases his position in the reality of everyday experience: his first account of justice is in fact true, observable in every city, everywhere; later on, he appeals to the reality that the unjust man and the tyrant are at a great advantage in life because of their injustice: they do in fact have more of what he takes to be good. Finally, it is with Thrasymachus that the political aspect comes to light—or rather, a political *problem*, for Thrasymachus begins by talking in political terms, but it becomes clear that he is focused only on the good of one individual, and that this individual will attain his good at the expense of the rest of the community. In the first book, we get the second-last argument (351a–352b), which deals both with a group of people and the individual, and begins to address this challenge, but the whole work will contain a response of a much more substantial kind, and the individual and the community will both be present throughout, in the city/soul analogy.

Thrasymachus' active interest in the good, and the active thought that follows from this, has thus produced a number of implicit challenges. An answer to Thrasymachus will have to be able to achieve a relationship to the good that is at least as successful as what he claims; we have already seen where Socrates is going in this regard. An answer to Thrasymachus will also have to take account of the basis he finds for his own views in reality; we shall see below how Socrates will take this up (see *Justice Based in Nature*, pages 248–9 below). It will also be necessary to address both the good of the individual and that of the community. Above all, Thrasymachus has presented a challenge concerning the credibility of any account of justice: clearly the pious imperatives we found in Cephalus will no longer do. We shall take this up in the conclusion.

The argument with Cephalus and Polemarchus did not make great demands on Socrates. Certainly nothing like the *Republic* was needed to answer them. With Thrasymachus, the matter is very different. He has thought deeply enough that an argument with him brings out major challenges. It is above all in this presentation of challenges that drives the argument on to the rest of the work—and indeed *requires* the sort of account we find in the rest of the work—that Thrasymachus is good.

THE LIMITS OF THRASYMACHUS

Thrasymachus is the most thoughtful of the three characters confronted by Socrates in book i, but still he exhibits two deficiencies as a thinker. In the first place, he has not adequately reflected on one crucially important question: what is good? Certainly, he has an answer to this question, but his answer has the same character as Cephalus' ethical world. That is, the matter of what is good is taken by Thrasymachus as simply *given*. He takes the nature of good things as *obvious*: nowhere does he try to justify the view that money and other possessions, as well as recognition from others, are good things. Instead he just proceeds as if this is an established fact. This is a most fundamental failing on his part: everything he says and does proceeds from his conception of the good, so that everything he says and does might well be based on a mistake.[65] We saw how his lack of thought on this matter explained his failure to respond to the last three arguments in book i.

A second defect comes in his relation to objective reality. On the one hand, he is remarkable for his focus on what he takes to be real. The bedrock of his world is his desire to get good things, and we have seen how much he wants *actual, objective* money, power, praise, possessions and so on, rather than merely imaginary, subjective realities (recall his rejection of Cleitophon's alternative). The same focus on objective reality is present in two of the advantages we saw in his position, both of which constituted challenges for the rest of the work: unlike the two preceding characters, he provides a compelling reason for action—again, the expectation of getting good things—and he is also able to give his position a foundation in the reality of everyday experience. On the other hand, the notion of liberating oneself from external constraints is another fundamental concern for Thrasymachus. Already in his first position (338c–339e), we note that a ruler is obliged to recognize no constraints at all, save whatever might be necessary to work with the other rulers (and the tyrant need not concern himself even with that). It soon becomes clear that this was no accident, for it is precisely because of a willingness to act in an utterly unrestrained manner that the unjust man or tyrant is able to do so well for himself. It is this connection that we should understand the claim that being "more free" (ἐλευθεριώτερον—344c5) is part of the unjust life.

The problem is that striving for an absolute liberation from constraint is not entirely compatible with a focus on getting objective goods. Every single argument that Socrates brings against Thrasymachus drives this point home, running the sophist's views against objective reality: both mistakes and skills presuppose objective reality, as does the good as Socrates understands it. Thrasymachus needs the world beyond himself to have a substantial existence insofar as he can acquire and dominate it, but he needs it to have an *in*substantial existence insofar as it might constrain his freedom of action. Thus Socrates' first question—do the rulers make mistakes?—effectively cuts Thrasymachus in half.

A certain liberation from the constraints of conventional or traditional thought is necessary to genuinely rigorous thinking, which must be free to perform a critical reexamination of every premise (recall that this is a thought we encountered in the *Gorgias*, in the theme of shame). Thrasymachus, however, has failed fully to think this through, for a liberation so absolute that it conflicts with objective reality is simply unintelligent. As with his focus on the good, he is impressive in the context of book i, but that context can make him seem rather more accomplished than he really is.

In fact, intelligence does not play such an important role for Thrasymachus' ideal individual: certainly some brainpower is required, but in practical life others might be far more intelligent and yet be helpless in the face of a proper

Thrasymachan, for the decisive intellectual moment for him is simply the recognition of the need for utterly unscrupulous, unconstrained behavior.

NOTES

1. On Thrasymachus, I have found Dorter, "Refutation of Thrasymachus," particularly helpful, as well as the treatment given by Schindler, *Plato's Critique*, 55–81, with which I am largely in agreement.
2. Cross and Woozley, *Plato's Republic*, 40–41, Joseph Maguire, "Thrasymachus—or Plato?" *Phronesis* 16, no. 2 (1971): 142–63, Annas, *Introduction*, 46, and Stephen Everson, "The Incoherence of Thrasymachus," *Oxford Studies in Ancient Philosophy* 16 (1998): 99–132, find Thrasymachus inconsistent. F. E. Sparshott, "Socrates and Thrasymachus," *The Monist* 50 (1966): 421–59, T. Y. Henderson, "In Defense of Thrasymachus," *American Philosophical Quarterly* 7, no. 3 (July 1970): 218–28, Lycos, *Justice and Power*, 40–53, and T. D. J. Chappell, "Thrasymachus and Definition," *Oxford Studies in Ancient Philosophy* XVIII (2000): 101–7, all find Thrasymachus consistent, though they differ as to his position.
3. W. K. C. Guthrie, *A History of Greek Philosophy Vol. IV* (Cambridge: Cambridge University Press, 1975), 88–97.
4. George F. Hourani, "Thrasymachus' Definition of Justice in Plato's *Republic*," *Phronesis* 7, no. 2 (1962): 110–20.
5. G. B. Kerferd, "The doctrine of Thrasymachus in Plato's Republic," in *Sophisitk*, ed. C. J. Classen (Darmstadt: Wissenschaftliche Buchgesellschaft, 1976), 545–63. P. P. Nicholson, "Unravelling Thrasymachus' Arguments in the Republic," *Phronesis* 19, no. 3 (1974): 210–32, follows Kerferd, but ends by saying that Thrasymachus' arguments "are in such disarray that no interpretation can be established beyond all doubt."
6. George Klosko, "Thrasymachos' Eristikos: The Agon Logon in Republic I," *Polity* 17, no. 1 (Autumn, 1984): 6–16, provides important considerations against the search for consistency in Thrasymachus beyond what I will say here.
7. I formulated these questions after reading G. J. Boter, "Thrasymachus and ΠΛΕΟΝΕΞΙΑ," *Mnemosyne* 39 (Fourth Series), no. 3/4 (1986): 261–81, who proceeds toward an understanding of Thrasymachus' position by working backwards, from Glaucon, to 343b–344c and then to the start of the conversation. See also Klosko, "Eristikos," 5–29, who draws attention to the importance of dealing with what Thrasymachus actually says, and thus of being aware of the difference between this and a position cobbled together from bits of what he says. The answer to the question I pose here is given in the conclusion, in particular under the heading *Proleptic Composition and the Cave in Republic I* (pages 238–40): the two different presentations of the Thrasymachan position are necessary to the structure of the *Republic*.
8. Schindler, *Plato's Critique*, 56, has come very close to this: "the problem with Thrasymachus is not so much a problem of character as it is, more fundamentally, a problem with what he takes to be real." This is correct, but what Thrasymachus takes to be real is wrapped up with his conception of the good. Schindler finds the account

of the Good in book vi relevant to Thrasymachus; I hope here to provide further textual support for this insight.

9. Of course, what ultimately underwrites this interpretation is my claim that we can explain the text by means of it.

10. The importance of being well-regarded by others also comes to light later on, when Thrasymachus mentions how the just man will be hated by relatives and acquaintances (343e6).

11. Dorter, "Refutation of Thrasymachus," 29, notes how Thrasymachus' initial definition, that justice is the advantage of the stronger, "is exceedingly vague . . . it can be taken to mean all things to all people . . . people who regard themselves as, in some decisive respect, stronger than the generality of men . . . would agree with Thrasymachus if they understand 'strength' in the way that suits them." Note just how richly appropriate it is from this perspective that Thrasymachus is soon forced into an argument from the "precise sense."

12. See Nettleship, *Lectures*, 27, who has understood this. Note also Socrates' exhortation that Thrasymachus not answer contrary to his actual opinion (346a), another suggestion that something different had occurred earlier.

13. Klosko, "Eristikos," 20, who makes reference to the *Meno* (75c8–d4), the *Theaetetus* (167e–168a) and the *Republic* (454a), among other dialogues. Klosko has established the eristic nature of the argument with Thrasymachus. In this paragraph I summarize certain of his main points; see his paper for more. He gives only a brief account (pp. 27–29) of the reason why Plato has given this character to the encounter with Thrasymachus, and allows that there is room for further work on the question. Here I think I can provide further insight by connecting this element to larger themes in the dialogue: see pages 233, 236–7, 239–40, 242 and 252–3.

14. Klosko, "Eristikos," 23. He notes the additional discussion of "the procedures for conducting and judging" the debate later on at 348a–b.

15. Klosko, "Eristikos," 24.
16. Klosko, "Eristikos," 24.
17. Klosko, "Eristikos," 20.
18. Klosko, "Eristikos," 21.
19. θέμεναι, which could even be: "*because* they legislated."
20. αὕτη . . . κρατεῖ, ὥστε . . . δίκαιον, τὸ τοῦ κρείττονος συμφέρον. Of course, κρατεῖ could also mean "is strong," so that the idea would be that the ruling party, which makes the laws (with its own good in mind), is strong, so that justice is the advantage of the stronger. This might soften, but does not fundamentally change, the point.

21. The argument at this point is analogous to that in the *Gorgias* from 488d–490a, where Callicles is forced to move from a straightforward focus on the basis of his position in observable facts to a question of intelligence.

22. C. D. C. Reeve, *Philosopher Kings—The Argument of Plato's Republic* (Princeton, NJ: Princeton University Press, 1988), 12–13, asks the same question, though he gives a different answer.

23. Dorter, "Refutation of Thrasymachus," 31, is correct to point to another aspect of the position that Thrasymachus rejects here, for if he follows Cleitophon, then "his

position becomes an innocuous equation of justice with law or decree. But clearly Thrasymachus has something more radical in mind than justice as obedience to law." What lies behind that "something more radical" is liberation in the service of "advantage," behind which, as we shall see, is a certain conception of the good.

24. The desire to win the argument without giving up the claim to actual advantage, and thus avoiding a position of mere belief, as suggested by Cleitophon, provides an example of Thrasymachus' double relation to objective reality—see *The Limits of Thrasymachus* below, pages 223–5.

25. The refutation of Thrasymachus proper will return to the matter of intelligence (from 348a).

26. Note how Thrasymachus speaks of ἢ σοφὸς ἢ ἄρχων ("either a wise man or one who rules") at 340e5: the phrase brings intelligence and rule together (note also ἐπιστήμη at 340e3). This will be echoed later by Socrates' similar use of intelligence-and-rule words together: σκοπεῖ οὐδ ἐπιτάττει (342c12, d5–6, e8); σκέψεταί τε καὶ προστάξει (342e3).

27. James Adam, *The Republic of Plato—Edited with Critical Notes, Commentary and Appendices, Vol. 1 (2nd edition)* (Cambridge: Cambridge University Press, 1965), 33, sees this, as does Alban Dewes Winspear, *The Genesis of Plato's Thought* (Montreal: Harvest House Ltd., 1974), 191, and Kerferd, "Doctrine," 551. Harrison, "Manipulation," 31, notes that "that strain of idealism which becomes a recurrent feature of the rest of the dialogue" begins with Thrasymachus' "exact sense;" further, "Socrates is here provided by his opponent with a term that will later play a considerable role in his exposition of the Theory of Ideas, where it will characterize the education of the philosopher-king (503d) and also distinguish the standards that apply at the end of the "longer way" from those of everyday discussion (504a–505b, cf. 435d)."

28. D. J. Allan, "Introduction," *Plato Republic I* (Bristol: Bristol Classical Press, 1996), 28. Cross and Woozley, *Plato's Republic*, 50, make a similar point; see also Klosko, "Eristikos," 25.

29. Dorter, "Refutation of Thrasymachus," 32: "pure knowledge does not enjoin self-interest, but is precisely *dis*interested."

30. Reeve, *Philosopher Kings*, 280, fn. 15. Lycos, *Justice and Power*, 113, makes a similar point. In the context of book i, one might respond that the precise shepherd will not be concerned with the definition of "good," but will be concerned only with bringing his sheep into the state demanded by his craft, which is "good" as he understands it (of course, this response avoids addressing the question of what is good, and what the essence of a shepherd is, for answers to such questions are not appropriate to this book: see *Proleptic Composition and the Cave in Republic I* below, pages 238–40).

31. I have been speaking of "everyday experience" rather than "the real world" in discussing the non-precise shepherd. This is because another issue lurking beneath the surface here is the question of what is really real, again a matter that looks to the rest of the work. It is true that the shepherd in the world of everyday experience would define "good" in terms of his own good rather than that of the sheep, but this is by no means a knock-down argument, for why should the precise sense be determined by reference to the world of everyday experience? We cannot simply assume that

everyday experience is what is really real: maybe experience should be measured by the ideal, that is, by the precise sense.

32. Reeve, *Philosopher Kings*, 19. In similar fashion, Beversluis, *Cross-Examining*, 235, finds an inconsistency between the account of the wage-earning art and Socrates' earlier argument that "every [art] exists to promote the interest of someone or something other than the [art] or its practitioner (342b1–7)." But a practitioner is not mentioned at 342b1–7.

33. Accordingly, to introduce examples of skills, such as murder or tennis (Allan, "Introduction," 28) or crime (Cross and Woozley, *Plato's Republic*, 50), that seem not to aim at the good of their object is not necessarily relevant to the argument.

34. Note that Socrates calls the non-wage-earners craftsmen (δημιουργοί—346c6, 10), as he earlier spoke of how rulers perform the activity of craftsmen (that is, δημιουργεῖν—342e9): this takes up Thrasymachus' talk of the craftsman (δημιουργός—340e3, 4, 5) who was said to be characterized by knowledge (ἐπιστήμη—340e3) and rule (ἄρχων—340e5, 6). Wage-earning, one presumes, is distinct from the activity of a δημιουργός.

35. This anticipation has often been noted: see Adam, *Republic of Plato*, 46, Kahn, "Proleptic Composition," 138, D. J. Allan, "Notes," *Plato Republic I* (Bristol: Bristol Classical Press, 1996), 104. The question of what motivates rulers to rule is one to which the *Republic* will return (e.g., at 412c–e, 420b–421c, 520a–d).

36. Nettleship, *Lectures*, 33: "that this analysis is true, and that we not only can but must thus distinguish the two products, is shown by the fact that a doctor may cease to take fees, and none the less continue to heal."

37. The claim with universal validity—πανταχοῦ ("everywhere"—343d3)—in Thrasymachus' new position is now that the just man has less than the unjust. The earlier universal claim—πανταχοῦ (339a3)—was that justice everywhere was the advantage of the ruling party.

38. Indeed, when Thrasymachus sets the just and unjust men beside one another at 343d1–344a3, he is also anticipating the two statues mentioned at 361d4–6, an image that itself looks ahead to books vii–ix: see Matthew Robinson, "Competition, Imagery, and Pleasure in Plato's *Republic*, 1–9," *Plato: Journal of the International Plato Society* 13 (2013): 51–75.

39. See Boter, "Thrasymachus," 273.

40. Everson, "Incoherence," 103, notes that this idea was current at the time, quoting in particular Antiphon B44: "justice consists in not transgressing the rules of one's state."

41. Socrates hinted at this conception of the good against Polemarchus (334c10, d1, d3, e2, 335a3), but there the word "good" (ἀγαθός) was used interchangeably with "useful" (χρηστός, as was "evil," κακός, with "base," πονηρός). We saw how this confusion was appropriate in relation to Polemarchus.

42. Of previous interpreters, Méron, *Idées Morales*, 138, seems to have gotten closest to this: she noticed that Socrates and Thrasymachus differ in their conceptions of advantage, and sees, further, that Socrates' conception of advantage here has a parallel in the *Gorgias*, particularly in the passage ending at 507a. This is exactly

correct; of course, in that passage in the *Gorgias*, Socrates is giving his own account of "good" rather than "advantage."

43. The account of rule by the good, who compete with one another not to rule at 347b–d looks ahead to the philosopher king, who will rule not by desire but by compulsion—519c–520e. The anticipation of the philosopher king here has been remarked upon since at least Adam, *Republic of Plato*, 46, who was writing at the start of the twentieth century.

44. Rowe, *Philosophical Writing*, 190, makes a similar point, without noting the difference between the Thrasymachan and Socratean conceptions of the good.

45. Cross and Woozely, *Plato's Republic*, 52. John Gutglueck, "From Pleonexia to Polupragmosune: A Conflation of Possession and Action in Plato's Republic," *The American Journal of Philology* 109, no. 1 (Spring 1988): 20–39, gives a detailed development of this criticism.

46. The focus on the verb πλεονεκτεῖν in this argument takes up Thrasymachus' use of it at 344a1. On this word, Dougal J. Blyth, "Polemarchus in Plato's Republic," *Prudentia* 25, no. 1 (1994): 62, fn. 16, notes that "the term *pleonexia* and cognates occur some eighteen times in *R*. Twelve of these are in Socrates' conversation with Thrasymachus in Bk I; yet five of the remaining six occur in Glaucon and Adeimantus' challenge to Socrates in the first half of Bk II to convince them that the just man is happier than the unjust under all circumstances. This indicates the centrality of *pleonexia* to the conception of injustice in the main structural project of *R*. That this is so is confirmed by the final usage, in Bk IX (586b1) where the comparison of the two kinds of life is finally made."

47. Here I do not entirely agree with Rowe, *Philosophical Writing*, 190 (also p. 191, fn. 15), when he claims that "two wise people—two equally, and perfectly, wise ones—will always do the same thing under the same circumstances." Rowe sees a difference between Socrates and Thrasymachus only in the particular good things that they aim at (e.g., Rowe says, "Socrates' wise person will be wise in his choice of *goods*"), but we have seen that the difference goes farther than this: Socrates is not interested in *acquiring* good things, but in *being* good. This is not an externally determined conception, and so external acquisitions and actions might vary within a certain range. Two good people might do different things in the very same circumstances—one might choose to eat steak, another fish—but would be the same in their attention to their own internal harmony, not eating too much or too little, and no doubt avoiding inappropriate foods.

48. Lycos, *Justice and Power*, 120–36, provides a useful defense of the argument at 349b–350c, answering objections, expanding on Socrates' statements, and finding that "within its limited scope the argument is successful" (p. 121). What he does not account for is the dense manner in which the argument has been expressed, and thus for the respect in which it fails: it leaves much unsaid that Lycos finds necessary to spell out in considerable detail. I agree with Lycos that the thinking behind this argument is sound and can be defended at length, but what Socrates has actually said (and failed to say) is also important, and the failure of the argument in this respect coheres meaningfully with the numerous indications (e.g., 354b–c, 358b–d) that book i has not presented a compelling case. See also Dorter, "Refutation of Thrasymachus,"

35-9, and Rowe, *Philosophical Writing*, 186-97. Nettleship, *Lectures*, 36-40, is also illuminating in certain regards.

49. We have seen that in the *Gorgias* at 503e7-504a2, where we get an account of what it means for something to be good, a very similar idea seems to be at work.

50. Dorter, "Refutation of Thrasymachus," 39. Dorter also suggests (p. 40) that Plato is purposely looking ahead to book iv here.

51. Note also the concern at 423b-d that the city might become too large, and thus lose its unity.

52. Reeve, *Philosopher Kings*, 20-21.

53. It is true that fear (as Cross and Woozely, *Plato's Republic*, 56, suggest), or the mere belief that one is receiving just treatment from other citizens (Reeve, *Philosopher Kings*, 21) can hold a community together, but these will contain a source of weakness: the instant people cowed by fear have a chance, they will take action against whoever has terrorised them (see Thucydides ii.3-4 for an example); similarly, if people falsely believe themselves to be treated justly, the danger will always be present that they may discover the reality behind this. Justice itself has no such source of weakness.

54. The verb στασιάζειν, which Plato uses thrice in this passage (351d12, 352a2, 352a7) recalls στάσις, a highly significant word in Thucydides (e.g., iii.82.2).

55. On the explanation of "function" here, see Dorter, *Transformation*, 49, who notes how the concept will be more fully developed in what follows.

56. Dorter, "Refutation of Thrasymachus," 40.

57. Lycos' detailed consideration of this argument, *Justice and Power*, 144-53, is worth reading as an attempt to push Socrates' side of things; *inter alia*, following Annas, *Introduction*, 54, it offers a convincing response to the insertion of the notion of purpose into the argument by Cross and Woozley, *Plato's Republic*, 56-60.

58. The *Republic* will, of course, take up the relation of justice and virtue at greater length later on (see especially 432b-434c).

59. Recall how we saw above that there was a truth hinted at by Socrates' account of the skill of wage-earning: everyone recognises that supremely excellent activity often fails to attain appropriate compensation. In the current examples, however, there is no such contingency: eyes with their proper virtues will always see well; a knife that is sharp will always, of its nature, cut well.

60. Annas, *Introduction*, 55; Cross and Woozley, *Plato's Republic*, 58-59. See also Nicholas Pappas, *Plato and the Republic*, 2nd edition (New York: Routledge, 2003), 48-49.

61. The passage at 433c-434c is instructive here: the principle that each person should do his own proper task—that is, justice—is at least a match for the other three virtues as regards the excellence of a city (ἀρετή πόλεως—433d5); if the three classes interfere with one another, that produces the greatest harm to a city (434c); see also 444d-445c. As for "function," it will be central to the account of justice: see 370b ff., 406c-407a; 433a-434c, 443b-d are also relevant.

62. Pappas, *Plato*, 16-17, suggests that the fact that Cephalus and Polemarchus do not speak of politics is related to their status as metics, who cannot participate in the

political life of the city they inhabit. "As a result, Cephalus and Polemarchus describe the good human life without mentioning politics." Thus the political aspect merely lies implicit with these two.

63. Beversluis, *Cross-Examining*, 221.

64. The notion of ruling will be central to both the account of justice and the virtue of moderation: see, for example, 430e–431d, 441e, 442d, 443b–d, 444b–d; see also 509d, where the sun and the good are both said to be king (βασιλεύειν) of their respective realms. Recall also the introduction of self-rule in the *Gorgias* (491d).

65. In book vi (494b–495b; see also 496a) we hear about a philosophical nature that goes astray. From such inverted philosophers come the greatest harm. The passage has been taken (no doubt rightly) to point to Alcibiades, but it is no less relevant to Thrasymachus. Of course, both characters stand for the third and final moment in the development set out in each text.

Republic I
Conclusion

The first book of the *Republic* presents a movement between two opposed standpoints. Cephalus exhibits real piety, while Thrasymachus would steal everything he can, "sacred and profane" (344a9). Cephalus displays no active interest in the good; Thrasymachus is so intently fixed on what he believes to be good that everything he says and does can be explained on this basis. Cephalus aims to conform himself to an externally given order; Thrasymachus aims to liberate himself as fully as possible from any such constraints—indeed, a character more liberated from external constraints wouldn't care what other people thought of him, and thus wouldn't have any interest in taking part to begin with.

Cephalus is the most passive and unreflective character who could be included in the argument—indeed, we saw how there is not really an argument so much as an agreement-oriented discussion with him. The instant Socrates poses a genuinely critical question, Cephalus withdraws. Thrasymachus, by contrast, presents a form of activity so extreme that he threatens to dominate the proceedings by means of emotions such as fear rather than by argument. We saw how this portion of the dialogue consequently becomes an eristic argument—that is, a contest to win. A difficult contest it is: in contrast with the swift withdrawal of Cephalus, Thrasymachus can repeatedly adjust his position to hold his own (for a time) in the face of Socrates' questioning. This difference in intellectual ability is reflected in the fact that Cephalus repeatedly appeals to authority figures while Thrasymachus never does. Cephalus requires almost nothing of Socrates; Thrasymachus requires the rest of the *Republic* for a proper answer.

In every respect just mentioned, Polemarchus represents an intermediate standpoint. He is caught between the order inhabited by his father and the liberation aimed at by Thrasymachus. He may not be seen to attend constantly to the sacrifices as his father does, but he aims to be a loyal heir, attempting a defense of his father's position, and turning away from his own definition as it becomes clear that it is entering unseemly territory. He brings out the word "good" on his own the instant he has to think on his own, though it soon becomes clear that he has given it little thought, having failed fully to distinguish it from the useful. He is more active and able in argument than Cephalus and less so than Thrasymachus, and the argument with Polemarchus is just that: an argument, not a comfortable conversation, nor a struggle for supremacy. Polemarchus appeals to the authority of Simonides at first, in the manner of his father, but after this does not appeal to authority again, just as Thrasymachus does not. The confused and divided nature of Polemarchus is also hinted at by certain concepts we saw conflated with one another: good and useful, virtue and skill, owed and fitting. With Polemarchus, the absolute liberation advocated by Thrasymachus is coming into view, and the traditional order has begun to lose its grip. We do not have a consistent position in Polemarchus, but rather tendencies toward both his predecessor and his successor.[1]

We thus have a change from one position (Cephalus) to another, very different position (Thrasymachus), with a third position in between that has something in common with each of the extremes: this is a *development*, an idealized representation of a gradual shift from one state of affairs to another. It has the same structure as the three-stage development we saw in Thucydides, where we saw a move from one position (Periclean Athens) to another position (Alcibiadean Athens), with a transitional position in between: the Mytilenian debate occupies a position just like that of Polemarchus (see pages 85–6). As noted earlier, three steps is the minimum necessary to portray such a historical development; any further steps would, in effect, be repetitions of the middle, Polemarchan, position.[2]

One detail concerning the arguments can be explained from this perspective: Socrates uses the same kind of arguments against Polemarchus and Thrasymachus. That is, in both cases, Socrates begins by showing how the definition can be misinterpreted (331e–332a, 338c–d), and this is followed by arguments from the τέχνη-analogy (332c–334b, 340d–347e) and the difficulty of human knowing (334c–335a, 338d–339e); finally, there is a difficult section which considers the matter in itself (335b–e, 347e–354a), removing the character in question from the argument. This is to be explained by the fact that Polemarchus represents the same thing as Thrasymachus (i.e., a liberation from the world of Cephalus), but in a less extreme form. Accordingly, one brings the same kind of arguments against both, though the order is different: the argument with Polemarchus turns gradually away from utility toward the good, so the τέχνη argument must be first; with Thrasymachus, the tendency toward unrestrained liberation is now so great that the most important matter is simply to bring some limit to bear on it, so that we begin with the argument from the difficulty of knowing.

THE ARGUMENT OF BOOK I

The first book of the *Republic* does not provide an argument in the sense of a demonstration of the truth of a doctrine. What it does provide is a picture of a historical situation—*Plato's* historical situation—in a manner that brings out the pressing problem contained therein. In this case, by understanding the problem we come to see a great deal of the form the solution must take. Briefly put, the problem is that the collapse of traditional authority has produced Thrasymachus. The answer will require understanding what makes his position so attractive, and responding in a manner that takes it up—and this without sacrificing the good contained in the traditional order.

But let us consider the matter more closely. The overall movement of the first book of the *Republic* should be deeply disturbing to anyone who believes that "the unexamined life is not worth living."[3] It is precisely such examination which produced the move from Cephalus to Thrasymachus. On the basis of the picture given in book i, it seems that the examined life brings about the collapse of conventional morality and the possibility of a peaceful community, reducing human interaction to a terrifying struggle for domination.

Of course, there is no absolute necessity here: it is not the case that *every* critical examination of conventional norms *must* produce this result. What we are presented with here is a particular historical movement: it proceeds according to a logic of its own, and it remains dependent on contingent aspects of the situation. The relevance of this movement is not, however, confined to one specific situation. Here we shall focus on what is peculiar to book i.

The progression from Cephalus to Thrasymachus tells a story of the decreasing authority of a traditional ethical order. Cephalus stands for an unreflecting acceptance of this order, and he still finds in the voice of tradition an adequate basis for a life. His lack of concern for the difficulty brought to light by Socrates' questioning is reflected in his laughter as he goes off. People of the next generation, however, represented by Polemarchus, will feel more deeply the inability of traditional wisdom to give an adequate account of itself, even though they may at the same time feel the pull of that older order. Once such an ambiguous position has been reached, all that is required to produce a Thrasymachus is the combination of unscrupulousness and an intellect active enough to grasp the full consequences of the failure of tradition. For a failure there is: one only avoids all that Thrasymachus represents to the extent that one turns away from thought, accepting the traditional ethical order as given. The whole movement thus tends *of its nature* toward Thrasymachus: given critical thought, he seems to be the logical endpoint of what precedes him.

Thus the first book of the *Republic* poses a problem: by presenting a particular historical situation, it brings out the pressing need to answer a question: is it possible to think deeply about how one ought to live, and yet not end up with Thrasymachus? That is, is it possible to show that the examined life might yet be reconciled to peace, trust, stability and the standards of behavior which are usually thought to be desirable and praiseworthy? There is in particular a question concerning the possibility of maintaining a political community, for we saw how the three steps of the movement involved a gradual decline in the political entity that would naturally be maintained: first a city (Cephalus), then parties (Polemarchus), and finally the individual (Thrasymachus from 343b).

There is more still at work in all this: the movement from Cephalus to Thrasymachus is a bad thing—but also good. Let us begin with the more obvious, negative side. Not only does Thrasymachus give voice to a position that takes the subjugation of other people to be the highest ideal (i.e., in the tyrant), there are also unsubtle hints that we are to understand this as a deeply irrational and inherently violent standpoint. Thrasymachus is thrice compared to dangerous animals—he is a "wild beast" (336b6), a "lion" (341c2) and a wolf (336d7)[4]—and must twice be restrained by some of those present in order that the argument may proceed (336b, 344d). These hints constitute a dramatic portrayal of a violent nature, which should color our understanding of his position, and which in any case has a fairly obvious connection to what he says. When we combine Thrasymachus' understanding of the good, which makes human interaction a zero-sum game, with his almost-total liberation from conventional normative restraints, we see that we have here a view of the world that *of its nature* can be expected to produce violence. His great outburst at 343b–344c, with its talk of enslaving others (344b7), is, if anything, understated as regards the brutality implied by his position.

From this perspective, how desirable the world of Cephalus seems! There was no hint of violence in him, and Socrates' explicit admiration for Cephalus made clear that whatever the old man's faults, we are nevertheless to understand there to be real good in him. We saw suggestions of the role moderation played in his life, and we saw his definition of justice attempted to do well by other people. The pleasant and agreeable nature of the conversation with Cephalus, with its expressions of mutual regard, is particularly conspicuous when compared with the insults that characterize the encounter with Thrasymachus. When Socrates spoke with Cephalus, both participants express the expectation that they will benefit (328c–e); with Thrasymachus, such hopes have disappeared, for he participates in the argument with a view to attaining praise by means of a victory over Socrates. If our aim is to find a way to maintain a peaceful polity, it would seem that we should look to Cephalus, whose position would produce a city at peace with itself. Thrasymachus' position, on the other hand, would of its nature undermine any city, putting it in conflict with itself. The movement from Cephalus to Thrasymachus is a movement from an essentially peaceful situation to an essentially violent one.

In these respects, the movement of the first book seems to be negative, a catastrophic loss of peace and stability (and one which mirrors the development we saw in Thucydides). A look at Polemarchus confirms this. Recall how, just after he was forced to abandon the authority of a poet and start thinking for himself, he introduced the notion of doing some evil to others (332b7–9), a suggestion that represented a step beyond anything Cephalus said. As Polemarchus' definition becomes clearer, we see that a vast canvas is being opened up for evil: to the extent that one is guided only by the words "helping friends and harming enemies," then any behavior at all, however unscrupulous or brutal, is in principle permissible against enemies, and this is soon clarified so that enemies are understood simply to be those who seem bad. This is certainly liberation from the shackles of traditional authority, but it is not clear that it is a good or desirable thing. Thus Polemarchus ends by turning away from the consequences of his own words. With Thrasymachus, however, this form of liberation, this readiness for unscrupulous or brutal behavior, is taken further, for it is a conscious policy rather than an unintended consequence: the ideal man, the tyrant, gets the most of what is good *precisely because* he is most fully liberated from that acceptance of the authority of tradition, and thus of conventional norms, by which Cephalus was bound. From this perspective, then, it would seem that the collapse of that authority was entirely undesirable.

Plato has painted a more complex picture than this, however, and we can see it as we turn again to the indications that he wants us to understand the development that results in Thrasymachus also to be a *good* thing, and more than this, that the movement is a good thing *insofar as* it abandons a reliance on convention or authority. We saw how the movement from Cephalus to Polemarchus to Thrasymachus involved an increasing interest in "good," and that Thrasymachus switches from "advantage" to "good" at the moment at which he is at his most antinomian, most fully at odds with traditional authority.

We have, then, an increasingly active relation to the good as we move forward, and increasingly active thinking.[5] By the time we reach Thrasymachus, we have someone who has thought things through for himself to such a degree that he poses the five challenges that require an account of the sort that we see in the rest of the *Republic*. These challenges could not have been made without a readiness to go beyond the limits of what is conventionally acceptable. Even Thrasymachus' unpleasantness is necessary to what is good about him: he accuses Polemarchus and Socrates of deferring to one another (336c2), and certainly excessive consideration for others can be a hindrance to a demand for convincing reasons for their beliefs (recall the same idea in the *Gorgias* in the notion of being "rather crude" (i.e., ἀγροικότερος), and also in the theme of shame and frankness). From this perspective, the liberation from conventional thinking, from traditional authority, are goods essential to the possibility of philosophy.[6]

Thus there is, at every stage of the movement, an inadequate mix of good and bad. Thrasymachus is good insofar as he thinks actively and strives toward what he thinks good, and these traits make him a kind of image of a philosopher. Cephalus lacks these virtues, but pleasantness and mutual goodwill—the sorts of things that tend to produce a community at peace with itself—are certainly goods we would want to retain. How, then, do we keep what is good about Cephalus and Thrasymachus while avoiding what is bad?

Cephalus is the head of the household in which the *Republic* takes place. In this sense, he is a king, the leader of a community.[7] But while he may provide an image of a king, he is certainly no philosopher. Thrasymachus may be an inadequate image of a philosopher, he is no king. The *Republic* will aim at a philosopher king, one who is fully thoughtful, most intent upon the good, and yet also intent on producing a peaceful and stable order in the city (and himself).

PROLEPTIC COMPOSITION AND THE CAVE IN REPUBLIC I

The proleptic nature of book i—that is, the way in which it anticipates doctrines found later in the work—has been treated elsewhere, and we have seen new examples of such anticipations in the course of our treatment of this book. There is no need to recite yet again all the instances of proleptic composition in book i.[8] There is, however, a connection still worth investigating between this aspect of book i and another aspect, the fact that it takes place in the cave.

The first word of the whole work—"this verb in preference to any other word"[9]—is κατέβην, "I went down." As the philosopher must go down κα ταβαίνειν (519d), καταβατέον (520c), καταβιβαστέοι (538e)—to the cave to turn people away from the images and toward the sun, so too does Socrates go down to the Piraeus. Continuing in this vein, the torches which will light the horse race at night might be thought to constitute an allusion to the fire which lights the images of the cave for the prisoners there. Indeed, there is night imagery in the opening scene which should remind us of the darkness of the cave: sunset is coming, and there will be an all-night festival (328a), and this festival is in honor of Bendis, who is herself a moon goddess.[10] The image of the moon again suggests the darkness of the cave (the moon being the replacement of the sun at night), its light but a reflection of that of the sun. While the conversation of the *Republic* takes place, while would-be philosophers strive to relieve themselves of darkness and see the true reality which Socrates will compare to the sun, others, illuminated by torches, will revel in darkness, worshipping a goddess whose proper realm is night, just like the prisoners in the cave, who are content to remain ignorant of the reality of the situation in which they dwell.

All this would be *mere* imagery if not for the fact that it dovetails with so much of what we have seen of the content of book i. If we understand book i as being in the cave—more specifically, looking at images on the cave's wall, the objects of the lowest section of the line (see 509d–511e)—we should expect that realities which will later be seen more clearly would be prefigured in an imperfect way, and that arguments and characters which resemble truths would be imperfect images of what is to come. This is just what the proleptic aspect of book i gives us. We get glimpses that are partial and unsatisfactory, scraps of content abstracted from the reasoning by means of which they make complete sense. So, for example, Cephalus gives voice to certain doctrines found later in the work without fully embodying, or being able to explain, their content. Thus Polemarchus' "helping friends and harming enemies" does grasp an aspect of justice as the work will later understand it, since his words capture the nature that one class in the city must have (i.e., gentle to their own people, and harsh to enemies—375c), but it is no more than an aspect. Thus Thrasymachus shows himself to be most fundamentally concerned with the good at the very moment he admits his admiration for tyranny, which will prove to be the lowest political and psychological mode of being. Obviously, one could go on at great length with other examples.[11]

Above all, we have seen images of arguments: Socrates argues *ad hominem*, or he argues on the basis of a conception of the good that hasn't been agreed upon; his arguments often focus on attributes rather than essences, and when he touches on truths, he does so without providing an account of the reasoning behind them (the treatment of ἔργον in the last argument would be the sole exception; I take it the idea here is that we are getting our first glimpse of something beyond images on the cave's wall). Of course, a truth without reasoning must simply be accepted on faith: the anticipations of what is to come later in the work can be nothing more than images. We have also noted repeatedly how, when one finds a flaw in Socrates' arguments, one finds that it has failed to investigate one of the questions that the rest of the work will seek to address: what is good? What is justice? What is human virtue? Can there be a sort of skill of living well? Even the overall argument of the first book, as it was described above, is appropriate to the cave in that it is contingent, dealing as it does with a particular situation: it does not establish any truth applicable to all times and places, as for example mathematics can do. We noted above that Thrasymachus represents the very worst sort of character who could be included in the argument: in the violence and irrationality we find in him, we should understand ourselves to be as close to the bottom of the cave as philosophy can go.

Later on, Socrates will say the following of the philosopher's return to the cave: "it is necessary to become accustomed to looking at obscure things. Having done so, you will see infinitely better than the people there, and you will recognize each of the images and what they are images of" (520c). This describes the relation of the person who has worked through the whole *Republic* to book i: it is only in light of the whole work that the first book can really be understood.

As we move into book ii we are no longer dealing with images on a wall, and so arguments of a more adequate nature can start to appear. More than that, Thrasymachus' challenge can receive a more straightforward expression through Glaucon and Adeimantus. This is why Plato has stated Thrasymachus' challenge twice: in book i, the Thrasymachan challenge is stated in a convoluted manner—that is, in a manner appropriate to cave-images—and in book ii, we have moved beyond this, giving us the more adequate form of expression we find there. Thrasymachus and his peculiar sort of challenge are necessary to the development set out in book i, to the overall argument of this first book (and through that to the rest of the work); Glaucon and Adeimantus, and the challenge as they set it out, are necessary to the rest of the work.

There is scarcely any aspect of the first book which does not look ahead to the rest of the work. On the basis of this immense wealth of anticipations, it is necessary to reject the claim that book i was once a separate dialogue that was revised and added to the front of the *Republic*: the revisions would have to be so thorough as to render the thesis meaningless.[12] But it is possible to go farther than this: recent scholarship has shown that the structure of the whole *Republic* conforms to the line (as described at 509d–511e), or to the analogy of the cave.[13] The place of book i in the cave is a necessary part of this overall structure.

SOCRATES IN REPUBLIC I

That there is a change in the nature of the characters confronted by Socrates as we move through the first book of the *Republic* has long been recognized.

There is another complementary change in Socrates himself, and this seems largely to have gone unnoticed.[14] Just as we saw in the *Gorgias*, Socrates becomes more active as the conversation progresses, in reaction to each of the characters with whom he speaks.

Against Cephalus, Socrates' questioning is a straightforward attempt to elicit the old man's views; at no point does Socrates put forth his own ideas. Against Polemarchus, his questioning takes on a rather different character, for we saw that the overall argument with Polemarchus had a structure, starting with a focus on utility, and turning toward the good. That is, Socrates is not merely trying to discover Polemarchus' views, but is starting to nudge his opponent in a particular direction. In the final argument against Polemarchus (335b–e), Socrates goes farther than this, for he produces a dense argument that includes two concepts—function (ἔργον) and virtue (ἀρετή)—that look ahead to the rest of the *Republic*. These represent active additions on the part of Socrates, corresponding to nothing in Polemarchus, and their introduction serves an argument that replaces Polemarchus' view, according to which justice might help or harm, with a view according to which it can only do good. But Socrates' argument does not only concern justice, and it introduces a more general, teleological conception of the world that will be included in subsequent Socratic arguments.

Against Thrasymachus, Socrates becomes more active, putting forward his own theory of the arts in the argument from the "precise sense." This theory builds on the final argument against Polemarchus: there is now said to be a single function to each skill (see 346d6). The precise doctor cannot make people ill.[15] After he has set out the "precise sense" account of skills, Socrates becomes still more active, for in response to an extended tirade from Thrasymachus (343b–344c), he gives an extended counter-speech (347b–e) of his own. This counter-speech puts forth, if only in embryonic form, major doctrines of the *Republic*, which are based on Socrates' own conception of the good, one quite different from that of Thrasymachus. The final three arguments are not an attempt to respond to Thrasymachus on his own terms, for they proceed on the basis on Socrates' own, quite different, assumptions, and they thus constitute a development of Socrates' own thought at least as much as a criticism of his opponent. The final argument, in which, for example, the eye accomplishes a single good, takes up once again the notion of function that was introduced against Polemarchus, but develops this notion more fully.

Thus Socrates begins book i with an attempt simply to elicit someone else's views and ends it with an attempt actively to assert his own thought (the conversation with Polemarchus, as usual, represents a midpoint in this development). Plato has indicated the cause of this Socratic development, for he has included ample detail by which we can see that Socrates is mirroring his opponents at each step, becoming more active as they do. Let us march once more through the movement of the first book from this perspective.

Cephalus begins the conversation in a welcoming and pleasant manner, and Socrates replies in kind. He goes farther than this, however, making clear that he sees in Cephalus a source of insight (328d9–e8), and then, after the old man has made a speech, expressing wonder at the insight provided (329d8). We saw how the conversation is characterized by continual agreement on both sides, to such an extent that even Socrates' criticism of Cephalus is preceded by the words, "you speak splendidly" (331c1). Nothing like this is found later in the work, for Cephalus himself is not present later in the work: Socrates is mirroring both the old man's manners, and also the *manner of knowing* that defines Cephalus. That is, for Cephalus, the whole ethical world is taken as *given*: it is precisely *not* grasped as the result of an active intellect making rigorous sense of the world (and we saw how this picture was confirmed and intensified when we look back to Cephalus from Thrasymachus, for Thrasymachus has effectively answered important questions that Cephalus failed even to ask). Just as Cephalus *simply accepts* the authority of poets and great men, so too does Socrates *simply accept* almost all of what Cephalus says. Critical demands of the sort that Socrates will later make of Polemarchus and Thrasymachus are entirely absent. The difference remains even in Socrates' single direct criticism of Cephalus, for we saw how the older man took an opposition Socrates had put forth and tried to blunt its force, allowing some truth to his opponents (329e2–7); this too is mirrored by Socrates, who does not say that Cephalus' conception of justice is simply false, but suggests rather that it is sometimes right and sometimes wrong (331c4–5). After Cephalus departs, Socrates swiftly ceases to be so generous.

There is an echo of this generosity as Socrates makes allowances for the wisdom of Simonides (331e6–7, 332a7–8, b10–c3, 335e8–10), but Polemarchus himself receives no such consideration. Nevertheless, Socrates does mirror Polemarchus as well, not only by proceeding with a genuine argument rather than an agreeable discussion but also in his implicit acceptance of the identity of certain concepts that are not obviously identical, such as the owed and the fitting or the good and the useful. That is, Socrates gives expression to these concepts *as they are present to Polemarchus*. This applies also to Socrates' treatment of skills at this point in the argument, which he paints (333e–334a) as equally capable of doing harm and good: this fits Polemarchus' conception of justice, which also can do harm and good.[16]

Socrates mirrors Thrasymachus by adopting the form of argument appropriate to this last opponent. Thrasymachus sees the argument as a sort of zero-sum game in which one side must win, and we saw how Socrates responds to this by turning to *eristic* argument: now we have a sort of verbal combat, in which the end is victory rather than the attainment of truth. This includes insults: Thrasymachus calls Socrates "offensive" (βδελυρὸς—338d), a "slanderer" (Συκοφάντης—340d) and even a nobody (οὐδεν ὤν—341c), and Socrates responds with some sarcastic words of his own (ἄριστε—338d; σοφώτατε—339e; μακάριε—341b). It is no wonder that in this context we have "an unusually combative Socrates."[17]

At every stage, then, Socrates mirrors his opponent. The changes we see in Socrates are thus to be understood as *reactions* to the changing situation in which he finds himself. Obviously, it took Plato some trouble to write in this way. He could have had Socrates simply remain the same throughout, asking pointed questions and no more of every character. What positive purpose has Plato accomplished by having Socrates develop like this? As in the *Gorgias*, where we saw the same development, we can understand this to be an indication to the reader that the positive content that Socrates begins to produce in book i is a reaction to the movement of this first book. Of course, Socrates' positive doctrines in this book imply and require the rest of the work, so that Plato is telling us that the whole *Republic* will be an answer to the movement of book i.

However, Socrates is not merely reacting. He also helps to push things forward. In each of his encounters with the three characters in book i, he does something new in the last moment, something that anticipates how he will proceed in the next step. Against Cephalus, he simply accepts everything until the conversation's last moment, when he asks a critical question. Against Polemarchus, he continues with such questions, but in the last argument he begins to put forth his own view of a teleological order of things. Against Thrasymachus, he continues to put forth his own views, building on what had been said against Polemarchus, but always in an obscure and question-begging manner, so that his arguments look to the rest of the *Republic* for a more adequate treatment of their premises. It is only in the last argument against Thrasymachus that we get a clear and straightforward treatment of an idea—that of function (ἔργον)—which can stand on its own. This treatment of function looks ahead to book ii, where we will continue to encounter ideas treated in a clearer and more straightforward manner. The effect of this activity on Socrates' part is to drive home one fundamental problem of book i: it is precisely the actively examined life that seems to drive the whole movement forward.

NOTES

1. That Polemarchus' position, if one were not to turn away from it as he does, would lead us to Thrasymachus is suggested by the mention of Periander, Perdiccas, Xerxes and Ismenias at the end of the argument with Polemarchus (336a5–7). Bloom,

"Interpretive Essay," 444, n. 29, notes that "Periander was a sixth-century tyrant of Corinth . . . Perdiccas II was king of Macedonia . . . Xerxes was the Persian king who led the great expedition against Greece;" Allan, "Notes," 92, notes that Ismenias was "a Theban well-known to have received large bribes from the Persians." We thus have a number of men known for their power though evidently not for their justice—just the sort of greatly capable, though unscrupulous, individual that Thrasymachus will praise, for example, in his words on the tyrant (344a–c).

2. The differences between Polus and Polemarchus are also instructive here. Polus is conspicuously different from Gorgias, above all for his lack of shame, for being more willing to push normative limits aside. With Polemarchus, by contrast, the emphasis falls much more heavily on his connection with Cephalus: he is the older man's heir. Thus while Polus is not moved by Socrates' arguments and sticks by his praise of the life of the tyrant, Polemarchus ends by accepting Socrates' argument and turning away from the new, liberated position he had started to open up. Polus and Polemarchus thus give us examples of how the middle position might be portrayed as embodying a greater or lesser liberation from the first.

3. Plato, *Apology*, 38a.

4. At 336d Socrates suggests that if he hadn't looked first, he would have become speechless. Bloom, "Interpretive Essay," 444, tells us that "there was a popular belief in antiquity that if a wolf sees a man first, the man is struck speechless."

5. Friedländer, *Plato*, 52, has seen a bit of this: "The line that runs from Kephalos through Polemarchos to Thrasymachos marks a progressive improvement in the skill of argument. But this skill is inversely proportional to the affinity of the partners with Socrates."

6. In the context of the first book of the *Republic* conventional thinking and traditional authority can be treated together. In real life, the content of convention can change as we move from group to group, and can differ from traditional conceptions, but this is not Plato's focus either in this book of the *Republic* or in the *Gorgias*. His interest in these texts lies elsewhere.

7. Perhaps our initial view of Cephalus, wearing a garland (i.e., a kind of crown—ἐστεφανωμένος—328c2), is meant to contribute to this picture.

8. See Kahn, "Proleptic Composition," who refers often to Adam, *Republic*. See also J. R. S. Wilson, "Thrasymachus and the Thumos: A Further Case of Prolepsis in *Republic* I," *The Classical Quarterly*, New Series 45, no. 1 (1995): 58–67, and Harrison, "Plato's Manipulation," 38. Clay, "Plato's First Words," *Yale Classical Studies* 24 (1992): 127: "Cephalus' conception of the passions as despots leads finally to the paradox of the tyrant as the slave to his passions [in book ix], and his uneasy fear that the tales the poets tell of the afterlife might prove true . . . leads to the . . . myth of Er (book x, 614b–621b)."

9. Diskin Clay, "First Words," 127. See also M. F. Burnyeat, "First Words: A Valedictory Lecture," *Proceedings of the Cambridge Philological Society* 43 (1997): 4–7, and John R. Kayser, "Prologue to the Study of Justice: *Republic* 327a–328b," *The Western Philosophical Quarterly* 23, no. 2 (June 1970): 256–65.

10. H. T. Peck, ed., *Harper's Dictionary of Classical Literature and Antiquities* (New York City: Harper & Brothers, [1898] 1965), 203.

11. Dorter, "Refutation of Thrasymachus," 26–27, gives one particularly important example: Cephalus, Polemarchus and Thrasymachus prefigure the three parts of the city and soul as they are set out later in the work. That is, Cephalus gives us an image of the artisan class, Polemarchus of the warrior class and Thrasymachus is a sort of perversion of the philosopher class. This explains, in my view, why Cephalus leaves the discussion while the other two stay: in his relation to wealth, he displays the virtue (moderation) appropriate to the appetitive soul or artisan class (on moderation, see 430d–432a). This being so, to be a good member of the artisan class, he does not need the discussion that follows. The other two do, and so they stay.

12. For the argument against book i as a separate book, an argument to which the present account has contributed additional evidence, see Kahn, "Proleptic Composition," who also addresses certain stylometric arguments. On book i as a separate book see Friedländer, *Plato*, 50, or the overview in Debra Nails, *The People of Plato* (Indianapolis: Hackett Publishing Co., 2002), 324.

13. Angus Johnston, "The Origin of the Constitutions in the *Republic*," in *Philosophy and Freedom: The Legacy of James Doull*, eds. David Peddle and Neil Robertson (Toronto: University of Toronto Press, 2003), 73–82, sees the structure in terms of the line: book i presents likenesses or guesses, the first section of the line; books ii–iv correspond to the second segment of the line; books v–vii to the third; and books viii–x to the final section of the line. Kenneth Dorter, "The Divided Line and the Structure of Plato's *Republic*," *History of Philosophy Quarterly* 21 (2004): 1–20, sees the structure of the work as an ascent followed by a descent, as in the cave analogy; see Dorter, *Transformation*, for a more detailed account along these lines. For our purposes, the important point is that both agree with the present account in finding the cave in book i. Note also that both Dorter and Johnson provide a basis for an answer to the supposed fallacy that David Sachs, "A Fallacy in Plato's *Republic*," *The Philosophical Review* 72, no. 2 (1963): 141–68, thought he saw in the *Republic*: it is to be expected that what we end up with in the end is of a fundamentally different kind from what we begin with—one cannot judge the forms by the standard of the cave. See also Schindler, *Plato's Critique*, 53, fn. 37.

14. Dorter, *Transformation*, 3, does note that in the argument with Thrasymachus, Socrates "makes a number of positive assertions."

15. This is a development from, and not a mere contradiction of, the view expressed earlier (333e7–8), that the person most able to make someone well is also most able to make them sick, for the earlier view was a mirroring of Polemarchus: see below.

16. Dorter, *Transformation*, 28, has noted this particular correspondence.

17. Beversluis, *Cross-Examining*, 221.

The *Gorgias* and the First Book of the *Republic*
Connections and Comparison

By now it should be clear enough that close parallels exist between the first part of the *Gorgias* (to 499c) and the first book of the *Republic*. The second book of the *Republic* provides a fitting final moment to this consideration of parallels. Of course, it does return to concerns from the preceding book— above all, Thrasymachus' position is explicitly taken up by Glaucon (358a– d)—but it also takes up concerns from the *Gorgias*, and it is worth pausing to show just how tight the connections to this other dialogue are. Certainly, it is nothing new to say that the *Republic* will return to and further develop many ideas from the *Gorgias*,[1] but there are also many specific phrases and ideas that are taken up in book ii.

In book ii, when Glaucon is restating Thrasymachus' challenge, he gives an account in which injustice is by nature (πεφυκέναι—358e3) good, whereas "justice" is merely an agreement between the less capable sort of people (358e–359b). This effectively takes up Callicles' distinction between nature and custom (*Gorgias* 482e–484a), as well as his account of the origin of conventional justice (*Gorgias* 484b4–c9). More specifically, Glaucon suggests that the best case is not to pay the penalty when one has done wrong (ἀδικῶν μὴ διδῷ δίκην—359a6), a matter also raised in the *Gorgias*, which is punctuated by the same phrase (e.g., 473b3–4, 479d5, e2–3, 480a6–8, c3–5, 480e8–481a1, 509b3).[2] Glaucon's focus on ability, specifically the ability to take vengeance when wronged (ἀδύνατος—359a7, also μὴ δυναμένοις—358e6; similarly, 359b1–2, b6) recalls Callicles' emphasis on ability (e.g., δύνατος—483c2, ἀδύνατος—522c5) and on self-*defense* (486a–c, 522c). The career of Gyges (360a8–b-2)—going from a menial position to ruler, killing the rightful ruler *en route*—follows the same path as the career of Archelaus as told by Polus (471a–c). Polus paints a terrible picture of the torments that can result if one is caught wronging a tyrant (473c); Glaucon's account of the terrible punishments that await the just man (361e4–362a2) is the equivalent in the *Republic*, and includes some common vocabulary (i.e., στρεβλόω—to put someone to the rack—or τοὺς ὀφθαλμοὺς ἐκκαίω—to put someone's eyes out). Glaucon's talk of the real man (ὡς ἀληθῶς ἄνδρα—359b2) reminds us of the emphasis Callicles put on the notion of being a man (ἀνήρ—see 483a8–b1; ὡς ἀληθῶς ἄνδρα at 512e1).[3] The liberated side of Callicles—the realist side, as we called it—was found ultimately to rest on the appetites (ἐπιθυμίαι—see 491e–492c), and Glaucon also effectively assumes that appetite (ἐπιθυμία—359c3) would move the just and unjust men if each had full resources. As the question in the *Republic* is a choice of life (κρίσις . . . τοῦ βίου—360e1), and this becomes a matter of setting apart the two extreme sorts of life (360e–361d3), so too does the question in the *Gorgias* come to one's way of life (βίος—488a2), to be decided by setting side by side the two lives (500c–d). Even Glaucon's talk of stripping the just man of everything but his justice (γυμνωτέος—361c3), so that his justice may be tested (βασανίζω—361c5–6) takes up Socrates' talk in the *Gorgias* of testing (βασανίζω—487a1, 4, e1) his own beliefs, and the talk in the myth of stripping the dead so that they may be judged (γυμνοὺς κριτέον—523e1). While treating the *Gorgias*, we noted the significance of the word ἀγροικία ("crudeness") to the theme of shame (see pages 110–1); in the *Republic*, Glaucon admits that those who praise injustice may speak rather crudely (ἀγροικοτέρως—361e1). Clearly this is not a matter of an incidental similarity of material: the *Republic* is taking up the same challenge as the *Gorgias*, and is expressing it by means of the same language.

JUSTICE BASED IN NATURE

One particularly important idea common to both dialogues is the question of the basis on which any account of justice might claim to be credible. When Callicles speaks of "the nature of justice" (φύσιν τὴν τοῦ δικαίου—485e2) he implicitly challenges Socrates to answer him with a contrary account of this nature; Glaucon in the *Republic* makes the same challenge concerning the nature of justice (φύσις δικαιοσύνης—359b4). When Callicles says that his account holds "in many places . . . among the other animals, and . . . in whole cities and tribes" (πολλαχοῦ . . . ἐν τοῖς ἄλλοις ζώοις καὶ . . . ἐν ὅλαις ταῖς πόλεσι καὶ τοῖς γένεσιν—483d3–4), he is pointing in the same direction as his direct claim concerning nature, to the basis in reality that gives his account credibility. Though Thrasymachus does not speak directly of the nature of justice, he does follow Callicles in emphasizing the universal applicability of his account: it holds true in all cities, everywhere (ἐν ἁπάσαις πόλεσιν—338e7; πανταχοῦ—339a3, 343d3). Both Callicles and Thrasymachus want to base their action on something *real*, rather than on fairy tales or wishful thinking. In this regard they represent a significant improvement over Gorgias and Cephalus, who simply took norms as given.

When we turn to the nature of the answer given by both works, the similarities continue. From 499c, the *Gorgias* begins to provide a response to the problem that has come to light. In similar fashion, the *Republic* from 468c (in book ii) is giving an answer to the problem that the work so far has set forth. The first thing to note about this answer is that it takes up an idea we saw at work in the *Gorgias*. The city comes to exist, we are told, not by some contractual arrangement as Glaucon suggested (358e–359b)—that is, its order is not a matter of convention, as Callicles might say—but it rather comes to be out of the nature of the individual.[4] The positive argument of the *Republic* begins when Socrates says that the city comes to be because each of us is not self-sufficient but in need of many things (369b).[5] His account does not begin on an intuitive, arbitrary, or contractual basis, but rather on the basis of a reality of nature—indeed, he later refers back to this as the "city founded according to nature" (κατὰ φύσιν οἰκισθεῖσα πόλις—428e9).[6] Accordingly, just as Socrates' account in the *Gorgias* took up a challenge from Callicles concerning a foundation in reality, so too does the account in the *Republic* begin on a similar basis (in the process taking up the challenge from Thrasymachus).[7] If all of this is correct, it would seem that the idea of finding a ground for action in reality, rather than on some arbitrary assumption or merely subjective intuition, is an abiding interest of Plato's. His view, then, would be that if the *Republic* consists in nothing more than a series of pious ought-to-be's, if it's just one man's vision, it is a worthless document. In the *Gorgias* we find this thought already at work.

ONE COMMON DEVELOPMENT

It is above all in the development running through the whole of each that these two works are similar to one another, and it is clear that Plato has the same basic idea in mind in both dialogues. The movement in both cases is from a standpoint that takes norms as simply given to a position that believes itself to be skeptical and thus to have transcended such unthinking acceptance. If the normative aspect of life—that is, how ought we to act? Why should we do anything at all?—is governed by nothing more than rules that have been accepted passively and uncritically, the fate of the entire normative edifice is sealed the moment it finds itself confronted with genuine skepticism and inquiry. This is true even if, as the presentation of Cephalus suggests, much of what is uncritically accepted is actually true: if it is present merely as a received truth, it will be incapable of self-defense when confronted with real criticism. This is not to say that an order of received truths will collapse and disappear right away, the instant it meets with skeptical inquiry. Rather, the hold it has over people will decay over time. Here we see the significance of the fact that the move from the first to the second step in both dialogues is from an old to a young man: the generation that has grown up within the older order will, in general, not abandon it the moment it is subject to effective criticism, but the *next* generation, less in the hold of that older order, will feel the changed situation more strongly.

Once the stories of Cephalus about the afterlife have been cast aside, or the declarations of Gorgias that "one ought" to act in a given way have been found wanting, what basis is there for living a life? The appetites are an ever-present fact of life, and in the absence of anything else, their indubitable reality will tend to assert its authority, even if only unconsciously. Both dialogues suggest how the appetites can become destructive when one focuses on them in a myopic manner, forgetting the importance of other considerations—and yet the situation at this point is precisely that other considerations are difficult or impossible to see, because the basis of so much of normative life has come to seem an empty illusion. The satisfaction of the appetites produces pleasure, and pleasure, precisely because it can be good, can lead us away from less momentary or directly present goods, such as friendship or the life of the community. The limits on appetite-satisfaction that are necessary to these less immediately obvious goods come to seem arbitrary and unjustifiable constraints on one's freedom. The result is the impulse toward tyranny that we find in Callicles and Thrasymachus. What we have in all this is a natural development, proceeding not by an iron necessity, but unfolding nonetheless according to a logic of its own. Given the starting point, the end can be no great surprise.

In both dialogues, the development has in the end the pretense of having thought things through, of having left behind the unthinking acceptance of norms that are merely given. In both dialogues, this pretense is partly misleading. Both Callicles and Thrasymachus can be defeated by Socrates because they have failed to think an aspect of their position through, because they have taken something to be obvious, in need of no further examination. In both cases, part of what they take as simply given comes down to the appetites and the pleasure these produce.[8] Of course, the focus on pleasure and the appetites is not simply wrong: we saw how Socrates, in the *Gorgias* (517b–519a), drew a picture in which a good life would be lived with constant appetite-satisfaction and pleasure, as these motivations were integrated into a wider framework in which so much depended on the ruling principle. The problem with pleasure and the appetites in Callicles and Thrasymachus is with the way in which they are present. A comparison with the starting point of the development is instructive here. Gorgias and Cephalus could not defend the normative constraints they took as given, but the fact that these were present—that is, that Gorgias took it as obvious that "one ought" not to do certain things, and that Cephalus accepted the wisdom of tradition—must mean that in practice, both men subjected their appetites to regular limits. With Thrasymachus and Callicles, the impulse is towards liberation from any such constraints, with the result that the appetites come into their own, in abstraction from any wider normative framework.

The difference between Thrasymachus and Callicles on the one hand, and a more adequate position (such as the one Socrates has begun to set out) can be summarized in language we developed in our reading of Thucydides: the former grasp truths in a *merely immediate* fashion. That is, (the realist) Callicles has plainly not related pleasure to other things he holds dear (i.e., to his aristocratic aspect). Rather, he has focused on pleasure on its own, as a fundamental principle from which all else is to be derived, rather than as a principle that has a place in the context of other important principles with which it must be held in balance; something similar is at work in the Thrasymachan conception of the good.

The parallel with Thucydides here should be made explicit: the relation of the Thrasymachan/Calliclean focus on the appetites to the account that we saw Socrates present in the *Gorgias* is like the relation of Alcibiades' skill at "expressing things" (ἑρμηνεῦσαι ταῦτα) to Pericles' possession of the same ability: the difference in both cases is between a principle grasped on its own, in abstraction from anything else, and a principle grasped in the context of a larger framework. Accordingly, both the *Gorgias* and the first book of the *Republic* present us with a historical development, and one that is, at least in one respect, a *movement towards the immediate*. In the *Republic*, the immediacy of the endpoint receives particularly vivid dramatic expression, as the aggressive behavior of Thrasymachus threatens to dominate the discussion through emotion rather than reason.

Nevertheless, despite their failure, both Callicles and Thrasymachus have moved the argument forward, forcing it to confront difficulties and bringing out truths that Plato clearly considers important. We thus have a paradox: the overall development is in one respect a move towards more rigorous thought, and in another respect a move towards the most immediate basis for action. This paradox coheres with what we have seen, on the one hand, in the fact that there are a number of regards in which both Callicles and Thrasymachus are good, and on the other, in the remarkably unsympathetic characterization Plato has given them.

TWO DIFFERENT PERSPECTIVES

Although the *Gorgias* and the first book of the *Republic* are focused on what is fundamentally the same development, there are significant differences in the manner in which they present it. A consideration of certain of the most important of these differences will help shed some light on an obvious question: why has Plato written two works that are so similar to one another?

We can see important differences between the two accounts as we focus on the consistency of the development, and on the theme of liberation. Let us begin with the first of these. The three characters of the *Gorgias* do not present an altogether consistent development in every regard. For example, if we consider intellectual ability, it does not consistently increase or decrease at each step as we move forward. Gorgias is an accomplished rhetor, who can boast that no one has asked him a new question in years. He is thus a figure of some intellectual stature, even though the dialogue subsequently shows that there is much he has not thought through at all. Polus, as we saw, is remarkable for his lack of intelligence; he represents a step beyond Gorgias not by virtue of his superior intellectual ability but rather in terms of his greater shamelessness. There is no suggestion that Callicles can approach the fame of Gorgias in the (intellectually demanding) discipline of rhetoric, and yet it soon becomes clear that he has thought more deeply on certain matters than the older man (e.g., on convention and nature). The three corresponding characters in the *Republic* present something quite different. Cephalus exhibits a minimum of intellectual ability, for Socrates' first genuinely critical question is sufficient to get him to leave the dialogue. Polemarchus is distinctly more impressive, as he is able to put up at least a little resistance to Socrates' questioning, while Thrasymachus is clearly far superior to his predecessors as regards intelligence, requiring far more from Socrates in response. Thus in the *Republic* we have a clear, step-by-step increase in intellectual ability as we move forward; in the *Gorgias* we do not.

The nature of the debate presents a similar case. In the *Gorgias* it is not the case that the conversation becomes less civil and more (or less) focused on the truth at each step as we move from one character to the next. Recall how we saw that against Gorgias and Callicles, Socrates expresses the hope that the conversation will lead to the truth, while against Polus his behavior is conspicuously different: he seems at this point to be intent on contradicting the younger man as completely as possible. In similar fashion, though Callicles, like Polus, expresses his exasperation with Socrates, the conversation does not become noticeably less civil as it moves from its second to its third stage. On the contrary, Callicles, "being an Athenian gentleman ... does not break rudely into the conversation as Polus did at 461b3, his question is first addressed as an "aside" to Chaerephon."[9]

The *Republic* presents a rather different case. As regards civility, we find a consistent development from the agreeable conversation with Cephalus, to the straightforward argument with Polemarchus, to the contentious face-off against Thrasymachus. We saw how this last portion of the book presents an eristic argument, a battle to win rather than an attempt to bring out the truth, comparable in this respect with the argument with Polus. The portion of the development concerned more with beating an opponent than with attaining the truth comes as a sort of interruption in the *Gorgias*; in the first book of the *Republic*, it comes at the culminating moment, cohering in obvious ways both with the characterization of Thrasymachus and with his conception of the good, and also with that aspect of the overall movement that proceeds toward the bottom of the cave in the first book.

On the basis of such considerations, the *Republic* might seem to offer a more consistent development than the *Gorgias*, but there is one respect in which the movement through Gorgias, Polus, and Callicles is quite consistent: each of these three characters is split down the middle, each characterized by an inner conflict between a world of conventional normative considerations and a liberation from the constraints of that world. The most fundamental difference between them lies in the question of how far they will go down the road of liberation, measured in part by the moment at which shame causes them to retreat from the argument. In addition, what we saw in Callicles could be found hinted at already in Gorgias; it is not going too far to say that Gorgias *is* Callicles in some sense, that Callicles is present *potentially* in Gorgias, that "Gorgias' teaching is the seed of which the Calliclean way of life is the poisonous fruit."[10]

In the *Republic*, we find quite another story: certainly Polemarchus is divided down the middle between the older order and the new liberation, but this is not true of the other two. Cephalus is entirely secure in his belief in traditional authority; there is no hint in him of what is to come, as there is with Gorgias. Thrasymachus represents a situation as fully opposed as possible to that of Cephalus: not an absolute liberation from the shackles of convention, but a liberation as complete as a person might attain while still being capable of taking part in an argument (any further liberation on Thrasymachus' terms would produce a fistfight instead). The two characters are simply opposites in many respects—for example, where Cephalus represents unreflective virtue, with only a passive relationship to the good, Thrasymachus represents thoughtful vice, and is quite actively focused on the good.

The notion of tyranny drives home this difference in the way in which the characters within each dialogue relate to one another. While we found a hint of tyranny—making others slaves—in Gorgias, and explicit attention to a tyrant (Archelaus) with Polus, in Callicles we find the aim of tyranny so fully developed that it receives a philosophical foundation in the appetites. A similar idea points to the very different relationship between the three equivalent characters of the *Republic*: Cephalus is content to have escaped a "raging and fierce master," and to be free of "many mad masters" (λυττῶνα τινα καὶ ἄγριον δεσπότην . . . δεσποτῶν . . . πολλῶν ἐστι καὶ μαινομένων ἀπηλλάχθαι—329c–d). Thrasymachus, by contrast, is focused on the "good of the masters" (δεσποτῶν ἀγαθὸν—343b): he would impose a relationship of the sort Cephalus is happy to have escaped. Whereas the *Gorgias* presents the development of "the same force"[11] throughout, the *Republic* moves from one situation to something fundamentally different.

The *Republic*, beginning from an uncomplicated representation of traditional authority, affirms that older posture as something good in its way. We saw this in our treatment of that dialogue on its own, but we can now see how this affirmation of the older order is conspicuous also by comparison with the *Gorgias*: the relationship of Cephalus to Thrasymachus is presented as a movement from one state to its opposite, not a straightforward relationship of potency to actuality as we find with Gorgias and Callicles. Thus Plato has not emphasized in the first book of the *Republic* how the first step is compromised by its relationship with the last. Cephalus, even though he's not at all a thoughtful person, is *simply* a virtuous man; with Gorgias, we are in morally ambiguous territory from the start.

The *Republic* also puts greater emphasis on the evil of the movement's final moment. Thrasymachus is more consistent than Callicles: we do not see a well-mannered "aristocratic" side to Thrasymachus, and so Socrates does not refute him by means of arguments that play nature and convention against one another, as he does with Callicles. Far from having an aristocratic side, Thrasymachus talks of force-feeding, and actually needs to be restrained so that the argument may continue.[12] Callicles certainly becomes frustrated as the argument proceeds, but his behavior is distinctly superior to that of Thrasymachus. Even if Callicles does find the practice of philosophy later in life unseemly and "worthy of a beating," still the insult to Socrates in this is indirect; the taunts and name-calling we see from Thrasymachus name-calling are a different matter. We noted above Callicles' polite entry into the argument; the contrast with Thrasymachus' explosive and aggressive entry could hardly be greater. Callicles initially makes a show of his friendly intention towards Socrates. There is no hint of friendship with Thrasymachus, and it is Thrasymachus, not Callicles, who is compared to various wild animals (336b6, 341c2, 336d7). The argument with Thrasymachus is by far the more acrimonious, coming the closest in the Platonic corpus to actual violence. In the *Republic*, then, Plato has given greater emphasis to the fact that something dangerous, destructive, and genuinely evil is coming to light in all of this.

And yet, even as the *Republic* gives us a darker vision of the movement's final moment, it also emphasizes more strongly the good in that moment. We found that both Callicles and Thrasymachus are good in some sense, but Thrasymachus is more intently focused on the good, and precisely because he does not have an aristocratic side: for Callicles, the matter of rule, of the appetites, of grounding action in reality—these are only the foundation of *half* of who he is (i.e., of his realist side). Thus Socrates complains that he gives into shame. Socrates makes no similar complaint against Thrasymachus, for he is entirely and only moved by the good as he understands it. Plato, then, has used the first book of the *Republic* to sharpen the paradox that he sees in all this: he presents us with a movement towards evil, a movement that is also towards good.

In all that we have now said, perhaps there is a basis for an answer to the question of why Plato would return, in the *Republic*, to a development that he had already treated in the *Gorgias*. The fact of this return is, of course, testimony to the importance that this development had for him, but the differences between the two movements suggest that he at least wanted a chance to emphasize different aspects. One difference in particular is worth noting: the *Gorgias* is focused on the development insofar as it lies implicit in the teaching of one of those intellectuals who travelled around from city to city in Plato's time. The *Gorgias* provides a reflection on what lies unseen in the sort of teaching they provided. The great promise of this new, antinomian intellectual movement had the effect of luring people away from their traditional sympathies, and thus it led, of its nature, to the poisonous fruit represented by Callicles. The version we see in the *Republic* does include one of these travelling teachers in Thrasymachus, but he appears only in the final moment: the same idea is present here, but as something that appears on the scene after the traditional order is already failing to give an account of itself—as an effect more than a cause.

What is remarkable about the version of the *Republic* is the clarity with which it brings out the theme of *authority and liberation*. That is, what it gives us, above all, is a move from a standpoint in which the authority of tradition is accepted without question to a standpoint defined by its liberation from that authority. It would be difficult to come up with clearer images of these two standpoints than Cephalus and Thrasymachus.

Perhaps Plato, having reflected further upon the matter, had come to a clearer view of what was most essential in the development: the most fundamental problem was the inability of the older order to give an account of itself. As a consequence, in the *Republic*, the development is from simple belief to an attempt to grasp everything through thought, from stability to competition, from an entirely passive acceptance of what is simply given to a position that sees such passive acceptance as intolerably confining, and strives instead to determine everything actively. Much of this is at least hinted at in the *Gorgias* as well, but it is the *Republic* that brings out what is most universal and essential in this particular historical situation—and also sharpens the view we get of Plato's own, ambiguous, relation to the whole development.

WHY THE DIALOGUE FORM?

At this point, one can venture to suggest what Plato has gained by writing two dialogues, rather than two treatises that set out his views in a straightforward and explicit manner. By giving us characters who stand for various stages of the collapse of an order of traditional belief, and doing so at the same time as he sets out arguments concerning justice, rhetoric, and related topics, he has been able to produce something that would be difficult or impossible to produce in any other way. For example, we can now simply speak of "Cephalus," and with that one word communicate the notion of resting with what is simply given, of an uncritical acceptance the authority of traditional wisdom, of a simple piety, of the possession of a content without the understanding necessary to defend or explain it—or even just an image of a conspicuous lack of intellectual activity. We should also recall the nuanced and paradoxical picture Plato has painted in each of these characters and in the overall movement of each dialogue: characters who have only partially thought things through, who present a highly realistic mix of important virtues and profound inadequacies; developments towards both good and evil, towards the immediate as well as towards more rigorous thought. Without the dialogue form, we could certainly explain these things, but it would take far more space to do so, and even then it would be difficult to attain so rich a picture as Plato has given. The more literary form of expression we find in the *Gorgias* and the first book of the *Republic* is helpful for certain kinds of content, such as the reflection on the historical process that runs through both and the contingent sort of argument they bring to light. In other contexts—one thinks, for example, of the hypotheses of Plato's *Parmenides*—a more direct and explicit form of expression is more appropriate. This no doubt helps to explain why not all of the dialogues are as rich in characterization, dramatic structure, and so on, as the two we have treated here.

NOTES

1. For example, Kahn, "Drama and Dialectic," 100, notes that Plato will develop in the *Republic* the idea, touched on at 490b–491c of the *Gorgias*, that "morally and intellectually superior men should rule;" Scott, "Platonic Pessimism," 31, speaks of "striking resemblances between *Gorg.* 491e2–492c8 and *Rep.* viii, 560d1–561a1"; Klosko, "Refutation of Callicles," 130, suggests that the view that Socrates sets out from 499b in the *Gorgias* "prefigures the central political teaching of the *Republic*." See also Beversluis, *Cross-Examining*, 371–75.

2. Book iii of the *Republic*, at 392b, takes up the same idea.

3. We touch on the theme of the real man below, in the section *A New Subjective Spirit*, pages 263–5.

4. Consider the perceptive comments of Robinson, "Competition," 55: "since the nature of each citizen is complete only in partnership with the others, it follows that there is no need for an artificially and externally imposed social contract to unify the citizens and to create justice. Nature already unifies them through natural necessity, and by doing so defines the good of each one as the good of the whole, rather than as the good of the discrete individual." Robinson further suggests that Socrates here begins to appropriate the term "nature."

5. It is later suggested that justice is to be found in the need that the elements of the city have for one another (372a).

6. In fact, there are numerous significant references in books ii–iv to nature (φύσις), above all at the end of book iv, where justice turns out to involve arranging the soul according to nature (κατὰ φύσιν) while injustice is an arrangement contrary to nature (παρὰ φύσιν—444d); the question of a disordered and ruined nature (ταραττομένης φύσεως καὶ διαφθειρομένης—444a–b) is decisive. Socrates speaks of "nature" (φύσις) at other important moments (for example, 375d–e, 376b–c, 408b, 443b).

7. Of course, the term "reality" is one that cannot be regarded as settled in the first two books of the *Republic*. If it turns out that Callicles and Thrasymachus have not been entirely correct on the matter of what is really real, it may prove necessary to ground justice in something more than the reality of everyday experience. Since the rest of the work lies beyond our focus here, the problems involved in all this can be left aside, although note that if the structure of the *Republic* is given by the line, as suggested earlier, it could allow Plato to resolve the problem here without contradiction.

8. In the case of Thrasymachus this point is not explicitly made, but given his conception of the good, it is difficult to see how it can be avoided. He is most fundamentally concerned with getting what is good, and what drives him to do this? Given the things he believes to be good—money, possessions, political power, praise—it is clear he is driven by his appetites, and thus by the pleasure he will get as he satisfies them.

9. Dodds (1990: 260).

10. Dodds (1990: 15).

11. Dodds (1990: 5).

12. There is nevertheless a residue of Callicles' aristocratic side in Thrasymachus, for despite his poor behavior, he does desire recognition from other people, and it is this that makes him subject to the argument. Plato does not seem to be interested in confronting a character who has no interest at all in his relations with others: a desire for good relations with other people is presumably one way in which we are not each self-sufficient, as suggested in book ii of the *Republic* (369b). See also the notion of friendship in Woolf, "Callicles and Socrates."

Conclusion

On the basis of the detailed treatment given to Thucydides' account of the decline of Athens, to Plato's *Gorgias* and to the first book of the *Republic*, we can now see how each work is concerned with a three-step development. In addition, it should be possible to appreciate the specific nature of each stage within each of these developments, as well as each development taken as a whole. Though it is impossible to be comprehensive, here we shall take up what seem the most interesting points of comparison.

JUSTICE AND POWER IN PLATO AND THUCYDIDES

One major theme in Thucydides is justice and power, which points to two fundamentally different ways of relating to other people. Although he often emphasizes how these two principles conflict, we have now seen that there is more to the matter than this: he is also interested in the way in which they can be held together in certain circumstances, and more than this, he is aware of the importance of their unity, of the power that can arise from justice.

The theme is directly relevant to Plato. The same ideas are present in the *Gorgias*, which begins with a question concerning the power (δύναμις) of Gorgias' art (447c2), but soon develops into a consideration of normative matters as well. Polus and Callicles, and to some extent even Gorgias, see power and conventional norms as tending to conflict, a view that receives particularly vivid expression in Polus' account of the life of the tyrant Archelaus (471a–c). This echoes one aspect of the theme in Thucydides. Just like other themes in the *Gorgias*, the matter develops as the work proceeds, and soon Socrates describes "good," the concept at the heart of normative concerns, in such a manner that it seems to be a power itself, and he even comes, in the end, to declare a need for a power to avoid doing injustice! This echoes the other side of this theme in Thucydides, the side that sometimes sees a power in justice.

Of course, it is in the *Republic* taken as a whole that Plato will give his fullest treatment of the question of the nature and relation of justice and power. The theme is introduced on the work's first page, where Socrates and Glaucon are confronted by Polemarchus and his group of young men, and Polemarchus asks, "Do you see how many we are? . . . become stronger than these fellows, or stay right here."

"Well," replies Socrates, "one possibility still remains, that we might persuade you that you ought to let us go."

"Would you be able to persuade us," says Polemarchus, "if we don't listen?" (327c)

In this exchange two different ways of relating to other people are put forward, the first based on force, the second on persuasion. Persuasion, of course, is the way of moving other people proper to relationships of trust. Thus we have trust and force, the very same idea that is work in Thucydides' "justice and power". The theme resurfaces later in book i with Thrasymachus, who must be forced to remain subject to the argument, so that he can be tamed by and become genuinely interested in it (as he eventually does: 450a–b, 498c–d). In book i the emphasis is on justice and power as they oppose and exclude one another. The rest of the work will aim to develop an understanding of justice according to which it is a sort of power, continuing a reflection of which we see the first hint in Thucydides.

PLATO AND THUCYDIDES COMPARED

Plato and Thucydides clearly disagree in the judgment they pass on the overall development in question, and this disagreement turns on their respective views on the first stage: Thucydides lives at a time when he feels the normative order of the city can still give an account of itself. Plato, a younger man, sees an older order that is accepted passively, or not at all. As a result, the movement in Thucydides is a straightforward falling-away from the initial unity of virtues and the fully adequate statesmanship of Pericles, while in Plato, although very similar evils arise over the course of the development, we also see evidence of increasingly active thinking as things move forward, so that the whole thing is partly good. If post-Periclean politicians failed to live up to the full reality of Periclean statesmanship, in Plato there are realities that only come fully to light because Thrasymachus and Callicles are ready to push things as far as they do. Thus where Thucydides sees the development as an unambiguous evil, in which thinking became ever less adequate, Plato sees something deeply ambiguous, in which thinking became ever more adequate.

Still, Plato and Thucydides are in agreement about the nature of the endpoint of this development. All three works give considerable emphasis to the destructive nature of the final stage, to its readiness to behave with unrestricted brutality, and to its consequent tendency to undermine any community based on trust and mutual recognition. We have already seen (page 251) how Plato sees a movement toward the immediate in just the same sense as Thucydides does: in their conception of ends, both Callicles and Thrasymachus are properly described as having a merely immediate focus in the relevant sense.

In all three works we come to what seems a paradoxical result in the final stage, for there is both a focus on a conception of justice which is supposed to follow directly from facts of the natural world, and also a radical focus on the subject, whose appetites (in Plato) and also inadequate perceptions (in Thucydides) become the moving force. That is, there seems to be an emphasis both on the reality of what is beyond the self and on what is peculiarly within the self. We shall take up this focus on the subject below, but its connection to this peculiar conception of justice merits a few words. In both Plato and Thucydides, the new, antinomian thinking gets going at least in part because convention comes to seem less real than observable facts of everyday experience, and as this apparently straightforward natural reality is pursued, there is a gradual liberation from the constraints that convention once supplied. It is at the moment that it believes itself to have found an adequate ground in nature for its normative novelties that this new way of thinking is completely liberated from the old, so that the individual comes into his own as a focus for action, no longer bound by obligations toward anything beyond the self.

In Plato, we find a double relation to objective reality: for both (the realist) Callicles and Thrasymachus, it must be substantial insofar as it can provide an object for their appetites, but it must be insubstantial insofar as it might hinder those same appetites. For example, both aim at tyranny, at an entirely active relation to the world around them (on this, see below), and in both cases, Socrates' first criticism forces the abandonment of the pretense that what is at work here is an attempt to ground norms on observable facts in a straightforward manner. Neither of them were prepared for this, because neither had thought so far, having been content to rest their minds once a look at facts observable by all had served its purpose. The purpose, of course, was to free them from the constraints inherent in convention. Both Callicles and Thrasymachus return to their focus on what they take to be real, Callicles in his focus on pleasure and the appetites (492a–c) and Thrasymachus in his final tirade (343b–344c), which makes claims about how things really are. In neither case, however, does this focus on reality ever bind the Calliclean or

Thrasymachan individual: it never plays the role of a constraining factor to which they must conform themselves and limit their appetitive activity. This is a peculiar sort of "reality."

The focus on "natural" justice is associated with inadequate thinking in Thucydides as well, for as it comes into its own, no longer limited by being a part in a whole, we also find a thinking characterized by fear and vicious circles—that is, by immediate reaction. The need for reality to be insubstantial in Callicles and Thrasymachus also finds a mirror in Thucydides: as the drives that Diodotus described, and the Athenian character, take over, they interfere with the accuracy of perception, coming to drive that as well.

In the end, the true emphasis here is on what is within the self. Even natural justice—that is, the view that it is a reality of nature that the strong dominate the weak—is instrumental. That is, it is not a straightforward attempt to describe or understand the world, but is brought forward in the service of the end of unconstrained action—nobody speaks of it when they believe themselves weak! The apparent concern with readily observable facts thus masks a purely subjective motivation.

There are, finally, points of connection with Thucydides peculiar to either the *Gorgias* or the first book of the *Republic*. Each takes up different aspects of the development as it is portrayed in the earlier work. We noted, in the conclusion to Thucydides, how the *Gorgias* takes up the historian's concern with convention and nature (νόμος and φύσις), but there is another connection running through the whole: the *Gorgias* emphasizes how the end of the movement is already present in the beginning, at least potentially. We saw this in numerous themes that developed as the dialogue progressed, above all in the three characters: in Gorgias we saw hints of the evil that was to follow, for example, in his talk of making others slaves (452d–e), but we also found that he accepted certain normative limits on behavior. Both these elements remain present in Polus, though the evil receives a fuller development, and they are also both characteristic of Callicles, who embraces the life of the tyrant with greater understanding than Polus, and yet is also an aristocrat. In Thucydides the end was potentially present in the beginning, though in a rather different way: the various echoes of Pericles' words that we find in Cleon or Alcibiades suggest how they took up certain aspects of the older statesman, though they did so always in a partial or inadequate way. And insofar as the difference between Pericles and his successors is explained by the logic of part and whole rather than the presence or absence of some particular element, then the crucial matter is not what is present, but rather how it is arranged, producing a point of connection with that crucial passage in the *Gorgias* in which Socrates gives his account of what "good" is (503d–504d).

The first book of the *Republic* presents a change from an initial state to its opposite, with the second stage as an incoherent mix of the first and last stages. This is just what we saw in Thucydides, but the second stage provides a particularly interesting point of comparison. We saw how in Polemarchus, a sweeping liberation from conventional constraint comes into view once he is forced to think for himself, and even a brief focus on the subject as the measure of right and wrong. Polemarchus turns away from these things, and Socrates suggests that the position he has abandoned is appropriate to certain tyrants (336a). All this looks ahead to Thrasymachus, who will take these things up with enthusiasm. The Mytilenian debate plays the same role as Polemarchus, for it introduces vicious circles, brutal punishments for subjugated cities, a limited temporal focus—and Athens (barely) turns away from all these: Cleon loses the debate. Of course, in Alcibiadean Athens, all of these elements are not only present, they are in the driver's seat. Thus in both works, crucial elements of the final stage make an initial appearance in the second stage, but are rejected, for the time being.

A NEW SUBJECTIVE SPIRIT

In all three works we have considered, the final stage presents a focus on activity together with a basis for action which is ultimately subjective, as well as a brutal policy of conquest (in Thucydides) or a preference for tyranny (in Plato). These elements are not related to one another incidentally but shed mutual light on one another, pointing to a new subjective spirit with its own peculiar nature.

One remarkable result of our treatment of Thucydides came as we examined Alcibiadean Athens. Here we found not only an extreme form of individualism as a political principle but also a *subjective* principle in the focus on appearances (which can only exist for a perceiving subject). This focus characterizes not just one individual but the whole city as it sets out on the Sicilian expedition. Together with this focus on the subject came the culmination of certain themes that ran from beginning to end of our consideration of Thucydides, one of which was the resolution of a balance of passive and active, in Pericles, into unrestrained activity, in Alcibiades (and in the Athenians at Melos).

This emergence of a new subjective principle, including the matter of unrestrained activity, is also present in the final stage in both Platonic works we treated. In the *Republic*, the theme of passive and active finds clear expression in Thrasymachus, who presents an extreme one-sided development of activity which parallels that found in Alcibiadean Athens. Thrasymachus' conception of the good is about getting good things, a notion that requires activity (in a manner that Socrates' conception does not), and it becomes clear that this is best done through his preferred form of government, tyranny, which is itself an extreme expression of activity in political terms: where all other forms of political association require some kind of negotiation and compromise with other people—that is, a mixture of activity and passivity—tyranny is characterized by an assumption of total activity on the part of the tyrant, while everyone else simply accepts orders—or must accept what happens to them. It is to just this kind of activity that Thrasymachus draws attention as he speaks of seizing the property of other people and even enslaving them (344a–b). His one-sided striving toward activity is evident from the start, as he bursts into the argument, threatening to dominate it by sheer emotional force. This tendency is conspicuous in its difference from the passive tendencies we noted in Cephalus, such as his desire not to do wrong unwillingly (331b), the way in which his conception of character was deficient, or his unquestioning acceptance of the wisdom of tradition. The *Republic* also touches on the matter of appearances that we saw in Thucydides, in the potent observation that the rulers can make mistakes (or that one can be mistaken about who is a friend or enemy), which led to what was identified as the appearance/reality form of argument used against both Polemarchus and Thrasymachus.

In the *Gorgias* too, the question of activity is at work, for example, in the theme of manliness.[1] Callicles introduces this theme when he declares that being wronged is not a characteristic experience of a man (ἀνήρ—483b1; see also 484a3, d2, 485c1, d3, d6, also ἄνανδρος—485c2, d4; ἀνανδρία—492b1). Socrates will later throw the matter of being a real man back at Callicles by using the word in certain significant places (e.g., 500c5, 512e1; ἄνανδρος—522e2), but he brings up the matter of the characteristic experience of a man most forcefully without using the word, at 494e in the question concerning catamites: here Callicles is made to imagine being passive in precisely the respect in which his real man would be most active. One remark made by Callicles is particularly revealing in this regard: "how would anyone be happy while a slave to anything at all?" (491e5–6) The aim here is to be subject to *nothing at all*, to enjoy *total* mastery and thus unbounded activity. Of course, Callicles aims at the life of a tyrant (492b) no less than Thrasymachus, with all the implications that carries. Like so many other themes in the *Gorgias*, the one-sided tendency of (the realist) Callicles toward activity is anticipated earlier, not only in Polus' admiration of Archelaus (471a–c) but also in Polus' entry into the dialogue—bursting in via an interruption—and his initial preference for asking questions rather than being asked (462b–467c).

There is a logic at work in all this. Adequate judgment must include a passive moment, in which unpalatable objective realities, which of their nature will clash with internal drives, can make themselves felt and thus be properly incorporated into an understanding. As the motivation for action moves into the subject alone, whether this involves basic drives such as greed or fear, or, in Plato, the appetites with their ground in pleasure, there arises a danger that what lies outside of the subject will be treated as less significant than it actually is. To the extent that people are driven by internal forces like greed or pleasure, they can easily fail to take adequate account of objective realities to which one must passively adjust oneself; to the extent that forces within the self take over and demand action, there will be nothing but activity. This is why we find the one-sided tendency toward activity in the final stage in all three works. The move toward the subject thus carries a danger of an intellectual failing, a danger which is realized in all three works.

All these aspects—a basis for action in the subject, intellectual deficiency, a one-sided tendency toward activity (and brutal activity at that)—all of them together paint a picture of the particular kind of subjective spirit that Plato and Thucydides thought characteristic of the endpoint of the development. Liberated from the bonds of convention—we saw above that this is the real point of "natural" justice, which does not bind the strong—this new subjective standpoint strives to be beyond the limits to which people ordinarily recognize themselves subject, but it has gone too far. No doubt as a reaction to the initial (first-stage) position against which it defines itself, it aims at a *total* freedom, an utterly unrestricted activity: it has lost sight of the importance of objective realities, to which one must passively adjust oneself. Intoxicated by, and myopically focused on, its new-found freedom, it has become caught up in appearances and impressions: its liberation is partly a liberation from reality.

LIBERATION AND AUTHORITY

Plato and Thucydides are united in depicting a development that strips away the restraints provided by convention and ends in an inadequate conception of liberation. The very nature of this inadequacy points to the need for something else, for something that limits and binds—that is, for some form of authority.

The attempt at absolutely unrestricted activity was connected above with an attempt (perhaps not always altogether conscious) to deny the significance of all limits, and these must include the limits inherent in objective reality. We should now consider the other side, the need for the acceptance of limits, for a character that is accordingly partly passive, and for the recognition that objective reality is not only substantial insofar as it offers something to our appetites but also insofar as it constrains us. All three works point the way to an orientation of this kind.

The *Gorgias* shows with particular clarity what is at issue here. In his account of "good" (503d–505b), Socrates contrasts the notion of something structured and ordered (503e7–504a2) with that of acting at random (εἰκῇ—503e1, 3).² The distinction here points to the difference between an objective order and the caprice of an individual will. The side of Callicles which seeks only to minister to the appetites will act more or less at random, depending on the degree to which the individual's desires happen to be ordered. What it will not do is accept any order as a limit on the appetites: "how could a man be happy if he's enslaved to anything at all?" (491e) The other standpoint, described by Socrates, will aim to bring about an order, whether building a house or a ship, or living a life. This latter conception accepts a whole host of restrictions upon one's activity—that is, it accepts the authority of something objectively real over that activity. The reward is something otherwise unattainable: a house that doesn't collapse, a boat that does not sink, and—if the analogy holds—a life well-lived.

The first book of the *Republic* returns to this idea, in the first of the three "glimpse-of-the-good" arguments advanced by Socrates (349b–350e). Here he gives an idea of why one might see authority of a certain kind to be a necessity, and pure liberation to be an evil: in real life, successful activity is to be compared to the tuning of an instrument because it aims to *attain*, rather than to exceed, a limit. The body that gorges itself excessively will fail to attain health, as will the body that starves itself too much—and one should add that in addition to consuming the right *amount*, one must also consume the right *kind* of thing. These restrictions on what must be consumed have an *authority* over anyone who aims to have a healthy body, and by virtue of this authority they limit such a person's freedom. Acceptance of this kind of authority, however, does not constitute *only* a loss of freedom, because it also *opens up* possibilities that would otherwise be closed. For example, those who attain a healthy body will be freed from the limits of a weak and diseased body, and will thus be able to do a great deal not possible for those who rejected the authority of the body's natural limits and needs. Those who successfully tune strings will then be able to play music. It should not be hard to see how this account can be applied more generally.

In Thucydides, we see the same idea worked out in political terms. Certainly, Alcibiades has a freedom in a sense that Pericles did not, for the younger man escapes the constraints of being a citizen in a particular city— and yet to say this is to answer nothing that we saw in the Periclean account of the need for the city. Just as attaining a limit—neither too much, nor too little food, nor the wrong sort—is necessary to attain a healthy body, so too must the individual who hopes to lead a life in which he can pursue his own affairs in a stable manner accept the normative limits of life in the city, in which his own interests can be balanced against the interests of others and against the need to maintain the whole.³ We saw how Thucydides is very clear indeed about the fatal role played by merely private interests (ἴδια); clearly, these are interests considered in abstraction from the limits imposed by city life—that is, interests understood as *liberated from* the constraints that the city must impose upon individuals.

Alcibiades, Callicles, and Thrasymachus, then, each implicitly point to a conception of freedom that regards people as more free insofar as they are not held back by any constraint. Thrasymachus makes the matter explicit when he describes injustice as "more free" (ἐλευθεριώτερον—344c5) than justice. This is freedom understood *immediately*: it sees that there are limits, and that there is therefore the possibility of being released from them; that is all. So simply considered, freedom seems to fall on the latter side, in a release from limits.[4]

The more sophisticated conception does not look at the matter so simply. It sees that there is a very great danger of catastrophe if we ignore the limits to which we are naturally subject. The best even a very talented individual might hope for from that orientation is what Alcibiades achieves: he is able to escape the likely consequences of his behavior for a time—until one night he cannot. Those who seek a more stable basis for a life well lived will accept that we are inevitably subject to certain constraints, so that the question is not simply a matter of how we might get beyond them, but rather how we attain the widest possible range of activity within them.[5] The need is to balance our desire for the greatest possible liberty of action with the need to accept the authority of objective limits.

And because people live in a world that consists not only of tasks and things like tuning a lyre or houses but also of other people, the limits to which we must subject ourselves do not only consist of the order inherent in things and activities to which Socrates points in the *Gorgias* and the first book of the *Republic*, but are also found in normative limits that inform our interaction with other people. Thucydides' remark concerning how Pericles restrained the populace freely (ἐλευθέρως—ii.65.8) offers a look at this latter notion: precisely because he so clearly subjected himself to the normative limits demanded by his city, he found himself free in a way that his successors were not, and had a form of influence and power that they lacked. Genuinely free action exists as part of a wider consideration just like the Periclean unity, in which competing principles are balanced against one another.

The freedom toward which Plato and Thucydides point us would free us from the likely consequences of the inadequate conception of liberation, from the "many mad masters" (*Republic* 329c) of the appetites. It would do this by integrating into the notion of liberation the need for authority: liberation, the release from limits, and authority, which requires an acceptance of limits, constitute an opposition of the sort we saw in Pericles, for here too we must find an appropriate balance between them. In fact, their fully adequate forms will inform one another: liberation, properly conceived, will free us from an unthinking acceptance of a merely arbitrary authority, and this will allow the authority that we do accept to be of the proper kind, the authority of actual limits of the real world—which will in turn free us from the confines of blind and incompetent action.

The historical development that Plato and Thucydides bring to light is not characteristic of all times, but it is characteristic of our own time, as is the particular subjective spirit they see at the end and its implicit conception of freedom. The realization that these works are so deeply relevant to our contemporary situation cannot be a cause for optimism.

NOTES

1. See Rutherford, *Art of Plato*, 164–65, on this theme.
2. Perhaps this passage gives us an initial hint of why Plato might take non-material things to be most real. (The realist) Callicles—like Thrasymachus and the Athenians at Melos—really is looking to the natural, material world, taking it to be what is really real. But once that focus proves to be inadequate and destructive, this orientation is destabilized. As Socrates describes what he takes "good" to be (503d–505b), his account certainly coheres with the natural world, but the real focus is on something beyond nature, on the *ordering principle* whose presence makes things good. It is the right ordering, not the material world, that provides an adequate basis for action, and anyone who is going to live while looking to this is assuming that this ordering must in some significant sense *be*, and in a more substantial sense than the natural world, which has been shown to be inadequate. If our treatment of Thucydides was correct in saying that the Periclean unity is the reality from which Pericles' successors fall short, then a basis for this line of thought is already hinted at in Thucydides: the natural drives of Diodotus may seem more real in an everyday sense, but if taken as a basis for action, they lead to catastrophe. (The focus on the need for order, and the horrors that its collapse had produced in the Peloponnesian War, no doubt goes some way to explain Plato's lack of sympathy for democracy.)
3. Note that the actual fate of Pericles or Alcibiades—both did die before their time—is not relevant here, for that will be determined to some degree by contingency. The question is what provides the most reasonable hope of a life that satisfies an individual's interests. Here the Periclean approach is clearly far superior.
4. Recall that we saw in our treatment of Plato how the relevant conception of appetite is itself immediate here, particularly in comparison to Socrates' account in the *Gorgias* (517b–519a).
5. It is in connection with this need for stability that we should remember Socrates' concern in the *Gorgias* with saying "the same things" (482a7–b1; see also 491b5–8 and 527d5–7) or remaining stable (527b3–4).

Works Cited

Adam, James. *The Republic of Plato – Edited with Critical Notes, Commentary and Appendices, Vol. 1 (2nd edition)*. Cambridge: Cambridge University Press, 1965.
Allan, D. J. "Introduction" and "Notes." *Plato Republic I*. Bristol: Bristol Classical Press, 1996.
Allison, June W. "Pericles' Policy and the Plague." *Historia* 32, no. 1 (1983): 14–23.
Andrewes, A. "The Mytilene Debate: Thucydides 3.36–49." *Phoenix* 16, no. 2 (Summer, 1962): 64–85.
Andrews, James A. "Cleon's Ethopoetics." *The Classical Quarterly* 44 (i) (1994): 26–39.
Andrews, James A. "Cleon's Hidden Appeals (Thucydides 3.37–40)." *The Classical Quarterly*, New Series 50, no. 1 (2000): 45–62.
Annas, Julia. *An Introduction to Plato's Republic*. New York: Oxford University Press, 1981.
Archie, Joseph Patrick. "Callicles' Redoubtable Critique of the Polus Argument in Plato's *Gorgias*." *Hermes* 112, no. 2 (2nd Qtr. 1984): 167–176.
Barney, Rachel. "Callicles and Thrasymachus." *The Stanford Encyclopedia of Philosophy*. Edited by Edward N. Zalta (Fall 2017 Edition), URL = https://plato.stanford.edu/entries/callicles-thrasymachus/.
Bender, Georg Friedrich. *Der Begriff des Staatsmannes bei Thukydides*. Würzburg: Konrad Triltsch Verlag, 1938.
Beversluis, John. *Cross-Examining Socrates: A Defense of the Interlocutors in Plato's Early Dialogues*. Cambridge: Cambridge University Press, 2000.
Bloom, Alan. "Interpretive Essay." In *Plato, Republic*. Trans. Alan Bloom, 305–436. Philadelphia: Basic Books [1991] 1968.
Blyth, Dougal J. "Polemarchus in Plato's Republic." *Prudentia* 25, no. 1 (1994): 53–82.
Bosanquet, Bernard. *A Companion to Plato's Republic for English Readers*. London: Rivington's, 1906.
Bosworth, A. B. "The Humanitarian Aspect of the Melian Dialogue." *The Journal of Hellenic Studies* 113 (1993): 30–44.

Boter, G. J. "Thrasymachus and ΠΛΕΟΝΕΞΙΑ" *Mnemosyne* 39 (Fourth Series), no. 3/4 (1986): 261–281.
Burnyeat, M.F. "First Words: A Valedictory Lecture." *Proceedings of the Cambridge Philological Society* 43 (1997): 1–20.
Cain, R. Bensen. "Shame and Ambiguity in Plato's *Gorgias*." *Philosophy and Rhetoric* 41, no. 3 (2008): 212–237.
Carone, Gabriela Roxane. "Socratic Rhetoric in the *Gorgias*." *The Canadian Journal of Philosophy* 35, no. 2 (June 2005): 221–241.
Cawkwell, George. "Thucydides' Judgment of Periclean Strategy." *Yale Classical Studies* 24, 1975: 53–70.
Chappell, T. D. J. "Thrasymachus and Definition." *Oxford Studies in Ancient Philosophy* XVIII (2000): 101–107.
Clay, Diskin. "Plato's First Words." *Yale Classical Studies* 24 (1992): 113–129.
Cogan, Marc. *The Human Thing*. Chicago: University of Chicago Press, 1981.
Connor, W. Robert. *Thucydides*. Princeton, NJ: Princeton University Press, 1984.
Cooper, John M. "Socrates and Plato in Plato's *Gorgias*." In *Reason and Emotion—Essays on Ancient Moral Psychology and Ethical Theory*, 29–75. Princeton, NJ: Princeton University Press, 1999.
Cornford, Francis M. *Thucydides Mythistoricus*. London: Edward Arnold, 1907.
Cornford, Francis M. "Introduction." In *The Republic of Plato*, edited and translated by F. M. Cornford, xv–xvi. New York: Oxford University Press, [1941] 1964.
Cross, R. C. and Woozley, A. D. *Plato's Republic: A Philosophical Commentary*. London: Macmillan Press, 1964.
Deininger, Georg. *Der Melier-Dialog*. M. Krahl: Erlangen-Bruck, 1939.
Dodds, E. R. *Plato: Gorgias—A Revised Text with Introduction and Commentary*. New York: Oxford University Press, [1959] 1990.
Dorter, Kenneth. "Socrates' Refutation of Thrasymachus and Treatment of Virtue." *Philosophy and Rhetoric* 7 (1974): 25–46.
Dorter, Kenneth. "The Divided Line and the Structure of Plato's *Republic*." *History of Philosophy Quarterly* 21 (2004): 1–20.
Dorter, Kenneth. *The Transformation of Plato's Republic*. Lanham, MD: Lexington Books, 2006.
Dover, Kenneth J. *Greek Popular Morality at the Time of Plato and Aristotle*. Berkeley: University of California Press, 1974.
Everson, Stephen. "The Incoherence of Thrasymachus." *Oxford Studies in Ancient Philosophy* 16 (1998): 99–132.
Flashar, Hellmut. *Der Epitaphios des Perikles: Seine Funktion im Geschichtswerk des Thukydides*. Heidelberg: Carl Winter, 1969.
Forde, Steven. *The Ambition to Rule: Alcibiades and the Politics of Imperialism in Thucydides*. Ithaca, NY: Cornell University Press, 1989.
Foster, Edith. *Thucydides, Pericles and Periclean Imperialism*. New York: Cambridge University Press, 2010.
Friedländer, Paul. *Plato, II*. Trans. Hans Meyerhoff. New York: Random House, 1964.

D. B. Futter, "Shame as a Tool for Persuasion in Plato's *Gorgias*." *Journal of the History of Philosophy* 47, no. 3 (July 2009): 451–461.
Gaiser, Konrad. *Das Staatsmodell des Thukydides*. Heidelberg: F. H. Kerle Verlag, 1975.
Gentzler, Jyl. "The Sophistic Cross-Examination of Callicles in the *Gorgias*." *Ancient Philosophy* XV (1999): 17–43.
Gifford, Mark. "Dramatic Dialectic in Republic Book I." *Oxford Studies in Ancient Philosophy* 20 (2001): 35–106.
Gomme, A. W. *A Historical Commentary on Thucydides, Vol. II*. Oxford: Oxford University Press, 1956.
Gomme, A. W, Andrewes, A., and Dover, K. J. *A Historical Commentary on Thucydides, Vol. V*. Oxford: Oxford University Press, 1956.
Gomme, A. W. "International Politics and Civil War." In *More Essays in Greek History and Literature*, edited by, David A. Campbell, 156–176. Oxford: Basil Blackwell, 1962.
Greenwood, Emily. *Thucydides and the Shaping of History*. London: Duckworth, 2006.
Grene, David. *Man in His Pride*. Chicago: University of Chicago Press, 1950.
Gribble, David. *Alcibiades and Athens*. Oxford: Oxford University Press, 1998.
Gutglueck, John. "From Pleonexia to Polupragmosune: A Conflation of Possession and Action in Plato's Republic." *The American Journal of Philology* 109, no. 1 (Spring, 1988): 20–39.
Guthrie, W. K. C. *A History of Greek Philosophy Vol. IV*. Cambridge: Cambridge University Press, 1975.
Harrison, E. L. "Plato's Manipulation of Thrasymachus." *Phoenix* 21, no. 1 (Spring, 1967): 27–39.
Henderson, T. Y. "In Defense of Thrasymachus." *American Philosophical Quarterly* 7, no. 3 (July 1970): 218–228.
Herter, Hans. "Zur Ersten Periklesrede des Thukydides." In *Studies Presented to D. M. Robinson, Vol. II*., edited by George E Mylonas and Doris Raymond, 613–623. St. Louis, MO: Washington University, 1953.
Herter, Hans. "Thukydides und Demokrit über Tyche." *Wiener Studien* 89, no. 10 (1976): 106–128.
Holladay, A. J. "Athenian Strategy in the Archidamian War." *Historia* 27, no. 3 (1978): 399–427.
Hornblower, Simon. *Thucydides*. Baltimore: Johns Hopkins University Press, 1987.
Hornblower, Simon. *A Commentary on Thucydides, Vol. I*. Oxford: Oxford University Press, 1991.
Hourani, George F. "Thrasymachus' Definition of Justice in Plato's *Republic*." *Phronesis* 7, no. 2 (1962): 110–120.
Irwin, Terence. *Plato's Ethics*. New York: Oxford University Press, 1995.
Irwin, Terence. "Notes." In *Plato—Gorgias*, translated and edited by Terence Irwin, 109–250. New York: Oxford University Press, 1979.
Johnson, Curtis. "Socrates Encounter with Polus in Plato's *Gorgias*." *Phoenix* 43, no. 3 (Autumn 1989): 196–216.

Johnston, Angus. "The Origin of the Constitutions in the *Republic*." In *Philosophy and Freedom: The Legacy of James Doull*, edited by David Peddle and Neil Robertson, 73–82. Toronto: University of Toronto Press, 2003.
Jeffrey, Andrew. "Polemarchus and Socrates on Justice and Harm." *Phronesis* 24, no. 1 (1979): 54–69.
Kagan, Donald. "The Speeches in Thucydides and the Mytilenian Debate." *Yale Classical Studies* 24 (1975): 71–94.
Kahn, Charles. "Drama and Dialectic in Plato's *Gorgias*." *Oxford Studies in Ancient Philosophy* 1 (1983): 75–121.
Kahn, Charles. "Proleptic Composition in the *Republic*, or Why Book I was Never a Separate Dialogue." *The Classical Quarterly* New Series 43, no. 1 (1993): 131–142.
Kahn, Charles. *Plato and the Socratic Dialogue*. Cambridge: Cambridge University Press, 1996.
Kaufmann, Charles. "Enactment as Argument in the *Gorgias*." *Philosophy & Rhetoric* 12, no. 2 (Spring 1979): 114–129.
Kayser, John R. "Prologue to the Study of Justice: *Republic* 327a–328b." *The Western Philosophical Quarterly* 23, no. 2 (June 1970): 256–265.
Kerferd, G. B. "The doctrine of Thrasymachus in Plato's Republic." In *Sophisitk*, edited by C. J. Classen, 545–563. Darmstadt: Wissenschaftliche Buchgesellschaft, 1976.
Klosko, George. "The Insufficiency of Reason in Plato's *Gorgias*." *The Western Political Quarterly* 36, no. 4 (December 1983): 579–595.
Klosko, George. "The Refutation of Callicles in Plato's *Gorgias*." *Greece & Rome* 31, Second Series, no. 2 (October 1984): 126–139.
Klosko, George. "Thrasymachos' Eristikos: The Agon Logon in *Republic* I." *Polity* 17, no. 1 (Autumn 1984): 5–29.
Kohl, Werner. *Die Redetrais vor der sizilischen Expedition (Thukydides 6,9–23)*. Meisenheim am Glan: Verlag Anton Hain, 1977.
Landmann, G. P. "Das Lob Athens in der Grabrede des Perikles—Thukydides II 34–41." *Museum Helveticum* 31, fasc. 2 (1974): 65–95.
Lloyd-Jones, Hugh. *The Justice of Zeus*. Berkeley: University of California Press, 1971.
Liebeschuetz, W. "Thucydides and the Sicilian Expedition." *Historia* 17, no. 3 (July 1968): 289–306.
Lycos, Kimon. *Plato on Justice and Power*. Albany: State University of New York Press, 1987.
Macleod, Colin. *Collected Essays*. Oxford: Oxford University Press, 1983.
Macleod, Colin. "Form and Meaning in the Melian Dialogue." *Historia* 23 (1974): 385–400. Also in *Collected Essays*, 52–67.
Macleod, Colin. "Rhetoric and History (Thucydides 6.16–18)." *Quaderni di Storia* 2 (1975): 39–65. Also in *Collected Essays*, 68–87.
Macleod, Colin. "Reason and Necessity: Thucydides 3.9–14, 37–48." *Journal of Hellenic Studies* 98 (1978): 64–78. Also in *Collected Essays*, 88–102.
Macleod, Colin. "Thucydides' Plataean Debate." *GRBS* 18 (1977): 227–246. Also in *Collected Essays*, 103–122.

Maguire, Joseph. P. "Thrasymachus – or Plato?" *Phronesis* 16, no. 2 (1971): 142–163.
Marshall, Morrison. "Pericles and the Plague." In *Owls to Athens—Essays on Classical Subjects Presented to Kenneth Dover*, edited by E. M. Craik, 163–170. Oxford: Clarendon Press, 1990.
McTighe, Kevin. "Socrates on Desire for the Good and the Involuntariness of Wrongdoing: *Gorgias* 466a–468e." *Phronesis* 29, no. 3 (1984): 193–236.
Méron, Evelyne. *Les Idées Morales des Interlocuteurs de Socrate dans les Dialogues Platoniciens de Jeunesse*. Paris: J. Vrin, 1979.
Michelini, Ann N. "Polle Agroikia: Rudeness and Irony in Plato's *Gorgias*." *Classical Philology* 93, no. 1 (January 1998): 50–59.
Moss, Jessica. "Shame, Pleasure and the Divided Soul." *Oxford Studies in Ancient Philosophy* 29 (2005): 137–170.
Moss, Jessica. "The Doctor and the Pastry Chef: Pleasure and Persuasion in Plato's *Gorgias*." *Ancient Philosophy* 27 (2007): 229–249.
Murray, James Stuart. "Plato on Power, Moral Responsibility and the Alleged Neutrality of Gorgias' Art of Rhetoric (*Gorgias* 456c–457b)." *Philosophy and Rhetoric* 34, no. 4 (2001): 355–363.
Nails, Debra. *The People of Plato*. Indianapolis: Hackett Publishing Co., 2002.
Nettleship, Richard Lewis. *Lectures on the Republic of Plato*. London: Macmillan & Co. Ltd., [1962] 1897.
Nichols, Mary P. *Thucydides and the Pursuit of Freedom*. New York: Cornell University Press, 2015.
Nicholson, Graeme. *Plato's Phaedrus—The Philosophy of Love*. West Lafayette, IN: Purdue University Press, 1999.
Nicholson, P. P. "Unravelling Thrasymachus' Arguments in the Republic." *Phronesis* 19, no. 3 (1974): 210–232.
Olympiodorus. *Commentary on Plato's Gorgias*. Translated and edited by Jackson, Robin, Lycos, Kimon and Tarrent, Harold. Boston: Brill, 1998.
Ostwald, Martin. *ANAGKH in Thucydides*. Atlanta: Scholars Press, 1988.
Palmer, Michael. "Love of Glory and the Common Good." *The American Political Science Review* 76, no. 4 (December 1982): 825–836.
Pappas Nicholas. *Plato and the Republic*, 2nd edition. New York: Routledge, 2003.
Parry, Adam. *Logos and Ergon in Thucydides*. New York: Arno Press, [1981] 1957.
Parry, Adam. "The Language of Thucydides' Description of the Plague." In *The Language of Achilles and Other Papers*, edited by H. Lloyd-Jones, 156–176. New York: Oxford University Press, 1989.
Parry, Adam. "Thucydides' Use of Abstract Language." In *The Language of Achilles and Other Papers,* edited by H. Lloyd-Jones, 177–194. New York: Oxford University Press, 1989.
Peck, H. T., ed. *Harper's Dictionary of Classical Literature and Antiquities*. New York City: Harper & Brothers, [1898] 1965.
Penner, Terry. "Socrates on Virtue and Motivation." In *Exegesis and Argument: Studies in Greek Philosophy Presented to Gregory Vlastos*, edited by E. N. Lee, A. P. D. Mourelatos and R. M. Rorty, 133–151. Assen: Van Gorcum & Comp. B. V., 1973.

Plenio, Wolfgang. *Die letzte Rede des Perikles (Thukydides II 60–64)*. Kiel: Christian Albrechts Universität, 1954.

Plutarch. *Plutarch's Lives, Vol. III: Pericles and Fabius Maximus, Nicias and Crassus*. Translated by Bernadotte Perrin. Cambridge, MA: Harvard University Press, [1986] 1916.

Pouncey, Peter R. *The Necessities of War*. New York: Columbia University Press, 1980.

Pozzi, Dora. "Thucydides ii.35–46: A Text of Power Ideology." *The Classical Journal* 78, no. 3 (February/March 1983): 221–231.

Rawlings, Hunter R. *The Structure of Thucydides' History*. Princeton, NJ: Princeton University Press, 1981.

Rechenauer, Georg. "*Polis nosousa*: Politics and Disease in Thucydides—the Case of the Plague." In *Thucydides—A Violent Teacher?*, edited by G. Rechenauer and V. Pothou, 241–260. Göttingen: V&R unipress, 2011.

Reeve, C. D. C. *Philosopher Kings – The Argument of Plato's Republic*. Princeton, NJ: Princeton University Press, 1988.

Rengakos, Antonios. *Form und Wandel des Machtdenkens der Athener bei Thukydides—Hermes Einzelschriften 48*. Stuttgart: Franz Steiner Verlag, 1984.

Rengakos, Antonios. "Fernbeziehungen Zwischen den Thukydideischen Reden." *Hermes* 124, no. 4 (1996): 396–417.

Robinson, Matthew. "Competition, Imagery, and Pleasure in Plato's *Republic*, 1–9." *Plato: Journal of the International Plato Society* 13 (2013): 51–75.

de Romilly, Jacqueline. *Thucydides and Athenian Imperialism*. Translated by Philip Thody. Oxford: Blackwell, 1963.

de Romilly, Jacqueline. "Les intentions d'Archidamos." *Revue des études anciennes* 64, no. 3–4 (1962): 287–299.

Rood, Tim. *Thucydides: Narrative and Explanation*. New York: Oxford University Press, [2004] 1998.

Rosen, Stanley. *Plato's Republic: A Study*. New Haven, CT: Yale University Press, 2005.

Rowe, Christopher. *Plato and the Art of Philosophical Writing*. Cambridge: Cambridge University Press, 2007.

Rutherford, R. B. *The Art of Plato: Ten Essays in Platonic Interpretation*. Cambridge, MA: Harvard University Press, 1995.

Saar, Hans-Georg. "Die Reden des Kleon und Diodotus und ihre Stellung im Gesamtwerk des Thukydides." PhD diss., University of Hamburg, 1953.

Sachs, David. "A Fallacy in Plato's *Republic*." *The Philosophical Review* 72, no. 2 (1963): 141–168.

Schindler, D. C. *Plato's Critique of Impure Reason*. Washington, DC: The Catholic University of America Press, 2008.

Schneider, Christian. *Information und Absicht bei Thukydides—Hypomnemata 41*. Göttingen: Vandenhoeck und Ruprecht, 1974.

Scott, Dominic. "Platonic Pessimism and Moral Education." *Oxford Studies in Ancient Philosophy* 17 (1999): 15–36.

Sesonske, Alexander. "Plato's Apology: Republic I." *Phronesis* 6, no. 1 (1961): 29–36.

Sparshott, F. E. "Socrates and Thrasymachus." *The Monist* 50 (1966): 421–459.

Stahl, Hans-Peter. *Thucydides: Man's Place in History*. Translated by David Seward. Swansea: The Classical Press of Wales, [1966] 2003.
Stahl, Hans-Peter. "War in Thucydides: Veneer Remover – Veneer Fabricator." In *Thucydides— A Violent Teacher?*, edited by G. Rechenauer and V. Pothou, 29–48. Goettingen: V&R unipress, 2011.
Stawell, F. Melian. "Pericles and Cleon in Thucydides." *The Classical Quarterly* 2, no. 1 (January 1908): 41–46.
Strasburger, Hermann. "Thucydides and the Political Self-Portrait of the Athenians." In *Oxford Readings in Classical Studies—Thucydides*, edited and translated by Jeffrey Rusten, 191–219. Oxford: Oxford University Press, 2009.
Strauss, Leo. *The City and Man*. Chicago: The University of Chicago Press, 1964.
Stauffer, Devin. *The Unity of Plato's Gorgias*. New York: Cambridge University Press, 2006.
Tarnopolsky, Christina. *Prudes, Perverts, and Tyrants: Plato's Gorgias and the Politics of Shame*. Princeton, NJ: Princeton University Press, 2010.
Taylor, A. E. *Plato: The Man and His Work*. London: Butler & Tanner Ltd., [1926] 1963.
Thorne, Nicholas. "Prediction, Probability, and Pessimism in Thucydides." In *Mouseion* LVIII—Series III 14, no. 1 (2017): 45–62.
Tompkins, Daniel P. "The Language of Pericles." In *Thucydides Between History and Literature*, edited by Antonis Tsakmakis and Melina Tamiolako, 447–464. Berlin: Walter de Gruyter GmbH, 2013.
Thucydides. *The Landmark Thucydides*. Translated by Richard Crawley. Edited by Robert Strassler. New York: Touchstone, 1998.
Thucydides. *The Peloponnesian War*. Translated, with notes, by Steven Lattimore. Indianapolis: Hackett Publishing Company, 1998.
Thucydides. *Historiae*. Vols. 1–2. Ed. Jones, Henry Stuart. Oxford: Oxford University Press, 1907.
Urwick, Edward J. *The Message of Plato: A Reinterpretation of the Republic*. London: Methuen & Co., 1920.
Weiss, Roslyn. "Killing, Confiscating and Banishing at *Gorgias* 466–468." *Ancient Philosophy* 12 (1992): 299–314.
Westlake, H. D. *Individuals in Thucydides*. Cambridge: Cambridge University Press, 1968.
White, Nicholas P. "Rational Prudence in Plato's *Gorgias*." *Platonic Investigations*, edited by Dominic O'Meara, 139–162. Washington, DC: The Catholic University of America Press, 1985.
Wilson, John F. *The Politics of Moderation*. Lanham, MD: University Press of America, 1984.
Wilson, J. R. S. "Thrasymachus and the Thumos: A Further Case of Prolepsis in *Republic* I." *The Classical Quarterly*, New Series 45, no. 1 (1995): 58–67.
Winnington-Ingram, R. P. "*Ta Deonta Eipein*: Cleon and Diodotus." *Bulletin of the Institute of Classical Studies* 12 (1965): 70–82.
Winspear, Alban Dewes. *The Genesis of Plato's Thought*. Montreal: Harvest House Ltd., 1974.

Woodhead, A. G. "Thucydides' Portrait of Cleon." *Mnemosyne*, Fourth Series 13, fasc. 4 (1960): 289–317.
Woolf, Raphael. "Callicles and Socrates: Psychic (Dis)Harmony in the *Gorgias*." *Oxford Studied in Ancient Philosophy* 18 (2000): 1–40.
Young, Charles M. "A Note on Republic 335c9–10 and 335c12." *The Philosophical Review* 83, no. 1 (January 1974): 97–106.
Zahn, Rose. *Die erste Periklesrede (Thukydides i.140-144)*. Leipzig: R. Noske, 1934.

Index

active, 2, 8–10, 12, 23–25, 83, 88, 108, 112, 119, 123, 145, 172–73, 178, 184, 189–90, 197, 202, 219, 222–23, 233–35, 237, 241–42, 253, 255, 260–61, 263–64
Adeimantus, 111, 210, 217, 240
ad hominem, 14, 48, 82, 94, 104–5, 107–12, 149–50, 155, 172, 177, 213, 239
Alcibiades, 5, 7, 9–11, 14–15, 18, 45, 50, 55, 57, 60–69, 75–76, 78–81, 83–86, 251, 262–63, 266–67
appearance, 57, 63–64, 66–69, 67n37, 84–85, 102, 120, 129, 131, 164, 193–94, 263–65
appetite, 110, 129, 134, 140, 146–48, 155, 158–59, 162–67, 182–83, 248, 250–51, 253, 255, 261, 264–67. *See also epithumia* as desire
Archelaus, 102, 128–29, 134, 140–41, 158, 247, 253, 259, 264
Aristotle, 8, 101
Athenians at Melos, 3, 14, 16, 56, 58–59, 69, 83–84, 86, 263
authority, 1, 27, 181–84, 186, 189–90, 204–5, 233–35, 237–38, 242, 250, 253–56, 265–68

Callicles, 2–3, 18, 48, 82–83, 94, 99, 101–5, 107–12, 117, 119, 121, 123, 128–34, 137–50, 155–62, 165, 167–68, 171–73, 205, 205n21, 247–55, 259–62, 264, 266–67; as good, 94, 103–4, 112, 155–59, 167, 251, 254
Cephalus, 2, 96, 111–12, 177–78, 181–86, 189–92, 194, 196, 204, 212, 215, 218, 221–23, 233–39, 241–43, 249–56, 264
circle, 45–46, 56–58, 69, 78, 85, 87, 262–63; circle of fear, 58, 69, 77–78, 87; circle of viciousness, 44, 46, 58, 78, 80, 87
Cleon, 2, 5, 14–15, 36, 41–50, 55–60, 63, 76–78, 85, 87, 262–63
convention, 2, 82–84, 94–95, 110–12, 123, 127, 129–31, 133, 138, 140–41, 143, 147–49, 155–56, 167, 196, 202, 211–13, 224, 235–38, 247, 249, 253, 259, 261, 263, 265
convention and nature, 110, 123, 131, 138–40, 148–50, 156, 252, 254, 262
custom and nature, 48, 82, 130, 247

democracy, 26, 42–43, 65
democracy and empire, 8, 26, 42, 44
Diodotus, 45, 47–51, 57, 59, 76, 78, 83, 262
divine, 34, 59, 83, 111, 181
divine order, 181, 185–86, 190. *See also* ethical order; traditional order

277

empire, 14, 26, 27, 42–43, 46–47, 49, 56–58, 65–68, 82–85, 88; democracy and empire. *See* democracy; expanding the empire, 9, 14, 35, 57–58, 66, 68, 84–85
epithumia as desire, 66–67
ethical order, 1, 117, 204, 235–36. *See also* divine order; traditional order

fear, 15, 30, 34, 42, 45, 49–50, 56–59, 61, 65, 67–69, 83, 85, 88, 122, 184, 202, 233, 262, 264; circle of fear. *See* circle
first speech, Pericles' (i.e., ii.60–4). *See* Pericles
frank, 109–10, 146–47, 149, 162, 167, 201, 203, 238
freedom, 1, 23, 26, 29, 31, 33, 69, 84, 110, 120, 122, 147, 152, 162, 182, 184, 204, 224, 250, 265–68
Funeral Oration. *See* Pericles

Glaucon, 111, 200, 210, 217, 222, 240, 247–49, 260
Gorgias (character), 2, 82, 99, 101–3, 107–12, 117–23, 127–28, 132–34, 137–39, 149, 158, 171–73, 249–50, 252–54, 259, 262
Gorgias (dialogue), 1–2, 83, 93–95, 99, 101–5, 107–10, 112, 117, 133, 144, 146, 150, 155–58, 167, 171–73, 177, 205n21, 215n49, 222n64, 224, 238, 241, 243, 247–56, 259, 262, 264–65, 267
Gyges, 247

holism, 9, 65, 84. *See also* unity; whole
holist, 5, 49, 93, 104. *See also* unity; whole

immediacy, 11–12, 14, 18, 25, 34–35, 56–57, 77, 251
immediate, 1, 11–13, 16, 25, 27, 31, 33–34, 43–44, 46–47, 51, 57–58, 77–79, 84–85, 117, 119, 159, 190, 251, 256, 261–62, 267
incorruptible by money. *See* Pericles
individual, 1–3, 5, 8, 11, 15, 28–34, 61, 63–66, 68, 78–81, 85, 88, 94, 112, 120, 131, 138, 140, 143, 147, 157, 164, 185, 216–18, 221, 223–24, 236, 249, 261–63, 266–67
Ismenias, 234n1

judgment, 6–7, 12n11, 15, 24, 26, 28, 31–33, 35–36, 43–45, 47, 49–50, 62, 66, 69–70, 77–78, 80, 108, 260, 264
justice and power, 8, 15, 18, 26–27, 42, 55, 80–82, 88, 129, 259–60

last speech, Pericles' (i.e., ii.60–64). *See* Pericles
liberate, 83–84, 197, 212, 221, 224, 233, 237, 248, 261, 265, 267
liberation, 1, 82, 84, 94, 127, 147, 149, 189, 193–94, 196–97, 204, 211–12, 224, 233–34, 236–38, 251–53, 255, 261, 263, 265–67
limit, 2, 69, 84, 121, 133, 148, 193–94, 196, 204–5, 215–17, 220, 223, 235, 238, 250–51, 262, 265–68

Melian Dialogue, 14, 17, 27, 47, 55–56, 58–60, 65, 68, 78, 81, 87
Mytilenian debate, 13–15, 41, 46, 48, 51, 55, 58, 75–78, 81, 85–86, 194n8, 234, 263

natural justice, 102, 111, 155–56, 167, 199, 205, 261–62, 265. *See also* objective order
Nicias, 14, 50, 60–63, 66–67, 69, 75, 78, 83

objective order, 110, 138–41, 143, 157, 160, 266. *See also* natural justice
older order, 2, 189, 235, 250, 253–55, 260. *See also* divine order; traditional order

opposition, 2, 7–8, 11, 23–25, 34, 42, 69, 75, 81–82, 85, 108, 127, 159–60, 171, 182–83, 213–14, 242, 267

partial, 11, 45, 60–61, 133, 163, 166, 189, 192, 239–41, 243, 247, 250, 253, 256, 262
passive, 2, 8–10, 12, 24, 66, 83, 107, 184, 233, 249, 253, 255, 260, 263–65
passivity, 9, 10, 24–25, 43, 65, 83, 184, 264
patriotism. *See* Pericles
Peloponnesian War, 1, 5, 17, 29–30
Perdiccas, 234n1
Periander, 234n1
Pericles, 1–2, 5–18, 23–36, 41–45, 47–50, 55–58, 60–61, 63–66, 69, 76–89, 160, 251, 260, 262–63, 266–67; expressing things, 6–7, 45, 50, 62–63, 66, 75, 86, 251; first speech (i.e., i.140-4), 17, 24–26, 28, 183; Funeral Oration, 8, 17, 23, 25–30, 33–34, 42; incorruptible, 6, 26, 49–50, 64, 80, 84; integrity, 14, 47–48, 55; last speech (i.e., ii.60-4), 5, 14, 25–26, 28–29, 32, 63, 77; patriotism, 6–7, 47, 50, 61, 64–65, 76; recognizing what is needed, 6, 44–45, 49–50, 60–61, 63, 75–76; speaking against the people, 6, 44, 61, 81; superior to the influence of money, 6, 50, 61, 76
personal, 16, 30, 32–34, 48, 61, 63–65, 68, 76, 79–80, 85, 132
pleasure, 30, 101, 103, 108, 129–31, 134, 140, 142, 146–50, 155, 158–64, 166, 182–83, 250–51, 261, 264–65
Polemarchus, 2, 177–78, 189–97, 202–5, 207, 212, 219, 221–23, 233–39, 241–43, 252–53, 260, 263–64; compared with Polus, 234n2
Polus, 2, 82, 99, 101–2, 107–10, 112, 117–18, 121, 127–34, 137–39, 149, 158, 160, 171–73, 247, 252–53, 259, 262, 264; compared with Polemarchus, 234n2

private, 23, 26, 31–35, 61, 64, 88, 201, 266
public, 23, 26, 31–34, 61, 201

Republic, 1–2, 86, 93–96, 102, 104, 111–12, 117, 157, 164, 167, 172–73, 177–78, 181–83, 185, 190, 192, 195–97, 201, 203, 207–9, 213–14, 223, 233, 235–41, 243, 247–49, 251–56, 259–60, 262–64, 266–67
rule, 34, 42, 46, 57, 65, 68, 83, 87, 120, 139, 144, 146–47, 155, 158, 163–64, 167, 203–10, 212–13, 222, 249, 254
ruler, 120, 145, 204–7, 210–11, 224, 247, 264
ruling, 25, 42, 95, 102, 110, 120, 144, 146, 155, 158–59, 162, 165–67, 203–4, 209–10, 219, 222, 250

shame, 103–4, 107–12, 122–23, 133, 149, 167, 224, 238, 248, 253, 255
shameful, 101, 108–9, 121, 123, 127, 129–31, 133–34, 138–39, 143, 149, 155, 158–59
Sicilian debate, 13–15, 59–60, 62, 64, 68–69, 75, 77–78, 83
Sicilian expedition, 9, 13, 32, 55, 58–59, 61–62, 65, 68–69, 75, 83, 218, 263
slave, 102, 120, 122–23, 128, 140, 143, 147, 158, 165, 253, 262, 264
subjective impression, 57, 63, 66–67
subjective spirit, 2, 18, 94, 263, 265, 268

temporal, 8, 12–14, 27–28, 56, 58, 69–70, 77–80, 85, 103, 263
Thrasymachus, 2–3, 18, 94, 96, 104, 111, 167, 172, 177–78, 192–96, 194nn8–9, 199–224, 233–43, 247–55, 260–64, 267; as good, 94, 104, 221–23, 236–38, 251
three stages/three steps, 1–3, 5, 13–15, 18, 58, 65n34, 78–79, 85, 93–94, 104–5, 107, 234, 236, 259
tradition, 186, 235, 237, 251, 255, 264

traditional, 1, 30, 181, 190, 224, 235, 237–38, 253–56; traditional order, 181, 205, 234–35, 255
tyranny, 26, 42, 46, 51, 65, 82, 84, 102, 155, 201, 204, 210–11, 221, 239, 250, 253, 261, 263–64
tyrant, 102, 120, 122, 128–30, 134, 138, 140, 147, 158, 182, 201, 204, 210, 212, 216, 220, 222, 224, 236–37, 247, 253, 259, 262–64

unity, 6–8, 10, 23–24, 41, 59, 61–63, 65, 75–77, 83, 85–86, 88–89, 103, 259–60, 267. *See also* holism; holist; whole
useful, 63, 87, 129–31, 163, 178, 185, 191–94, 197, 234, 242

utility, 130, 185, 193–94, 234, 241

vicious circle. *See* circle

whole, 1, 3, 5–8, 10–12, 18, 29, 31–32, 41, 43, 45, 50, 56, 60n15, 61, 66–68, 80, 86–87, 93, 95–96, 99, 120, 129, 144, 158, 164, 172, 177–78, 181, 185, 189–90, 192–93, 195–96, 206, 209, 213, 215, 223, 236, 238, 240, 242–43, 248–49, 255, 259–60, 262–63, 266. *See also* holism; holist; unity

Xerxes, 234n1

About the Author

Nicholas Thorne received his BA and MA in classics from Dalhousie University and his PhD in classics and ancient philosophy from the University of Pittsburgh. He previously taught at the University of Tennessee in Knoxville. He lives in Munich, Germany.